Clinical Case Formulation

Clinical Case Formulation

Varieties of Approaches

Edited by

Peter Sturmey

WILEY-BLACKWELL

A John Wiley & Sons, Ltd., Publication

This edition first published 2009
© 2009 John Wiley & Sons, Ltd.

Wiley-Blackwell is an imprint of John Wiley & Sons, formed by the merger of Wiley's global Scientific, Technical, and Medical business with Blackwell Publishing.

Registered Office
John Wiley & Sons Ltd, The Atrium, Southern Gate, Chichester, West Sussex, PO19 8SQ, UK

Editorial Offices
The Atrium, Southern Gate, Chichester, West Sussex, PO19 8SQ, UK
9600 Garsington Road, Oxford, OX4 2DQ, UK
350 Main Street, Malden, MA 02148-5020, USA

For details of our global editorial offices, for customer services, and for information about how to apply for permission to reuse the copyright material in this book please see our website at www.wiley.com/wiley-blackwell.

The right of the editor to be identified as the author of the editorial material in this work has been asserted in accordance with the Copyright, Designs and Patents Act 1988.

Library of Congress Cataloging-in-Publication Data

Clinical case formulation : varieties of approaches / edited by Peter Sturmey.
       p.   cm.
   Includes index.
     ISBN 978-0-470-03291-6 (cloth) – ISBN 978-0-470-03292-3 (pbk.)
   1. Clinical psychology–Methodology.   2. Counseling–Case studies.   3. Psychotherapy–Practice.
   I. Sturmey, Peter.
     RC467.C574 2009
     616.89–dc22   2009013397

A catalogue record for this book is available from the British Library.

Set in 11/13pt Times by Aptara Inc., New Delhi, India
Printed and bound in Singapore by Fabulous Printers Pte Ltd

1   2009

For Tony Crisp

Someone who knows how to formulate cases

Contents

About the Editor

Peter Sturmey is Professor of Psychology at Queens College and the Graduate Center, City University of New York. He has published over 100 peer-reviewed articles and numerous book chapters. He is on the editorial board of several journals, including *Research in Developmental Disabilities* and *Research in Autism Spectrum Disorders*. Previous books include *Functional Analysis in Clinical Psychology* (1996, Wiley, UK), *Offenders with Developmental Disabilities* (with Lindsay and Taylor, 2004, Wiley, UK), *Mood Disorders in People with Mental Retardation* (2005, NADD Press), *Autism Spectrum Disorders: Applied Behavior Analysis, Evidence and Practice* (with Fitzer, 2007, ProEd Inc.), *Functional Analysis in Clinical Treatment* (2007, Elsevier), *How Teach Verbal Behavior* (2008, ProEd), *Behavioral Case Formulation* and intervention (2008, Wiley, UK), *Applied Behavior Analysis and Language Acquisition in People with Autism Spectrum Disorders* (with Fitzer, 2008, ProEd). His main research interests are in staff and parent training, developmental disabilities and applied behaviour analysis including applications to clinical psychology.

List of Contributors

Marna S. Barrett is Assistant Professor in the Department of Psychiatry at the University of Pennsylvania School of Medicine. Her main research interests are in the area of therapist characteristics, attrition and psychotherapy outcome. Her current studies include investigations of factors predictive of early engagement and attrition in community mental health settings, cultural influences on mental health service use and the use of a modified motivational interviewing to increase commitment to treatment.

Nigel Beail is Consultant Clinical Psychologist and Head of Psychological Services for Barnsley Learning Disability Service and Honorary Professor of Psychology at the University of Sheffield in the United Kingdom. His clinical work includes providing psychological interventions to meet the needs of people with learning disabilities who present with a wide range of problems. He specializes in work with clients who self-injure, those that offend or have significant mental health problems. He has a particular interest in the provision and evaluation of psychological therapies for people who have intellectual disabilities and has pioneered outcome research in the area.

Betsey A. Benson is Adjunct Associate Professor of Psychology, and Director, Adult Behavior Support Services, Nisonger Center, a University Center of Excellence in Developmental Disabilities, Ohio State University. She directs the Adult Behavior Support Services programme at the Nisonger Center at Ohio State University. She has published on the topics of aggression, anger management and depression in persons with intellectual disabilities. She is a Fellow in the American Association on Intellectual and Developmental Disabilities, an Associate Editor for the *Journal of Mental Health Research in Intellectual Disabilitie*s and a member of the Advisory Board of the *Journal of Intellectual Disability Research.*

Richard Bentall is Professor of Clinical Psychology at the University of Bangor, Wales. He obtained a PhD in experimental psychology at Bangor in 1983, and then undertook training in clinical psychology at the University of Liverpool. After a brief period working in the British National Health Service, he took up a lecturing job at Liverpool in 1986, and was eventually promoted to professor there before moving to the University of Manchester in 1999 and then returning to Bangor in 2007. Professor Bentall is highly critical of standard approaches to psychiatric diagnoses (especially the DSM) and advocates research on particular types of psychotic behaviours and experience as a methodology that avoids the limitations of current symptoms of psychiatric classification. With collaborators throughout the United Kingdom, he has conducted large-scale randomized controlled trials of cognitive behavioural interventions for patients suffering from psychosis, most recently a trial using cognitive behaviour therapy to prevent psychosis in those at ultra-high risk of a first breakdown. His book, *Madness Explained: Psychosis and Human Nature* (Penguin, 2003) won the British Psychological Society book prize for 2004.

Mari Brannigan is the Director of Nursing NHS Greater Glasgow and Clyde, Scotland. On completion of training in cognitive behavioural therapy at the University of Dundee, Mari has developed clinical expertise in providing CBT in a range of NHS settings. She has considerable experience of supervising and training others and has been involved in the development and delivery of a number of training courses across Scotland. She has a particular interest in the role of mental health nursing in contributing to the delivery of psychological interventions at both specialist and non specialist level.

David A. Casey is Associate Professor and Vice Chair of the Department of Psychiatry and Behavioral sciences. His interests include geropsychiatry, psychopharmacology, substance abuse and psychodynamic psychotherapy.

Myra Cooper is Senior Research Tutor and Consultant Clinical Psychologist on the Clinical Psychology Doctoral Training Course, University of Oxford. She is an internationally recognized expert on eating disorders, and has had an important role in developing and testing new cognitive models of the disorders. She conducted some of the pioneering early information-processing research in eating disorders. She is the author of numerous research papers and book chapters as well as a well-received book *The Psychology of Bulimia Nervosa: A Cognitive Perspective* and (with Gillian Todd and Adrian Wells) a pioneering self-help book, *Bulimia Nervosa; a Client's Guide to Cognitive Therapy* which made her innovate core belief work accessible to patients with eating disorders. She is currently preparing *A Clinician's Guide to Bulimia*

Nervosa (also with Gillian Todd and Adrian Wells), which will present an updated cognitive theory. Recently, with colleagues in Oxford, she has expanded her research work to investigate the neural correlates of cognitive and emotional processing in eating disorders.

Helen DeVries is Professor of Psychology and Director of the Doctoral Programme in Clinical Psychology at Wheaton College, Illinois. She received her PhD in Counselling Psychology from Virginia Commonwealth University and completed her internship at the Palo Alto VA Hospital, with a focus on geropsychology and family therapy. She completed a 1-year NIMH postdoctoral fellowship in geropsychology through the Stanford University School of Medicine and Palo Alto VA Hospital, followed by additional postdoctoral training in neuropsychology and rehabilitation psychology at the Medical College of Virginia. Her areas of interest and research include: family/marital functioning in mid- and late-life families, midlife transitions and training issues in clinical geropsychology. She collaborates with a local community agency serving economically disadvantaged older adults to supervise practicum students in their clinical work with older adults and to carry out research and support clinical services at the agency. She teaches courses in family systems theory/therapy, geropsychology and neuropsychology.

Robert Didden is a professor (Intellectual Disabilities, Learning and Behavior) at the Behavioural Science Institute of the Radboud University Nijmegen. He also is head of Trajectum Knowledge Center and psychologist at Trajectum Hanzeborg at Zutphen, a center for clients with mild to borderline intellectual disabilities and severe behavioral and psychiatric problems, The Netherlands. His research and clinical interests include applied behaviour analysis, especially as applied to behavioural and mental health problems, and instructional procedures for children and adults with developmental disabilities. He serves as an associate editor for *Perceptual and Motor Skills* and the Dutch-language journal *Nederlands Tijdschrift voor de Zorg aan Verstandelijk Gehandicapten.*

Anthony DiMech is a Specialist Registrar in Psychiatry and an honorary lecturer at the Department of Psychiatry, University of Southampton. He has a special interest in cognitive therapy for severe mental conditions including substance use disorders. He graduated in Medicine at the University of Malta in 1997 and was elected member of the Royal College of Psychiatrists in 2004. He was awarded a Master of Science degree in Clinical and Public Health Aspects of Addiction at the Institute of Psychiatry, King's College, London in 2006. His thesis focused on physical health problems in individuals with substance use disorders. In 2007, he was awarded a postgraduate Diploma in cognitive therapy for severe mental health problems at the University of Southampton and specialized in personality disorders.

Mark Dunn is a Clinical Psychotherapist trained as a psychotherapist at Guys Hospital and specializes in cognitive analytic therapy. He teaches psychotherapy and is an experienced clinical practitioner and supervisor in a range of therapeutic models. He retired at Consultant level from the NHS in 2004, after running an outpatient psychotherapy service for 15 years. He is now director of a private psychotherapy service in Central London. In addition, he works with the Metropolitan Police and other organizations in coaching, employee assistance and executive support roles.

Tracy D. Eells received his doctorate in clinical psychology at the University of North Carolina, Chapel Hill and completed a postdoctoral fellowship at the John D. and Catherine T. MacArthur Foundation Programme on Conscious and Unconscious Mental Processes of the University of California, San Francisco. He is currently a Professor of Psychiatry and Behavioral Sciences and Associate Dean for Faculty Affairs at the University of Louisville School of Medicine. He has a busy individual and group psychotherapy practice and teaches psychotherapy to psychiatry residents and clinical psychology graduate students. Dr Eells has published several papers on psychotherapy case formulation and has conducted workshops on the topic for professionals. He is editor of the *Handbook of Psychotherapy Case Formulation*. He is on the editorial board of *Psychotherapy Research, American Journal of Psychotherapy* and *Pragmatic Case Studies in Psychotherapy*. He currently serves as an Executive Officer of the Society for Psychotherapy Research.

Tyish S. Hall Brown is a graduate student in clinical psychology at the University of Maryland, College Park. She began her graduate career at the Maryland Center for Anxiety Disorders where she worked with school-aged children diagnosed with Social Phobia. Currently, she is a member of the CAPER lab under the direction of Carl W. Lejuez where her interests include risk-taking propensity in pre-adolescents, the effects of sleep loss on daytime function in adolescents and the comorbidity of sleep disorders and mood disorders in school age children. Additionally, Tyish has been an extern at Children's National Medical Center in Washington, DC for the past 2 years where she has gained experience in early childhood development as well as paediatric sleep. She is scheduled to attend Brown University for the 2007–2008 pre-doctoral internship year with a special focus on paediatric psychology.

Stephen N. Haynes is Professor of Psychology at University of Hawaii at Manoa. He has published extensively in the area of behavioural assessment, clinical case formulation, assessment instrument development, functional analysis, psychometrics, health psychology and family functioning. He is the author of 13 books and special journal sections, has served on 12 editorial boards and is the previous editor of *Psychological Assessment*, a journal of the American psychological Association.

Derek R. Hopko is Associate Professor of clinical psychology at The University of Tennessee-Knoxville. He graduated from West Virginia University and completed his residency and postdoctoral training at the University of Texas Medical School in Houston. His research and clinical interests focus on the behavioural assessment and treatment of mood and anxiety disorders. Dr Hopko has strong interests in health psychology, and conducts behavioural treatment outcome research with cancer patients diagnosed with clinical depression. He is a recipient of grant funding from the National Institute of Mental Health, the National Cancer Institute and the Susan G. Komen Breast Cancer Foundation. He has over 70 peer-reviewed publications and serves on the editorial board of five journals.

Kevin Howells is Professor of Psychology and Head of the Peaks Academic and Research Unit in the Nottinghamshire Healthcare Trust, one of the four national units for the assessment and treatment of Dangerous and Severe Personality Disorder. He is a Chartered Clinical and Forensic Psychologist Fellow of the British Psychological Society. He has researched treatment of anger, violence and antisocial behaviours, cognitive behaviour therapy, assessment of psychological problems, service evaluation, particularly in forensic settings and idiographic methods.

Tom Jackson is a clinical psychologist supporting adults with intellectual disabilities in Barnsley, England. He graduated from Sheffield University, England in 2004, after completing a doctoral thesis investigating the nature and practice of individual psychodynamic psychotherapy with people with intellectual disabilities. He has longstanding interests in psychodynamic psychotherapy and the emotional experiences of people with intellectual disabilities, and contributes regularly to teaching and training of postgraduate psychologists in clinical training.

Lawrence Jones is the Lead Psychologist in the Peaks unit, Rampton Hospital, UK, a Chartered consultant clinical and forensic psychologist and former Chair of the Division of Forensic Psychology in the British Psychological Society. He has published on case formulation approach to motivation, therapeutic community models for intervention, iatrogenic interventions with personality-disordered offenders and offence analysis. He has previously worked in community, prison and mental health settings with personality-disordered offenders.

David Kingdon is Professor of Mental Health Care Delivery at the University of Southampton, UK, and honorary consultant adult psychiatrist for the Hampshire Partnership NHS Trust. His research interests are in cognitive therapy of severe mental illness and mental health service development on which he has published about 100 papers, chapters and books including lead authoring of *Cognitive Behaviour Therapy in Schizophrenia* (1994, Guilford Press), *A Case Study Guide to Cognitive Behaviour Therapy in Psychosis* (2002, Wiley), *Cognitive Therapy in Schizophrenia* (2005, Guilford Press) and *Tackling Mental Health Crises* (2006, Routledge).

Raimo Lappalainen is Professor in Clinical Psychology and Psychotherapy, at the Department of Psychology, University of Jyväskylä, Finland. He is a licensed psychologist and psychotherapist, and supervisor in cognitive behaviour therapy and acceptance and commitment therapy. He has written and researched in the area of behavioural analysis of eating, cognitive behaviour therapy and acceptance commitment therapy.

Carl W. Lejuez is currently an Associate Professor in the Department of Psychology and Director of the Center for Addictions, Personality, and Emotion Research (CAPER) at the University of Maryland, College Park. His academic work may be best described within the framework of translational research focused on understanding the mechanisms underlying the development and maintenance of affect disturbances and addictive behaviours, with an explicit goal of linking these findings to assessment and treatment. He is the co-founder of the Brief Behavioural Activation Treatment for Depression which is based directly in behaviour theory and basic behavioural principles.

Cory F. Newman is the Director of the Center for Cognitive Therapy, and Associate Professor of Psychology in Psychiatry at the University of Pennsylvania School of Medicine, a Diplomate of the American Board of Professional Psychology, with a specialty in Behavioural Psychology and a Founding Fellow of the Academy of Cognitive Therapy. Dr Newman has served as protocol cognitive therapist and supervisor in a number of psychotherapy outcome studies. In addition to being an international lecturer, Dr Newman is the author of dozens of articles and chapters as well as four books on cognitive therapy.

Jonathan T. Newton is Professor of Psychology as Applied to Dentistry, King's College London. He leads the Oral Health, Workforce and Education Research theme at King's College London, a group which is involved in cutting edge research in the behavioural sciences as applied to dentistry. Outside the dental field, he is interested in research into individuals with severe mental retardation and those with eating disorders. He was Chair of Trustees of a National Charity for Eating Disorders in the United Kingdom and has published on public understanding of and the role of self-help in the management of eating disorders.

Peter Sturmey is Professor of Psychology at Queens College and the Graduate Center, City University of New York. His main research interests are in staff and parent training, developmental disabilities and applied behaviour analysis including applications to clinical psychology.

Maged Swelam is a Specialist Registrar in Psychiatry with a special interest in psychotherapy. He graduated from the University of Alexandria school of Medicine in 1997 and joined Wessex Deanery postgraduate training programme in Psychiatry in 2002. He was awarded the Membership of the Royal College of Psychiatrists in 2004 and was recently awarded a postgraduate Diploma in Cognitive therapy for patients with severe mental health problems from the University of Southampton. Other research interests include the role of Mindfulness and Spirituality in people with mental health problems.

Tero Timonen is the Research Director and Adjunct Professor at the University of Joensuu, Finland, and is a licensed psychologist, cognitive behavioural psychotherapist and supervisor both in Finland and Sweden. His working area is to develop practical therapeutic applications and do research in the area of neurological and cognitive disorders as well as with severe psychological problems in children, adolescents and young adults. As a psychotherapist, he has also worked with adult psychiatric clients with the emphasis on personality problems, psychoses as well as problems in memory, perception and psychological control.

Priyanthy Weerasekera is Associate Professor and Postgraduate Psychotherapy Coordinator in the Department of Psychiatry and Behavioural Neurosciences, McMaster University. She obtained her MD from McMaster, and her MEd in Counselling and Consulting Psychology from Harvard. Along with her colleagues, she has developed a broad-based empirically oriented psychotherapy programme that trains residents in a variety of psychotherapies. She has been invited to present this Programme, and her Multiperspective Formulation Model at numerous academic institutions and professional meetings. She has published articles on these topics as well as a book *Multiperspective Case Formulation: A Step towards Treatment Integration* designed to assist clinicians with this challenging process.

David A. Wilder is Professor of Psychology at Florida Institute of Technology. Dr Wilder has two areas of research interest. The first is in the assessment and treatment of behaviour problems. His second area of interest involves the assessment and improvement of employee performance problems.

Christopher J. Williams is Professor of Psychosocial Psychiatry, University of Glasgow. His main clinical and research interest is in the development and evaluation of ways of providing wider access to CBT approaches, including the *www.livinglifetothefull.com* life skills course, and *www.fiveareas.com* practitioners resources. He has developed written and computer-based self-help treatments for anxiety, depression and bulimia and is a well-known CBT trainer and teacher. He is a Past-President of the British Association for Behavioural and Cognitive Psychotherapies, Director of Glasgow Institute of Psychosocial Interventions (GIPSI), a Trustee of the charity Triumph over Phobia and a Patron of the National Phobics Society in the United Kingdom. He has published a number of self-help packages addressing depression, bulimia and anxiety (www.calipso.co.uk).

Paul Willner is Emeritus Professor of Psychology at University of Wales, Swansea, UK. After an undergraduate and doctoral training at Oxford University, he worked as an academic psychologist in London and Wales, and in 2004 was awarded a higher doctorate from Oxford University for 25 years of research on the psychobiology of depression and addiction. He trained as a clinical psychologist in the late 1990s and has worked as a full-time clinician, supporting adults with intellectual disabilities, since 2000. His major current research interests are in the application of CBT to people with intellectual disabilities, forensic issues and mental capacity.

Preface

When mental health practitioners are faced with a new client they have to predict the best treatment for this particular person. This is not an abstract question concerning the efficacy of treatments in general, but a highly specific question about one particular person and his or her unique set of circumstances right here and now. Many mental health practitioners answer this question by using psychiatric diagnosis as a predictor of best treatment. But for many reasons, mental health practitioners often reject this approach. Rather, the clinician takes the information he or she has concerning this specific person's unique set of problems, assets and circumstances, and using the clinician's experience, knowledge of the outcome literature, theoretical perspective creates a hypothesis or series of hypotheses that will guide them to the most effective treatment for this person.

Case formulation is a commonly taught clinical skill and many clinicians use it routinely. Although there is some agreement about the general features and common general principles that underlie case formulation, the content of different formulations is often quite different depending upon the theoretical orientation of the clinician. Clinicians may make formulations from cognitive, cognitive-behavioural, behavioural, psychodynamic, psychiatric and eclectic approaches. Even within each of these orientations, the specific technologies and concepts used to develop a formulation may vary considerably.

This book provides examples of contrasting formulations of the same case for five different clinical problems: depression in a middle-aged woman, psychosis, an eating disorder, hoarding in an older adult and anger in a person with intellectual disabilities. Each pair of formulations is followed by an independent commentary and the final chapter in the book comments upon the entire volume and endeavour of case formulation.

I thank all the authors of the chapters, especially those who wrote case formulations. The authors of case formulation chapters were brave enough to expose their clinical skills to the world, to knowingly write a formulation that would be contrasted with another unknown formulation and that would be critiqued both by the authors of the commentary chapters as well as book's readers. The authors of the commentator chapter also deserve special thanks: they had to balance honesty with tact. I asked the authors to carry out very specific tasks: they all succeeded in doing so.

PART I
Overview

1

Case Formulation: A Review and Overview of This Volume

PETER STURMEY

Case formulation is a basic clinical skill for many mental health professionals. It is often included in professional training (Page and Strizke, 2006; Page, Stritzke and McLean, 2008) and continuing education for many mental health professionals (Kendjelic and Eells, 2007; Kuyken *et al.*, 2005; Sim, Gwee and Bateman, 2005). Various professional bodies, such as the British Psychological Society (British Psychological Society Division of Clinical Psychology, 2000, 2001), the American Psychiatric Association (2004) and the American Psychological Association (APA) (2005), identify this as a professional competency that practitioners should have and the professional training courses should teach. Within cognitive-behavioural approaches to mental health, case formulation is seen as a core skill for all practitioners. The first part of this chapter provides an overview of what is meant by case formulation. The second part of the chapter describes how authors in this book made their case formulation and highlights some of the links and contrasts across different formulations in this book.

CASE FORMULATION

Rationale and importance of case formulation

Clinicians must determine which treatment is best for which client. There are now a very large number of treatments available for all the common mental

Clinical Case Formulation: Varieties of Approaches. Edited by Peter Sturmey.
© 2009 John Wiley & Sons, Ltd.

health disorders. Clinicians may well be perplexed as to which treatment to select for each particular client.

One approach to solve this problem is to use psychiatric diagnosis to predict treatment. The terms used to describe both pharmacological and psychological treatments often refer to diagnosis. Psychotropic medications are called 'anti-depressants', 'anti-psychotics' and 'anxiolytics'. Psychological treatments also often refer to diagnosis, for example when we refer to treatment groups as 'anxiety management groups' or 'support groups for eating disorders' and so on. Treatment algorithms, randomized controlled trials (RCTs), reviews of the outcome literature and reviews of evidence-based treatment, such as Cochrane reviews, National Institute for Clinical Excellence guidelines and the APA guidelines (APA, 2005), all are organized around diagnostic categories. Many mental health advocacy groups are also organized around specific diagnostic groups. Thus, the notion that diagnosis predicts effective and ineffective treatment is pervasive. This model suggests that diagnosis 1 predicts that treatment A will be relatively effective for this diagnosis and treatment B will be relatively ineffective for this diagnosis, and diagnosis 2 predicts that treatment A will be relatively ineffective and treatment B will be relatively effective for this diagnosis. Thus, we might recommend anti-depressants for people with Major Depression, but not for a Psychotic Disorder. Likewise, we would place people with anxiety disorders in an anxiety management group, not in a support group for people with eating disorders. This model is based on an interaction between diagnosis and treatment.

This model of predicting treatment efficacy has many limitations. First, most outcome research using RCTs does not address the question of diagnosis by treatment interaction. Rather, most RCTs merely compare one treatment with some other procedure, such as a waiting list control, or, more rarely, some placebo or perhaps a second treatment. Researchers select participants to ensure that they all meet the *same* diagnosis. Thus, these kinds of RCTs permit us to conclude that treatment A may be effective for diagnosis 1. They tell us nothing about the effectiveness of this treatment for diagnosis 2 and nothing about whether this treatment is the *most* effective treatment for this diagnosis. Wilson (1996) proposed a contrary argument. He has noted that some standardized, manualized treatments for eating disorders are highly effective. He suggested that treatment determined by diagnosis might be highly desirable because the clinician can learn one highly effective treatment procedure to a high degree of proficiency. Further, there may be little room left for individualization of treatment – which in any case might be unreliable and capricious – to improve over this standard treatment. (Ghaderi [2006] presented some evidence to the contrary.)

A second limitation to this model of predicting which treatments might be effective is that response to treatment is highly varied. RCTs emphasize statistical significance – changes that are unlikely to be due to chance – and changes in the score of the average, but non-existent, subject. Statistically significant results may emerge from many patterns of response to treatment. For example, a statistically significant result might occur if 50% of the treatment group have a large, positive response to treatment, 25% have no response and 25% have a modest *negative* response to treatment, if the experiment has a large enough number of participants and if the dependent measures are sufficiently sensitive. A statistically significant result may also emerge if most of the participants make a modest improvement but one that has no practical significance for any particular person. The average client does not exist: the clinician will never treat this mythical person. The clinician treats specific clients. Even when there is a strong evidence base for a particular treatment, it may be unclear at the outset of treatment if the clinician is working with someone who will respond positively, not respond or respond negatively to this particular treatment.

A third limitation is that clinicians frequently work with clients who have apparently already had standard, diagnosis-based treatment and who did not respond to any meaningful degree. For example, it is common for clinicians to work with people who have taken anti-depressants or anxiolytic medication for many years and still have significant problems; indeed their failure to respond to standard treatments is often the reason for referral. Further, after standardized psychological treatments, such as anger management, cognitive behaviour therapy for depression and so on, a significant proportion of clients have residual problems, did not respond or responded badly to standard treatment.

A fourth limitation in diagnosis predicting the most effective treatment for each client is that many clients meet diagnostic criteria for more than one diagnosis. When a clinician works with a client who meets diagnostic criteria for Major Depression, Substance Abuse and Generalized Anxiety Disorder, which of these three diagnoses predict the most effective treatment for this client? If all three predict effective treatments, in which order should the clinician implement these treatments? Will effective treatment of the Major Depression result in a generalized improvement in the client's functioning, or will treatment of the Generalized Anxiety Disorder result in the broadest spread of treatment effects?

The ability of psychiatric diagnosis to predict the most effective treatment depends on the reliability and validity of that diagnosis. The developers of the third edition (revised) of the *Diagnostic and Statistical Manual* (DSM) trumpeted its arrival as a triumph of science (Kutchins and Kirk, 1997). The number of psychiatric diagnoses has expanded considerably with each edition of DSM (Houts, 2002) and the developers of DSM did not conduct reliability trials for almost all the hundreds of diagnoses in DSM-III-R (Kutchins and Kirk, 1997). Where researchers did conduct diagnostic trials, they were conducted *after* the diagnostic criteria had already been set; thus, the results of reliability trials did not inform the development of the diagnostic criteria. Indeed, careful examination of the reliability of DSM-III-R revealed that the reliability of the new diagnostic criteria may not have been very much different from the reliability of the old criteria (Kutchins and Kirk, 1997). In any case, this may be of limited relevance, since the reliability of diagnosis by routine practitioners may have little to do with the diagnostic practices of eager, well-trained government-funded researchers. Some structured clinical interview procedures may result in quite high reliability. However, most clinicians do not use these assessment methods routinely. In any case, the *validity* of these measures to differentially predict an effective treatment is still little researched.

Clinicians may often work with clients with rare, idiosyncratic, subclinical problems or other problems that do not meet diagnostic criteria. In these situations too, psychiatric diagnosis may be of limited use to predict treatment.

Finally, some clinicians often feel that they have something more to offer than skilled, but technocratic, application of diagnostic algorithms and manualized treatment. Whether true or not, many clinicians believe that their input into understanding the case and designing treatment for each individual client has something to contribute to treatment.

These limitations to predict treatment based on diagnosis, if true, are serious. Consequently, clinicians and professional training standards have argued that case formulation is a better way to guide selection of the most effective treatment. So what is case formulation?

Definitions of case formulation

There are many definitions of case formulations. Eells (2007a) defined case formulation as

> a hypothesis about the causes, precipitants, and maintaining influences of a person's psychological, interpersonal and behavioral problems ... [which] helps organize information about a person, particularly when that information contains contradictions or inconsistencies in behavior, emotion and thought content ... it contains structures that permit the therapist to understand these contradictions ... it also serves as a blueprint guiding treatment ... It should help the therapist experience greater empathy for the patient and anticipate possible ruptures in the therapy alliance ... The nature of this hypothesis can vary widely depending on which theory ... the clinician uses ... (p. 4)

Eells' definition is deliberately broad and attempts to avoid any theory-specific constructs. His definition specifies that case formulations serve several functions, such as unifying information concerning development and maintenance of the presenting problems, resolving conflicting information, guiding treatment and improving the relationship between the therapist and client.

Others have defined case formulation from the perspective of specific theories. For example, McWilliams (1999) noted from a dynamic formulation that when her supervisor first asked her to make a dynamic formulation of a case she should

> suggest how the person's symptoms, mental status, personality type, personal history, and current circumstances all fit together and make sense ... (p. vii)

Later, she noted that we put all the assessment information into

> a narrative that makes this human being and his or her psychopathology comprehensible to us, and we derive our recommendations and our way of relating to the client from that narrative ... (p. viii)

Thompkins (2007) gave this definition of case formulation from the cognitive-behavioural perspective:

> [A] hypothesis about the patient's disorders and problems, and which is used as the basis for intervention ... it is parsimonious; that is, it offers the minimum detail necessary to accomplish the task of guiding treatment ... (p. 291)

Turkat (1990) defined problem formulation from a behavioural perspective as

> (1) [a] hypothesis about the relationship among the various problems of the individual; (2) [h]ypotheses about the aetiology of the aforementioned difficulties; (3) [p]redictions about the patient's future behaviour ... (p. 17)

From an eclectic perspective, Weerasekera (1996) wrote that

> 'formulation' is defined as a provisional explanation or hypothesis of how an individual comes to present with a certain disorder or circumstances at a particular point in time ... [that] include[s] biological, psychological and systemic factors ... (p. 4)

As these definitions illustrate, researchers and clinicians have offered definitions of case formulation from an atheoretical stance and from the perspective of both specific and eclectic approaches to case formulation. These definitions come from very different authors. Yet, they share several features. First, most of them emphasize that a formulation abstracts out key features of the case. A formulation is not a list, chronology or summary of all the details of the case. Persons and Thompkins hit the nail on the head when they suggested that a formulation should have enough detail to guide treatment, and, by implication, nothing more. A second related idea is that case formulations should integrate all the information about the case into a unified and related idea or set of ideas. The formulation should tie together the onset, development, maintenance of the problem(s) and should link these ideas to the treatment that should grow out of and relate to the formulation. Third, these definitions note or imply the tentative and provisional nature of case formulation. A case formulation is only based on what the clinician knows so far. Further assessment, events, response to treatment and relapses may all cause a formulation to be revised in some potentially significant way. For example, Haynes and O'Brien (2000) pointed out that formulations have boundaries. Finally, one of the key functions of case formulation is to guide treatment. Specifically, case formulations should predict individually designed treatments that will be more effective than treatments that would otherwise have been implemented.

Different approaches to case formulations share these several features. However, the authors' differing theoretical perspectives result in very significant differences between approaches to case formulation. Specifically, approaches to case formulation differ in terms of the following: (1) the nature of the behaviour that therapy should change; (2) which independent variables are important in a case formulation; (3) the role of history in a case formulation; (4) how to use the case formulation with the client; (5) the role of psychiatric diagnosis, if any, in case formulation; and (6) how prescriptive the definitions of case formulation are (see Table 1.1).

Current status

There are now at least two handbooks and many individual volumes available on case formulation. Most are cognitive and cognitive-behavioural approaches to formulations, although this literature does address all major theoretical approaches. For example, Eells' *Handbook of Psychotherapy Case Formulation* (Eells, 1997, 2007b) presents case formulation and many examples of case formulation from psychoanalytic, eclectic, cognitive, cognitive-behavioural and behavioural perspectives. Hersen and Rosqvist (2008) published a large

Table 1.1 A summary of different theoretical orientations in psychology and how they may apply to various aspects of case formulation.

Orientation	Relevant variables	Cause of behaviour	Role of client history	Assessment	Prototypical treatment	Therapeutic relationship
Behavioural	Observable behaviour, including what people do, say and feel is central. Thoughts and feelings are important too since they are private behaviour. Private behaviour is accessible only to one person. Self-report of behaviour and other information are regarded with suspicion, as such verbal behaviour is often controlled by other people's behaviour and may be inaccurate reports of both public and private behaviour	The current environment controls public and private behaviour. Controlling variables for respondent behaviour include unconditioned and conditioned stimuli. Controlling variables for operant behaviour include reinforcer deprivation and satiation, antecedent stimuli and contingencies. Private verbal behaviour, such as rules, private antecedents and contingencies may also be important, but may be hard to access and change	The current environment controls behaviour because of the organism's learning history. History may be less important than the current environment as only the current environment can be modified to change behaviour	Focuses on reliable observation of behaviour and experimental manipulation of independent variables to detect reliable functional relationships between the environment and behaviour. Self-report data alone is insufficient	Teaching skills, other behaviour, including self-regulation, as alternatives to problematic behaviour and poor self-control repertoires. Direct treatment of the target behaviour may also take place, for example, through operant extinction, and through changing the behaviour of relevant others, such as family members and friends	The therapist must establish himself or herself as a powerful source of reinforcement by demonstrating that his or her advice results in client relief from aversive behaviour and situations. The therapist should carefully teach the client more effective ways of behaving and self-regulation

(Continued)

Table 1.1 (Continued).

Orientation	Relevant variables	Cause of behaviour	Role of client history	Assessment	Prototypical treatment	Therapeutic relationship
Cognitive	Current problems and current thinking are the focus of cognitive therapy. The therapist tries to infer patterns of faulty thinking, such as attributions and negative automatic thoughts, and cognitive structures that cause the presenting problem(s)	Client's current problem behaviour is caused by faulty cognition. This faulty thinking may be precipitated by a stressful event. The clients may have learned these inappropriate cognitions earlier in life	The client may have learned maladaptive ways to think and stressful life events may have precipitated current maladaptive patterns of thinking	The therapist should identify the faulty patterns of thinking, beliefs, attributions, perceptions and other faulty cognitive processes. This may be done by carefully interviewing the client, questionnaire measures of thinking and attributions, self-recording and behavioural experiments to disconfirm faulty thinking	Maladaptive patterns of thinking are changed by teaching the client to identify them, retraining thinking and conducting behaviour exercises to challenge maladaptive beliefs. Skills teaching and some forms of exposure therapy may also be included	The relationships should be supportive, collaborative, open and active in order for the client to participate in assessment, understand the formulation and participate in treatment

Psychodynamic	The current problems are symptoms of an underlying conflict that likely dates back to infancy or early childhood. The relationship between the client and others, including the therapist and client, may mirror historical relationships, such as those with caretakers. Therapist feelings concerning the client may also provide valuable insights	Historical trauma, often early in development, and subsequent defences cause the presenting problem	Client history is central to case conceptualization and treatment. Only when the original trauma is uncovered and revealed through interpretations will real change in the current problem occur	Assessment focuses on whether the client is suitable for psychodynamic psychotherapy, on interpreting current symptoms and defences in order to uncover the original trauma	Client and therapist meet together individually. The therapist is a reflective sounding board for the client, reflects what the client says and does and occasionally makes interpretations. The transference of client feelings and therapist feelings about the client are important. The therapist reveals little of himself or herself	The relationship is the vehicle for therapeutic change. This relationship may become very significant to the client. Therapist's feelings regarding the client may be useful in understanding the client's problems

(Continued)

Table 1.1 (Continued).

Orientation	Relevant variables	Cause of behaviour	Role of client history	Assessment	Prototypical treatment	Therapeutic relationship
Psychiatric	Symptom clusters that correspond to mental illnesses; psychiatric histories that are typical of different mental illnesses	Presenting problems are symptoms of mental illnesses described in manuals of mental disorders caused by biochemical disorders of the brain, genes and their interaction with the environment	A client history is usually taken. Sometimes a history may be characteristic of a particular mental illness and may be a part of a comprehensive psychiatric case formulation	Assessment typically takes place during an interview with a psychiatrist. Assessment may also include record reviews, questionnaires and input from team members	Mental illnesses are treated primarily with psychotropic medications. Other treatments are adjunctive, but may be considered	The psychiatrist is a physician who like other physicians treats illnesses. The relationship should be professional, respectful and supportive. The psychiatrist may educate the client about his or her illness, medication and the side effects of medication
Eclectic	'Eclectic' refers to several approaches to case formulation that combine perspectives from two or more schools of therapy. Hence, many variables may be relevant	Many causes of behaviour may be considered, such as biological, learning, cognition, interpersonal and psychodynamic and so on	If this particular version of eclecticism includes perspectives that incorporate a school of psychology that addresses history than it may be important	Many forms of assessment may be included. Some forms of eclecticism include methods to combine assessment information from different schools of psychology	Many treatments are possible. Some forms of eclecticism borrow interventions from many schools of psychology and may also include psychiatric interventions, such as psychotropic medications	This varies from one form of eclecticism to another, but many forms of eclecticism include the therapeutic relationship as being important in various ways

handbook on case conceptualization and treatment in adults which covers all the common DSM diagnostic categories and includes many examples of case formulation, largely from a cognitive-behavioural perspective. Sturmey (2007) also provided examples of behavioural approaches to conceptualization and case formulation of all the major DSM-IV diagnoses. There are also several other smaller volumes that also focus on cognitive and cognitive-behavioural approaches to case formulation (Bruch and Bond, 1998; Gauss, 2007; Nezu, Nezu and Lombardo, 2004; Persons, 1989; Tarrier, 2006; Tarrier, Wells and Haddock, 1998). These cognitive and cognitive-behavioural approaches to case formulation are one of the most active areas of publication on case formulation at this time. Others have published on case formulation from a psychotherapeutic (Horowitz, 1997; McWilliams, 1999), behavioural (Cipani and Schock, 2007; Dougher, 2000; Turkat, 1985, Skinner, 1953, 1971; Sturmey, 1996, 2007, 2008) and eclectic perspectives (Weerasekera, 1996). In the specific area of functional assessment and analysis of behaviour problems, where behavioural approaches are sometimes mandated in American law, there are also specific resources on case formulation to address this need in both special education (O'Neill *et al.*, 1997) and mainstream settings (Umbreit *et al.*, 2006; Watson and Steege, 2003). There are also individual examples of case formulation scattered throughout clinical journals, including some dedicated to case studies and some, such as *Cognitive and Behavioral Practice*, that have presented case formulations with subsequent commentaries and responses by the original case formulation authors.

Most of these books present only one theoretical perspective. Several books, Eells (1997, 2007b) in particular, present case formulations from different perspectives, but in order to contrast different approaches to case formulation the reader must compare formulations across different cases in different parts of the book. No books directly contrast different approaches to case formulation. Thus, educators providing professional training in case formulation, students and practitioners lack resources to learn about these differences.

THE CURRENT VOLUME

I designed this book to address this gap. The aims of this volume are to (1) provide models of different approaches to case formulation, (2) highlight the differences in approaches to case formulation, (3) provide models of case formulation for common clinical problems that were varied in terms of the referred problem, population and context, (4) identify the significant issues in alternate approaches to case formulation, and (5) stimulate debate on alternate approaches to case formulation.

The authors' tasks

I did not ask authors to write literature reviews on case formulation. Several are already available (e.g. Tarrier and Calem, 2002). These reviews have many virtues, but they do not meet the needs identified above. I therefore devised the following format. First, one or more authors wrote a case description. Each case description was structured with standard headings. I provided some guidelines as to what authors should write in each section. Table 1.2 summarizes these guidelines. Once the authors had completed their case studies, I sent them out to two new sets of authors who independently wrote formulations of the case. Again, I provided predetermined sections and guidelines for each of the authors to follow. Table 1.3 summarizes these guidelines. I gave formulation authors these standard guidelines to facilitate comparison of the formulations by the commentator authors and readers. In order to allow a

Table 1.2   The case study guidelines given to authors of the case study chapters.

The word limit is 4000 words: there are no exceptions! Please use the following standard headings in your chapter
1. *Presenting complaint*. Describe the main presenting complaints and any other problems the client presents with. If relevant describe the reasons that the client would give for seeking help. Do not organize the material too much. Let the case formulators in each chapter do that
2. *Client demographic data*. Briefly describe the client's relevant demographic data
3. *Client demeanour and personal appearance*. Describe the client's demeanour, behaviour, affect and personal appearance in so far that it is relevant to the case
4. *Client current lifestyle*. Describe the client' current lifestyle including education, work or other daily patterns of living, relationships and social support, family status and the impact of the client's problems on these factors. Include information on those variables that are likely to be of interest to the two authors writing the case formulations. If the client currently received treatment for the presenting problems, describe them
5. *Client history*. Describe the client history close to the way the client would describe his or her own history. Again, include information on those variables that are likely to be of interest to the two authors writing the case formulations. If there are previous treatments describe them and the client's response to these treatments
6. *Client goals*. If the client has goals for therapy state them in the client's own terms
7. *An event*. Describe an event that might occur during assessment or early during therapy that might confirm a current formulation or give rise to an opportunity to reformulate

Table 1.3   The guidelines for authors writing case formulations.

4500 word limit – no exceptions! Each case formulation chapter will use a standard series of headings used to illustrate what is important to each approach to case formulation. The aim is to not only show your formulation, but how and why you arrived at this formulation. These will include the following sections

1. *Theoretical orientation and rationale.* State the theory that frames your formulation. State the rationale for your case formulation

2. *Relevant and irrelevant variables.* Identify the relevant and irrelevant variables in your case formulation. Justify your selection. Which variables do you give most weight to and why?

3. *Role of research and clinical experience.* What is the role of research versus clinical experience and intuition in this approach to case formulation? State very briefly what research, if any supports this approach

4. *The formulation.* Concisely state your formulation

5. *History.* Describe the status you give the client's history and its significance, if any, in your formulation

6. *Current factors.* Describe the status of current factors in your formulation of the case and their significance, if any, in your formulation

7. *Treatment plan.* Describe the treatment plan implied by your formulation. Describe how this plan is linked to your formulation. Describe how your formulation changes the treatment plan from a standard treatment plan to an idiographic treatment plan for this particular person

8. *The event.* Your case description includes an event. Interpret that event in the light of your formulation. Does this event confirm your formulation or cause you to reformulate. Justify your decision. Does the event and its associated reformulation, if any, change your treatment plan?

9. *Other issues.* Are there any other issues in formulating this case?

10. *Summary.* Briefly summarize your formulation in 200 words

clear examination of differences in approaches to case formulation, I selected authors from different and contrasting theoretical perspectives. Finally, once these authors have completed their two independent formulations, I gave the case study and the two formulation chapters to another author and asked him or her to comment upon the two independent formulations. Again, I attempted to find commentator authors from theoretical perspectives that differed from those of both authors of the two case formulations. Table 1.4 summarizes the commentators' guidelines.

In selecting authors and commentators, I attempted to address some common theoretical and clinical questions and to address potential strengths and weaknesses of different approaches to case formulation. (The final authors also reflect the vagaries of recruiting authors.) For example, the two formulations of the depression case contrast cognitive-behavioural with behavioural

Table 1.4   The guidelines for authors writing comments.

The main purpose of the comments is to highlight the similarities and differences between
the two case formulations. This can relate to the variables that are considered relevant –
the target behaviours, proximate and distal causes – the role of research versus
experience and intuition, the role of the therapeutic relationship, the kinds of treatment
implied by the formulation and so on

There is no specific format or headings for the comments chapters

When writing your commentary, bear two things in mind. First, you may disagree with one
(or both) of the case formulations. If you do have critical comments make them
respectfully and in a way that addresses the ideas, not the author. Second, the word limit
you have is very tight – only 3000 words. Stick to it! You can only do this by being quite
concise and structured in your comments

---

approaches to formulating depression. These are two common approaches
which have some similarities, but also have fundamental differences. Likewise, the contrast of a cognitive analytic therapy formulation with psychodynamic formulation allows the reader to consider the merits and limitations of
one eclectic approach to case formulation, which includes elements of psychodynamic approaches, with another purely psychodynamic approach. Sometimes the differences between different approaches to case conceptualization
are said to be modest and make little fundamental difference to treatment.
However, the contrast between psychodynamic and cognitive-behavioural approaches to case formulation of anger in a man with intellectual disabilities is
quite remarkable. One places the causes of the problem largely in the past and
one largely in the present; one results in a treatment plan consisting of weekly
psychotherapy sessions and one results in a 16-week anger management plan
that includes skills teaching and cognitive therapy. Table 1.5 summarizes
these chapters and their theoretical orientations.

Overview of the volume

Two chapters frame the five sections on case formulation. This chapter describes the general issues in case formulation and the final chapter by Tracy
Eells reacts to the entire book, identifies emerging themes and suggests future directions for research. I invited him to do so because of his extensive experience in editing the two editions of his *Handbook of Psychotherapy Case Formulation* (Eells, 1997, 2007b) and extensive research in case
formulation, including research on professional training in this area (Eells,
Kandjelic and Lucas, 1998; Eells and Lombart, 2003; Eells *et al.*, 2005).

Table 1.5 A summary of the theoretical orientations and authors in Sections 1–5 of the book.

Case	First formulation	Second formulation	Commentary
Depression Brannigan and Williams	Cognitive Newman	Behavioural Lejuez *et al.*	Cognitive-behavioural Williams
Psychosis DiMech, Swelam and Kingdom	Psychiatric Casey	Behavioural Wilder	Anti-psychiatry/cognitive Bentall
Eating disorder Newton	Eclectic Weerasekera	Behavioural Lappailanen *et al.*	Cognitive Cooper
Hoarding in older adults DeVries	Cognitive Dunn	Psychodynamic Barrett	Cognitive-behavioural and cognitive analytic Howells and Jones
Anger in a person with intellectual disabilities Benson	Psychodynamic Beail and Jones	Cognitive Willner	Behavioural Didden

Depression

Depression is often referred to as the 'common cold' of mental health; hence, a chapter on formulation of depression is a good place to begin. Brannigan and Williams describe a middle-aged woman with low mood, lack of confidence, sleep disturbance and physiological discomfort, such as tension and tachycardia. She also has poor relationships with her family and at work. Her husband works away from home a lot and her children have left home: the nest is mostly empty and an affair is on the near horizon. She has a history of high academic achievement and professional training, but, after giving up her career to raise her family, she cannot get back into a job commensurate with her training. Further, she performs poorly in this job that is well below her capacity because of repeatedly checking her work. Thus, in two areas that are of key importance to her – her family and profession – she does poorly.

Cognitive and cognitive-behavioural approaches to case formulation now dominate clinical practice and educational training and there is an extensive literature on the effectiveness of cognitive and cognitive behaviour therapy with depression. Yet, behaviourism has a long history of formulating and treating depression (Ferster, 1973; Lewinsohn, 1974; Skinner, 1953, 1971) and some research suggests that the mechanism behind cognitive and cognitive-behavioural treatment of depression is behavioural activation, rather than cognitive restructuring. For example, Jacobson *et al.* (1996) conducted a component analysis of cognitive-behavioural treatment of depression. They found that, despite greater therapist allegiance to cognitive therapy, behavioural activation was more effective than cognitive therapy. Further, this was true for several outcome measures, including cognitive measures. Recently, there has been a revival of interest in behavioural activation for treatment of depression. For example, a recent meta-analysis of behavioural activation based on 16 RCTs with 780 subjects found a large effect size for behavioural activation, no evidence of loss of effect at follow-up and a small, non-significant difference in favour of behavioural activation over other psychological treatments (Cuijpers, van Straten and Warmerdam, 2007). Thus, the first formulation by Newman is a Beckian cognitive formulation of this case and the second is a behavioural formulation by LeJuez, Hopko and Hall Brown.

Newman's cognitive formulation focuses on negative automatic thoughts, such as 'I am fat'. These thoughts result from the client's assumptions and schemata, such as 'flaws are intolerable', which appear to date back to the client's early learning history. The therapist and client work collaboratively and empirically to make this formulation. Research and clinical experience are both important and this formulation would use many kinds of data, such as weekly monitoring of mood using psychometric instruments, and activity logs to monitor specific problems, such as alcohol use. The formulation notes that loneliness, avoidance of disappointing others, cognitions about abandonment are all key factors in understanding this client's problems. The treatment implied by this formulation includes addressing avoidance, cognitive restructuring for both negative automatic thoughts and core beliefs, teaching communication skills using role play and preparation for upcoming potentially difficult situations and regular homework assignments. Newman remains neutral on the issue of the affair and would offer discussions about it as well as opportunities to improve her marital relationship.

LeJuez, Hall Brown and Hopko's behavioural formulation of this case focuses on the loss of contingent reinforcement for healthy behaviour, especially in the areas of family role and relationships. They use problematic thoughts to identify target behaviours that produce these problematic thoughts, for example, behaviour that results in lack of confidence. Their treatment plan begins with building a good therapeutic relationship, identifying the functions of depressed behaviour in order to subsequently increase valued activities that serve the same function as depressed behaviour, such as maintaining an important role in her daughter's life in a healthy fashion. This is done by identifying long-term valued goals, small weekly goals and daily self-recording of those small goals. Since family roles are so important to Sally, they explicitly argue against the affair and instead recommend interventions to strengthen the marital relationship. LeJuez *et al.* note that progress should be evaluated comprehensively, not only in terms of increased activity.

Williams was one of the authors of the case study and a noted expert in cognitive behaviour therapy, so his commentary on the two formulations is especially pertinent. He begins by noting the similarities in these two approaches to formulations, such as an emphasis on strong therapeutic alliance, active collaboration between client and therapist, empiricism, both in terms of an evidence base for selection of treatment and for developing the formulation and evaluating treatment with the client, a focus on current functioning and emphasis on change outside of the weekly therapy session. The formulations differ in the way they conceive of cognitions, the role of other people, and how to handle the potential affair. Some of the issues he identifies include how to use a formulation with a client, including presenting the information in a readable, readily interpretable manner, and a relative neglect of issues such as client strengths, religious belief and potential medical issues in both formulations.

Schizophrenia

Kingdom, Swelam and DiMech describe a case of psychosis in a 29-year-old man, Zeppi, with an unusual developmental history characterized by deprivation, absent or abusive family and other inappropriate social relationships. He is isolated, unemployed, suspicious and unkempt. He believes that there is a conspiracy in which others are trying to kill him by focusing electromagnetic waves on him. Following an incident in which a neighbour called the police because he was carrying a large knife, the police detained him and they found that he had two knives with him. Following admission to a psychiatric hospital, Zeppi did not take his psychotropic medication and during the third week of admission Zeppi experienced unusual physical sensations and attacked a nurse and broke her nose.

Psychiatrists commonly formulate cases and often do so using a medical-diagnostic model; this is especially true in the area of schizophrenia, which is often seen as largely biological illness. Casey provides a prototypical psychiatric formulation of this case. He presents classical rationales for the medical-diagnostic model. Namely, there are discrete illnesses described by symptom patterns codified in the APA's (1994) *Diagnostic and Statistical Manual* (DSM) and presented in multi-axial classification. These symptom patterns reflect underlying brain pathology and disturbances in neurotransmitters. The existence of these illnesses is supported by a vast amount of biomedical research and the effectiveness of psychotropic medications. Psychiatrists are skilled at detecting these symptom patterns and prescribe medications that correspond to the diagnosed illness. Casey presents several common criticisms of this approach and finds them all unsatisfactory. He presents a formulation that is the DSM multi-axial classification of the illnesses. This guides treatment in identifying anti-psychotic medication as the treatment plan. Additionally, a multi-disciplinary team would provide other interventions, such as re-establishing family contact.

Behavioural approaches are often pitted as the opposite to medical models, since they construe behaviour as the thing in and of itself to be treated, rather than a symptom of an underlying illness (Sturmey, 2007, 2008). Hence, contrasting a behavioural formulation of this case highlights the characteristics of each approach. Wilder describes how a behavioural approach to the case would identify specific behaviours of interest and their relationship to environmental events such as antecedents and consequences as well as any skills deficits that Zeppi might have. Wilder notes that early behavioural models used arbitrary consequences, such as food, which were unrelated to the variables maintaining the behaviour. In contrast, contemporary behavioural interventions for schizophrenia are based on an understanding of which variables influence the target behaviour. Thus, treatment involves restructuring the environment based on this assessment. Other variables, such as history and genetics, may well be important, but the clinician cannot manipulate them. Wilder suggests that assessment includes ruling out medical problems, accurately identifying the function of the somatic complaints by individual experiments and identifying skills deficits. Wilder also demonstrates how the event can be analyzed using an antecedent–behaviour–consequent chart. The treatment plan would include teaching a skill to replace the somatic complaints that served the same function, teaching and motivating social, self-care and vocational skills.

Bentall, well known for his anti-psychiatry analysis of schizophrenia (Bentall, 2003), comments on the case and these formulations from a cognitive perspective. Bentall noted the limitations of psychiatric diagnosis of psychotic disorders, especially in terms of validity and the ability of psychiatric diagnosis to predict treatment. Likewise, he notes the limitations of this behavioural formulation because of the possibility of limited scope of the analysis and the possibility that treatment effects of operant interventions may be limited. He also notes that both formulations fail to address the content of the delusions. He suggests that two kinds of delusions are 'poor me' delusions, in which the person feels like an innocent victim, as in Zeppi's case, and 'bad me' delusions, in which a person feels that persecution is deserved. He goes on to reformulate the case, including both the presenting delusions, history and event, and goes on to suggest alternate cognitive interventions, such as testing the veracity of strange, but potentially true, beliefs.

Anorexia nervosa

Eating disorders are a common referral, and, like depression, clinicians should be able to formulate these common problems. Newton presents a case study that exemplifies many of the presenting problems and complexities of Anorexia Nervosa. These include reduced and restrictive eating, excessive exercise, various kinds of perfectionism and low weight that is not problematic for the client, but problematic for those around them. Additionally there are social problems, including complex family dynamics, poor friendships and avoidance of adult roles. Newton captures some of the common dynamics of anorexia, when at the second appointment, Antoinette's mother – a former ballerina who gave up her career to help her former husband's career – announces that she too has had anorexia since adolescence! and seeks the therapist's help for her problems.

Weerasekera (1996) has published on one particular form of eclectic case formulation called 'multi-perspective' case formulation. This is a version of the application of the biopsychosocial model of mental health applied to case formulation and involves consideration of biological, psychological and social factors and consideration of the individual and the system in which they behave. These different perspectives are integrated into one integrated formulation. Weerasekera argues that no one theoretical perspective is adequate to account for the full complexity of any case and thus all relevant theoretical perspectives should be used.

Weerasekera's formulation notes that Antoinette has biological vulnerabilities to Anorexia Nervosa, Obsessive Compulsive Personality Disorder and parent–child problems. Her developmental history and family dynamics may have contributed to the development of her problems although her performance at school, at least until recently, was a strength. Precipitating factors include attention from her mother for eating problems and avoidance of her father with his new wife. Her defences include displacing her feelings of loss onto activities she can control, such as exercise. Initial treatment includes establishing a positive therapeutic relationship and behavioural intervention to establish clear goals for change and cognitive therapy. This will then set the stage for an integrated treatment plan which will include cognitive-behavioural and psychodynamic therapy to address eating, facilitation of expression of affect, family therapy, medication to maintain weight gain and social activities at school.

Haynes has also developed a very characteristic approach to case formulation (Haynes and O'Brien, 2000). This approach involves multi-modal behavioural assessment, clear specification of which variables are causes, correlates and target behaviours. This method then classifies these causal variables in terms of degree of manipulability, magnitude of effect and whether their effects are direct or intermediate. The formulation is then summarized in a Functional Analytic Clinical Case Model (FACCM) vector diagram. Lappailanen, Timonen and Haynes presented a second formulation of this case. Noting that diagnostic-based explanations of clinical problems are often circular, they go on to note that clinicians often fail to acquire the necessary, reliable and valid information to make a rigorously valid formulation. Thus, they recommend expanding the limited assessment information in the case to include many different forms of assessment, such as direct observation of mother–daughter interaction in analogue situations, such as eating a meal, self-monitoring many aspects of eating behaviour and so on. This information is used to systematically identify the status of relevant variables and potential causal chains of events and behaviour. They then use the resulting FACCM diagram to identify key causal variables that are readily manipulable and have a large effect on the target behaviours. For example, one of their FACCM formulations suggests that cognitive distortions, low calorie intake, control behaviours are the variables that are most modifiable and would result in the largest impact on excessive weight loss.

Cooper, an author with extensive experience in the area of eating disorders, provides a measured and careful analysis of the similarities and differences between these two approaches. For example, Weerasekera's formulation is eclectic, embraces diagnosis, global and specifies treatment in rather general terms, whereas Lappailanen *et al.*'s formulation is based on learning theory, explicitly rejects diagnosis, highly detailed and molecular and specific in treatment strategies. At the same time, she carefully eschews judgement about the relative merits of either formulation.

Hoarding in an older adult

All the other cases presented in this volume are commonly encountered clinical problems. But, clinicians must formulate unusual problems too. DeVries case study of hoarding objects in an older adult is an uncommon problem, so it presented its formulators with the challenge of adapting their clinical skills and pre-existing frameworks to a novel or at least rare problem.

DeVries describes Mrs Lewis, a 76-year-old woman who is about to be ejected from her apartment. She has thrown almost nothing out of her apartment for many years. Every surface, other than one chair in which she sleeps, is covered with piles of newspapers, bills and books. She is meek, timid and strives not to offend. She is socially active in that she attends activities as a volunteer, but observes others rather than interacting with them. She has no friends in the residence where she lives, even though she has lived there for

10 years, and has little contact with her two daughters. She has a long history of broken relationships dating back to childhood and after her divorce she has had little money. She has tried to throw things away as part of a simple contingency contract with her psychologist, but was unable to do so. When her daughter visited recently, her daughter took things to storage, but Mrs Lewis was convinced that she threw many valuable things away, but did not know what they might be. When her psychologist begins to ask about important things that she has lost in her past, Mrs Lewis began talking about losses of family members throughout her life and agreed to discuss this further.

The formulation of this case contracts eclectic and pure forms of psychodynamic formulation. Cognitive analytic therapy (CAT) is a popular form of eclectic therapy that combines elements of cognitive, analytic and other therapies. Dunn notes that CAT is based on the idea that ideas of the self and consciousness consist of dialogues between the self and others and society and between the self and the self. CAT formulation too is a dialogue between the therapist and the client. This takes time. Therapy does not begin until a good working alliance has developed and quick simple solutions are avoided. Formulations consist, in part, of a number of typologies which are then fine-tuned to the individual person. The formulation is summarized in a letter to the client and sometimes in a diagram called a Sequential Diagrammatic Reformulation. In this case, the formulation typology is called 'Cinderella' in which it is characterized as 'submissive[,] serving[,] striving to please[,] avoiding conflict[,] needs not met[and] self sufficient'. Dunn's letter summarizes the client's life history of losses and how it may be linked to her present problems. It states that part of her problem is that she cannot tell what things are valuable and so throws nothing away, but now the building supervisor is trying to throw her away. The CAT treatment plan is relatively standardized, at least in terms of the approximate sequence of events over a standard 16-week course of CAT.

A more classic and pure psychodynamic formulation of this case comes from Barrett who uses Luborsky's core conflictual relationship theme (CCRT) paradigm to formulate the case. The central idea in CCRT is that patterns of relationships recapitulate themselves across the lifespan. These patterns consist of client wishes, responses of others and the client's responses. Current interpersonal problems can be understood in those terms. Luborsky and colleagues developed supportive–expressive psychotherapy to use with CCRT formulations. Barrett concludes that Mrs Lewis is suffering from a Schizoid Personality Disorder, underlying depression and Obsessive Compulsive Disorder. Her history discloses consistent patterns of interaction. Treatment consists of supportive–expressive psychotherapy which reveals the formulation to the client gradually and in which she would learn better ways to defend against unacceptable emotions, express her own needs and respond to others in a way that does not result in feelings of depression and anxiety.

Howells and Jones comment on these two psychodynamically influenced formulations primarily from a cognitive-behavioural perspective, although both authors state that they are influenced by other schools of psychology, such as CAT and personal construct theory. They apply Kuyken's and colleagues criteria for the adequacy of case formulation to these formulations (Bieling and Kuyken, 2003; Kuyken, 2006; Kuyken *et al.*, 2005). They note that the two formulations each generate a number of hypotheses and argue that there is overlap between some hypotheses from different formulations, such as concurrent on the role of problems to avoid distress associated with loss, but not for other hypotheses that seem to be quite different between formulations. They also note the possibility that both formulations do not emphasize evidence and may not actively test and attempt to disconfirm their hypotheses.

Intellectual disabilities and anger

Anger (or is it mere aggression?) is one of the most common threats to effective community adaptation and personal well-being in people with intellectual disabilities. Benson describes a 30-year-old, single man with mild intellectual disabilities and cerebral palsy living with his grandmother who is sociable, relaxed and friendly upon first meeting. His most prominent difficulty is interpersonal difficulties at work, but also at home with his grandmother. These include difficulties resolving minor interpersonal challenges, such as another client knocking over his soda or following instructions from his job coach, and other problems, such as difficulties understanding work schedules. He has a variety of work skills and he has not lost jobs because of not performing the basic elements of the job. These problems have resulted in him loosing his job on several occasions over the last few years. He agrees that he sometimes has problems controlling his temper. His personal goal is to obtain a better job.

In the past, behavioural approaches dominated case conceptualization and treatment with people with intellectual disabilities and it continues to be the most active area of assessment and treatment research (Didden, Duker and Korzilius, 1997; Didden *et al.*, 2006). However, British practitioners have now adopted a variety of approaches which remain a point of controversy (Sturmey, 2005, 2006a, 2006b, 2006c), and this case study provides several interesting opportunities to contrast these approaches directly. Beail and Jackson write a psychodynamic formulation and Willner writes a cognitive-behavioural formulation. These formulations allow the reader to examine the application of psychodynamic and cognitive-behavioural formulations to a problem that is not typically included in books on cognitive-behavioural and psychodynamic formulation. Didden's commentary gives a behavioural perspective on these approaches to case formulation.

Beail and Jackson note that psychodynamic case formulation is based on the model that current problems reflect hidden historical sources of anxiety that the client may be largely unaware of. The job of the therapist is to uncover these hidden feelings through transference and link the past with the present in therapy. This is done through individual weekly sessions with a therapist in a private setting away from work. The patient talks and freely associates and the therapist's job is to be a blank screen who does not give advice and who does not reveal personal information. The therapist also observes his or her own reaction to the client (counter-transference) and also uses this information in his or her formulation. Beail and Jackson speculate that this man had not integrated all the parts of his psyche. His problem may result from the absence of a father figure in his development which resulted in an absence of boundaries for his behaviour and in a rejection of the pain associated with disability. This is shown by defences, such as denial of his disability and the pain associated with this loss, and omnipotence, in which he presents himself as a physically fit and competent person without problems. Intervention would consist of weekly sessions of psychodynamic psychotherapy which will reveal and link the hidden past to the current feelings and problems and in this way result in integration of all parts of the person's psyche.

Willner's cognitive-behavioural formulation of this case uses both be- havioural concepts, such as antecedents, behaviours and consequences, elements from cognitive therapy, such as dysfunctional cognitions causing problems with anger, and the 4P (predisposing, precipitating, perpetuating and protective) factors that Weerasekera used in an earlier formulation of eating disorder. Willner suggests that predisposing factors include intellectual disability, autism and attention hyperactivity disorder, precipitating factors include triggers, such as interpersonal slights, perpetuating factors, such as anger being effective at obtaining items from shopkeepers, and protective factors, such as his grandmother. Willner presents both a complex diagram- matic formulation and a simple linear graphical formulation of the case and argues for the superiority of the former. He suggests that treatment should include a standard anger management package modified for people with intellectual disability (Taylor and Novacco, 2005) with various individual elements, such as teaching relevant skills, such as stopping and thinking, assertiveness and hobbies.

Didden's commentary notes that these two formulations share some sim- ilarities, such as using self-reports of feelings, and both note that he has problems with relationships and presents himself in a manner that minimizes his disabilities. Didden comments that there are many differences between these two approaches to case formulation, such as whether the analysis and treatment should focus on the present or past, whether presenting problems are things of interest in themselves or symbols or symptoms of underlying problems and the extent to which treatment is clearly described and manual-ized or not. Didden goes on to comment that both approaches to formulate this case suffer from circular arguments, by inferring underlying but unobservable causes, such as cognitive structures or hidden trauma that are inferred from behaviour and then used to explain behaviour. Finally, Didden goes on to suggest how a functional approach to this case might be used to develop an alternate case formulation.

Eells final chapter, *Contemporary Themes in Case Formulation*, comments and reacts to the earlier chapters in the book. He identifies five emerging themes: the limited quantity of research on the reliability and validity of case formulation research; the commonalities and differences between approaches to formulations in terms of what is formulated; the roles of evidence and theory in different approaches to case formulation; how different approaches to case formulation differ in the way information is organized; and the different ex-planatory mechanisms that are used in the various approaches to case formu-lation. In his final section, he outlines future directions in research including work on the psychometric properties of formulations, the roles of evidence-based practice, psychotherapy integration, clinical judgement and cross-cultural issues in case formulation. His chapter identifies links and themes that cross the various chapters of this volume, sometimes in surprising ways.

STRENGTHS AND LIMITATIONS OF THIS PROJECT

Strengths

All the authors made competent formulation which clinicians can use as models for their own work. The formulations are highly characteristic of the theoretical approaches that the authors adopted. They are good exem-plars of different approaches to case formulation. The presence of more than one formulation from the same theoretical approach enables the reader to compare how one theoretical approach deals with different populations and problems. For example, the reader may compare psychodynamic for-mulations of anger in a person with intellectual disabilities, and psychody-namic approaches to hoarding in an older adult, cognitive-behavioural ap-proaches to formulating depression and to anger in a person with intellectual disabilities, and behavioural approaches to formulating depression and psychosis. The contrasting pairs of formulations also allow the reader to directly compare cognitive-behavioural and behavioural approaches, psychiatric and behavioural approaches, psychodynamic and cognitive-behavioural approaches, and psychodynamic and eclectic approaches to case formulation. The commentary chapters offer detailed critiques – both positive and some less so – of the preceding formulations. Some commentaries offer yet another case formulation. Others avoid offering specific critiques, but comment generally on the issues related to case formulation.

Limitations

The format of this book is in some ways quite limited. The formulators only responded to a written case description. None of the formulators ever met these clients or experienced the clinical context in which the cases were presented. They did not get to observe the client's behaviour, hear their pattern of speech, or experience their own reactions or observe them with family members or staff. Although a couple of the authors asked for additional information from the case study authors, almost all did not request additional information. The strain of this method shows in some formulations, for example, when some authors commented upon missing information or indicated what they might do, depending upon the results of assessment information they did not have.

Yet, they all made formulations! Perhaps they may have made different formulations or proposed different treatment plans if they had met the clients or used different assessment methods. Even so, the formulations they made and the treatment plans they proposed look like prototypical and credible clinical work.

SUMMARY

Clinicians face the daunting task of predicting the most effective treatment for each of their clients. In many situations diagnosis fails to do that. Many authors agree that case formulation must be brief, abstract, integrated and guide treatment. However, there are many approaches to this task that differ from one another in which variables are relevant to making a formulation. This volume illustrates these different approaches to case formulation by presenting two contrasting formations of a case, commentaries upon these formulations and a final chapter that identifies emerging issues and comments up the entire endeavour.

REFERENCES

American Psychiatric Association (1994) *Diagnostic and Statistical Manual of the Mental Disorders*, 4th edn, DSM-IV-TR, American Psychiatric Association, Washington, DC.

American Psychiatric Association (2004) *Practice Guidelines for the Treatment of Psychiatric Disorders*, American Psychiatric Association, Washington, DC.

American Psychological Association (2005) *Report of the 2005 Presidential Task Force on Evidence-Based Practice*, APA, Washington, DC.

Bentall, R.P. (2003) *Madness Explained. Psychosis and Human Nature*, Penguin, London.

Bieling, P.J. and Kuyken, W. (2003) Is cognitive case formulation science or science fiction? *Clinical Psychology: Science and Practice*, **10**, 52–69.

British Psychological Society Division of Clinical Psychology (2000) *Understanding Mental Illness and Psychotic Experiences. A Report by the British Psychological Society Division of Clinical Psychology*, British Psychological Society Division of Clinical Psychology, Leicester.

British Psychological Society Division of Clinical Psychology (2001) *The Core Purpose and Philosophy of the Profession*, British Psychological Society Division of Clinical Psychology, Leicester.

Bruch, M. and Bond, F.W. (1998) *Beyond Diagnosis. Case Formulation Approaches in CBT*, John Wiley & Sons, Ltd, Chichester.

Cipani, E. and Schock, K.M. (2007) *Functional Behavioral Assessment, Diagnosis and Treatment. A Complete System for Education and Mental Health Settings*, Springer, New York.

Cuijpers, P., van Straten, A. and Warmerdam, L. (2007) Behavioral activation treatments of depression: a meta-analysis. *Clinical Psychology Review*, **27**, 318-26.

Didden, R., Duker, P. and Korzilius, H. (1997) Meta-analytic study of treatment effectiveness for problem behaviors with individuals who have mental retardation. *American Journal on Mental Retardation*, **101**, 387–99.

Didden, R., Korzilius, H., van Oorsouw, W. and Sturmey, P. (2006) Behavioral treatment of problem behaviors in individuals with mild mental retardation: a meta-analysis of single-subject research. *American Journal on Mental Retardation*, **111**, 290–8.

Dougher, M.J. (2000) *Clinical Behavior Analysis*, Context Press, Reno, NV.

Eells, T.D. (1997) *Handbook of Psychotherapy Case Formulation*, Guilford, New York.

Eells, T.D. (2007a) History and current status of psychotherapy case formulation, in *Handbook of Psychotherapy Case Formulation*, 2nd edn (ed. T.D. Eells), Guilford, New York, pp. 33–2.

Eells, T.D. (2007b) *Handbook of Psychotherapy Case Formulation*, 2nd edn, Guilford, New York.

Eels, T.D., Kandjelic, E.M. and Lucas, C.P. (1998) What is in a case formulation? Development and of a content coding manual. *Journal of Psychotherapy Research*, **7**, 144–53.

Eells, T.D. and Lombart, K.G. (2003) Case formulation and treatment concepts among novice, experiences, and expert cognitive-behavioral and psychodynamic therapists. *Psychotherapy Research*, **113**, 187–204.

Eells, T.D., Lombart, K.G., Kendeljelic, E.M. *et al.* (2005) The quality of psychotherapy case formulations: a comparison of experts, experiences, novice cognitive – behavioral and psychodynamic therapists. *Journal of Consulting and Clinical Psychology*, **73**, 579–89.

Ferster, C.B. (1973) A functional analysis of depression. *American Psychologist*, **28**, 857–70.

Gauss, V.L. (2007) *Cognitive Behavioral Therapy for Adults with Asperger Syndromes*, Guilford, New York.

Ghaderi, A. (2006) Does individualization matter? A randomized trials of standard (focused) versus individualized (broad) cognitive behaviour therapy for bulimia nervosa. *Behaviour, Research and Therapy*, **44**, 273–88.

Haynes, S.N. and O'Brien W.H. (2000) *Principles and Practice of Behavioral Assessment*, Kluwer, New York.

Hersen, M. and Rosqvist, J. (2008) *Handbook of Psychological Assessment, Case Conceptualization and Treatment, Volume 1. Adults*, John Wiley & Sons, Inc., Hoboken, NJ.

Horowitz, M.J. (1997) *Formulation as a Basis for Planning Psychotherapy Treatment*, American Psychiatric Association, Washington, DC.

Houts, A.C. (2002) Discovery, invention and the expansion of modern diagnostic and statistical manuals of mental disorders, in *Rethinking the DSM. A Psychological Perspective* (eds L.E. Beutler and M.L. Malik), APA, Washington, DC, pp. 17–65.

Jacobson, N.S., Dobson, K.S., Truax, P.A. *et al.* (1996) A component analysis of cognitive-behavioural treatment for depression. *Journal of Consulting and Clinical Psychology*, **64**, 295–304.

Kendjelic, E.M. and Eells T.D. (2007) Generic psychotherapy case formulation training improves formulation quality. *Psychotherapy: Theory, Research, Practice, Training*, **44**, 66–77.

Kutchins, H. and Kirk, S.A. (1997) *Making us Crazy: DSM: The Psychiatric Bible and the Creation of Mental Disorders*, Free Press, New York.

Kuyken, W. (2006) Research and evidence base in case formulation, in *Case Formulation in Cognitive Behaviour Therapy: The Treatment of Challenging and Complex Clinical Cases* (ed. N. Tarrier), Routledge, London, pp. 12–35.

Kuyken, W., Fothergill, C.D., Musa, M. and Chadwick, P. (2005) The reliability and quality of cognitive case formulation. *Behaviour, Research and Therapy*, **43**, 1187–201.

Lewinsohn, P.M. (1974) A behavioural approach to depression, in *The Psychology of Depression: Contemporary Theory and Research* (eds R.M. Friedman and M.M. Katz), John Wiley & Sons, Inc., New York, pp. 157–78.

McWilliams, N. (1999) *Psychoanalytic Case Formulation*, Guilford, New York.

Nezu, A.M., Nezu, C.M. and Lombardo, E. (2004) *Cognitive-Behavioral Case Formulation and Treatment Design. A Problem-Solving Approach*, Springer, New York.

O'Neill, R.E., Horner, R.H., Albin, R.W., *et al.* (1997) *Functional Assessment and Program Development for Problem Behavior: A Practical Handbook*, 2nd edn, Brooks/Cole, Pacific Grove.

Page, A. and Strizke, W. (2006) *Clinical Psychology for Trainees*, Cambridge University Press, Cambridge.

Page, A.C., Stritzke, W.G.K. and McLean, N.J. (2008) Toward science-informed supervision of clinical case formulation: a training model and supervision method. *The Australian Psychologist*, **43**, 88–95.

Persons, J.B. (1989) *Cognitive Therapy in Practice. A Case Formulation Approach*, Norton, New York.

Skinner, B.F. (1953) *Science and Human Behavior*, MacMillan, New York.

Skinner, B.F. (1971) *Beyond Freedom and Dignity*, Knopf, New York.

Sim, K., Gwee, K.P. and Bateman, A. (2005) Case formulation in psychotherapy. Revitalizing its usefulness as a clinical tool. *Academic Psychiatry*, **29**, 289–92.

Sturmey, P. (1996) *Functional Analysis in Clinical Psychology*, John Wiley & Sons, Ltd, Chichester.

Sturmey, P. (2005) Against psychotherapy with people with mental retardation. *Mental Retardation*, **43**, 55–7.

Sturmey, P. (2006a) On some recent claims for the efficacy of cognitive therapy for people with intellectual disabilities. *Journal of Applied Research in Intellectual Disabilities*, **19**, 109–18.

Sturmey, P. (2006b) In response to Lindsay and Emerson. *Journal of Applied Research in Intellectual Disabilities*, **19**, 125–9.

Sturmey, P. (2006c) Against psychotherapy with people who have mental retardation: in response to the responses. *Mental Retardation*, **44**, 71–4.

Sturmey, P. (2007) *Functional Analysis in Clinical Treatment*, Elsevier, Burlington, MA.

Sturmey, P. (2008) *Behavioral Case Formulation*, John Wiley & Sons, Ltd, Chichester.

Tarrier, N. (2006) *Case Formulation in Cognitive Behaviour Therapy. The Treatment of Challenging and Complex Cases*, Routledge, London.

Tarrier, N. and Calem, R. (2002) New developments in cognitive behavioural case formulation. Epidemiological, systemic and social context: an integrative approach. *Behavioral and Cognitive Psychotherapy*, **30**, 311–28.

Tarrier, N., Wells, A. and Haddock, G. (1998) *Treating Complex Cases. The Cognitive Behavioral Therapy Approach*, John Wiley & Sons, Ltd, Chichester.

Taylor, J.L. and Novacco, R.W. (2005) *Anger Treatment for People with Developmental Disabilities. A Theory, Evidence and Manual Based Approach*, John Wiley & Sons, Ltd, Chicheter.

Thompkins, M.A. (2007) Cognitive-behavioral case formulation, in *Handbook of Psychotherapy Case Formulation*, 2nd edn (ed. T.D. Eells), Guilford, New York, pp. 290–316.

Turkat, I.D. (1985) *Behavioral Case Formulation*, Pergamon, New York.

Turkat, I.D. (1990) *Personality Disorders. A Psychological Approach to Clinical Management*, Pergamon, New York.

Umbreit, J., Ferro, J., Liuapsin, C.J. and Lane, K. (2006) *Functional Behavior Assessment and Function-Based Intervention: An Effective, Practical Approach*, Prentice Hall, Upper Saddle, NJ.

Watson, T.S. and Steege, M.W. (2003) *Conducting School-Based Functional Behavior Assessment: A Practitioner's Guide*, Guilford, New York.

Weerasekera, P. (1996) *Multiperspective Case Formulation. A Step Toward Treatment Integration*, Krieger, Malabar, FL.

Wilson, G. (1996) Manualized-based treatments: the clinical application of research findings. *Behaviour, Research and Therapy*, **34**, 295–314.

PART II
Depression

2

Sally: A Case of Depression

MARI BRANNIGAN AND CHRISTOPHER WILLIAMS

BACKGROUND

The following case illustrates the complexities that can be present when someone seeks help for problems of depression.

PRESENTING COMPLAINT

At initial assessment, Sally complained of a 3-year history of depressive symptoms. These included low mood, tiredness, increasing tearfulness, impaired concentration, poor sleep pattern, social withdrawal and feelings of guilt, shame and failure. In addition, she reported feeling tense and anxious at times and experienced physical symptoms of anxiety including dry mouth, slight nausea and palpitations. Her eating was also affected. Although these symptoms had been present to varying degrees over the previous 3 years, they had become worse in the preceding 6 months. For the last 6–7 months she had felt progressively more depressed. She expressed feeling down and low in her mood with a distinct loss of confidence.

Her previously bubbly personality now seems very subdued. She is increasingly anxious about doing things, particularly when in social situations with others. When she meets people for the first time she worries that they will see her as unattractive or boring, and she also doubts her ability to cope when on new work placements. She has not experienced any form of panic attacks; however, sometimes her anxiety does reach quite high levels and causes her to feel physically tense and shaky. When she feels like this she also notices a slight feeling of sickness, a rapid heart beat and slightly increased breathing, which makes her feel somewhat spaced out and cut off from things. This strengthens her fears that she is not connecting well with others or coping with her job. She believes that 'unless I cope all the time then I'm a failure'.

She feels that she has lost all confidence in her abilities and worries about the effect this has on her family. Both her children left home in the last 2 years, and she has become increasingly distressed about this in the last 6 months. The focus of the distress is currently based around her concerns about her daughter's relationship. She completes the Beck Depression Inventory-II and scores 30 – a low severe level of depression.

DEMOGRAPHIC DATA

Sally is a 55-year-old woman who lives with her husband, Dave, on the outskirts of town. They have two children: Mary, aged 23, and Jack, 21. Mary moved out of the family home 2 years ago in order to live with her boyfriend, and Jack is studying at university some 350 miles away. Jack started this course some 6 months ago.

Sally and Dave live in a large four-bedroom house. She has always taken pride in her home, but lately has lost interest in this and feels it is too big for just her and her husband.

Sally returned to work 5 years ago after having given up her job as an accountant in order to raise her family. She found it difficult to find work at that time and therefore signed up with a temping agency as a bookkeeper. She does not find this satisfactory, as the positions are often short term. She finds her job unfulfilling, as the work is intermittent and there is no regular money and few other benefits. Again this leaves Sally feeling that she has failed to live up to her own expectations. Sally's husband, Dave, is a businessman and is employed as a Director of a local packing company. His work involves significant travel and time away from home.

DEMEANOUR AND PERSONAL APPEARANCE

Sally is a petite lady who looks slightly younger than her years. She has always prided herself on her appearance, but over the last 4–5 months has stopped taking as much care over this. Her previous activities of swimming and going to the gym have also decreased, and she reports that she has begun to put on weight. She feels very unhappy with how she looks and sometimes stands in front of the mirror making comments to herself that she looks 'fat' and 'unattractive'. She has put on a small amount of weight. At initial assessment she is wearing clean clothes and appears well presented.

To begin with, she finds it quite difficult to discuss how she feels with the therapist. She apologizes repeatedly for this saying she finds it 'difficult to describe' how she feels. She says the reason for this is because she has always been someone who is 'private' and does not like to talk about her emotions. She sees talking about depression as evidence of her lack of coping and of personal failure.

Sally reports that over the past 4–5 months other people have noticed that she was not her usual self. Up until then nobody appeared to have noticed any change, even though she herself described a general worsening of her feelings for the last 3 years.

Over the last 2 years she has lost a lot of confidence. Her friends comment that she now looks more anxious than before and a number of people have remarked that she does not look her usual self. Sally sees herself as being a woman who is a shadow of her former self because of this loss of confidence. She looks in the mirror and thinks 'I have completely changed.'

Objectively, she appears less anxious than perhaps she describes. There is some variability in her mood and she is able to smile wryly as she describes some of the aspects of her history. She becomes increasingly upset, however, when describing her worries about her daughter's relationship, her children having left home and also her thoughts about embarking on an extramarital affair.

CURRENT LIFESTYLE

Sally describes feeling progressively worse over the last 3 years, especially since her children left home. She knew before they left home that life would feel emptier and had done some planning for things to fill her life. She signed up for an evening class about discovering local history, which she enjoyed at first. At the same time she kept working although she had found it difficult to get a permanent job. The temp agency kept offering her short 2–4 week placements doing bookkeeping work. This was work far below her normal skill level as a qualified accountant. However, because of looking after the children she had not been able to keep up her accreditation as a working accountant and at this stage in her life does not wish to spend time completing update courses in this. When doing work in the various different companies where she has been placed, she rarely gets to know anyone in the office in a meaningful way. Because of her reduced confidence in the last 2 years, she now finds it increasingly difficult to attend new places of work where she predicts that no one will talk to her and that she will be unable to cope.

When she is at work, she also finds herself drinking more cups of coffee during the day to make her feel 'sharper'. She blames this lack of sharpness on her poor sleep and she feels tired with poor concentration. She finds it difficult to complete bookkeeping tasks and she loses her place in the various columns in the sheets. She finds herself having to double- and triple-check things to make sure that things have been added up correctly and on some occasions has had to stay very late to check for errors that she fears she may have made. Her most recent boss made a comment to her about being slow and was slightly impatient with the speed at which she was working. This caused Sally to dwell on this comment for the next week or two, and she sometimes cried in bed as she remembered the humiliation of what was said. As a result she has said no to any offers of work by the agency for the last 6 months.

Sally has found that when she is upset she tends to eat more. She has noticed that she particularly finds that eating chocolate and shortbread biscuits helps her feel better. As a consequence, she has been eating more and more of these to soothe how she feels, but unfortunately has put on weight as a result. She stands in front of the mirror each day saying 'you're fat and lazy' to herself. She has also been tempted to spend more money on clothes and was buying more clothes for a time until she became even more depressed some 2–3 months ago after which she began going out less and less. She struggles to do food shopping these days and Dave is increasingly critical when he gets home tired from work to find the larder and fridge empty. He keeps saying to her that they should get in some additional home help to clean the house if she is finding things to be a struggle. Sally finds it 'completely humiliating' to have someone come into her house and see how messy it is. She thinks she 'should be able to do it myself'.

She has also noticed a significant change in her sleep so that when she goes to bed at 10.30 p.m., as usual, she tosses and turns for at least an hour before getting off to sleep. She then sleeps fitfully, waking up in the early hours of the morning on several occasions to go to the toilet at 2.00 a.m. and 4.00 a.m. before waking finally at around 5.00 a.m. When she wakes she is unable to get back to sleep and feels immediately tense. She has taken to listening to the radio in bed or switching on the television. To overcome her problems of sleeplessness, she tends to sleep in during the day and not get up before 10 o'clock. She also tends to have a nap in the early afternoon and also drinks more alcohol at night, particularly when David is away. She has developed a taste for Chardonnay, and what started out as a single glass has now extended to between half a bottle and a bottle, which she drinks at night when she is alone. She persuades herself that it helps her to relax and also to go off to sleep. However, she has noticed that when she drinks a whole bottle this causes her to wake up earlier to go to the toilet in the middle of the night.

Sally continues to feel tired. Previously she enjoyed walks to the local park and to the local nature reserve. However, she is finding this more and more difficult to do. She now rarely goes out and her previous trips to the swimming pool stopped soon after Jack left to go to university. She no longer feels confident putting on a swimming suit and feels embarrassed in the changing rooms surrounded by younger women, all of whom appear to be slimmer and fitter than she is. The reduced activity strengthens her belief that she has become lazy.

Dave tends to be at home only every other week and when he is away he is often away for three to four days in a row on various training conferences and sales events. Sally sometimes lies awake in bed wondering where Dave is and whether he is being faithful. Three years into their married life she had suspicions that he was having an affair and, although Dave denied this, she still has her suspicions that something went on. She eventually accused Dave of seeing a colleague at work. Dave initially denied this, but then admitted that something happened 'just once'. Although there was much upset at the time, they were able to talk things over and Dave convinced Sally that everything was over. She has no evidence that Dave is currently seeing anyone; however, the doubts often come at night when she is alone. She thinks of other people that she has known who have ended up divorcing and splitting up because of affairs. She knows that Dave is an attractive man who is very sociable and fears that while he is away he may forget his commitments at home. She wonders whether Dave could possibly love her in spite of how she looks. When she thinks of this she often becomes very weepy and almost convinced that Dave views her as unattractive and too old and will leave her for 'a younger model'. She secretly checks his mobile phone to see who he has called when he is out.

Over the past few years, Sally has developed a close relationship with John who is a friend she has made at the local history class. John is divorced and in his early 60s. They hit it off immediately when they first met. They share the same interests and are able to relax in each other's company. Although nothing has ever happened, she is tempted to begin an affair with him. He has hinted that he would enjoy this too and has invited her for evening meals on several occasions. She accepted the first time and really enjoyed it but decided to leave early rather than having after-dinner coffee. John and she phone each other regularly and Sally finds she often confides in John about her feelings.

Sally is also critical of her husband for being away so much and finds that John has a sympathetic ear. She finds herself physically attracted to John and often fantasizes about what it would be like to be with him. She has the distinct impression that John would like things to progress further to a sexual relationship and they have kissed and hugged on a number of occasions. As she has thought about taking things further, she feels very guilty about the possible consequences. She views an affair as being 'bad', 'wrong' and 'not her'. She is someone who was brought up by parents who took her to church and she still occasionally goes to church some four or five times a year. Since she has found herself tempted and having these guilty thoughts, she has avoided going to church because of these thoughts.

CLIENT HISTORY

Figure 2.1 summarizes Sally's history. Sally was born and brought up in an apartment building in the heart of a large city. She was an only child and was always the focus of her parent's attention. Her parents are both dead, her father some 15 years ago and her mother 10 years ago. She thinks back of happy memories of her parents and has their photo on view in her house. When she consider her current state, she remembers things that her parents have told her over the years about 'you have to stick at things' and 'do your best' and that 'when the going gets tough, the tough get going,' a saying much loved by her father. In many ways, she is quite like her father who always kept to himself and never showed signs of weakness. She admired this in him, however, but is finding it increasingly difficult to appear to be strong. Her parents remained together until they died, and she believes it is important that married couples stay together. She remembers her mother's words, 'If you make your bed you can lie in it.' There was no history of early childhood trauma or abuse.

She went to local schools and always did well, scoring amongst the top marks in the class. She remembers her parent's comments about report cards and good scores in exams that 'you should always push yourself and do your best.' She notes that throughout her life she has been someone with high standards and she sees this as a positive aspect about her personality. She has always dressed well and has always strived to 'do her best'. To date she has largely succeeded in this.

Sally married well, had two lovely children and has also kept herself busy socially as well as at home. She has taken pride in keeping her house neat and tidy and in being able to entertain her husband's business associates on a regular basis. Her own work life had also been successful until she left to look

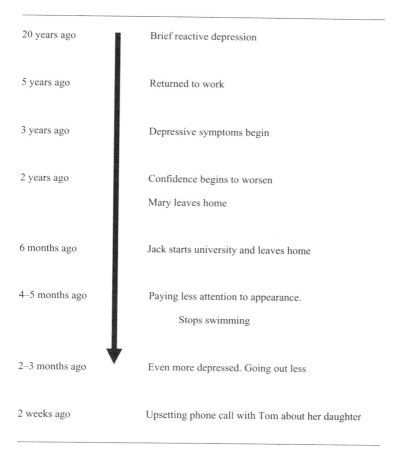

20 years ago	Brief reactive depression
5 years ago	Returned to work
3 years ago	Depressive symptoms begin
2 years ago	Confidence begins to worsen Mary leaves home
6 months ago	Jack starts university and leaves home
4–5 months ago	Paying less attention to appearance. Stops swimming
2–3 months ago	Even more depressed. Going out less
2 weeks ago	Upsetting phone call with Tom about her daughter

Figure 2.1 A timeline of Sally's history.

after her children. She has never resented this, however, but now realizes that she has not achieved what she could have done if she had not had children. This reinforces her belief that she has failed to reach her potential.

There is no family history of psychiatric illness, alcoholism or self-harm. Sally herself had a short episode of depression around the time she suspected her husband's affair, and she received some support from her community physician, who prescribed an antidepressant tablet, which seemed to help. Apart from that she has felt well.

The main concerns that pre-occupy Sally at present are worries about her daughter Mary. She is concerned that Mary is wasting her life and that Mary's boyfriend 'is pulling her down'. She has high ambitions for Mary and hopes that she will go to university, get a good degree, have a good career and eventually marry someone who is hard working and ambitious to get on in life. Mary, however, does not share these aspirations. Mary seems happy with Tom, who does not have a regular job and plays in a local band. Sally is also concerned about how Tom looks as he is quite overweight and has very long hair. Mary has also put on weight and neglects her appearance in ways that Sally does not approve of. Whenever Sally has mentioned this to Mary in the past they have ended up having blazing rows. The biggest concern Sally has is that Mary will become pregnant and 'ruin her life'. She finds herself thinking about these concerns again and again and feels that she has failed as a mother.

CLIENT GOALS

When Sally first attended therapy she said that her goal was to 'feel better'. The two main things she said she really wanted to work on were to rebuild her confidence and also to try and improve her relationship with Mary once again. She realized that loneliness had become an issue and that she had withdrawn from seeing any of her friends. She said that she wanted to rebuild these relationships. At the same time she said that she was confused and wanted to talk through what she should do regarding the affair that she was tempted to have with John. She said that a key problem for her was that there were just so many things going on she did not know where to start.

AN EVENT

Sally described in detail an event that happened 2 weeks ago, which left her feeling very upset, depressed, anxious and guilty. She had phoned Mary to try and make up with her. The phone had been answered by her boyfriend Tom. Sally had been somewhat taken aback by this and asked to speak to Mary; however, Tom's immediate response was to say that Sally's previous call to her had left Mary feeling upset and Mary did not want to speak to her.

Sally immediately felt quite angry and loudly demanded to speak to Mary over the phone. Tom kept repeating to her that Mary did not want to speak to her at the moment and advised her that Mary preferred her to keep away. Tom said that Mary should be allowed to live her own life and he said this in a tone that Sally felt was very sarcastic and lacking in respect.

Sally then felt very angry, began to shout at Tom and demanded she speak to Mary. Tom hung up the phone. Afterwards Sally felt a mixture of anger and frustration. She went upstairs and lay on the bed sobbing. She tried to phone her husband to talk about what had happened, but his phone was on the answering service. She went downstairs and had a couple of glasses of wine to try and calm herself and sat there trembling and crying. She blamed herself for having 'messed up the conversation'. She looked back on how Mary had been as a child and all the potential that she had and realized that 'Mary will never amount to anything,' 'I've let her down as a mother and failed completely,' 'I should have been able to prevent her from meeting someone like Tom.' She also started to blame herself for letting the conversation go so badly wrong. She believed that she should have been more conciliatory and apologized early on in the phone conversation to try and make things up to Mary. She immediately tried to call Tom back again some four or five times, but the phone went straight to an answering machine. She feared that Mary would never want to see her again and that she would not be allowed to be there for her as a mother. She worried that if Mary ever has a child she will never be allowed to see her grandchild or Mary ever again. She was very tempted to drive over at once to Mary's house and knock on the door but because of the wine she decided against that.

Two days later when Dave arrived home she immediately told him what had happened, insisting that they do something now to try and contact Mary. Dave felt quite against this as he had just got in and was tired. They had a further argument about how they should best respond. She found Dave's suggestions to let things calm down and give it a week or so unsatisfactory, and felt that he was blaming her. As she told her therapist her story, her therapist warmed to her and was sympathetic.

She asks you – 'what can I do?'

3

Cognitive Formulation of Depression: Case of Sally

CORY F. NEWMAN

THEORETICAL ORIENTATION AND RATIONALE

This case conceptualization of Sally is written from the perspective of cognitive therapy (Beck, 2005), in which the client's maladaptive or otherwise erroneous thought processes represent particularly fruitful points of assessment and intervention. In depression, dysfunctional thinking typically takes the form of unwarranted pessimism, excessively negative self-assessments, overgeneralized assumptions about hardships for oneself and the world and a tendency to overlook opportunities for hope in solving problems. Such negative biases in thinking manifest themselves in 'automatic thoughts', a silent dialogue that depressed persons have with themselves in specific situations, such as Sally's thought that she is 'fat and unattractive' when she looks in the mirror. These automatic thoughts themselves emanate from more general, underlying beliefs and assumptions, such as Sally's steadfast notion that flaws are intolerable, and that she must always present herself favourably in public or else she is a failure. As a result, depressed persons such as Sally will experience ongoing emotional symptoms, and will engage in problematic behavioural strategies, such as avoiding previously enjoyable activities for fear of being judged harshly by others. Depressive thinking styles tend to be rigid and self-sustaining, as the propensity for depressed individuals to think in all-or-none, overgeneralized terms inhibits their making important distinctions across situations, or designing new solutions to old problems.

Clinical Case Formulation: Varieties of Approaches. Edited by Peter Sturmey.
© 2009 John Wiley & Sons, Ltd.

Cognitive therapy is designed to assess, monitor and modify such maladaptive automatic thoughts and underlying beliefs, with the goal of improving the clients' quality of emotional life, and expanding their adaptive behavioural repertoire. In Sally's case, she may learn to spot and modify her assumptions that co-workers would not like her, and that she would necessarily fail in a new job; thus, she would be more apt to seek and attain suitable employment. She may become less apt to denigrate herself for being overweight, and thus feel better about going back to the gym and pool, activities which make her feel better about herself and improve her health. Cognitive therapists want to understand the possible etiological factors pertinent to the clients' thoughts and beliefs, and thus will examine important historical data from the clients' lives. Similarly, cognitive therapists examine the ways that clients try to cope with their psychological distress. Cognitive therapists attempt to assess how adaptive or maladaptive these 'compensatory strategies' may be (Beck, 1995). At the same time, cognitive therapists are keen to study the manifestations of the clients' full range of psychological strengths and weaknesses in everyday life, in the here-and-now, and to try to implement interventions that will produce favourable results in a time-effective manner.

The therapeutic relationship is a very important consideration in cognitive therapy (Gilbert and Leahy, 2007), in which developing and maintaining a spirit of collaborative empiricism is a high priority. In other words, the therapist and client share the responsibility – in a positive atmosphere of teamwork – of examining the client's objective life situation and subjective phenomenology, towards the goal of testing new, psychologically healthier ways for the client to think and act in everyday life. Cognitive therapists are also mindful of addressing and repairing 'alliance ruptures' in ways that will be educational and validating for clients and therapists alike (Newman, 1998). For example, if a client becomes angry as a result of believing that the therapist is trying to control him, a cognitive therapist would try to avoid simply denying this assertion, or becoming angry in return. Rather, he or she would caringly offer to explore how the process of their therapeutic relationship took a negative turn, and would express optimism that through understanding their interactional process and mutual interpretations thereof they can work things out, and learn something useful along the way.

RELEVANT AND IRRELEVANT VARIABLES

If one looks at case conceptualization as an ongoing exploration, then therapists would be ill-advised to assume that any variable is irrelevant. There is

45

considerable detective work in formulating a case, and – in the parlance of private investigators – 'no clue is too small, and all leads should be pursued.' Of course, in the interest of keeping the treatment to a reasonable time limit, it is important to use clinical judgement and objective data in order to *prioritize* the variables in question. We have already seen how the client herself reports that 'so many things are going on' that she does not know where to start. Thus, we need to have a short list of variables, which will feed nicely into a list of goals for treatment.

High-priority variables would be those factors that can be measured, tested and corroborated in some reliable and valid way. An obvious example is diagnostic data, gathered by means of a structured, standardized, clinical interview (e.g. the *Structured Clinical Interview for the Diagnostic and Statistical Manual, Fourth Edition: SCID*; First *et al.*, 1995). In the case of a clinically depressed individual such as Sally, it would be advantageous to obtain her responses on the *Beck Depression Inventory* (BDI; Beck, Steer and Garbin, 1988), *Beck Anxiety Inventory* (BAI; Beck *et al.*, 1988) and *Beck Hopelessness Scale* (BHS; Beck *et al.*, 1974) on a session-by-session basis. We know that Sally has scored 30 (severe) on the BDI at the outset of therapy, and we would like to see how she scores on the above measures of anxiety and hopelessness as well, with an eye towards assessing progress over the course of treatment. Given that Sally exhibits marked symptoms of anxiety and anger, we may find that she evidences co-morbid diagnoses.

Naturally, cognitive therapists place a high premium on ascertaining the clients' key cognitions associated with their emotional distress. In the case of Sally, these would include her overtly stated beliefs in the here-and-now, such as 'Unless I cope all the time, then I'm a failure', and her more implicit beliefs that are reflected by her behavioural patterns, such as 'If I avoid a situation then I will avoid failure'. It is also important to explore the possible historical genesis and maintenance of Sally's maladaptive beliefs. For example, Sally may believe that she is a bad person, on the basis of her desire to pursue a relationship with a particular man who is not her husband, a desire which is at odds with her mother's teachings that one should always remain true to one's marriage through thick and thin.

Additional variables would be measures of Sally's alcohol intake, and a log of her eating and sleeping habits. It would also be advantageous to obtain a general charting of Sally's daily activities, identifying avoidance behaviours and triggers for symptom exacerbation, as well as to identify moments of pleasure and mastery. Given that Sally's communication problems with her daughter and perhaps her husband Dave are quite germane to Sally's poor mood, self-reproach and sense of loneliness, it might be useful for the therapist to gain permission to read Sally's printed e-mail exchanges with her daughter and perhaps husband Dave as well. At the very least, such information would allow the therapist to compare and contrast the way that Sally portrayed her interactions with significant others with the way she actually communicated with the relevant parties *in vivo*.

There are also a number of variables that may be somewhat more difficult to measure objectively, but that can be explored through general questioning. These include an exploration of memorable childhood experiences that may have made a lasting impression on Sally's self-image and unwritten rules for how to run her life, and her feelings for her husband and would-be boyfriend John.

ROLE OF RESEARCH AND CLINICAL EXPERIENCE

Research findings and clinical experience are vital, complementary aspects in the development and delivery of effective therapy. Clinical experience is often a rich source of hypotheses about the nature of various psychopathologies and their treatment, while research trials can put these hypotheses to empirical tests (DeRubeis *et al.*, 2005; Hollon *et al.*, 2005). Indeed, there is a voluminous literature supporting the efficacy of cognitive therapy for acute, mild-to-moderate depression, and a growing body of research suggesting that cognitive therapy can produce favourable outcomes even in the cases of severe and/or chronic depression (see Hollon and DeRubeis, 2004, for a review). The ideal outcome is a positive feedback loop, whereby clinical and research data build on each other, thus helping cognitive therapy to develop, advance and become applicable to a wider range of clinical problems across multiple cultural contexts.

Good therapists use their years of clinical experience to sharpen their observational skills, such as pattern recognition, and detection of incongruities between clients' verbal and non-verbal communication. Experience also helps therapists to develop a broader and more client-friendly repertoire of questions, feedback and homework assignments, as well as to gain practice in applying a wide range of clinical techniques and strategies, such as guided imagery, cognitive restructuring and role-playing. These clinicians also think like social scientists in that they use the research literature as a guide in utilizing empirically supported methods, viewing their clinical judgements as hypotheses that can be supported or falsified by objective evidence, and evaluating clients' condition and progress via psychometrically sound measures over time.

THE FORMULATION

In the case of Sally, we have a good foundation upon which to construct some preliminary hypotheses. For example, we see that Sally's two reported periods of acute clinical depression have co-occurred with periods of loss, or threat of loss. The first was 20 years ago when Sally was worried that she might lose her husband to another woman. The present episode became exacerbated 6 months ago with the departure of her youngest son Jack to university, though it began a year in advance of her older daughter Mary leaving the household 3 years ago. Combined with her husband's penchant for being away from home on business trips, this development left Sally alone at home for much of the time. We may then hypothesize that *loneliness* is an important issue with which to deal in therapy. If Sally's responses to loneliness are severe, disproportionate to the situations and result in a wide range of dysfunction, such as suicidal ideation, inappropriate pursuit of others and anger, we might also hypothesize that Sally maintains beliefs such as 'People I love always abandon me', or 'I am nobody without someone who needs me'. More data would be needed in order to explore these hypotheses.

We may also readily hypothesize that Sally is very concerned with keeping up appearances, in that she learned from her father to withhold sharing potentially sensitive personal information with anyone, including friends. Thus, it would stand to reason that Sally would be quite vulnerable to the circumstance of a diminishment of her outward appearance, such as gaining weight. Indeed, this problem has become one of her most negative preoccupations, as demonstrated by her stated cognitions: 'I have completely changed' and '[I am] fat and lazy'. Further, we might posit that Sally has many acquaintances, but few close friends, given that she is loath to discuss deep, personal matters. It is likely that Sally has constructed a life in which she looks good to the casual outside observer, and in which she knows many people, but in fact she still feels lonely. Now that these acquaintances are beginning to notice that Sally 'has not been herself', even this compensatory benefit – being seen as 'well put together' – is ebbing, thus leaving Sally with little on which to prop her self-esteem. Sally would be expected to be especially drawn to a relationship with John, who listens to her and expresses desire for her, during a time when she may be feeling otherwise lonely, unattractive and emotionally deprived.

We know that Sally is dissatisfied with her work life, having left the field of accounting many years ago in order to raise her children, and now believes that she is incapable of going through the rigours of updating her certification. As a part-time bookkeeper, Sally feels unfulfilled. Moreover, her thoughts have turned to what might have been had she continued with her career as an accountant. Such ruminations would surely call up feelings of regret, and perhaps anger at herself for not attempting the challenging feat of both working and raising children. Sally told her therapist that she had low self-confidence, and the therapist would be helped by knowing if this has been a theme in Sally's life. For example, did Sally exhibit excessive anxiety about her academic performance during her years as a schoolgirl, even though her grades were good? If the answer is 'yes', this finding would mean that Sally has a longstanding cognitive bias towards expecting that she will fail. A related belief is that mistakes and flaws are intolerable, such that Sally would rather avoid people than risk having her shortcomings exposed. Such a rigid, maladaptive belief may have been fomented by her religious upbringing, with its focus on sinfulness and her mother's admonitions to stay with a husband no matter what the circumstances.

Now that her children are out of the house, Sally might feel somewhat resentful that everyone else in the immediate family seems to be doing what they wish, while she is stuck in a situation that leaves her unhappy. This resentment may also lead her to feel guilty – after all, she may ask herself ruefully how she can possibly hold her family responsible for her own choices, and 'What kind of terrible mother and wife would I be to feel this way?' At the same time, Sally's feelings of guilt may have something to do with her attraction to John. Simple and sensitive therapeutic questioning could begin to tease this apart.

Another area of concern is Sally's maladaptive use of avoidance as a compensatory coping strategy. As she began to feel more self-conscious about her appearance, Sally decreased doing her usual and customary activities, such as going to the gym and pool. Predictably, Sally's resultant sense of being less physically fit contributed to an exacerbation of her belief that her appearance was declining, and increased her tendency to avoid situations in which she might be exposed as unattractive.

In order to conceptualize Sally's psychological condition with some degree of sophistication, we must try to understand those aspects of her functioning that seem contradictory or paradoxical. One such area of apparent inconsistency is Sally's attraction to John, combined with her lack of attention to her physical appearance. At first blush, we might expect that a person in Sally's life circumstance – feeling lonely, unfulfilled and low in self-esteem – might become rejuvenated by the attentions of a potential romantic partner. Even if a strong sense of right versus wrong and its attendant guilt prevented Sally from acting on such extramarital desires, we might nonetheless expect Sally to take actions that would enhance her appearance. This is especially true in the context of Sally's lifelong habit of valuing how she looks to the outside world, irrespective of how she actually might feel. Instead, we learn that Sally is uncharacteristically paying *less* attention to her physical fitness, and yet she has hugged and kissed John on some occasions. We might ask ourselves, 'Is Sally deliberately staying away from the gym and pool, and choosing to eat more fattening foods so as to prevent John from finding her attractive? Is Sally – who already appears to be on a slippery slope towards an affair – tormented with conflict, such that she is trying to make *John* be the one who will lose interest? Is she testing John to see if he will still care about her even if she gains weight? On the other hand, if John loses interest, might Sally not be aware that this would further exacerbate her loneliness and low sense of self-worth? This is quite a conundrum for Sally, and the therapist would do well to give her a great deal of empathy for being in this state, whilst not necessarily telling her what she *ought* to do.

A cognitive case conceptualization is fluid. It develops, changes and otherwise modifies to accommodate new data as treatment progresses (Needleman, 1999; Persons, 1989). Thus, the therapist should be open to revising and updating the case conceptualization, perhaps as a result of information acquired through Sally's homework assignments, or perhaps in response to the direct input of Sally's husband in a conjoint session.

HISTORY

Although cognitive therapy focuses a great deal on the client's problems in the present time, with an eye towards creating positive changes in the future, the past is not neglected. Sally's history provides rich information that can inform the case formulation and suggest treatment options. For example, we have evidence that Sally took her parents' golden rules for proper living very seriously, including the notions that one should keep up appearances, strive for success and not let adverse situations ruffle one's feathers. This probably plays a significant role in Sally's propensity for feeling like a failure when she reflects on her disappointing career status, problems with her husband and daughter, her weight, her depression and her need to consult a therapist.

Sally's history of depression in response to loss and the threat of loss is important. She became depressed early in the marriage when she ascertained that her husband might have been tempted to stray, and she became depressed pursuant to her adult children leaving home, combined with renewed fears that her husband might want to leave.

CURRENT FACTORS

Current factors include the following: (a) Sally's *decrease* in doing things for self-efficacy and healthy enjoyment, such as going to the gym and pool, and finding suitable employment; (b) her *increase* in consumptive, addictive behaviours, such as eating and drinking as means by which to regulate her mood, leading to sleep disturbance, weight gain, poorer decisions and further self-reproach; and (c) the significant periods of time she spends alone and ruminating, for example wondering if her husband is with a woman while on his business trip, and imagining that her daughter will become pregnant and ruin her life (further evidence of Sally's catastrophic style of thinking). The *event* described below brings together a number of such current factors, and thus has the potential to be fodder for productive conceptualization and intervention.

Another important factor in the here-and-now is Sally's growing distance from many of the people in her life, including her husband Dave, her female friends whose social invitations she usually rejects and her adult children, especially her daughter, with whom she is in conflict. This leaves John, her good and great friend, with whom she is perilously getting closer.

TREATMENT PLAN

Sally stated that her goals for therapy were to 'feel better' and 'build her confidence'. One of the tasks of the cognitive therapist will be to help Sally expound on these goals, towards comprehensiveness and specificity. The treatment plan will focus on the following targets:

- Sally's compensatory strategy of *avoidance* is a major problem. It includes not taking work assignments, withdrawing from friends, using food and alcohol as an escape from her feelings, abandoning formerly healthy activities such as going to the gym and pool and not being forthcoming about thoughts and feelings that might make her feel ashamed. Sally will need exposure to these avoided activities and subjective experiences, along with constructive modifications in how she thinks about them.
- In terms of the *process* of Sally's thinking, she is prone to engage in catastrophic, 'all-or-none' thinking. She tends to ruminate, therefore creating worst-case scenarios in her mind, becoming more and more distressed, and then responding to others either with avoidance and/or demands. This thinking style also makes her apt to believe that she is an abject failure whenever she detects an imperfection in herself. The cognitive therapist would teach Sally to utilize Socratic questions in order to help herself

moderate the extremity of her thinking, and to generate more benign ways of viewing her various problems. These questions include 'What are some other perspectives I can take about this situation?' 'What concrete evidence supports or refutes my negative assumption?' and 'What constructive action can I take to deal with this problem?' among others (see Beck, 1995).

- In terms of the *content* of Sally's thinking, her most salient depressive beliefs centre on her sense of being a failure, alone and abandoned, and perhaps deserving of punishment owing to her budding extramarital relationship and her rift with her daughter. She berates herself for her perceived flaws, from her weight to her difficulties in employment and important relationships. A cognitive therapist would not merely dispute Sally's negative thoughts and beliefs about herself and her life. Rather, the therapist would help the client distinguish between objective problems such as the daughter's unwillingness to talk to her, and her subjectively biased interpretations, such as she failed as a mother in that daughter Mary was wrecking her life. By doing so, the therapist could help Sally learn ways to question, test and modify her biased beliefs, while beginning the process of doing systematic problem-solving on those problems that have been objectively confirmed. In order to assist Sally in boosting her sense of hope and self-efficacy, the therapist would need to help her take stock of her personal strengths and past successes.
- Sally's communication skills need considerable work. She has difficulty articulating her thoughts and feelings, is wont to make demands and to get angry when her negative beliefs are triggered by stressful situations and appears to lack the know-how to make collaborative and/or conciliatory gestures, for example to daughter Mary.
- Sally's excessive use of alcohol is too important to overlook, especially as it impinges on her sleep, her mood and her judgement.

Homework will be a vitally important part of treatment (Rees, McEvoy and Nathan, 2005), as it will help Sally learn new coping skills, gain a sense of self-efficacy, decrease undue dependence on the therapist and increase the chances that her therapeutic improvements will be maintained for the long run. An example of a homework assignment for Sally might be to experiment with refraining from ringing up her daughter, while taking the time to write down a conciliatory dialogue to use if and when Mary would call *her*. In the meantime, Sally would use the *dysfunctional thought record* (DTR; Beck, 1995) to write down her automatic thoughts associated with her urges to contact Mary, as well as other episodes of high emotionality associated with Mary, such as anger, guilt, sadness, anxiety and shame. Sally would also be instructed and guided in coming up with rational responses to help her put the entire matter in a less hopeless perspective, to do more problem-solving and less catastrophizing. Similar homework assignments might be to accept social invitations from friends, to seize upon opportunities for part-time work and to use the DTR to combat the sort of automatic thoughts that might otherwise convince her to remain at home. For example, Sally can write down her automatic thought, 'I can't let anybody see me like this', followed by a series of rational responses such as 'My friends care about me, and that's more important than my insecurities about my weight'. The intended result would be that Sally would indeed go out with her friends, thus improving her morale, and incrementally reducing her reliance on avoidance as a strategy to cope with her negative self-evaluations.

Additional take-home tasks could focus on communication experiments with Dave, perhaps after doing preparatory role-play exercises in session, and scheduling time at the pool and/or gym. The list could go on and on, depending on the collaboration and creativity of Sally and her therapist. The goals are to improve Sally's mood, sense of self-efficacy and to expand her adaptive behavioural repertoire, while simultaneously reducing the risk that she will become too dependent on therapy sessions themselves.

Of all the problems that Sally presents, perhaps the thorniest of them all is her extramarital relationship with John. They have already hugged and kissed, which means that they have moved towards an affair. While responsible therapists would surely engage Sally in a discussion of the pros and cons of her relationship with John, collaboratively evaluate potential consequences and engage in advance problem-solving, they would have no illusions that they could tell Sally to cease and desist from pursuing the object of her affection. A therapist can no more demand that Sally stay away from John than Sally herself can tell her daughter Mary to stay away from her boyfriend Tom. Perhaps the therapist can make this point overtly in session. Sally and Mary are both grown women who have to make their own decisions, though caring others can offer support, concern and the means by which to weigh factors and anticipate consequences, as the therapist can do for Sally, and perhaps Sally can do for Mary. Nevertheless, the therapist can ask Sally if she would like to take small, gradual steps to enhance her marriage, such as by inviting Dave to go to the gym with her.

THE EVENT

Sally's series of unfortunate events with daughter Mary is a rich area for conceptualization and intervention. Sally phoned Mary ostensibly to make up with her, but she had not done the necessary cognitive and behavioural rehearsal in advance of making this gesture. When Sally was caught off guard by Tom's intercepting the call and telling her that Mary did not wish to speak to her, Sally's negative beliefs about abandonment, being a failure as a mother, and predicting catastrophic outcomes for her daughter were triggered. Sally's maladaptive response was to become irate and make demands, resulting in Tom's hanging up. Sally repeatedly attempted to ring up her daughter again, whereas a single conciliatory voice message would have sufficed. Sally then used alcohol as a means by which to reduce her arousal and to anaesthetize her emotional pain, but this served only to exacerbate her depression. Later, when her husband returned from his business trip, Sally viewed his recommendation to give Mary some time before trying once again to communicate as being patently unsympathetic. Again, Sally felt abandoned and alone, yet there were alternative ways that Sally could have viewed and handled this event more effectively and benignly.

OTHER ISSUES

Although Sally does not complain about going through menopause, it would be prudent to consider the possibility that hormonal changes associated with this stage of life may be playing a role in Sally's irritability, her disturbances in eating, sleeping and body image, as well as her sluggishness and mood decline. It may be useful to inquire about Sally's most recent visit to her gynaecologist, and/or to consider the advisability of a referral to an endocrinologist. This medical consideration is consistent with the empirical spirit of cognitive case formulation and therapy.

Sally may also be excessively focused on the issue of weight, both in herself and in daughter Mary. Sally's inability to tolerate this particular flaw may explain the 'blazing rows' Sally has had with her daughter over this issue.

SUMMARY

This cognitive case formulation has focused on Sally's vulnerabilities in how she thinks about herself and life situation. Her chief compensatory strategy of *avoidance* has ultimately exacerbated her sense of isolation, including turning down social invitations, and failure, such as not taking part-time jobs, and not going to the gym or pool. Sally's depressive episodes have been linked to times of loss, and her current empty nest represents such a loss. She is now vulnerable to the attention of a man outside her marriage, which both temporarily assuages her loneliness and makes her feel like a bad person, creating quite a conflict for her. Sally's excessive alcohol use disturbs her sleep, worsens her mood and impairs her judgement. The client's attempts to control her grown daughter's life are backfiring, with the daughter distancing herself from the client, and the client feeling more abandoned, alone and as having failed as a mother.

Cognitive therapy will help Sally to combat her catastrophic thinking style. An important goal is to encourage Sally to gain exposure to constructive activities that will give her a sense of mastery and pleasure, while helping her to modify her eating, sleeping and drinking habits. Sally also needs to improve her communication skills, for example with her husband and daughter, and her problem-solving skills, such as those regarding plans for work life and in considering the pros and cons of her relationship with John. Homework will be a vital part of therapy, and the therapist will measure the client's progress both by objective means (e.g. the various Beck Inventories; observing her success in solving problems in her family life) and subjective data (Sally's self-report of her symptoms, and changes in her maladaptive beliefs). The possible contribution of hormonal changes associated with menopause should be considered in assessing Sally's emotional difficulties.

The cognitive therapist's goal is to work diligently to help Sally receive and retain the 'goods' that cognitive therapy has to offer. If the techniques of cognitive therapy are analogous to the 'cargo', then the case conceptualiza-tion is the map that helps make certain that the techniques are well-directed, and the healthy therapeutic relationship is the smooth road or calm waterway used in the service of this well-mapped delivery. A good case conceptu-alization enables cognitive therapists to provide accurate empathy, because their in-session comments will demonstrate an understanding of the clients' subjective views of themselves, their lives and their future. The therapists' interventions will be well targeted, such as honing in on Sally's unfortunate habit of avoiding situations that might otherwise give her a sense of mastery and pleasure were it not for her negative beliefs. Similarly, a well-formulated case conceptualization will enable the cognitive therapist to be sensitive to the client's unique vulnerabilities, such as Sally's fears of abandonment, and propensity for believing she is a failure. Thus, the therapist will take great care to inform Sally about necessary breaks in therapy well in advance, while discussing the potential opportunity for Sally to practise her skills on her own. Likewise, the therapist will be mindful of Sally's concerns about failing her homework assignments, and will describe the between sessions assignments as win–win scenarios where much useful information can be obtained, even if Sally faces difficulties in completing the agreed-upon tasks. Thus, the case conceptualization creates a positive synergy with both the technical aspects of cognitive therapy as well as with the therapeutic relationship. If Sally is like many other depressed clients in cognitive therapy, it should be expected that she will make significant progress, and will maintain her gains long after regular sessions have concluded.

REFERENCES

Beck, A.T. (2005) The current state of cognitive therapy: a 40-year retrospective. *Archives of General Psychiatry*, **62**, 953–9.

Beck, A.T., Epstein, N., Brown, G. and Steer, R.A. (1988) An inventory for measuring clinical anxiety: psychometric properties. *Journal of Consulting and Clinical Psychology*, **56**, 893–7.

Beck, A.T., Steer, R.A. and Garbin, M.G. (1988) Psychometric properties of the Beck Depression Inventory: twenty-five years of evaluation. *Clinical Psychology Review*, **8**, 77–100.

Beck, A.T., Weissman, A., Lester, D. and Trexler, L. (1974) The measurement of pessimism: the Hopelessness Scale. *Journal of Consulting and Clinical Psychology*, **42**, 861–5.

Beck, J.S. (1995) *Cognitive Therapy: Basics and Beyond*, Guilford Press, New York.

DeRubeis, R.J., Hollon, D., Amsterdam, J.D. *et al.* (2005) Cognitive therapy vs. medications in the treatment of moderate to severe depression. *Archives of General Psychiatry*, **62**, 409–16.

First, M.B., Spitzer, R.L., Gibbon, M. and Williams, J.B.W. (1995) *Structured Clinical Interview for DSM-IV. Axis I Disorder with Psychotic Screen*, Psychiatric Institute, New York.

Gilbert, P. and Leahy, R.L. (eds) (2007) *The Therapeutic Relationship in the Cognitive Behavioral Psychotherapies*, Routledge-Brunner, London.

Hollon, S.D. and DeRubeis, R.J. (2004) Effectiveness of treatment for depression, in *Contemporary Cognitive Therapy: Theory, Research, and Practice* (ed. R.L. Leahy), Guilford Press, New York, pp. 45–61.

Hollon, S.D., DeRubeis, R.J., Shelton, R.C. *et al.* (2005) Prevention of relapse following cognitive therapy vs. medications in moderate to severe depression. *Archives of General Psychiatry*, **62**, 417–22.

Needleman, L. (1999) *Cognitive Case Conceptualization: A Guide for Practitioners*, Erlbaum, Mahwah, NJ.

Newman, C.F. (1998) The therapeutic relationship and alliance in short-term cognitive therapy, in *The Therapeutic Alliance in Brief Psychotherapy* (eds J.D. Safran and J.C. Muran), American Psychological Association, Washington, D.C., pp. 95–122.

Persons, J. (1989) *Cognitive Therapy in Practice: A Case Formulation Approach*, W.W. Norton, New York.

Rees, C.S., McEvoy, P. and Nathan, P.R. (2005) Relationship between homework completion and outcome in cognitive behaviour therapy. *Cognitive Behaviour Therapy*, **34**, 242–7.

4

Behavioural Formulation of Depression: The Case of Sally

CARL W. LEJUEZ, TYISH S. HALL BROWN,
AND DEREK R. HOPKO

THEORETICAL ORIENTATION AND RATIONALE

The conceptual foundation for a behavioural approach to depression can be traced back to the original behavioural models of depression. Specifically, Skinner (1953) initially proposed that depression involved an interruption of established sequences of healthy behaviour that had been positively reinforced by the social environment, with this extinction resulting in a variety of emotional side effects that could be characterized as depressed behaviour. Further extensions of this work also included the role of reinforcement available for depressed behaviour including a two-phase process (Ferster, 1973; Lewinsohn, 1974). Specifically, it was hypothesized that depressed affect and behaviour initially could be maintained through positive and negative reinforcement (e.g. extra attention from a loved one and removal of responsibilities at the onset of a depressive episode). Although aversive consequences including social isolation would begin to occur in place of more positive consequences (Coyne, 1976), the depressed individual's symptomatic behaviour might actually increase to regain lost reinforcement in a paradoxical 'deviation-amplifying' process resulting in a vicious cycle of further negative consequences and exacerbated depressive symptoms. Based on these etiological models, conventional behavioural therapy aims to increase healthy behaviour through contact with response-contingent reinforcement, while simultaneously decreasing punishment for such behaviour and reducing access

Clinical Case Formulation: Varieties of Approaches. Edited by Peter Sturmey.
© 2009 John Wiley & Sons, Ltd.

to reinforcement for depressed behaviour (Lejuez, Hopko and Hopko, 2003; Lewinsohn and Graf, 1973; Martell, Addis and Jacobson, 2001).

In considering a behavioural conceptualization of depression, it is important to note that 'behaviour' is not limited to overt behaviour, as thoughts, feelings and actions are all a function of one's environment, including the positive and negative consequences experienced as well as the environmental stimuli currently present. Behavioural theory suggests that causality resides in the environment and its impact on thoughts, feelings and overt behaviour. For this reason, it is crucial for a behaviour therapist to assess and understand the thoughts and feelings of the client, not because these will be viewed as causal variables to be targeted by an intervention, but rather because they provide a comprehensive picture of the client's experience within his or her environment.

RELEVANT AND IRRELEVANT VARIABLES

Using the provided case study, several key variables can be identified that fit within the behavioural approach outlined above. The chronology of Sally's symptoms suggests that her current state is not merely a temporary reaction to an isolated event. In fact, the depression began initially 3 years ago as she began to prepare for her first child leaving home, and increased significantly in severity once both had left home. This is especially relevant for Sally because success had always been strongly reinforced from her parents and therefore a priority for her, with self-punishment for perceived failures as a by-product. Skinner (1971) described this phenomenon in terms of the development of negative emotional side effects (i.e. guilt, shame and a sense of sin) in response to unachieved goals. Because motherhood was one of the few areas in her adulthood in which she could take some pride and feel some sense of accomplishment as she once had with schoolwork in her youth, her loss of that role and the reinforcement that accompanied it likely have played an important role in her depression in general and loss of confidence specifically.

This focus on the client's beliefs and other private events is important, not because they will be targeted directly as the mechanism for behaviour change, but instead because they may be used to identify targets for change in her environment and experiences that would influence these beliefs and the resulting feelings. In what appears to be an effort to maintain this mother role, she has become quite involved in the life of her daughter, who she believes is making choices that keep her from living up to her potential. Thus, it may be the case that Sally is reasserting herself in the role of the mother with her daughter both to hold on to this role for which she has had some success and to help her daughter achieve the type of life success that Sally feels she herself has not achieved. However, instead of achieving these desired goals, this approach has had a destructive effect and has pushed her daughter further away – an added loss of reinforcement leading to thoughts of failure and additional feelings of depression.

Several other behaviours that Sally has evidenced have served to increase the likelihood and intensity of negative outcomes; ironically, these behaviours are those which she consciously utilizes to achieve some goal or to reduce the likelihood of negative outcome. For example, although she has held a series of jobs that are below her skill level, her performance has been disappointing. She attributes this to having low confidence, and feeling anxious/jittery and tired/sluggish. She reports a string of compensatory behaviours intended to help her address her concerns at work, beginning with drinking excess coffee to keep her 'sharp'. However, the coffee increases her anxiety and jitters, and actually impairs her performance in the long run, as well as making it difficult for her to sleep at night. To address her sleep difficulties, Sally has begun to drink excessive amounts of alcohol in the evening, which has created further sleep problems. She then wakes up tired and repeats this cycle throughout the day, with each attempt aimed at temporarily preventing or removing negative consequences while exacerbating her depression. This pattern is evident in other aspects of her life as well. For example, she avoids swimming due to the fear that others will judge her as overweight in a bathing suit, but this leads to her getting less exercise and paradoxically getting heavier. These types of behaviours are clear targets for intervention.

Beyond her increasingly strained relationship with her children, it is also extremely relevant that Sally has little connection with her husband, further reducing access to interpersonal reinforcement, and thereby making her vulnerable to an extramarital affair which goes against her religious beliefs. In providing Sally with increased access to meaningful experiences, it will become important to target her relationship with her husband and to reenergize her relationships with her friends. In addition, despite the fact that it may decrease some immediate positive reinforcement, it will be important for Sally to limit her interactions with John reducing the level of intimacy that has developed between the two, allowing her to refocus on rebuilding a similar connection with her husband and moving in a valued direction away from being an adulteress.

Although one might be led to believe that a behavioural approach would find Sally's report of anxiety and a loss of confidence as less relevant, these variables are in fact quite relevant. Sally indicates a loss of confidence which now appears to pervade most aspects of her life and has led to a pattern of behaviours which have only made matters worse. In contrast to a cognitive approach that focuses directly on the lack of confidence itself, our focus is on her previous experiences and the link between these previous experiences and her current circumstances. In this way, a lack of confidence itself is not the problem, but instead serves as a starting point for discovering which behavioural experiences produced this lack of confidence. Because anxiety and a loss of confidence are at the root of the problem from Sally's perspective, the success of behavioural therapy will depend in large part on helping her understand that improving her interactions with the world around her will ultimately lead to more confidence, increased self-efficacy and reduced anxiety, as opposed to the other way around where she would need to think and feel better before making changes in her environment and experiences.

ROLE OF RESEARCH AND CLINICAL EXPERIENCE

With increased interest in cognitive theory in the last quarter of the twentieth century, interventions based exclusively on a behavioural approach are now regarded as insufficient to address the complexity of human experience. Despite the documented efficacy of cognitive and cognitive-behavioural therapies (Dobson, 1989), several recent findings along with evolving socioeconomic and professional developments raise the question of whether purely behavioural approaches to treating clinical depression were abandoned too hastily. For example, managed care organizations have established the need to develop and utilize psychosocial interventions that are both time-limited and empirically validated (Peak and Barusch, 1999), both features that exemplify the behavioural model. Second, empirical data demonstrate that behavioural interventions lead to behaviour change and to lasting changes in thoughts and feelings (Jacobson *et al.*, 1996; Jacobson and Gortner, 2000; Simons, Garfield and Murphy, 1984). Third, therapeutic benefits most often occur in the initial sessions of cognitive-behavioural therapy, a period during which behavioural interventions often are more prominent than cognitive ones (Hollon, Shelton and Davis, 1993; Otto, Pava and Sprich-Buckminster, 1996). Taken together, these data suggest the value of an approach based primarily on behaviour theory that provides a comprehensive approach to treating a client's depression, both at the level of overt behaviour and at the deeper level of one's inner world and experience. Of course, clinical experience affects the manner in which the intervention is implemented, but a hallmark of the behavioural approach is the use of the empirical literature to develop a conceptualization and design the appropriate intervention.

THE FORMULATION

At initiation of therapy, Sally scored 30 on the Beck Depression Inventory (BDI; Beck *et al.*, 1961), which places her in the low severe level of depression. The depressive symptoms she reported include persistent low mood, fatigue, increasing tearfulness, impaired concentration, poor sleep patterns, increased appetite and social withdrawal, as well as feelings of guilt, shame and failure. Specifically, Sally reported that she had stopped engaging in almost all proactive activity at home, including recreational activities (e.g. exercising) and household responsibilities (e.g. cleaning clothes and washing dishes). She stated that although she had always taken pride in her home, lately she had lost interest in doing so. Additionally, she reported loss of interest in her career as well as in her appearance. The latter issue resulted in a weight gain that exacerbated her already-lowered self-confidence.

Our formulation is based upon her loss of contingent reinforcement for healthy behaviour and the emergence of coping behaviours that have some immediate negative reinforcement value, but that actually produce greater negative consequences including the development of anxiety and a lack of confidence. An interesting aspect of this case from a behavioural perspective is the clear belief of the client that her thoughts, feelings and mood states are driving her behaviour and that the goal of therapy is to make changes at this level. For example, she states that her goal is to 'feel better' and a primary goal of therapy is to rebuild her confidence. A good behaviourist must be aware of the naturalness of considering these phenomena as causal. As such, directly challenging the client's beliefs on this point early in therapy is not recommended. Instead, the therapist must work to develop good rapport by acknowledging these feelings and how they are correlated with the behavioural problems she is reporting, while still remaining aware of and staying true to the approach that behaviour change will lead to changes in thoughts and feelings. In this way, identifying attainable behaviour-change goals may be useful to help the client push past initial fears and apprehension. Further, changing maladaptive behaviour depends upon understanding how such behaviour is functional within the client's previous experiences and current environment, and how changes in the environment and her experience within it can lead to a change in overt behaviour as well as thoughts and feelings.

TREATMENT PLAN

Given the clear indication for loss of reinforcement, we propose a targeted behavioural activation (BA) approach (Lejuez, Hopko and Hopko, 2003), modified to include a focus on her anxiety symptoms (Hopko, Lejuez and Hopko, 2004). As defined by Hopko *et al.* (2003), BA is a therapeutic process that emphasizes structured attempts at engendering increases in overt behaviours that are likely to bring the client into contact with reinforcing environmental contingencies and to produce corresponding improvements in thoughts, mood and overall quality of life (see also Martell, Addis and Jacobson, 2001 for a detailed historical account of the roots of BA). Although BA strategies generally have been utilized in the context of treating individuals with clinical depression, they also have relevance to treating anxiety, both to facilitate naturalistic *in vivo* exposure (Hopko, Lejuez and Hopko, 2004), as well as to initiate proactive behaviour to add a sense of control and to address anxiety-provoking situations in more active and effective ways. This relevance fits well with the inter-relatedness of depression and anxiety (Merikangas, Risch and Weissman, 1994; Mineka, Watson and Clark, 1998), as well as the functional similarity that involves an avoidance of environmental stimuli that are either aversive or presumably non-reinforcing.

The successful implementation of this type of pragmatic activity-based protocol may be overwhelming for some clients at first, especially for a client like Sally, who states that she wants to 'feel better' and 'get back her confidence' before she can make changes in her life. Thus, as outlined by Lejuez *et al.* (2006), treatment must begin with an initial focus on developing a therapeutic relationship, as it is necessary for Sally to trust the therapist and to agree with the rationale that productive action towards creating more healthy environments is in fact possible, even before she feels less depressed and anxious. A strong working alliance can also limit the likelihood of her losing motivation and slipping back into the types of immediate affect reduction strategies outlined above, which have generally served to exacerbate her problems rather than helping her move in a more positive direction.

Assessment of current activity level and environmental factors maintaining depression

As a first step in the implementation of BA, it is useful to develop an understanding, both for the client and the therapist, of the client's overt behaviour as well as the thoughts and feelings associated with these behaviours. Towards this end, treatment begins with self-monitoring of already occurring daily activities. Daily monitoring logs are useful in obtaining a baseline activity level within the first few sessions, and serve as an educational instrument whereby individuals can examine their lack of activity and potential desired non-depressed activities.

In coordination with the assessment of already occurring activities, early sessions of BA should involve a special focus on the individual needs of the client. In addition to assessing what is and is not occurring, it is equally crucial to understand why she is engaging in the current pattern of depressed behaviour (i.e. the functional aspects of the depressed pattern of behaviour). In Sally's case, there is a clear absence of effective and enjoyable behaviours, as well as the emergence of ineffective, depression-related behaviour. Specifically, she has stopped cleaning her home, taking as much care of her appearance as she had previously, engaging in pleasurable activities such as swimming, going out with her friends, going to church, eating healthy and accepting offers of work by her temping agency. Additionally, she has increased engagement in unproductive behaviours, including critical overevaluation of her daughter's choices, seeking attention of another man (thereby developing an emotional intimacy previously reserved for her husband) and frequent checking of her husband's mobile phone to see who he calls when he is out of the house.

Based on these starting points for therapy, an initial goal will be to help Sally determine why these behaviours are occurring and to start considering how to replace them with more effective behaviours that meet the same functional needs. The extent to which these behaviours are linked to other individuals in her life, behavioural contracts may be used to help the other individual understand how he or she may be helpful in supporting more effective behaviour in the client. For example, therapy might be used to help Sally realize that initiating critical interactions with her daughter allows her to maintain at least some type of connection with her daughter now that she has moved away, despite the fact that her criticisms are actually eroding their relationship. Although this might involve some form of cognitive challenging and correction, it is done for the goal of altering her interaction with her environment. As this approach progresses, Sally may be encouraged to identify other strategies for preserving this role in her daughter's life, with a contract used for her daughter requesting her to respond positively to more positive efforts on her mother's part. In this way, both will benefit and Sally may achieve the same goal without the need for criticism and other control-related behaviours.

Identifying values and goals to construct the activity hierarchy

Following from the insights that emerge from the initial stages of BA, the emphasis shifts to identifying a person's values and goals within a variety of life areas that include family, social and intimate relationships, education, employment/career, hobbies/recreation, volunteer work/charity, physical/ health issues and spirituality. Activities are then generated through a

collaborative effort by the client and therapist to facilitate movement towards these goals. This effort begins with the construction of an activity log
that is hierarchically arranged. That is, activities are ranked according to their
perceived difficulty with Level 1 activities the easiest and Level 5 the most
difficult. Typically, a list of 15 activities is compiled with three activities in
each level. For each activity, the client and therapist collaboratively determine
what the final goal will be, in terms of both frequency and duration of the
activity in minutes per week. Clients are encouraged to make these decisions,
thereby taking responsibility for resulting therapeutic gains and to promote
self-regulation of their own behaviour. Usually, prior to the end of this second
session, clients select the number of times in the following week that they
aspire to engage in each of the activities from the first category. These goals
are recorded on the behaviour checkout. Additionally, these goals are also
recorded on a master log that stays with the therapist. As each activity is
introduced into treatment, weekly goals initially will be lower than the final
goal. For example, Sally's activity hierarchy would begin with relatively easy
goals targeting both necessary life activities such as organizing her home,
getting to bed by a certain time and engagement in social activities such as
calling friends on the telephone. Higher level goals include loosing weight,
improving her occupational circumstances by accepting manageable temping jobs, rebuilding her relationship with her daughter by participating in
value-free activities and rebuilding her relationship with her husband through
increased interaction and intimacy. It is useful to note that activities typically
include things the client will do, though it can also include a deliberate action not to engage in an unproductive behaviour such as not drinking alcohol
prior to bed or not drinking coffee after 1–2 p.m. in the afternoon. As weeks
progress, weekly goals are increased until the final goal is achieved.

Charting weekly activity using the behaviour checkout

After the therapist and client agree upon the homework, the client is given
instructions on how to complete the behaviour checkout. On each day of the
following week, preferably at a specified time, the client circles the 'Y' (i.e.
yes) for each activity that he or she was engaged in during the day. Similarly,
if an activity was not performed during the day, an 'N' (i.e. no) is circled.
Circling the letters is important for two reasons: progress towards weekly
goals can be monitored by the therapist, and circling the letters may serve as a
conditioned reinforcer through pairing with praise from the therapist as well
as a natural reinforcer that eventually begins to occur as a result of completing
an activity. Furthermore, to serve as an additional and possibly more salient
conditioned reinforcer, clients are instructed to circle the 'G' (i.e. goal) on

each day once the goal is met, regardless of whether or not they were engaged in the activity on the days following goal attainment. This strategy provides clients with additional conditioned reinforcers and signifies that the goal is not perfection in a given category (i.e. completing every activity every day), but rather setting and meeting reasonable goals. To illustrate this component, the therapist and Sally could develop a plan for Sally to complete her daily behaviour checkout at 8:00 p.m. each evening before getting ready for bed. If her initial goals for the week were to spend 1 h a day cleaning the house for 3 days and to call two friends once during the week for a 15–30 min conversation, she would monitor whether or not she completed these goals by circling the 'Y' on each day she completed the task and the 'N' on the days she did not. So for example, if Sally called a friend on Monday and then called the second friend on Wednesday, she would circle the 'Y' on Monday and Wednesday, the 'N' on Tuesday, Thursday, Friday, Saturday and Sunday, and the 'G' on Wednesday, Thursday, Friday, Saturday and Sunday, denoting that she had completed the goal for that week. This may be especially important for someone such as Sally for whom success is of great value.

Assessing progress and treatment modification

At the start of each therapy session, the therapist examines the client's behaviour checkout and verbally reinforces weekly goal attainment through praise. The following week's goals are then adjusted based on the client's reported ease or difficulty. For example, if difficulties are encountered (e.g. the local nature reserve was closed due to poor weather conditions), the therapist and client work to resolve the problem. For each target activity, if the weekly goal was achieved, the goal is increased for the following assessment period. Goals are evaluated and increased until the assessment period goal is consistent with final goals. Once the final goal is achieved for three consecutive weeks, mastered activities are no longer monitored, the rationale being to increase generalization of increased activity once therapy is terminated. This is also done to eventually move Sally away from her focus on success and towards simply experiencing the benefits of the more positive activities. At the conclusion of each session, the client and therapist determine which new activities will be monitored for the coming week. So if Sally successfully made two phone calls to two different friends during week one, week two might require that Sally make two phone calls again to two friends and have lunch with one of them on one day for at least an hour. These goals will continue to progress until Sally is consistently involved in some type of outside social activity on a weekly basis and in contact with her friends regularly. The structure from the programme and therapist-delivered reinforcers are used to encourage this behaviour, with the goal that, over time, more naturalistic reinforcers will begin to strengthen these new behavioural patterns and more positive thoughts and feelings would emerge.

In assessing client progress, it is again important to focus on more than simply increased activity: comprehensive assessment of covert behaviour is crucial. In line with the concept of desynchrony, it may be the case that initially the client will not experience improvement in thoughts and mood, and may be discouraged by the difficulty of changing ingrained behaviour patterns. However, it is crucial that changes in behaviour eventually correspond with changes in negative thoughts and feelings. For example, in Sally's case it would be important to eventually progress from a simple reduction in anxiety symptoms to a self-reported increase in overall confidence. To the extent that this disparity between thoughts and actions does not change over time, it is important to return to the activation approach to ensure that the activities selected by the client are equally in line with his or her own values and goals and not the values and goals of other people.

THE EVENT

The event brings together several of Sally's problem domains. Although clearly distressing and pertinent to identifying treatment goals, it does not change the overall case formulation or course of treatment. In fact, it confirms the general formulation of the case in that multiple aspects of Sally's depressive symptomatology were evidenced in the encounter. The event was consistent with her reported fears of abandonment and a lost connection with her daughter tied to a boyfriend she considered to be a poor choice, combined with a lack of support and validation from her husband. In addition, the lack of support in dealing with the situation appears to be consistent with previous reports and another indicator of the possible need for supplemental marital therapy. Thus, the event provides a concrete example to utilize in therapy that nicely summarizes some of her key issues and targets.

SUMMARY

Sally is a 55-year-old woman who has experienced elevated depressive symptoms over the past 3 years, with these symptoms escalating over the past 6 months. She reports feelings of anxiety and low self-confidence and reports a loss of connection with her children and husband. Our formulation is based upon a loss of contingent reinforcement for healthy behaviour and the emergence of affect-based coping behaviours that have some immediate negative reinforcement value but with greater long-term negative consequences. Her treatment plan was based on BA which emphasizes structured attempts at promoting increases in overt behaviours aimed at increasing contact with reinforcing environmental contingencies to produce corresponding improvements in thoughts, mood and overall quality of life. Rather than indiscriminately increasing contact with events that are presumed to be pleasant or rewarding, this approach involves an idiographic assessment of Sally's goals and values, and the subsequent initiation of BA to increase her access to reinforcement. Finally, although thoughts and feelings were not regarded as proximal causes of overt behaviour to be targeted directly for change, the BA procedures utilized with Sally addressed cognitions and emotions indirectly by bringing her into contact with more positive consequences for overt behaviour.

REFERENCES

Beck, A.T., Ward, C.H., Mendelson, M. *et al.* (1961) An inventory for measuring depression. *Archives of General Psychiatry*, **4**, 561–71.

Coyne, J.C. (1976) Toward an interactional description of depression. *Psychiatry*, **39**, 28–40.

Dobson, K.S. (1989) A meta-analysis of the efficacy of cognitive therapy for depression. *Journal of Consulting and Clinical Psychology*, **57**, 414–9.

Ferster, C.B. (1973) A functional analysis of depression. *American Psychologist*, **28**, 857–70.

Hollon, S.D., Shelton, R.C. and Davis, D.D. (1993) Cognitive therapy for depression: conceptual issues and clinical efficacy. *Journal of Consulting and Clinical Psychology*, **61**, 270–5.

Hopko, D.R., Lejuez, C.W. and Hopko, S.D. (2004) Behavioural activation as an intervention for co-existent depressive and anxiety symptoms. *Clinical Case Studies*, **3**, 37–48.

Hopko, D.R., Lejuez, C.W., Ruggiero, K.J. and Eifert, G.H. (2003) Contemporary behavioral activation treatment for depression: procedures principles, and process. *Clinical Psychology Review*, **23**, 699–717.

Jacobson, N.S., Dobson, K.S., Truax, P.A. *et al.* (1996) A component analysis of cognitive-behavioural treatment for depression. *Journal of Consulting and Clinical Psychology*, **64**, 295–304.

Jacobson, N.S. and Gortner, E.T. (2000) Can depression be de-medicalized in the 21st century: scientific revolutions, counter-revolutions and the magnetic field of normal science. *Behaviour, Research and Therapy*, **38**, 103–17.

Lejuez, C.W., Hopko, D.R. and Hopko, S.D. (2003) *The Brief Behavioural Activation Treatment for Depression: A Comprehensive Patient Guide*, Pearson Custom Publishing, Boston, MA.

Lejuez, C.W., Hopko, D.R., Levine, S. *et al.* (2006) The therapeutic alliance in behavior therapy. *Psychotherapy: Theory, Research, Practice, Training*, **42**, 456–68.

Lewinsohn, P.M. (1974) A behavioural approach to depression, in *The Psychology of Depression: Contemporary Theory and Research* (eds R.M. Friedman and M.M. Katz), John Wiley & Sons, Inc., New York, pp. 157–78.

Lewinsohn, P.M. and Graf, M. (1973) Pleasant activities and depression. *Journal of Consulting and Clinical Psychology*, **41**, 261–8.

Martell, C.R., Addis, M.E. and Jacobson, N.S. (2001) *Depression in Context: Strategies for Guided Action*, W. W. Norton, New York.

Merikangas, K.R., Risch, N.J. and Weissman, M.M. (1994) Comorbidity and co-transmission of alcoholism, anxiety and depression. *Psychological Medicine*, **24**, 69–80.

Mineka, S., Watson, D. and Clark, L.A. (1998) Comorbidity of anxiety and unipolar mood disorders. *Annual Review of Psychology*, **49**, 377–412.

Otto, M.W, Pava, J.A. and Sprich-Buckminster, S. (1996) Treatment of major depression: application and efficacy of cognitive-behavioural therapy, in *Challenges in Clinical Practice: Pharmacologic and Psychosocial Strategies* (eds M.H. Pollack and M.W. Otto), Guilford, New York, pp. 31–52.

Peak, T. and Barusch, A. (1999) Managed care: a critical review. *Journal of Health and Social Policy*, **11**, 21–36.

Simons, A.D., Garfield, S.L. and Murphy, G.E. (1984) The process of change in cognitive therapy and pharmacotherapy: changes in mood and cognitions. *Archives of General Psychiatry*, **41**, 45–51.

Skinner, B.F. (1953) *Science and Human Behavior*, The Free Press, New York.

Skinner, B.F. (1971) *Beyond Freedom and Dignity*, Alfred A. Knopf, Inc., New York.

5

Commentary on Cognitive and Behavioural Formulations of Anxiety–Depression

CHRISTOPHER J. WILLIAMS

Clinical Case Formulation aims to provide contrasting viewpoints in helping practitioners and clients make sense of the client's presentation. As a reader and commenter on both formulations, I am struck by how much is shared by the cognitive and radical behavioural perspectives. As well as some significant commonalities – perhaps more than what might, at first, be expected – there are also some important differences in perspective, emphasis and intervention. My approach here is to summarize these and to ask questions of both approaches. In the case of Sally, it seems clear that there are many potential targets for intervention – some cognitive and some behavioural – but importantly there are other areas of her experience that are also significant to her.

THE PURPOSES OF A FORMULATION

To start with, I would invite readers to consider the purpose of a formulation. Who is it for – the practitioner or client? Is it shared openly with the client or held by the practitioner? Is it authoritative or collaborative in construction? Who gets to keep a copy of the summary? Whose language is it in – the technical language of the practitioner or the words of the person himself? Formulation has a dual goal of providing a model of understanding for both the patient and practitioner and of informing change by providing a road map

Clinical Case Formulation: Varieties of Approaches. Edited by Peter Sturmey.
© 2009 John Wiley & Sons, Ltd.

for potential treatment. The longer I have spent as a practitioner the more I have come to realize that formulation actually does not pre-date intervention, and this traditional conceptualization is inaccurate. Instead, formulation is the first intervention on which all else is based. For example, Skinner (1953) suggested that by asking the client to do the work necessary to develop a formulation, this was itself already changing behaviour. Similarly, by asking a client to begin to record thoughts can helpfully change unhelpful styles of thinking. Also, by asking a client to begin to notice thoughts and their impact on emotion and activity, this in itself may change those thoughts by helping convince the client how unhelpful getting caught up in such patterns really is. Likewise, from a behavioural perspective, by teaching the client to discriminate environment–behaviour relationships, the therapist aids discrimination training.

Most people like Sally feel scared. They are scared by their symptoms, by the possibility of change, scared to talk about things and to see people, including practitioners like us. Depression makes people feel scared. It puts them off working on their problems. If the person does not feel that people listen to and understand his or her problems, he or she may less likely to engage in change. If we encourage the person to work on problems that we consider, as practitioners, important but that remain unimportant to the client, then he or she is far less likely to engage in therapy. Crucial to engagement is a formulation that identifies problems that the client himself or herself wishes to tackle. A shared formulation is so important because it sells the therapeutic model. Formulation therefore really matters to clients as well as practitioners.

The language used to introduce it also matters. The language of a *shared* formulation is different from the language used by professionals. Ultimately, what is needed is an approach that provides an evidence-based approach by offering a treatment approach that is effective, acceptable and engaging. This is best achieved by (a) helping clients make sense of why they feel as they do by providing them with a model – either cognitive therapy (CT) or behaviour therapy (BT) in this case – that has an evidence base, (b) addressing problems clients themselves wish to tackle and (c) adopting an effective and collaborative therapeutic relationship. Both authors (Chapters 3 and 4) rose admirably to the challenge and both chapters fulfil these key criteria.

COMMONALITIES AND DIFFERENCES

Commonalities

There are a number of shared principles in both CT and BT approaches.

Change does not just happen – it needs to be planned

Many readers will identify with the different New Year resolutions that we are all prone to make at the start of the year. For example, look at the number of cars outside gyms and sports clubs in the opening weeks of January. Contrast that with how full these car parks are only a few weeks later. Good intentions are not enough: a plan with support is more effective. So, those people who commit themselves to change, plan realistic targets in using the gym, or who use a personal trainer, family member or friend to help them keep on track are more likely to be successful. They plan for change.

Change is based on a trusting, warm and effective therapeutic relationship

Both authors emphasized the need for joint, collaborative working. In terms of the keep-fit analogy above, both CT and BT approaches provide the thera-peutic support of a practitioner (or mental health trainer!) in planning change. This support includes trust, warmth, empathy, genuineness, good commu-nication skills and the ability to pitch things in ways that engage the client in change. Both authors emphasized the need to listen and respond to Sally's concerns. Terms such as 'empathy', 'sensitivity' and the need to take great care are mentioned in both the summaries.

Formulations are not fixed – they evolve with time

Information is gathered, changes are planned and understanding of what is going on changes with time. Both practitioner and client learn from and make discoveries from their plans to bring about change. Therefore, the understanding of why the person feels as he or she does and how to change this changes over time in both CT and BT.

The therapy does not just take place in the 1 h a week session with the therapist

Therapy involves the other 167 h in the week as well. Whether termed *home-work* or a *putting into practice plan* (Williams, 2009), both approaches en-courage the person to make changes in his or her life outside the therapy session. This involves putting into practice what he or she has learned. Plans are made, problems anticipated and activities then reviewed to identify what has gone well and any difficulties that have arisen. From this, the practitioner and client plan how to build from this to some next steps that will take things forward. Specific tools can help structure this work such as the *dysfunctional thoughts record* (DTR) in CT and the activity diaries and plans in BT. In both cases, the things the client writes down in between therapy sessions can become a shared focus between the therapist and client in order to develop and evaluate a clear plan for change.

Writing things down offers other advantages. It can encourage the client to adopt an observer stance. Sometimes writing things down helps the client see things differently and more objectively. It can help clarify understanding. Importantly, it provides a written record to allow change to be identified and to tackle problems of poor memory.

In both approaches it really matters how Sally feels

Instead of just guessing whether there is an improvement, the therapist uses rating scales of mood and measures of activity in both approaches. The purpose is both to monitor progress and to aid the process of change. This focus on empirical measured outcomes is a real strength of both CT and BT and has built the foundation of evidence-based practice which is at the centre of both models.

Both therapies challenge common stereotypes that they focus only on the here-and-now

In both therapies, important historical factors are asked about and other possible aetiological factors identified. These may be viewed as data. However, another way of seeing things is that it helps the person tell his or her story, thereby helping himself or herself to begin to see and understand things differently. This idea of narrative is not a concept directly mentioned in either formulation, but in itself can be part of the process of understanding and change. Writing things down also helps the person tell his or her story, which is something that can itself be therapeutic (Smyth, 1998; Smyth and Pennebaker, 1999).

Are there any really significant differences between the approaches?

CT and BT have very significant differences in emphasis. Each brings a different model which makes sense of presentation and each model brings a different range of interventions. These clear differences are being lost in practice as therapists increasingly adopt cognitive-behavioural formulations drawing heavily on both models (see later).

How thoughts, rules and fears are conceptualized

The CT approach places greater emphasis on thinking. Thoughts are seen as worsening how the person feels and affecting what he or she does and how he or she lives his or her life. Therefore, helping Sally to begin to notice and begin to question her unhelpful and upsetting thoughts is very important. There is significant creativity in the CT approach in working with Sally to help her change her upsetting thoughts. Specific questions and strategies, such as using the DTR, structure this process. The greater focus on cognition in CT leads to interventions to test out thoughts and behaviour, such as comparing and contrasting her perceived versus actual responses. For example, Sally could ask others how she comes over to see how others may perceive her. So, at work this would allow her to check to what extent she comes over as someone who is failing to cope – something which she currently fears. In many instances, the person finds that others' opinions are far more positive than he or she would have predicted.

CT sees core beliefs such as *'People I love always abandon me'* and *'I am nobody without someone who needs me'* as driving Sally's feelings and behaviour. They may become targets for change. Planned changes in behaviour are used to experiment and test out beliefs to discover whether they are accurate or not. They would not be given such a primary role in BT; however, it would be incorrect to think that BT does not address thoughts. Some contemporary forms of BT such as acceptance commitment therapy also address private behaviour such as thoughts as a primary target for change (Hayes, Strosahl and Wilson, 2003).

In contrast, in the BT model thoughts, feelings and actions are seen as a function of one's environment so that causality resides in environmental factors. Less emphasis is placed on the ongoing role of beliefs in keeping Sally's feelings of distress going. However, it would be incorrect to state that BT overlooks beliefs: it clearly does not. Beliefs are challenged in order to allow behaviour change. Behaviour change is also focused on the person's values and goals. Here the process of change is very specific. It involves altering behaviour and making changes in small steps called 'attainable behaviour change goals'. Eventually, changes in behaviour correspond with changes in negative thoughts and feelings (LeJuez, Brown and Hopko; Chapter 4, Section 'Assessing Progress and Treatment Modification', pp. 65–66). However, the driver for change is altered behaviour.

How problem behaviours are conceptualized

Any presentation – physical or mental health in focus – can be summarized as one of four circles (Williams, 2009). These circles are (a) reduced activity,

(b) avoidance, (c) backfiring/unhelpful or behaviours and (d) strengths and helpful responses.

Reduced activity

In the BT formulation, there is a strong emphasis on reduced activity and changes are introduced not only to boost mood *but also* to change thoughts, such as beliefs of self-efficacy. CT also emphasizes such changes – with the aim of increasing activities that provide a sense of pleasure (fun/enjoyment) and mastery (a feeling of achievement). This is described differently in behavioural activation where an emphasis is on planning activities that are valued by the person. This idea of value is surprisingly cognitive in focus, yet is central to the BT approach of planning activity changes. It is likely to draw people into making changes and lead to effective engagement. It also respects the person's own goals and gives meaning to the activity. The use of words like mastery and pleasure in CT seems (to me) to fail somehow to encapsulate this idea of value.

A perspective overlooked by both formulations is the idea that it can be helpful to help people plan activities that build closeness to others. For example, loneliness is seen as a *problem of thought* in the CT formulation and *of behaviour* in the BT approach. Neither really focuses on identifying the importance of closeness to others as an important factor that affects how people feel.

There are problems and issues in both Sally's thinking and behaviour. However, another conceptualization that could be used is to see this as an issue of problem-solving. Problem-solving therapy can be an effective treatment for depression (Mynors-Wallis *et al.*, 2000; Nezu, 1986). Sally's loneliness could also be conceptualized as a practical problem that she can plan to tackle. Doing this may well involve both thinking and behaviour changes, and builds on a motive that is potent for many people – a need to love and be loved. The concept of a systemic problem-solving approach to tackling her problem relationship is mentioned in the CT formulation, as is the need for some skills-based training such as communication skills. However, again, there is little more here than a few single line comments suggesting that an external focus on relationships and skills training is not especially emphasized in the CT formulation. In view of the widespread integration of problem-solving approaches into clinical treatment models, this may be, however, more an issue of editing and issues to do with a lack of space.

Both models show how Sally's reduced activity creates a vicious circle causing her to feel more and more low and scared. Both models also show other consequences of reduced activity such as social consequences and reduced fitness and some weight gain as a result of going less to the gym. The greater focus on tackling reduced activity in the BT approach is shown by the length of time spent working through how behavioural activation could benefit Sally – and how in doing this Sally's fears/concerns and values all need to be addressed.

Avoidance

Both formulations see avoiding scary people, places and situations as a part of the problem. In both approaches, the treatment involves exposure such as facing up to fears in a planned step-by-step way in BT, with a more cognitive focus on challenging fears in CT. In BT, fears are still acknowledged as potential blocks. However, the way of changing these is by altering behaviour. In contrast, in CT the focus is on specifically identifying and challenging fears and linking this to experiments to change behaviour and test beliefs.

Backfiring/unhelpful or effective/ineffective behaviours

Both formulations agree that Sally shows a wide range of unhelpful behaviours. However, the models differ in explanation as to why she presents these different behaviours. In CT, the patterns of behaviour may be seen as driven by underlying beliefs or rules that lead the person to act in ways that prove his or her failure and unlovability. The BT approach takes a more developmental view in which the response is seen as one that may have been helpful or partially helpful at some stage but now no longer is so. In BT, the language used is that of a 'compensatory behaviour' and there is a far more detailed focusing on unhelpful behaviours.

Sally needs to discover more about why her responses are sometimes part of the problem. The BT model provides a clearly argued rationale for this. Here, the immediate benefits (reinforcers) are seen as driving the behaviour. Sally's use of alcohol to reduce her emotional pain helps boost how she feels in the short term. However, in the medium to longer term it makes her feel worse emotionally, physically and socially. A similar model can help Sally discover how her other varying unhelpful responses, such as her discussion on the phone with her daughter's partner, can again be part of the problem. Her responses create difficulties for her, and also importantly with those around her.

Sally's strengths and helpful responses

A criticism of these two formulations is that they tend to emphasize only on problematic thoughts and behaviours. In both formulations, there is little emphasis placed upon what Sally is doing well at present. Relatively little is made of Sally's potential past strengths or personal resources. A virtuous circle of helpful behaviours (Williams, 2009) could be helpfully identified here. This would help her identify and build on what she is doing well currently or has done well in the past in similar situations.

How the environment and other people are conceptualized

Both models address the key people and relationships around Sally; however, the emphasis made differs in the two models. CT is defined as *'designed to assess, monitor and modify such maladaptive automatic thoughts and underlying beliefs, with the goal of improving the clients' quality of emotional life, and expanding their adaptive behavioural repertoire'* (Newman; Chapter 3, Section 'Theoretical Orientation and Rationale', pp. 43–44). This clearly emphasizes thoughts and behaviour. However, there is little emphasis in this definition of the importance of others around the person.

The impact of others

Sometimes people are distressed because of their thoughts. However, sometimes it is realistic to be distressed when life is tough and upsetting. People can let us down. We can be hurt. We can end up with incurable illness or face debts we struggle to pay. In these circumstances looking at how we view things is important, but tackling these external problems is also important. In both conceptualizations, there is a mention of tackling external problems but in neither does this seem especially important. Given the evidence that problem-solving approaches can be effective (Mynors-Wallis *et al.*, 2000; Nezu, 1986), it might be considered that overly focusing on cognition (CT) or behaviour (BT) in the formulation may overlook the need for skills-based interventions using a problem-solving framework.

External relationships can be a source of distress, as is shown in Sally's relations with her daughter, husband and daughter's partner at present. They can also be a source of support. Sometimes this support can be helpful and sometimes unhelpful, for example wrapping the person in cotton wool or trying to force him or her to do things. Both CT and BT formulations were very able to conceptualize the problematic relationships that Sally has around her.

How the two models handle the potential affair

There are marked differences in how the two formulations approach the potential affair. In the CT formulation, the issue is viewed as something that is a decision which is entirely down to Sally and the therapist would not dream of telling her to desist. In contrast, in the BT formulation her flirtation is clearly seen as unhelpful behaviour because it will end up worsening how she feels. It also has the possibility of hurting far more people around her.

It could be commented that the CT formulation here tries to adopt a value-free approach. However, the focus that the CT formulators place on respecting the person's own beliefs and values negates this. Instead, it values the person's autonomy. This issue is seen as a decision for Sally not for the therapist. The therapist may ask her questions to help her clarify her thoughts, but it is still fundamentally her decision. It is clearly stated that the therapist should not tell her what to do. In contrast, the BT formulation recognizes that such behaviour goes against her religious beliefs and other values. It suggests planning ways of improving her relationship with her husband and friends and to reduce her intimacy with John. Again, this respects her values and beliefs and does not impose the practitioner's own beliefs. However, it seems more actively to engage her in an issue which is causing her distress and which has the potential, if it develops further to a full affair, to cause even more distress for Sally and those around her.

How do the two models address her religious faith?

Related to her dilemma about the possible affair is the impact of her spiritual beliefs and faith. In surveys in the US, around one in five psychiatric patients have some beliefs that sin/moral guilt and wrongdoing are wrapped up in their sense of depression (Sheehan and Kroll, 1990). Her beliefs about the affair involve her faith. The CT formulation sidesteps this discussion of *right* versus *wrong* and seems to move the discussion to one of whether the response is *helpful* for her or not. It is noteworthy that both formulators pick up on at least the presence of her religious faith. Larson, Pattison and Blazer (1986) showed that in many cases a person's spiritual beliefs are not focused upon in case summaries. Their review showed that only 3% of the published papers in key psychiatric journals during a 5-year period had included among the items they had studied any variables referring to the religious faith of the studied population.

In contrast, the BT approach specifically mentions a sense of sin. It may be argued that in US culture, it may be more likely that religious faith aspects be considered than in the United Kingdom. However, faith-based beliefs and behaviours can be important sources of potential support and difficulty for clients and it seems entirely appropriate to consider the clients' beliefs routinely in assessment. Sally's potential affair is stated as going against her religious beliefs. Because being an adulteress will make her feel worse, interventions are planned to reduce the likelihood of this occurring. This ties in with discussion elsewhere in choosing targets for change in BT that target behaviours that are valued by her. This use of the word *valued* when introducing targets is refreshing as it emphasizes an important part of this BT approach: it is compassionate. It is not solely interested in the behaviour of an automaton, but that of a person. This is also true of the CT approach; however, the language of CT does not make this clear. Compassion is now increasingly a focus for CT practitioners (Gilbert, 2005).

What about biological factors?

Neither formulation focuses on biological risk factors. A danger is that of 'psychologization', which may occur with 'the overemphasis and exaggeration of the role of psychological factors in illnesses which are generally considered to have a predominantly physiological and/or biochemical aetiology' (Goudsmit and Gadd, 1991, p. 449). Of course, any mental health presentation can, on occasion, have a physical aetiology. Perhaps Sally has anaemia, a thyroid problem or undiagnosed diabetes? An argument can be made that every assessment for depression and anxiety should contain a recommendation that a brief physical examination and core blood tests, such as full blood count, plasma viscosity, blood sugar and thyroid function tests, should occur in collaboration with a physician.

What about language?

CBT and BT have a potential problem. That problem is the technical language used in formulation by professionals (Williams and Garland, 2002). This technical language can sometimes be either blaming or too technical. The language of CT can be blaming. For example, the DTR and other terms commonly used are a language that could be perceived as engendering shame, critical or undermining. As well as feeling depressed, now Sally is potentially at risk of seeing herself as thinking or behaving wrongly too. This may be reinforced by terms often used in the CT approach such as 'maladaptive' and 'erroneous'. The language of formulations may also be too complex and involve overgeneral assumptions. It is not made clear whether Sally is expected to learn this language before being able to engage in therapy or whether the practitioner would 'translate' and pitch concepts at the right level for her. For example, the therapist could introduce 'problematic behavioural strategies' as 'shall we try to work out if some of the things you do may be backfiring?' Similarly, trying to jointly agree problems and issues that Sally can feel engaged in working on is described as identifying 'high priority variables'. This language is very important for use in a technical summary of Sally, but is a hard language for some clients to learn. The reading ages of both formulations reflect this. The reading ages were 19.1 and 21 years for the CT and BT summaries, respectively – for higher than the 11–12 year old level of popular newspapers. The Flesch reading scores are also low. Both were below 40 compared with an accessible text score of 60+. The reading ease test rates text on a 100-point scale; the higher the score, the easier it is to understand the document. For most standard texts, a score of 60–70 should be aimed for.

Both points raise important issues again of exactly who the formulation is for. If it is for the practitioner then the technical language is just that – technical. It can be translated when used with clients. On comparing the use of language in the two approaches, it does seem to me that the BT approach has the most immediately accessible and less overtly blaming language. However, how these concepts are introduced will allow practitioners to adjust the language by taking into account the individual clients needs.

Can both approaches be integrated?

Part of the artificiality of presenting supposedly pure CT and BT summaries is that in many ways CT and BT are rarely purely practised when a worldwide perspective is taken. Most often cognitive-behavioural therapy (CBT) is the term used to describe a drawing together of approaches from both models. This coming together of ideas is also seen in both pure CT and BT here: the radical BT model addresses thoughts and fears, the CT model addresses behaviour. Making changes in either area also benefits the other.

Some final thoughts on working flexibly

I remember training on the Newcastle CBT course in the United Kingdom in the early 1990s. During the first 3 months of this one-year postgraduate course, my fellow course members and I often felt quite deskilled. The ways we thought and made sense of clients were slowly stripped away and rebuilt through the process of reflective learning and clinical supervision. After 3 months or so we were fully steeped in the model.

It was at that time when we were shown several video tapes of well-known leaders and practitioners such as Professor Aaron Beck working with clients. We all agreed that he was not very good! Our judgement was based on our feeling that he failed to use the clear structure of therapy that we had learned from his classic work *Cognitive Therapy of Depression* (Beck, Rush and Shaw, 1979) and on the course. This book is perhaps both one of the best and the worst things to have been published in this field. Beck *et al.* manualized the CT model and interventions so that the approach could be taught and delivered worldwide. It led to research trials and evaluations. At the same time his flexibility, creativity and use of everyday language and terms used by the clients themselves at times were not perhaps as well captured. Our judgement as naïve trainees was clearly wrong. Beck was and is a brilliant clinician. In the tape he (a) worked with a clear approach, but not rigidly; (b) listened and engaged the person on problems relevant to himself or herself; and (c) did so with warmth and understanding. These same three components shine out of both formulations. As such they have more in common than might at first sight be perceived. Formulation is not a straight jacket to be fitted and forced on the client. Instead, it helps clients make sense of how they feel using an empirically based model – a model that helps them understand and change.

Sally, I would suspect, will gain from working with either approach. Her goals are to feel better and regain confidence. There are various evidence-based ways of doing this. CT and BT are two such ways. Whatever is offered, unless it is built on the bedrock of a good therapeutic relationship, the impact will be less than it otherwise would have been. Formulation, no matter how good, is an interactive task between individuals. These two formulations show how good this can be.

CONCLUSION

The two formulations contain much richness in understanding how Sally feels. They provide a clear model and structure of working. Both pay attention to cognitions and behaviour. Both also consider Sally in the wider context of her family, friends and work life. Crucially, both work gently with her in a truly collaborative way to bring about change. Both show elements of a CBT approach, but differ in their emphasis. Crucially, both pay attention to Sally. She is not just a mix of altered behaviours and thinking: she is a person who is distressed and wants to change. Both formulations provided an effective basis for helping her change and that is the real goal of formulation!

REFERENCES

Beck, A.T., Rush, J.A., Shaw, B.F. *et al.* (1979) *Cognitive Therapy of Depression*, Guilford Press, New York.

Gilbert, P. (2005) *Compassion*, Brunner-Routledge, London.

Goudsmit, E. and Gadd, R. (1991) All in the mind? The psychologisation of illness. *The Psychologist, Bulletin of the British Psychological Society*, **4**, 449–53.

Hayes, S., Strosahl, K.D. and Wilson, K.G. (2003) *Acceptance and Commitment Therapy: An Experiential Approach to Behavior Change: An Experimental Approach to Behavior Change*, Guilford Press, New York.

Larson, D.B., Pattison, E.M. and Blazer, D.G. (1986) Systematic analysis of research on religious variable in four major psychiatric journals, 1978–1982. *American Journal of Psychiatry*, **143**, 329–34.

Mynors-Wallis, L., Gath, D., Day, A. and Baker, F. (2000) Randomized controlled trial of problem solving treatment, antidepressant medication, and combined treatment for major depression in primary care. *British Medical Journal*, **320**, 26–30.

Nezu, A.M. (1986) Efficacy of a social problem-solving therapy approach for unipolar depression. *Journal of Consulting and Clinical Psychology*, **54**, 196–202.

Sheehan, W. and Kroll, J. (1990) Psychiatric patients' belief in general health factors and sin as causes of illness. *American Journal of Psychiatry*, **147**, 112–3.

Skinner, B.F. (1953) *Science and Human Behavior*, The Free Press, New York.

Smyth, J.M. (1998) Written emotional expression: effect sizes, outcome types, and moderating variables. *Journal of Consulting and Clinical Psychology*, **66**, 174–84.

Smyth, J. and Pennebaker, J.W. (1999) Sharing one's story. Translating emotional experiences into words as a coping tool, in *Coping: The Psychology of What Works* (ed. C.R. Snyder), Oxford University Press, New York, pp. 70–89.

Williams, C.J. (2009) *Overcoming Depression and Low Mood: A Five Areas Approach*, 3rd edn, Hodder Arnold, London.

Williams, C.J. and Garland, A. (2002) A cognitive behavioural therapy assessment model for use in everyday clinical practice. *Advances in Psychiatric Treatment*, **8**, 172–79.

PART III
Psychosis

6

Zeppi: A Case of Psychosis

ANTHONY DIMECH, DAVID KINGDON, AND
MAGED SWELAM

PRESENTING COMPLAINT

Zeppi was seen by a psychiatrist and a social worker in a Police Station following his arrest for the possession of two offensive weapons without licence. These consisted of a 26-inch machete and a 7-inch dagger. Three Police Officers had raided his two-room basement apartment following concerns raised by a neighbour who had spotted him on some occasions bizarrely leaving the block with a sizeable knife hanging out of his coat. The Police Sergeant had tried to interview him but then decided that the detainee required a medical assessment. Zeppi was known to the Police through a number of reports he had made over the previous months, regarding his belief that organized crime groups wanted his demise.

Zeppi appeared very guarded and reiterated that the Police had made a gross mistake and the culprits were still at large. On the other hand, he felt relieved that finally the Police were taking his case seriously and were giving him protection. He had felt at a significant risk of losing his life for almost a year and had sought the help of the Police on a number of occasions. His fear started when he was still working for his cousin. He began to feel vulnerable working on the counter in his cousin's take-away restaurant and refused to work late night shifts or to have direct contact with customers. His cousin initially tried to accommodate his preferences, but the normal running of the business became incompatible with Zeppi's requests and thus his cousin had to employ someone else. Zeppi complained to his cousin that the new employee had tried to put his life at risk. Zeppi believed the same man was using a high-tech electronic device that fired magnetic waves at his body. As a result

Clinical Case Formulation: Varieties of Approaches. Edited by Peter Sturmey.
© 2009 John Wiley & Sons, Ltd.

of these waves, Zeppi experienced palpitations and believed that his killer intended to make him suffer a heart attack and make it look as if it was a natural death. He also described burning sensations in various parts of his body and attributed these to the magnetic waves. His cousin's scepticism of the situation initially puzzled Zeppi, and he later came to believe that the cousin was also involved in the conspiracy. Zeppi claimed that this made him see things more clearly. At that point, it was obvious that both his cousin and the new employee belonged to an international crime organization that had some sort of connection with Malta. He believed they were instructed by the parish priest of his village of origin to kill him slowly and make him suffer tremendously in the process. Zeppi believed that his cousin, to whom he started referring as "the traitor," had been the one who informed the parish priest of his whereabouts. His cousin wanted him to seek help but Zeppi felt that this was part of the organization's plan to lock him up and proceed with the torture plan more liberally.

Zeppi then found a new apartment, which he could just afford, after spending a few nights sleeping rough. Up to that point he was living in a converted garage in his cousin's house. He had managed to save most of his earnings as his cousin never charged him for rent and he used to have most meals at the take-away. Zeppi never turned up for work following the altercation with his cousin.

Despite this, Zeppi claims that he continued to experience the same attacks by his persecutors. He believed that other invisible devices were installed in his room. Though he never met again with the cousin and his collaborator, they persistently controlled these devices to prolong his misery. At times, he would experience the burning sensations, which he believed were caused by the magnetic waves, while he was sitting on a bench in the park. He was convinced that other members of the organization whom he had never met before were following him and using similar handheld devices to prolong his suffering.

Zeppi reported these events to the Police repeatedly. He claimed that the persecutors were very crafty and knew the movements of the Police, whose investigations were unsuccessful. He admitted that the Police could not possibly provide him with the level of protection he required and decided to look after himself. In the last couple of months he took to carrying arms whenever he left his apartment.

CLIENT DEMOGRAPHIC DATA

Zeppi was a 29-year-old single, unemployed man who originally came from Malta and had lived in London for the previous $1^{1}/_{2}$ years. He lived alone in a basement apartment of a 12-storey block of flats in the east of the city.

His mother lived in Malta but he had not spoken to her for over 5 years. His closest relative was an aunt to whom he spoke on the phone sporadically.

CLIENT DEMEANOUR AND PERSONAL APPEARANCE

The patient, a Caucasian man of short stature and slightly overweight, was seen in a Police interview room at around midnight. Zeppi appeared almost 10 years older than his age. He sported a light brown camouflage suit, which consisted of a pair of trousers and a long jacket that covered up to his mid-thighs. He also wore a matching baseball cap. His glasses were grey but one could still see his eyes. Long dark-brown hair fell from under his cap, almost touching his shoulders, and appeared somewhat unkempt. The overall impression of dishevelment was supported by his long and scruffy beard and various stains on his cap, jacket and trousers. The temperature in the room was quite warm, but Zeppi did not bother to unbutton his jacket. After a few minutes, his unpleasant body odour became obvious, confirming further the initial impression.

Initially he sat quietly and appeared fairly guarded. He was anxious and hesitant in answering the introductory questions. However, he became increasingly articulate and affable as the interview proceeded and in those circumstances, a reasonable rapport was established. Eye contact was maintained throughout the assessment. No abnormal movements were observed. At the end, he seemed calm and content. At no point did he give the impression of responding to abnormal stimuli.

CURRENT LIFESTYLE

Zeppi spent most of his days in his apartment, watching TV, listening to the radio and reading newspapers. He went out late in the evenings to do his shopping and take an occasional short walk in park just before it was stark dark. At times he would spend an afternoon at the local library reading about electronic devices and magnetic radiation. He did not register with the library or set up an Internet account and never borrowed any books.

The day he stormed out of his cousin's restaurant was his last day of work and he had sought no further employment since. He lived on his savings, although his aunt sent him some money every now and again. His diet consisted mostly of canned food and bread but occasionally he got himself a take-away meal on his way home. He did consume alcohol almost every night and this amounted to a couple of glasses of normal strength cider. He tended to buy his supplies from different shops and avoided talking to others as much as he could. He also avoided using buses or other means of transport because of the CCTV cameras, though he admitted that the CCTVs were inevitable in shops. He used to hide his dagger under his trousers in a pocket attached to his right leg when he intended to go shopping.

Zeppi had had no contact with his mother, who lived in the same village of the parish priest he thought was his chief persecutor. He appeared hesitant to discuss their relationship. However, he maintained telephone contact with an aunt on average every other month but had never visited after his move to the United Kingdom. This aunt lived on Malta's sister island, Gozo, where Zeppi had spent his later childhood. Zeppi had made no friends in the United Kingdom and his cousin was his only next of kin there. He lived in almost complete isolation.

CLIENT HISTORY

Zeppi's childhood was punctuated by a number of traumatic life experiences. To start with, he was the outcome of an abusive and incestuous relationship between his mother—a 13-year-old girl—and her grandfather. His mother lived on a farm on the outskirts of a little village in the north of the island. Her father had passed away a couple of years previously and she lived with her mother, uncle and grandfather. She had stopped attending school at the age of 12, which was quite common at the time, and was expected to dedicate her life to the demands of the farm. She led a very busy life feeding the animals, washing, cooking and also caring for her mother, who suffered from some sort of a quite disabling mental illness. The uncle spent very little time at home because he trekked to villages and towns trading the farm products.

Zeppi claimed that his mother had successfully managed to hide all the details of his early life for many years and that he had received almost all his information from his aunt when he was almost 18.

Apparently the pregnancy came to light only after the onset of labour. A local GP was called as his mother complained of severe abdominal pain and Zeppi was delivered at home. Zeppi's grandmother had been too unwell to notice his mother's body changes and his aunt had left home years prior to the pregnancy and never visited. The grandfather was most probably too scared to do anything about it and after the birth he decided to avoid a big scandal by concealing Zeppi's existence from the rest of the community. As a result, Zeppi was neither baptized nor registered at birth. The grandfather's decision was final and his mother and uncle never contested it. Zeppi remembered being told to hide away in the stables when the man in black visited. This was the parish priest who visited Zeppi's sick grandmother every couple of months.

Zeppi spent his first years living a hard, but somewhat serene, farm-life completely cut from the rest of the world. He described his mother as always on the go with very little time for him. His uncle was always away and his grandfather, frequently inebriated, ignored him completely to the point that he could hardly remember an instance when they spoke face to face. Zeppi felt closer to the animals than to human beings. In spite of this, Zeppi felt quite happy spending days running through the fields with the dogs, counting the freshly laid eggs and the hatched chickens and having a go at milking goats. Food was plenty; he had freshly baked bread for breakfast every day, one or two large fried eggs and cheese for lunch, minestrone for supper and meat once a week. The only person who seemed to show some interest in him was his grandmother, although he was strictly not allowed to be alone with her in her room. She spent her days sitting on a bench in a veranda doing nothing. He remembers her saying words to him that he could hardly grasp although she always seemed very friendly.

His seclusion from the rest of the world went on until he was 8. Up to that point, he had had very little contact with boys of his age except for the very infrequent visits by other farmers and their children who came to the farm for the sole purpose of exchanging cattle and products. School was an unknown concept and none of his relatives went to church.

The death of his grandfather brought about major changes in Zeppi's life. He met his aunt for the first time at the funeral. She was warm and affectionate and seemed to be the first person to show genuine and persistent interest in him. He liked her straight away. Following the funeral, he remembered very hot discussions between his mother and her sister, with a lot of screaming and crying and the unusual intervention of his uncle. Zeppi ended up leaving the farm with his aunt and a small box with some of his clothes in it. His mother cried her eyes out, but did not utter a word as he was leaving. He did not remember any hugs or kisses from her, which would have been very much out of character. As he described this important episode in his life, he claimed that he could still feel the stare of her red eyes.

The aunt lived in Gozo, Malta's sister island. Although he liked the affection of his aunt, Zeppi felt scared of his new environment. His aunt had a townhouse where she lived with her two sons. She was the eldest, around 12 years older than his mother, but her younger son was only 3 years his senior. She was separated from her husband and had a job as a teaching assistant in a local school.

Zeppi wanted to go back to the farm immediately and became quite disturbed. He felt that he had never settled at school nor had he made any friends. He was frequently targeted by other boys and severely punished by his teachers. His reactions to bullying were deemed out of proportion, and more often than not he had to endure the physical abuse of his peers and the stick of his teachers. Bullying went beyond the usual playground taunts, throwing of stones and punches and kicks. He described that on a few occasions, at the age of 12–13, he was attacked on his way home by a group of boys from his class. He described being awfully humiliated by his classmates who forcefully held him on the ground and pulled down his trousers whilst each and every member of the group spat on his genitals. Such group activity was not unheard of at the time and his cousin tried to sell it to him as 'friendly' bullying, a sort of initiation ritual to those outside the group. His cousin encouraged him not to react adversely to it but to take a more humorous point of view since it might be an opportunity for being accepted within the group. His cousin confessed that it had happened to him as well. However, Zeppi never accepted his cousin's perspective and became increasingly detached from the other boys in his class.

His visits to the farm were very rare and a few years later it was sold. After his mother got married, contact with her became even less frequent. However, for many years he had very vivid dreams about his life on the farm, which he did not share with anybody else.

His aunt put a lot of effort into helping him to catch up with his schoolwork and his younger cousin also helped him out. But his older cousin was very critical and abusive. He was 9 years older than Zeppi and had moved in with his father. This same cousin was also frequently abusive to his own brother and mother. Zeppi hated him for this. Once he asked Zeppi if he knew who his father was. Zeppi had always been told that his father had died before his birth. He remembered that his aunt intervened immediately and a big row started between the two. After that episode, his cousin's behaviour deteriorated further and he became even more abusive of Zeppi. On one occasion, Zeppi was alone in the house with a fever whilst his aunt and other cousin were at school. His elder cousin turned up and pretended to be nice to him. At one point the cousin pulled his own trousers down and started to masturbate in front of Zeppi. He tried to force Zeppi to have oral sex with him but Zeppi strongly refused. Then the cousin ejaculated on a piece of bread, pulled his trousers up and started to hit Zeppi with a belt. He did not stop until Zeppi ate a piece of the bread. Zeppi vomited several times after the incident but was too ashamed to tell anyone about it.

Zeppi left school at the age of 15 and started to work part-time in a local bakery. The owner was a friend of his aunt and gave him considerable support. His younger cousin also worked at the same place and for the first 2 years he thought he coped well. But after his cousin left and went to work abroad Zeppi felt very lonely and lost interest in work. He claimed that the other employees did not like him, told lies about him and made him leave. This was shortly followed by a formal admission to hospital where he spent many months. He reported that he refused medications, was given electric shocks in his head, and injections. His aunt visited him regularly but for the first time she did not take his side and encouraged him to have the injections and shocks. Eventually he was discharged back to his aunt's custody. He was not interested in going back to work and spent many days doing very little. When his younger cousin visited he became more active and spent more time outside with him. It was this cousin who suggested he should try his luck abroad. Zeppi agreed to work for his cousin and the aunt had no objections.

CLIENT GOALS

Zeppi was of the opinion that he was perfectly well and did not require any treatment, including regular visits and support from the Home Treatment team. It was not possible to agree on any treatment goals.

THE EVENT

Zeppi was formally admitted to an open ward for acutely ill patients. Initially, he was very reluctant to accept oral medications, but when he realized that unless he complied with treatment he was not going to be granted any leave, he started to take one tablet of an antipsychotic daily. He was scared of the prospect of being restrained and injected with medication. However, concerns were raised by the nurses about his compliance with treatment as tablets of Zeppi's prescribed medication were repeatedly discovered in the ward bins.

On the third week of admission, Zeppi was sitting in the television room of the ward. Two other patients and a male nursing assistant were sitting in the same room. Suddenly Zeppi lashed wildly at the nursing assistant and one of the patients. The patients managed to flee but the nursing assistant ended up with a broken nose and had to be taken to hospital. Zeppi was restrained and taken to the seclusion room on the same ward. A staff meeting was held shortly after the incident and it was decided that this attack was completely unexpected and unprovoked. A risk assessment form filled in a couple of hours prior to the incident had not identified any risks for violence.

Zeppi was taken to the psychiatric intensive care unit. He remained agitated and threatening, and intramuscular medication was administered. He refused to answer any questions and was observed closely for the following 3 days during which he agreed to take the prescribed medications orally. Zeppi was questioned about the violent incident by his psychiatrist. He apologized repeatedly, and it appeared that he had truly regretted the attack. He claimed that this was out of character for him as he considered himself a very peaceful person but that he needed to protect himself. He explained that on the days before the incident he had again started experiencing the magnetic wave attacks. He knew that the nurses and some of the patients were receiving orders from "the traitor's" criminal organization. He described the attacks as more intense than usual and involving other organs in addition to his heart. He believed that the hospital ward was all made up and the building was really a torture chamber. He felt the magnetic waves affecting his bowels and genitalia to prolong his suffering. Zeppi believed that the nurses had gained control of his penis. During the night before the incident the nurses had humiliated him by using electronic devices to make his penis erect and cause an ejaculation. They laughed at him repeatedly and Zeppi felt very embarrassed. Just before the incident happened Zeppi was sitting on a chair watching television when he started to experience the burning sensation of the waves on his lower abdomen. He saw the nurse assistant and two patients laughing at him. He thought that they were trying to use the waves to cause a cancer in his bowels. Zeppi felt that they gained control of him on his passing of flatus. At that stage, Zeppi felt he had to do something to stop the attack.

7

A Psychiatric Approach to Case Formulation

DAVID A. CASEY

THEORETICAL ORIENTATION AND RATIONALE

Formulation is the process by which psychiatrists take the raw information obtained by interview and other sources and organize it in order to make a diagnosis. Formulation requires applying an organizing principle or principles in order to logically synthesize and assign meaning to disparate bits of information (Mellsop and Banzato, 2006). Such organizing principles may be described as models or 'paradigms' (Kuhn, 1962). All scientific disciplines have one or more paradigms, which evolve over time to fit new data, but also represent an evolution of systems of thought. Psychiatric formulation also plays an important role in presenting a case; that is, systematically communicating information about a patient to other clinicians. Medical students and psychiatric residents are taught formulation as a key part of their training, sometimes explicitly but often implicitly by constant interchange with other clinicians, including more senior supervisors. Although formulation is a basic skill in psychiatric practice, residents often struggle with their ability to cogently formulate and present a case, given the endless variation and complexity of mental illness (McClain, O'Sullivan and Clardy, 2004; Ross et al., 1990). Psychiatric formulation cannot be understood without understanding the underlying paradigms which are applied. Because there are several paradigms in modern psychiatry, it has proven difficult to precisely define and describe what constitutes a psychiatric formulation.

Clinical Case Formulation: Varieties of Approaches.   Edited by Peter Sturmey.
© 2009 John Wiley & Sons, Ltd.

In the practice of psychotherapy, formulation involves an understanding of the relevant aspects of a case as they apply to a particular psychotherapeutic approach, such as cognitive behavioural or psychodynamic. In psychiatry, however, a complete formulation also includes making a psychiatric diagnosis, which can be a basis for a variety of other interventions, including decisions about psychopharmacology, hospitalization or medico-legal determinations (Mellsop and Bansato, 2006). The process of psychiatric diagnosis will be described further later in the chapter.

Psychiatric paradigms

The paradigms which are currently prevalent in psychiatry have evolved over many years, influenced by advancement in neuroscience as well as psychology, sociology and other disciplines. However, much of the data utilized by psychiatrists and other mental health practitioners have an inherently subjective element which leaves room for varying interpretations based not only on scientific theories of mental illness but also on a host of other influences. Because of this, psychiatric paradigms can be quite controversial. Although many psychiatrists agree on certain important elements of formulation, by no means is there unanimity of opinion. In fact, individuals as well as various groups of psychiatrists hold views substantially different than the mainstream. Many critics of psychiatry from outside the discipline have also vehemently objected to the major paradigms of thought, particularly the biomedical model. A historical perspective is useful to understand these issues, which will be explored further in this chapter.

There is not a single unitary paradigm in psychiatric formulation today. For example, many psychotherapeutically inclined psychiatrists utilize a psychodynamic formulation while others subscribe to a cognitive-behavioural model. Perhaps, the most influential and ambitious paradigms include the biomedical model and the biopsychosocial model. The *Diagnostic and Statistical Manual of the American Psychiatric Association, Fourth Edition, Text Revision* (DSM-IV TR; American Psychiatric Association, 2000) also serves as an organizing principle for psychiatric diagnosis. Although ostensibly atheoretical, DSM-IV TR may be regarded as a paradigm of psychiatric diagnosis and case formulation. These paradigms may overlap and may even be applied simultaneously. For instance, psychodynamic thinking may well influence the psychological component of the biopsychosocial model. Likewise, DSM-IV TR incorporates a multi-axial approach which derives largely from the biopsychosocial model. In this chapter, the biomedical and biopsychosocial models of psychiatric formulation as well as the DSM-IV TR will be further explored and applied to the case of Zeppi, a young man with a psychotic illness.

The biomedical model

The biomedical model, often also known as biological psychiatry, derives from an application of traditional medical modes of thinking, as applied to psychiatric illness (Guze, 1992). This model largely assumes that mental illnesses involve some pathological condition within the individual sufferer, which ultimately affects brain function, leading to psychiatric symptoms. Mental illness is thought of as occurring in more or less separate, discrete categories such as schizophrenia and bipolar disorder. In this model, illnesses are thought of as having recognizable clusters of symptoms (syndromes), a recognizable time course (e.g. acute, chronic and episodic) and a particular pattern of response to treatment. The biomedical model has been applied most often to the severe, disabling mental illnesses such as schizophrenia or major affective disorders. It has been more controversial when applied to personality disorders, substance abuse disorders, post-traumatic stress disorders and culture-bound syndromes. In these conditions, the assumptions made by the biomedical model might be problematic. Since this approach is analogous to that used in many other fields of medicine, it is appealing to many medically trained psychiatrists. Of course, the biomedical model is also supported by the vast and growing body of scientific data describing the biology of mental disorders. The relative success of psychopharmacology has also contributed to the rise of the biomedical model. The biomedical model may also tend to destigmatize mental illnesses by categorizing them as innate, no-fault chemical imbalances.

Critics of the biomedical model

The biomedical model has had many critics. Critics of this model have viewed it as too narrow, not admitting sufficiently to social, cultural and experiential influences on mental illness. It has been described as a 'deficit model', meaning that it focuses on individual pathology, rather than a holistic view of an individual's strengths and place in society, as well as weaknesses. Some authors have expressed a concern about the potential negative effects of attaching a psychiatric diagnosis or label to a patient. According to this view, this negative label may become a self-fulfilling prophecy. Some of psychiatry's critics have rejected the biomedical model entirely, viewing mental illness as largely a social phenomenon, perhaps resulting from an oppressive society. These theorists tend to downplay or even reject the role of brain function in mental illness. Critics of the biomedical model have come from both the right and the left of the political spectrum, as well as academia and certain religious groups.

Thomas Szasz, an American psychiatrist originally from Hungary, in *The Myth of Mental Illness* (Szasz, 1961) as well as many other publications, popularized his belief that mental illness does not exist. Using the concept of hysteria as an example, he argued that the mind is a construct, not synonymous with the biological entity of the brain, and that using medical concepts and terminology for mental phenomena is erroneous. Szasz takes a libertarian point of view and believes that individual behaviour is largely self-determined, and that individuals should bear the consequences of their behavioural choices. He sees 'medicalizing' of behaviour as taking away these concepts of free will, responsibility and self-determination. Civil commitment and the insanity defence are highly problematic from Szasz's point of view. Szasz is also concerned about potential abuses of psychiatric authority, such as those which occurred under the Nazi regime in Germany and its occupied countries. He believes that a reductionist, biological paradigm makes such abuses more possible by labelling some individuals as inherently dysfunctional.

Some authors, such as the Scottish psychiatrist Laing (1960), described psychosis as a form of personal growth rather than a state of illness. From this point of view, psychotic symptoms may be viewed as a creative response to an individual's struggle to cope with an irrational society. Laing also believed that schizophrenia could be viewed as a response to growing up in a dysfunctional family, particularly one in which the child received mixed or contradictory messages from the parent.

Others, including the leftist French philosopher and historian Foucault (1965), have claimed that mental illness did not exist in anything approaching its current form until the advent of an oppressive, modern Western society (despite much historical evidence to the contrary). Foucault believed that through most of history a relatively small number of eccentric or irrational individuals existed, who were tolerated or even embraced by society. He asserted that the definition of insanity shifted over the years to meet the needs of society, and reflected these social or political needs rather than any biological reality. According to Foucault, these eccentric individuals were seen as a threat to the social order and, in a sense, reinvented as 'madmen' during the Enlightenment period, which celebrated reason and order. Foucault challenged the conventional view that psychiatric patients were liberated from inhumane treatment during this period. He believed that large numbers of people were confined to psychiatric asylums for the first time during the Enlightenment. Foucault was a tremendously influential thinker in French political circles, and his teachings contributed to the social foment of the 1960s. His ideas are still influential in post-modernist academic thought.

The most extreme of these anti-psychiatry critics have suggested that psychiatrists invent illnesses which they are then paid to treat, or serve the state as oppressors of the socially unacceptable or troublesome. Many critics of the biomedical model believe that psychiatrists are too close to the pharmaceutical industry. Breggin (1991), a well-known American psychiatrist, is an outspoken critic of biological psychiatry as well as the pharmaceutical industry and its relationships with physicians, particularly psychiatrists.

Finally, some religious groups view mental dysfunction as a spiritual matter, rejecting the illness model. The most extreme anti-psychiatry views among religious groups are espoused by the Church of Scientology, headquartered in the United States. Scientology completely rejects psychiatry and psychology as 'pseudosciences'. Scientology has its own methods of self-help and counselling but opposes psychiatric medications and electroconvulsive therapy (ECT). However, some fundamentalist Christians as well as other religions view mental symptoms as a consequence of a lack of faith, demonic influences or punishment for sinful behaviour.

In part, critics of the biomedical model were reacting to perceived abuses of the commitment laws and inadequate care in state hospitals or asylums. This point of view can be seen in the context of the liberation movements of the 1960s, when criticism of psychiatry and the biomedical model reached its peak. Critics of psychiatry certainly served a useful function in forcing the discipline to closely examine itself. Partly as a result of these efforts, commitment laws were formalized with guarantees of due process and long-term custodial hospitalization was deemphasized. However, some critics of the biomedical model have tended to ignore voluminous scientific information and clinical experience documenting the reality of mental illness and the suffering it causes for patients, their loved ones and society at large. Generally, they see themselves as championing the oppressed and protecting them from psychiatric exploitation. As such, this anti-psychiatric paradigm derives partly from political or philosophical thought rather than primarily from scientific analysis or empirical data. As these critics come from many contrary points of view, they also do not present an alternative, coherent, workable model of care. The problems of the deinstitutionalization period such as homelessness and incarceration of the mentally ill partly result from rejection of the biomedical model without provision of a workable alternative.

The scientific approach utilized in advancing the biomedical model has been influenced heavily by our growing, but incomplete, understanding of a few key neurotransmitter systems (e.g. serotonin, norepinephrine, dopamine) and the evolution of drugs interacting with these systems. Many other areas of neurophysiology remain poorly understood, so that our theories of brain function in health and illness will need to continue to evolve. In fact, much of our early knowledge of brain function in mental illness occurred by working backwards to understand the effects of medications which had been discovered by serendipity.

With increasing knowledge of brain function, it has become obvious that the brain is not a fixed entity but continuously remodels itself throughout the life span in response to all sorts of inputs, including experiences mediated by family, society and culture as well as psychotherapy (Gabbard, 2000). Clearly, genetic factors govern certain givens, for each individual, while the maturing brain is shaped extensively within these limits by experience, health and illness, nutrition and other factors. Both adherents and critics of the biomedical model have failed to fully grasp that the biology of the brain is influenced by the experiences and social environment of the individual. The debates about the relative importance of nature, nurture, society and culture in mental illness can probably never be fully resolved. However, the absolute dichotomies assumed in these earlier debates are also not likely to be supported by further research.

The Biopsychosocial model

In the early 1970s, the biopsychosocial model was promulgated as a more comprehensive model of formulation, largely by George Engel. Engel was an American, originally trained as an internist who developed an interest in psychosomatics. His work was influenced by systems theory, such as the work of American psychiatrist and psychologist James Grier Miller on living systems. These theories described a hierarchy of systems. Using a systems theory approach, Engel argued that a biomedical, reductionistic approach was a necessary underpinning to understand mental illness, but a more inclusive, higher level integrative system was required to understand the full manifestation of psychiatric dysfunction (Engel, 1977).

This paradigm quickly became accepted in psychiatry and has been influential in other fields of medicine as well. Rather than proposing a unique new scientific theory or school of psychology, this model posits that patients are best understood by considering biological, psychological and social factors simultaneously (Borrell-Carrio, Suchman and Epstein, 2004). As developed in psychiatric practice, the biopsychosocial model also encompasses developmental, cultural, family, religious, legal, sexual, educational and other factors. Ideally, this model examines a patient's strengths as well as weaknesses. The individual is to be viewed in the contexts of personal development and experience. The stressors which influence the development of symptoms are also to be identified. Obviously, the notion of an inclusive formulation was not entirely original to Engel's work. Previous authors espoused similar points of view. For example, in the early decades of the 1900s, Meyer (1957) developed the concept of 'psychobiology' which entailed exhaustive interviewing and workup of each patient, to develop a thorough contextual framework for diagnosis.

The biopsychosocial model has also had its critics. For example, in application it has often proven to be additive rather than truly integrative. Psychiatrists can pick and choose points of view pragmatically to serve a particular diagnostic or therapeutic situation. This tendency has sometimes been described as 'eclecticism'. In fact, many training programmes in psychiatry describe themselves as eclectic. The term eclectic usually refers to a training programme which teaches several models, such as biological psychiatry as well as several systems of psychotherapy. (Chapter 11 by Priyanthy Weerasekera provides a specific example of an eclectic case formulation of a person with an eating disorder.) In order to achieve accreditation, American psychiatry training programmes must provide such an education. Critics of eclecticism suggest that our current paradigms are simply inadequate to address the wide array of clinical problems and that new paradigms need to be developed (Ghaemi, 2003).

DSM-IV TR diagnosis

DSM-IV TR is the current diagnostic handbook of American psychiatry, published by the American Psychiatric Association (APA). It is widely used in the United States in clinical practice, academia, government and by private insurance plans. The use of DSM-IV TR is not limited to the United States, however. It is influential in psychiatric diagnosis throughout the world. The APA has published three previous editions of this diagnostic handbook as well as several interim revisions of various editions.

DSM-IV divides diagnoses into five dimensions or 'axes'. This approach is commonly described as a 'multi-axial diagnosis'. The major psychiatric illnesses are recorded on axis 1, the personality and developmental disorders on axis 2, medical disorders on axis 3, level of psychosocial stressors on axis 4 and global assessment of functioning (GAF) on axis 5. Axis 1 and axis 2 disorders are described and explicit diagnostic criteria for each disorder are presented. An individual patient may receive one or more than one diagnosis on axes 1 and 2, or no diagnosis may be made. DSM-IV presents levels of psychosocial stressors for axis 4 as well as a descriptive guide of levels of global functioning numerically presented as 1–99 for the GAF on axis 5. Typically, axis 5 is presented as current GAF as well as the highest level of functioning within the past year.

The basic approach of DSM-IV evolved from its predecessor, DSM-III. The publication of DSM-III in 1980 was a watershed moment in the history of psychiatry. The preceding editions of DSM were descriptive in nature and did not have specific diagnostic criteria for each disorder. While not officially described as a psychoanalytic approach to diagnosis, psychoanalytic nomenclature was widely used in these documents. In the 1960s and 1970s, a variety of problems with DSM-II evolved. Psychiatric research began to focus on the biology of illness. Researchers had developed diagnostic criteria for many major psychiatric illnesses, and wanted these codified to facilitate standardized diagnosis among various research groups. The psychoanalytic paradigm was becoming less influential, and other paradigms such as the biomedical model, behaviourism and cognitive therapy became more accepted. Psychiatrists of that era expressed a desire to reformulate the profession as more clearly a part of medicine. Government and insurance programmes demanded a more scientifically based diagnostic handbook which took into account concepts such as validity and reliability of diagnosis. At the same time, the critics of the biomedical model harshly criticized the direction of psychiatric practice.

DSM-III was developed to take the new scientific findings of biological psychiatry into account, adopting modern views of medical diagnosis and categorization, while also embracing the biopsychosocial model (Wilson, 1993). Explicit diagnostic criteria were developed for each disorder and the multi-axial model was introduced. The diagnostic criteria were intended to be observable and empirical, rather than inferences about internal dynamics as was the case in the analytically influenced predecessors. DSM-III was intended to be atheoretical, meaning that psychiatrists from any school of thought could use it. DSM-III and its successors, DSM-III R, DSM-IV and DSM-IV TR have proven to be highly influential documents, much more widely accepted than the earlier versions. However, critics of the DSM-III approach regard these handbooks as overly reductionistic and dependent on the biomedical model. Even a carefully made DSM-IV diagnosis does not tell the whole narrative story of an individual with a mental illness. Some also object to the notion of dividing psychiatric illnesses into discrete categories rather than viewing disturbances as overlapping dimensions or points on a spectrum or spectra. The use of explicit, observable diagnostic criteria, which has obvious advantages, may not turn out to accurately reflect underlying brain function. For example, individuals with similar symptoms may have different underlying brain dysfunctions while individuals with different symptoms may have similar brain disorders. Clusters of symptoms which suggest that an individual may have several distinct and different DSM-IV diagnoses may actually reflect a single underlying brain disturbance.

RELEVANT AND IRRELEVANT VARIABLES

Psychiatric formulation is an inductive process. A large amount of information is collected, mostly from interview of the patient but also from interview of family, other informants and the medical record. The psychiatrist attempts to sort through this information to make a classification or diagnosis. In performing this task, the psychiatrist must seek out recognizable patterns in the information and prioritize, sometimes, contradictory data. The psychiatrist is searching for patterns which fit recognized 'syndromes', which are collections of symptoms which often occur together to form a broad diagnostic category.

The psychiatrist also utilizes the concept of differential diagnosis. This is a process of collecting all the syndromes which might fit the available data and selecting the most likely working diagnosis, attempting to rule in or rule out this diagnosis by collecting more information, including course of illness over time and response to interventions. Thereby, psychiatric diagnosis is not a static event but a process of refinement as more information is developed over time.

PSYCHIATRIC FORMULATION: THE CASE OF ZEPPI

A psychiatric formulation of the case of Zeppi can be organized using the biopsychosocial model, the syndrome approach and ultimately the DSM-IV TR framework. In this section, these various elements of the formulation will be presented.

The complete multi-axial DSM-IV diagnosis will be presented in Table 7.1.

Biopsychosocial model: biological factors

In modern psychiatry, psychotic symptoms are widely viewed as evidence of brain dysfunction. In the case of Zeppi, a variety of delusions are present, primarily paranoid in nature but also containing referential, somatic and sexual content. These delusions are prominent, pervasive and persistent. They have a bizarre element (i.e. patently absurd or impossible, such as the belief that waves sent from others might cause bowel cancer). Hallucinations are less prominent in the case presentation. Also of significance is the strong family history of chronic, debilitating psychosis. The role of incest in concentrating genetic influences is also important. Genetic influences are believed to be important in psychotic illnesses, particularly schizophrenia. There were no apparent significant developmental issues, medical illnesses, malnutrition, head injury or neurological symptoms. At the time of presentation, he was not taking medications, psychiatric or otherwise. Sleep and appetite were not noted to be disturbed.

Psychological factors

The content of Zeppi's belief system was primarily paranoid. Zeppi perceived his life to be threatened and controlled by others, despite the lack of objective evidence. His mood was anxious and fearful and he had a history of previous depression. He suffered a lack of the normal supportive family structure during childhood development. He was the victim of sexual and physical abuse and trauma. He frequently felt abandoned and humiliated. Although of seemingly normal intelligence, he received a spotty education. Violation of trust, abandonment and sexual confusion were elements of his personality, understandable given his life experience. He had violent fantasies and his behaviour in the hospital became overtly violent. He did not express suicidal thoughts or plans. His personality style was not obviously pathological, but may have had schizoidal elements.

Social factors

Zeppi was an immigrant from an essentially Third World culture and a highly dysfunctional family. He was socially isolated and focused his paranoia on the only family which might have supported him. His social and vocational skills were highly limited and he had no ongoing income. His religion had become a source of fear rather than support. He had never been married or had a sustained personal relationship outside of close relatives. He came from a tightly knit conservative culture in which family and church might normally be expected to form the main supportive network.

Differential diagnosis

The differential diagnosis of Zeppi would include illnesses which are characterized by persistent psychosis. Schizophrenia, Schizoaffective Disorder and Delusional Disorder are the illnesses which most closely resemble his disorder in terms of significant psychotic symptoms, persistence over time, lack of insight, logical disturbances and ideas of reference. Family history is also consistent with such an illness.

Zeppi has suffered from depressive symptoms but no overt mania, and his psychosis has not been limited to periods of affective illness, making schizophrenia a more likely diagnosis than schizoaffective disorder. His most significant symptoms are paranoid delusions which are bizarre and pervasive, with sexual, somatic and referential elements. He does not describe voices or auditory hallucinations, as typically found in schizophrenia. However, the degree and pervasiveness of his illness, the social regression and the bizarre nature of the delusions suggest schizophrenia as a more likely diagnosis than delusional disorder. As paranoid delusions form the core of the illness, chronic paranoid schizophrenia would be the diagnosis most closely fitting the picture.

Other illness which can include psychotic symptoms can more readily be ruled out. In Major Depression with Psychotic Features, the psychotic symptoms are limited to periods of severe depression and tend to have a depressive content. He did not display mood cycling or clear manic symptoms suggestive of a Bipolar Disorder. He did not have a history of Substance Abuse Disorder, neurological symptoms, medical history or cognitive symptoms which might suggest a Delirium, Dementia or Substance-Induced Disorder.

In DSM-IV, personality disorders are diagnosed on axis 2 according to diagnostic criteria, analogous to the major mental disorders diagnosed on axis 1. DSM-IV presents general criteria for the diagnosis of a personality disorder, and specific criteria for each individual disorder. An individual may have no axis 2 disorder, or may be diagnosed with one or more axis 2 disorders. If a patient meets the general criteria for a personality disorder but does not meet the full criteria for any specific disorder, Personality Disorder Not Otherwise Specified may be diagnosed. Personality disorders are grouped into clusters. Cluster A disorders are those with a psychotic-like element and include Paranoid Personality Disorder, Schizoid Personality Disorder and Schizotypal Personality Disorder. Schizoid Personality Disorder entails a persistent pattern of detachment from social relationships and a restricted range of emotional expression. This pattern probably best describes Zeppi's premorbid personality type. However, making an axis 2 disorder during an acute psychotic episode is often tentative, at least until sufficient information is available about premorbid function to solidify the diagnosis.

TREATMENT PLAN

Treatment planning in psychiatry ideally follows the biopsychosocial model. In the case of Zeppi, such a plan would initially involve a biological approach including a thorough medical and neurological evaluation. Particularly in newly diagnosed psychosis, it is important to consider the possibility of a somatic illness or substance abuse. Individuals with chronic psychosis have a high incidence of medical illnesses, such as diabetes and cardiovascular disease, as well as comorbidity with alcohol, tobacco or substance abuse. Much more rarely, a brain tumour or other central nervous system disorder is discovered. Psychotic patients often have limited access to medical care as well as poor nutrition and health habits. Antipsychotic medication is a standard part of therapy for such patients, but requires monitoring of body weight, blood glucose and lipid profile. Such medications are widely utilized for psychotic symptoms regardless of specific diagnosis. Psychological therapy would be supportive and pragmatic, avoiding insight-oriented or anxiety-provoking approaches which might actually exacerbate psychosis. Recently, cognitive-behavioural approaches to psychosis have also been developed. Social interventions would focus on reconnecting Zeppi with family and community resources, and planning for future needs in terms of housing and follow-up care. Especially in the hospital setting, psychiatric treatment plans are formal, written documents. These treatment plans are multi-disciplinary involving psychiatrists, nurses, social workers, psychologists and other therapists as well as input from the patient. A specific problem list is developed, with explicit short and long-term goals, a timeline and identification of the responsible professional. Strengths as well as problems are identified. Treatment plans must be developed as soon as possible after admission and updated at regular intervals. Staff members must utilize and refer to the treatment plan in their interventions and documentation.

THE EVENT

In the case history, Zeppi suffers an acute psychotic episode with marked paranoid elements. He feels threatened by processes beyond his control and arms himself against his persecutors. Fortunately, he does not take any overt violent action. However, his behaviour comes to the attention of the authorities who place him in a psychiatric facility. While hospitalized, his psychotic beliefs extend to those caring for him, and ultimately result in violent behaviour. Zeppi believes completely in his delusions, and feels that he must protect himself. He is compelled to accept treatment, even though he does not perceive the need. Unfortunately, experiences such as these are common in the lives of patients with schizophrenia. For many patients, a series of such hospitalizations occur. Treatment may lead to a reduction in symptoms in the short run, but lack of follow-up or failure to continue outpatient treatment and medication contributes to a cycle of re-hospitalization known as the 'revolving door'. Patients may object to continuing medication because they do not accept the diagnosis, or because of side effects such as weight gain.

Table 7.1   A psychiatric formulation of Zeppi's psychotic illness using the DSM-IV TR.

Axis 1
Schizophrenia, chronic paranoid type
Axis 2
Consider schizoid personality disorder
Axis 3
No diagnosis
Axis 4
Moderately severe: psychosocial isolation, lack of resources
Axis 5
Current GAF 20
Highest in past year 60

THE FORMULATION

Formulation in psychiatry involves a systematic, biopsychosocial synthesis of the available data into a coherent view of the case, including, but not limited to, a multi-axial DSM-IV diagnosis. Table 7.1 presents such a formulation of Zeppi's psychotic illness. Such a formulation may be used to help make therapeutic decisions such as psychotherapy, psychopharamacology or hospitalization. Psychiatrists should be aware of both the strengths and limitations of current paradigms in psychiatric formulation. In the future, perhaps one or more new paradigms will develop, taking into account new scientific developments in brain functioning as well as evolving social concerns about the mentally ill.

REFERENCES

American Psychiatric Association (2000) *Diagnostic and Statistical Manual of Mental Disorders, Fourth Edition, Text Revision (DSM-IV TR)*, American Psychiatric Association, Washington, DC.

Borrell-Carrio, F., Suchman, A. and Epstein, R. (2004) The biopsychosocial model 25 years later: principles, practice, and scientific inquiry. *Annals of Family Medicine*, **2**, 576–82.

Breggin, P. (1991) *Toxic Psychiatry: Why Therapy, Empathy and Love Must Replace the Drugs, Electroshock, and Biochemical Theories of the "New Psychiatry"*, Martin's Press, New York.

Engel, G. (1977) The need for a new medical model: a challenge for biomedicine. *Science*, **196**, 129–36.

Foucault, M. (1965) *Madness and Civilization: A History of Insanity in the Age of Reason*, Pantheon, New York.

Gabbard, G. (2000) A neurobiologically informed perspective on psychotherapy. *British Journal of Psychiatry*, **177**, 117–22.

Ghaemi, S. (2003) *The Concepts of Psychiatry: A Pluralistic Approach to the Mind and Mental Illness*, John's Hopkins University Press, Baltimore, MD.

Guze, S. (1992) *Why Psychiatry Is a Branch of Medicine*, Oxford University Press, New York.

Kuhn, T. (1962) *The Structure of Scientific Revolutions*, University of Chicago Press, Chicago, IL.

Laing, R.D. (1960) *The Divided Self: An Existential Study in Sanity and Madness*, Tavistock, London.

McClain, T., O'Sullivan, P. and Clardy, J. (2004) Biopsychosocial formulation: recognizing educational shortcomings. *Academic Psychiatry*, **28**, 88–94.

Mellsop, G. and Banzato, C. (2006) A concise conceptualization of formulation. *Academic Psychiatry*, **30**, 424–5.

Meyer, A. (1957) *Psychobiology: A Science of Man. Collected papers*, Charles C. Thomas, Springfield, IL.

Ross, C.A., Leichner, P., Matas, M. and Anderson, D. (1990) A method of teaching and evaluating psychiatric case formulation. *Academic Psychiatry*, **14**, 99–105.

Szasz, T. (1961) *The Myth of Mental Illness: Foundations of a Theory of Personal Conduct*, Hoeber, New York.

Wilson, M. (1993) DSM-III and the transformation of American psychiatry. *American Journal of Psychiatry*, **150**, 399–410.

8

A Behaviour Analytic Formulation of a Case of Psychosis

DAVID A. WILDER

THEORETICAL ORIENTATION AND RATIONALE

The behaviour analytic model focuses on operationally defined specific behaviours that may be exhibited by an individual with a psychotic disorder. That is, as opposed to assessing the presence or absence of the disorder, the behaviour analytic model focuses on specific behaviours exhibited by the individual, such as bizarre behaviour, perseverative or hallucinatory speech, odd facial expressions or body movements or social skills deficits. Assessment involves determination of the antecedent and consequential environmental events that influence these behaviours. Once the variables controlling the target behaviours have been identified, an intervention that is designed specifically to address the variables responsible for maintenance of each behaviour is implemented. Although the behaviour analytic model does not make use of biological explanations, the model does not deny that such variables are important. However, instead of *focusing* on a biological cause and corresponding intervention, the model analyzes the environmental events that may occasion and/or maintain each specific behaviour that makes up the individual's diagnosis (Wilder and Wong, 2007).

In a behaviour analytic account, psychotic behaviour stems from an individual's genetic history, his current biological condition, his history of interaction in and with the world around him (i.e., the environment) and immediate

Clinical Case Formulation: Varieties of Approaches. Edited by Peter Sturmey.
© 2009 John Wiley & Sons, Ltd.

environmental events (or immediate contingencies). Of these variables, immediate environmental contingencies are most amenable to manipulation. Thus, these are the focus of behaviour analytic assessment and treatment.

Individuals with a diagnosis of a psychotic disorder typically exhibit behavioural excesses as well as skill deficits. Behavioural excesses are responses occurring at unusually high rates that disrupt social relations, or activities of daily living, or both. Behavioural deficits are responses occurring at unusually low rates that are insufficient to maintain independent living. Specific behavioural excesses and skill deficits commonly seen in individuals with a psychotic disorder are described below.

Current practice guidelines recommend combining behavioural programmes, such as social skills training, independent living skills training and token economies with psychotropic drugs in the treatment of some psychotic disorders, including schizophrenia (American Psychological Association, 1997; Lehman *et al.*, 2004). These behavioural programmes derive from a behaviour analytic model of the assessment and treatment of psychotic disorders. Early behavioural programmes for individuals with psychotic disorders included procedures such as the token economy mentioned above. These programmes often used arbitrarily selected consequences (e.g., token reinforcement exchangeable for food or privileges and timeout from reinforcement) to override existing environmental contingencies and thereby promote desired behaviour or weaken undesired behaviour. In contrast to these early behavioural programmes, more recent behaviour analytic work with individuals with psychotic disorders has emphasized the investigation of various hypotheses about contingencies currently maintaining problematic behaviour. In addition, these hypotheses are often formally evaluated in analogue assessments known as functional analyses. These analyses lead to different combinations of treatment procedures applying *the same reinforcers that originally maintained the problematic behaviour* to either decrease or increase the behaviour of interest. So, instead of using token reinforcement or token fines to reduce bizarre behaviour that was maintained by escape from demands, a modern behaviour analytic model would restructure the environment to allow escape from demands for appropriate behaviour, such as asking for a break or for a different assignment (Wilder and Wong, 2007).

A behaviour analytic rationale for Zeppi's case is that his behaviours serve a purpose, or are functional. That is, Zeppi's complaints of magnetic waves affecting his body, his attack on the nursing assistant and his bizarre descriptions of his cousin's link to organized crime are the ways in which he obtains access to some preferred items, activities and situations and avoids other, non-preferred items, activities and situations in his environment. These behaviours are the result of skills he has learned and are exhibited because other, more socially appropriate ways of obtaining and avoiding items, activities and situations have not been learned.

RELEVANT AND IRRELEVANT VARIABLES

From a behaviour analytic standpoint, the most relevant variables in Zeppi's case are the specific behaviours he exhibits (e.g., somatic complaints), the contexts in which these behaviours occur, the antecedent events which immediately precede these behaviours, and most importantly, the consequences which result from his behaviour. By focusing on these variables, the clinician can change stimuli and events so that the target behaviours are less likely to occur and more socially appropriate behaviours take their place. For example, it is possible that the function or purpose of Zeppi's somatic complaints is to gain access to attention in the form of medical care; the medical care might, in turn, alleviate any aversive physical condition Zeppi may be experiencing. A modern behaviour analytic model might test this hypothesis by systematically providing medical care contingent upon somatic complaints/talk about magnetic waves and measuring the reoccurrence of complaints. Data from such an evaluation would be compared to data on complaints collected during a situation in which medical care was provided independent of somatic complaints/talk about magnetic waves. A treatment package based on these (and other) results would then be developed and implemented.

As described above, although genetic history, current biological state and history of interaction with the environment certainly contribute to behaviour (and psychotic behaviour in particular), from a behaviour analytic standpoint these variables are less relevant in Zeppi's case. The reason for this is that the clinician cannot actively manipulate any of these variables (with the possible exception of current biological state); thus, potential for behaviour change is lessened with a focus on these.

ROLE OF RESEARCH AND CLINICAL EXPERIENCE

Research plays a substantial role in a behaviour analytic case formulation of psychosis in that the model is based on applied research which demonstrates its utility. Behaviour analytic research focusing on the assessment and treatment of behaviours common to the diagnosis of psychosis has been conducted for many years. This research is best described according to its focus on behavioural excesses or behavioural (i.e., skills) deficits.

Behavioural excesses

In individuals with psychotic disorders, behavioural excesses tend to take the form of bizarre behaviour (e.g., unrealistic statements, inappropriate laughing, peculiar mannerisms), oppositional behaviour and stereotypic (i.e., repetitive) behaviour. Of these, bizarre behaviour (specifically, bizarre speech) has perhaps received the most attention from behaviour analytic researchers. Wilder *et al.* (2001) provided the first empirical demonstration of an experimental analysis of the function of bizarre speech in an individual with a psychotic disorder. Using 10-min exposures to various environmental contingencies, these authors showed that bizarre speech exhibited by a 43-year-old man with schizophrenia occurred more often when it was followed by attention from a therapist. A treatment consisting of differential reinforcement of appropriate speech plus extinction was then applied and found to be effective in decreasing the occurrence of bizarre speech and increasing appropriate speech.

This assessment and treatment procedure has since been replicated (Wilder, White and Yu, 2003). Figure 8.1 depicts a graph of the participant's behaviour in Wilder, White and Yu (2003). The top panel shows the results of a functional analysis of bizarre vocalizations exhibited by the participant, a woman with schizophrenia. The data suggest that her vocalizations were maintained by therapist attention. The bottom panel shows the results of a treatment evaluation based on assessment results. The treatment consisted of awareness training (showing her a videotape in which she performed the bizarre vocalizations), competing response training (teaching her to emit an alternative, more socially appropriate phrase in place of bizarre vocalizations), differential reinforcement (therapist delivering attention contingent upon use of alternative phrase) and extinction (therapist not attending to bizarre vocalizations) and was conducted across two therapists. This treatment ultimately reduced her bizarre vocalizations and increased her appropriate vocalizations.

Oppositional behaviour exhibited by individuals with psychotic disorders has also been successfully treated using a behaviour analytic model. Ayllon and Azrin (1965) used contingent access to tangible items to increase compliance among institutionalized individuals with psychotic disorders. Stereotypic behaviour exhibited by individuals with psychosis has also been successfully treated by behaviour analysts. Corrigan, Liberman and Wong (1993) reduced repetitive posturing by individuals with schizophrenia. Specifically, the authors used directed recreational activity and access to tokens contingent on appropriate behaviours to decrease stereotypic self-talk, mumbling and laughter. The directed recreational activity appeared to be the intervention component most responsible for reductions in stereotypy.

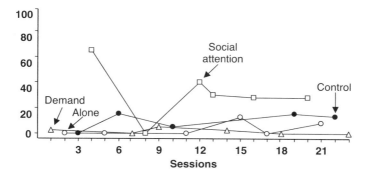

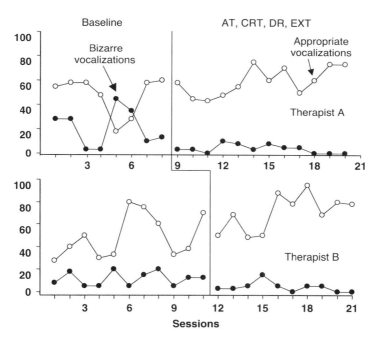

Figure 8.1   Percentage of intervals in which bizarre vocalizations occurred across all conditions of the functional analysis (top panel); percentage of intervals in which bizarre and appropriate vocalizations occurred during baseline and treatment (awareness training (AT), competing response training (CRT), differential reinforcement (DR) and extinction (EXT)) conditions across therapists A and B of the treatment evaluation (bottom panels). *Source*: Wilder, D.A., White, H., Yu, M. (2003). Functional analysis and intervention for bizarre speech exhibited by an adult with schizophrenia: A replication and extension. In *Behavioral Interventions*, 18, 43–52 © 2003 John Wiley & Sons. Reproduced with permission.

Behavioural deficits

Many individuals with psychotic disorders have social skills, personal hygiene and self-care skills and vocational skills deficits. Using a behaviour analytic model, a number of these skills have been successfully taught. Researchers have focused on teaching improved eye contact and facial expression (Eisler *et al.*, 1978), simple greetings (Kale *et al.*, 1968), conversational skills (Wilder *et al.*, 2002) and assertive behaviour (Hersen and Bellack, 1976). Behaviour analytic interventions designed to improve bathing, grooming and dressing among individuals with psychotic disorders have also been shown to be effective (Liberman, King and De Risi, 1976). Behavioural clinicians have also developed 'job clubs' to assist individuals with psychotic disorders in obtaining and maintaining employment (Azrin and Besalel, 1980).

Clinical experience also plays a role in a behaviour analytic case formulation for individuals with psychotic disorders. From the beginning of the formulation, clinicians with much experience are often more adept at identifying and defining the target behaviours to focus on, developing testable hypotheses about the function or purpose of target behaviours, carrying out the appropriate analysis of behaviours and devising and evaluating appropriate treatments.

THE FORMULATION

Zeppi does not have the skills required to appropriately obtain access to what he wants and to avoid those things he wants to avoid. First, Zeppi needs to be evaluated by a physician. His complaints about magnetic waves burning various parts of his body and his heart palpitations could be real physical symptoms of a medical problem. A thorough evaluation should be conducted, and Zeppi should be asked to describe in more detail the bodily location and intensity of the burning sensations. If a medical cause for these sensations is found, the appropriate medical treatment should then be provided. In addition, Zeppi may require a number of follow-up appointments with a clinician to ensure that he continues to appropriately self-administer any medical treatment (e.g., medication) which is prescribed.

If a medical cause is not found and Zeppi's complaints about magnetic waves burning his body continues and prevents him from obtaining and/or maintaining employment or establishing relationships, a functional analysis of these complaints would be conducted. This analysis involves developing hypotheses about the environmental variables which may maintain Zeppi's complaints. In a controlled setting, Zeppi's complaints would be measured across a number of different environmental circumstances or conditions. Each condition would be 10–15 min in duration and it would be conducted multiple times. It might be necessary to extend the duration of these conditions if the results were vague. In some cases, conditions which are longer in duration (e.g., 20 min or more) produce clearer data because the client has prolonged exposure to the contingencies operating in the condition. Due to this prolonged exposure, the client may more easily learn to discriminate among the contingencies in each condition.

One of these conditions would be an 'attention' condition in which a therapist would immediately provide a lot of attention contingent upon Zeppi's complaints and ignore all of his other behaviour. If Zeppi's level of complaining increased in this condition relative to the control condition (described below), this would suggest that the function or purpose of his complaining might be to obtain some form of attention from others. Another condition would be a 'demand' condition in which Zeppi would be asked to perform some difficult activity (e.g., completing paperwork). Contingent upon Zeppi's complaints, the therapist would provide Zeppi with a brief break from the activity. If Zeppi's level of complaining increased in this condition relative to the control condition (described below), this would suggest that the function or purpose of his complaining might be to obtain a break from a non-preferred activity. In a third condition, Zeppi might be left alone in the room (called the 'alone' condition) while his complaints are measured. If Zeppi continued to complain in the absence of a therapist, this might suggest that the function or purpose of his complaining might be to obtain 'self-stimulation'. That is, high levels of complaining in this condition relative to the control condition (described below) might suggest that Zeppi's complaints might simply provide a way for him to 'entertain himself'. Finally, a control condition would be conducted in which a therapist would provide Zeppi with attention on a regular basis (regardless of his complaints) and no demands. Often, low levels of behaviour are observed in the control condition. Zeppi's complaints in the other conditions would be compared to this control condition to determine the environmental events which are most likely to increase his complaints. Based on the results of this analysis, a treatment would be evaluated (see 'Treatment Plan', p. 115).

In these conditions, an 'establishing operation' or motivational condition may be created. That is, the condition is designed such that it might establish an event as something the client wants to obtain and makes behaviours that have historically produced access to that event more likely to occur. In the attention condition, for example, the therapist does not interact with Zeppi throughout the condition, unless complaints occur. This lack of interaction might establish attention as something Zeppi wants to obtain, and if complaining has been effective at producing attention in the past, Zeppi may be more likely to complain in that condition. Another feature of these conditions is 'discriminative stimuli' or cues. For example, the presence of a therapist ignoring Zeppi might serve as a cue for complaining in the attention condition. These cues signal to Zeppi that engaging in a target behaviour (i.e., complaining) will produce access to something he likes (i.e., attention).

Next, Zeppi's social, self-care and vocational skills would be assessed. This assessment would involve asking Zeppi to demonstrate a number of social skills (such as initiating a conversation, responding appropriately to a question, making eye contact, etc.), self-care skills (such as bathing, applying deodorant, shaving, appropriately dressing, etc.) and vocational skills (such as spelling, writing, categorizing items and following multi-step instructions). Zeppi's performance on each skill would be carefully observed to determine which skills he has mastered and which skills he needs to acquire. Based on the results of this analysis, a skills-training-based treatment would be evaluated (see *TREATMENT PLAN* section below).

History

Zeppi's history plays an important role in the case formulation described above. First, Zeppi had no formal schooling until the age of 8 years, and he left school at the age of 15 years. Thus, he experienced only 7 years of 'classroom instruction'. This has undoubtedly contributed to his poor social, vocational and self-care skills. In addition, Zeppi had virtually no contact with other children until the age of 8, which likely hindered his social development. During his school years, Zeppi had a number of experiences in which he was poorly treated by other children and has likely never developed and maintained a friendly relationship with a peer. Furthermore, it sounds as if Zeppi rarely even interacted with people until he went to school. His mother and his grandfather largely ignored him and his uncle was away much of the time. During these important early years of development, Zeppi never learned the skills necessary to interact with others. Vocational skills, many of which are taught during formal schooling, were likely also never learned by Zeppi. Finally, Zeppi probably never even learned many self-care skills given the environment in which he was raised.

Current factors

Zeppi's near complete isolation from other people is likely contributing to some of the behavioural excesses and skill deficits he currently exhibits. The contingencies in Zeppi's environment do not support learning and maintaining social, self-care or vocational skills. Because he is living on savings and gifts from his aunt, he does not need to work. Therefore, he does not need to exhibit the vocational or social skills necessary to seek and maintain employment. There is little need for Zeppi to learn and/or maintain self-care skills either, given that he rarely sees or interacts with others.

TREATMENT PLAN

Treatment for Zeppi largely depends on the results of the assessments described in the case formulation. If his complaints are not related to a medical condition, then a functional analysis of his complaints would follow. Depending on the condition in which complaints occurred most often, Zeppi would be taught an alternative way of getting access to what he wants or avoiding what he does not want. For example, if Zeppi's complaints occurred more often in the attention condition relative to the control condition, initial treatment would involve teaching Zeppi an alternative way of interacting with people/getting attention. If Zeppi's complaints occurred more often in the demand condition relative to the control condition, Zeppi would be taught a more socially appropriate way of avoiding activities which he does not like. If Zeppi's complaints occurred more often in the alone condition relative to the control condition, Zeppi might be taught more socially appropriate ways of 'entertaining' himself.

The results of the social, self-care and vocational skills assessment described in the case formulation also have implications for treatment. The specific skills that Zeppi has not mastered will be taught to him, first in a very controlled environment and then in more naturalistic settings. Skill training usually proceeds systematically in three steps. First, the skills would be described to Zeppi by the clinician. Next, the skills would be modelled for Zeppi. Finally, Zeppi would perform the skills being taught and receive feedback on his performance from the clinician. Zeppi will have mastered each skill when he has met a formal mastery criterion established by the clinician.

In addition to this, the clinician will attempt to create a motivational system to increase Zeppi's use of the skills taught to him. This system might be similar to a token economy in that Zeppi would be able to earn access to preferred items or activities (e.g., money, food, clothing and entertainment) contingent upon his appropriate use of the skills taught to him. The system would be developed in collaboration with Zeppi.

THE EVENT

During his admission to an open acute ward, Zeppi aggressed towards a nursing assistant and another patient. Although the patient managed to escape,

Table 8.1 An example of the use of 'ABC' analysis to analyze the event in Zeppi's case formulation.

Antecedent	Behaviour	Consequence
1. Nursing assistant and patient were in the corner of the room laughing	Zeppi hits the nursing assistant	1. Nursing assistant stopped laughing 2. Nursing assistant and patient exited the room

the nursing assistant suffered a broken nose as a result of the incident. When later asked about the incident, Zeppi claimed that the burning sensations in his body were more intense and that he thought the nursing assistant was controlling the magnetic waves producing the sensations. In order to stop the nursing assistant's alleged attack, Zeppi hit the nursing assistant.

Zeppi's behaviour during this event is consistent with the case formulation described above in that he wanted to avoid or stop something (the burning sensations or the laughing about the burning sensations), so he engaged in one of the few forms of behaviour in which he is somewhat skilled (i.e., aggression). Alternative, more appropriate forms of behaviour, such as telling a nurse or physician about the burning sensations and asking them to evaluate the areas of Zeppi's body in which the sensations were occurring, must be specifically taught to Zeppi.

Events like the one described above are commonly analyzed by behaviour analysts. An analysis of this event would involve describing the relevant antecedents, the behaviour itself and the consequences of the behaviour, using an 'ABC (i.e., antecedent, behaviour, consequence)' format. Descriptions of incidents in this format enable therapists to develop hypotheses regarding the reason or function of the behaviours described. An example of the use of 'ABC' analysis to analyze this event is provided in Table 8.1. Based on the events described in this table, a therapist might hypothesize that Zeppi's aggression functioned to produce escape from the nursing assistant/patient and/or their laughter.

The use of ABC or 'descriptive' analysis (as it is also called) methods of determining the function of problem behaviour is often contrasted with experimental methods (described in 'The Formulation', pp. 112–115) of determining the function of problem behaviour. Although they are fairly easy to conduct, the results of descriptive analysis methods may sometimes be misleading because they only identify correlations among environmental events and behaviour. Experimental methods, on the other hand, can be difficult to conduct because they involve intentional manipulation of events which may be related to behaviour. However, experimental methods may generally be more accurate in determining behaviour function. Often, descriptive analysis methods are used to identify the stimuli and events which are manipulated in an experimental analysis. When used in this way, the two methods complement one another.

Other issues

The formulation described above should not be taken to imply that Zeppi does not need (antipsychotic) medication to address some of his behaviours. Often the assessment and treatment procedures described above are combined with medication. In some cases, the proper medication can make learning alternative, socially appropriate behaviours easier for clients.

SUMMARY

To summarize, a behaviour analytic formulation of Zeppi's case would focus on the function or purpose of his behavioural excesses (i.e., somatic complaints), and on the skill deficits he exhibits. Although behavioural clinicians recognize that behaviour is complex and is likely due to genetic/biological variables as well as historical and immediate environmental contingencies, immediate environmental contingencies are most easily manipulated and thus are the focus of treatment. Therefore, once medical reasons have been ruled out for Zeppi's somatic complaints, systematic assessment would begin. After assessment in which the function or purpose of Zeppi's bizarre complaints is examined and his current social, self-care and vocational skills are evaluated, treatment would ensue. Treatment for Zeppi would be based on assessment results and would emphasize teaching Zeppi alternative, more socially appropriate means of getting access to items, activities and interactions he wants and avoiding items, activities and interactions he does not want. This formulation of Zeppi's case does not preclude (antipsychotic) medication; oftentimes a behaviour analytic approach is combined with medications to treat psychosis.

REFERENCES

American Psychiatric Association (1997) Practice guidelines for the treatment of patients with schizophrenia. *American Journal of Psychiatry*, **154** (Suppl. 4), 1–63.

Ayllon, T. and Azrin, N.H. (1965) The measurement and reinforcement of behavior of psychotics. *Journal of the Experimental Analysis of Behavior*, **8**, 357–83.

Azrin, N.H. and Besalel, V.A. (1980) *Job-Club Counselors Manual: A Behavioral Approach to Vocational Counseling*, University Park Press, Baltimore, MD.

Corrigan, P.W., Liberman, R.P. and Wong, S.E. (1993) Recreational therapy and behavior management on inpatient units: is recreational therapy therapeutic? *Journal of Nervous and Mental Disease*, **181**, 644–6.

Eisler, R.M., Blanchard, E.B., Fitts, H. and Williams, J.G. (1978) Social skills training with and without modeling for schizophrenic and non-psychotic hospitalized psychiatric patients. *Behavior Modification*, **2**, 147–72.

Hersen, M. and Bellack, A.S. (1976) A multiple-baseline analysis of social-skills training in chronic schizophrenics. *Journal of Applied Behavior Analysis*, **9**, 239–45.

Kale, R.J., Kaye, J.H., Whelan, P.A. and Hopkins, B.L. (1968) The effects of reinforcement on the modification, maintenance, and generalization of social responses of mental patients. *Journal of Applied Behavior Analysis*, **1**, 307–14.

Lehman, A.F., Kreyenbuhl, J., Buchanan, R.W. *et al.* (2004) The schizophrenia patient outcomes research team (PORT): updated treatment recommendations 2003. *Schizophrenia Bulletin*, **30**, 193–217.

Liberman, R.P., King, L.W. and De Risi, W.J. (1976) Behavior analysis and therapy in community health, in *Handbook of Behavior Modification and Behavior Therapy* (ed. H. Leitenberg), Prentice Hall, Englewood Cliffs, NJ, pp. 566–603.

Wilder, D.A., Masuda, A., Baham, M. and O'Conner, C. (2002) An analysis of the training level necessary to increase independent question asking in an adult with schizophrenia. *Psychiatric Rehabilitation Skills*, **6**, 32–43.

Wilder, D.A., Masuda, A., O'Connor, C. and Baham, M. (2001) Brief functional analysis and treatment of bizarre vocalizations in an adult with schizophrenia. *Journal of Applied Behavior Analysis*, **34**, 65–8.

Wilder, D.A., White, H. and Yu, M. (2003) Functional analysis and treatment of bizarre vocalizations exhibited by an adult with schizophrenia: a replication and extension. *Behavioral Interventions*, **18**, 43–52.

Wilder, D.A. and Wong, S.E. (2007) Schizophrenia and other psychotic disorders, in *Functional Analysis in Clinical Treatment* (ed. P. Sturmey), Elsevier, Burlington, MA, pp. 283–305.

9

Formulating Zeppi: A Commentary

RICHARD P. BENTALL

The story of Zeppi, as told by Kingdon and DiMech, describes a fairly typical example of psychotic behaviour, as might be encountered on any psychiatric ward. Casey provides a standard psychiatric formulation of this behaviour, using the DSM system, arriving at the conclusion that Zeppi suffers from chronic schizophrenia, but offering additional insights about his pre-morbid personality (possibly schizoid personality disorder), current stressors (described as moderate to severe) and his current level of functioning (a GAF score of 20 indicating marked impairment). Wilder, on the other hand, offers a more speculative behavioural analysis which emphasizes the functions of Zeppi's behaviour and which suggests some possible avenues for psychological assessment and intervention, for example the use of contingency management to increase Zeppi's social and occupational skills. While both of these formulations will be considered useful by clinicians adopting the relevant approaches, they share a number of limitations. First, I will argue that both fail to provide a sufficiently detailed description of Zeppi's difficulties. Second, I will question whether either account gives an adequate explanation of how Zeppi's history led to these difficulties or the assault on the nurse that highlighted the need for a better understanding of his behaviour. Third, there are some fairly obvious treatment recommendations that are overlooked by both Casey and Wilder. A final, overarching limitation is that neither formulation makes use of the rich research literature on paranoid delusions – Zeppi's most obvious complaint – which has emerged over the last 10 years (for up-to-date reviews, see Freeman, Bentall and Garety, 2008).

Clinical Case Formulation: Varieties of Approaches.   Edited by Peter Sturmey.
© 2009 John Wiley & Sons, Ltd.

DESCRIPTIONS OF ZEPPI'S COMPLAINTS

Diagnostic formulations attempt to classify the behaviour of patients by means of a categorical system that has evolved since the late years of the nineteenth century, when the German psychiatrist Kraepelin (1899/1990) first proposed the concept of *dementia praecox*, subsequently renamed *schizophrenia* by Bleuler (1911/1950). It is fair to say that the usefulness of this kind of formulation has been a topic of dispute ever since (Kendell, 1975).

Prompted by concerns about the reliability of psychiatric diagnoses, the extent to which different clinicians assign them consistently (Spitzer and Fliess, 1974), the third edition of the American Psychiatric Association's diagnostic manual (DSM-III; American Psychiatric Association, 1980) introduced operational criteria for each disorder, an approach that is used in the current fourth edition (American Psychiatric Association, 2000) and also in its major international competitor, the 10th edition of the World Health Organization's International Classification of Diseases (ICD-10; World Health Organization, 1992). Whether this has led to an improvement in diagnostic reliability remains moot (Kirk and Kutchins, 1992). Some critics have argued that disagreement between clinicians is still common, especially when they use different methods of collecting data from their patients (McGorry *et al.*, 1995). Others have pointed out that the proliferation of competing criteria for schizophrenia (the diagnosis Casey uses to describe Zeppi) has resulted in 'a babble of precise but different formulations of the same concept' (Brockington, 1992, p. 121). Hence, when three different diagnostic systems (including the DSM-III and ICD-10) were used with the same 700 patients, the numbers diagnosed as schizophrenic according to the different criteria varied between 268 and 387 (van Os *et al.*, 1999).

The usefulness of the diagnosis as a description of behaviour is also called into question by research on its validity. Factor analyses have consistently reported that schizophrenic behaviour is best described by at least three independent dimensions: positive symptoms (delusions and hallucinations), negative symptoms (flat affect, social withdrawal, apathy) and symptoms of cognitive disorganization (including incoherent speech) (Andreasen, Roy and Flaum, 1995; Liddle, 1987). If these dimensions had been used to describe Zeppi's complaints they would probably have provided better predictions of his social functioning and long-term outcome (van Os *et al.*, 1999). An even more serious limitation of psychiatric diagnoses is their very poor ability to predict the effects of specific treatments (Johnstone *et al.*, 1988); hence patients with a wide range of diagnoses respond to dopamine antagonist (antipsychotic) medication, the pharmacological treatment recommended by Casey (Tamminga and Davis, 2007).

Some researchers have responded to these kinds of limitations by attempting to study the causes of specific complaints (symptoms in the language of psychiatric formulations, and behaviours in the language of behavioural analysis). The guiding idea is that the problem of explaining schizophrenia will disappear once we have plausible causal models for each of the relevant complaints. This approach has led to considerable progress in understanding the origins of paranoid delusions (Bentall *et al.*, 2001; Freeman *et al.*, 2002), auditory hallucinations (Alleman and Laroi, 2008) and incoherent speech (McKenna and Oh, 2008). (For an attempt to construct a comprehensive theory of psychosis on this basis, see Bentall, 2003.) Wilder might be expected to sympathize with this approach, but unfortunately describes Zeppi's primary complaint as *bizarre speech*, as if its content is unimportant. This may be the consequence of adopting a methodological behaviourist position which, I believe, is not consistent with Skinner's (1945, 1957) sophisticated analysis of verbal behaviour or mental processes.

That the content of Zeppi's speech is important is evident for three main reasons. First, as we will see, the relationship between Zeppi's speech and his history can only be understood if we take into account content; it is important that Zeppi says that he is the victim of some kind of malevolent conspiracy, rather than the recipient of secret communications from strangers. Second, and related to this, different kinds of delusional beliefs appear to be the consequence of different causal processes. For example, referential delusions of communication seem to involve abnormal interpretations of others' gestures whereas paranoid delusions do not (Bucci *et al.*, 2008). Even within the broad category of paranoid delusions, important differences are discernable, for example between *poor-me delusions*, such as Zeppi's, in which the individual feels an innocent victim, and *bad-me delusions*, in which the individual believes that persecution is deserved (Chadwick *et al.*, 2005). Finally, there is the worry that any attempt to suppress bizarre speech without reference to its content, in Skinnerian terms, to eliminate verbal behaviour rather than to change it, will merely affect the overt expression of beliefs, rather than beliefs *per se*. Of course, a methodological behaviourist might object that we can never know whether this has happened. However, if beliefs change we might expect verbal behaviour to remain changed across a wide range of environments whereas, if mere expression is being extinguished, the beliefs might be expected to resurface when the original stimulus conditions, such as a sympathetic listener, are reinstated. It is therefore interesting to note that Wilder's own approach to treating psychotic speech (Wilder *et al.*, 2001) was anticipated by a much earlier study by Ayllon and Michael (1959) in which this is exactly what happened.

ZEPPI'S HISTORY

Casey's psychiatric formulation, like all diagnostic accounts, makes little reference to Zeppi's history whereas Wilder attempts to signpost some important historical influences, albeit in not much detail. Here, I will briefly point to some important findings in the research literature that make Zeppi's paranoid beliefs understandable.

Zeppi was born into a family that might fairly be described as dysfunctional. The product of an incestual relationship, he was ignored by his mother during his early years, and treated as a cause for shame by other members of his family. There is good evidence that disrupted attachment relationships can lead to increased risk of psychosis and, in particular, paranoid symptoms. For example, population surveys suggest that psychotic symptoms are associated with insecure attachment styles (Berry *et al.*, 2006; Cooper, Shaver and Collins, 1998; MacBeth, Schwannauer and Gumley, 2008; Mickelson, Kessler and Shaver, 1997), and recent studies have shown that this association is specific to paranoid beliefs (Meins *et al.*, 2008; Pickering, Simpson and Bentall, 2008). Similar findings have been reported in the studies conducted with severely ill psychiatric patients (Dozier, Stovall and Albus, 1999). In a population-based cohort study, it was found that being unwanted, as recorded *before* birth, led to a fourfold increased risk of psychosis at 26-year follow-up (Myhrman *et al.*, 1996). Separation from parents in early life has also been found to predict an increased risk of psychosis in genetically vulnerable children (Agid *et al.*, 1999; Parnas, Teasdale and Schulsinger, 1985) and also the children of migrants (Morgan *et al.*, 2007) who are known to be at high risk of psychosis (see below). These associations are not hard to understand as, at the risk of oversimplifying the vast and rich literature on attachment processes, the insecure styles of relating reflect the profound difficulty in trusting others that is the consequence of the absence of a 'secure base' in early life.

Of course, an insecure attachment style on its own is not likely to lead to psychosis and other factors are certain to be important. For example, cognitive deficits may contribute to the development of illness. There is some evidence that paranoid patients experience difficulties with 'theory of mind' skills, the ability to infer the mental states of other people (Brune, 2005; Corcoran, Mercer and Frith, 1995; Corcoran *et al.*, 2008) and also have a tendency to jump to conclusions when reasoning about probabilistic information (Corcoran *et al.*, 2008; Freeman, Garety and Kuipers, 2001; Garety, Hemsley and Wessely, 1991), handicaps which probably increase the risk of misunderstanding the intentions of other people. It would be interesting to know how Zeppi performed on formal assessments of these abilities.

As Zeppi grew up, further adverse experiences added to his troubles. When attending school in Gozo he was repeatedly bullied. He was also treated badly by his cousins, one of whom sexually abused him. Population-based studies (Mirowsky and Ross, 1983) and longitudinal investigations (Janssen *et al.*, 2003) have shown that paranoid beliefs typically arise following this kind of history of chronic victimization. Studies in which animals have been deliberately exposed to experiences of social defeat have shown that hypersensitivity of the basal ganglia dopamine system, which seems to play a role in threat anticipation, may be an important physiological process mediating between these kinds of adverse experiences and psychotic functioning (Selten and Cantor-Graae, 2005). This observation helps to explain why dopamine antagonist drugs are effective treatments for paranoid beliefs (Moutoussis *et al.*, 2007).

When Zeppi began work at age 15, he coped well at first, perhaps because of the support he received from his aunt, who appears to have been the only consistent attachment figure in his life. However, after his cousin left for the United Kingdom, he 'felt very lonely and lost interest in work'. Kingdon and DeMech give little information about the first episode of illness that followed soon afterwards. However, it is likely that unstable self-esteem contributed to this crisis. There is evidence from numerous studies that paranoid delusions typically emerge in the context of self-esteem that is low (Bentall *et al.*, 2008) and highly fluctuating (Thewissen *et al.*, 2007, 2008), which in turn may be a consequence of the kinds of experiences suffered by Zeppi earlier in his life (Bentall and Fernyhough, 2008; see Figure 9.1). In the case of bad-me paranoid beliefs, the individual embraces a negative view of the self and

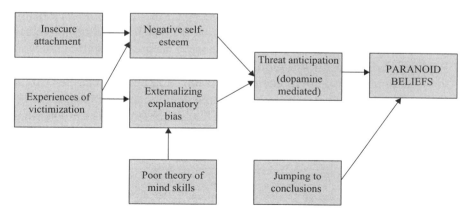

Figure 9.1 Processes leading to paranoid delusions. *Source*: Reprinted from Bentall and Fernyhough (2008).

assumes that others, sharing this view, have malevolent intentions towards the self. In the case of poor-me paranoia, the individual attempts to avoid negative thoughts about the self by constructing external attributions (explanations that implicate powerful others) for negative experiences, leading to a partial restitution of self-esteem but exacerbating paranoid thinking (Bentall, Kinderman and Moutoussis, 2008).

After recovering from this first episode, Zeppi decided to try his luck in the United Kingdom. However, this attempt to escape an environment that had been punishing and unsupportive did nothing to improve his mental health in the long term. Research in the United Kingdom and elsewhere has shown that the risk of being diagnosed as psychotic is increased by a factor of at least 4 in migrant populations (Bresnehan *et al.*, 2007; Cantor-Graae *et al.*, 2003; Fearon *et al.*, 2006; Harrison *et al.*, 1988; Selten *et al.*, 2001; Smith *et al.*, 2006; Zolkowska, Cantor and McNeil, 2001). Incidence rates are greatest when migrants live in neighbourhoods in which they form a clear minority (Boydell *et al.*, 2001; Veling *et al.*, 2008), suggesting that discrimination (Janssen *et al.*, 2003; Veling *et al.*, 2007), experiences of social defeat and powerlessness (Selten and Cantor-Graae, 2005) play a critical role in provoking illness. Socially isolated and in an unfamiliar environment, Zeppi became increasingly paranoid, creating friction with his cousin who, at that time, was his only friend. When that relationship broke down a psychiatric crisis was probably inevitable.

The account I have given of the events leading up to Zeppi's admission to hospital in the United Kingdom has focused on only one of his complaints: his belief that there is a conspiracy to harm him. I have not addressed Zeppi's other complaints, but these may also yield to an evidence-based psychological interpretation. For example, it seems that Zeppi's belief that he was being influenced by magnetic rays appeared late in the development of his illness and it is possible that it arose as a consequence of misinterpreting somatic experiences (either stress symptoms, the side effects of medication or both). As Wilder points out, a comprehensive account of Zeppi's difficulties would also have to address his social and vocational deficits, which may need to be targeted in treatment, not merely to afford him better strategies for obtaining attention, but also in order to build up his self-esteem and to facilitate his ability to form satisfying relationships with the wider social universe.

THE EVENT

Casey and Wilder attempt to understand Zeppi's assaultive behaviour in terms of their respective formulations. Casey suggests that attention needs to be given to the way in which Zeppi's delusional system led him to misconstrue and react to the intentions of those around him. Wilder, on the other hand, again draws attention to Zeppi's social deficits, arguing that, 'He wanted to avoid or stop something (the burning sensations or the laughing about the burning sensations), so he engaged in one of the few forms of behaviour in which he is somewhat skilled (i.e. aggression).' Once more the research literature is illuminating.

The question of whether or not severely ill patients like Zeppi constitute a danger to others has been a source of continuing controversy, but most current commentators hold that there is a genuine association between psychosis and violence (O'Kane and Bentall, 2000). However, it is important not to overstate this relationship – for example in a recent study in the United Kingdom it was estimated that only about 5% of homicides are committed by people with a history of psychosis (Shaw *et al.*, 2006). Moreover, this issue is obscured by many confounding factors – for example dysfunctional family relationships, experiences of victimization, homelessness and substance abuse, which are associated with violence in the general population and which are often present in the histories of patients with mental illness (Bonta, Law and Hanson, 1998; Shaw *et al.*, 2006). Interestingly, and consistent with Casey's assumption that the content of Zeppi's symptoms is important when interpreting his aggression, research has specifically highlighted paranoia and other so-called *threat/control override symptoms* (in which the individual feels threatened and controlled by other people) as being causally implicated in violent acts (Hodgins, Hiscoke and Freese, 2003; Hodgins *et al.*, 1996; Link, Stueve and Phelan, 1998; Stompe *et al.*, 1999).

The assault was described as 'completely unexpected and unprovoked' but it is unlikely that it was entirely spontaneous. Although the majority of the research on violence in psychiatric settings has focused on patient characteristics, there is some evidence that situational factors, particularly the presence of nursing staff who are either hostile or unavailable, may play a provoking role (Whittington and Wykes, 1994, 1996). Furthermore, Zeppi's outburst followed a period in which he experienced treatment that he, with some reason, perceived as coercive.

Link and Stueve (1994) have argued that violent acts by psychotic patients can often be understood using a principle of *rationality-within-irrationality*, according to which, 'Once one suspends concern about the irrationality of psychotic symptoms and accepts that they are experienced as real, violence unfolds in a "rational" manner.' Zeppi's behaviour certainly seems to ac- cord with this principle. Indeed, given his background, his beliefs and the circumstances in which he found himself, it is little wonder that he became so angry.

TREATMENT RECOMMENDATIONS

It will be apparent from what I have said so far that any attempt to treat Zeppi without addressing the content of his beliefs will be flawed, almost certainly unsuccessful in the long term, and, because it would amount to a profound disrespect for his autonomy, ethically questionable. (For a discussion of the key role of respect for autonomy in ethical health care see Beauchamp and Childress, 2001). In recent years, there has been an ideological shift in the provision of care for patients with severe mental illness, and the patient's need to develop his own goals and plan for recovery has been increasingly recognized (Anthony, 1993). Within this framework, it is important that the patient is offered interventions that are meaningful, collaborative and grounded in a strong therapeutic alliance (Priebe and McCabe, 2006).

In the United Kingdom, cognitive-behaviour therapy is rapidly becoming the standard psychotherapeutic method of addressing delusional beliefs, and is currently recommended for the treatment of psychosis by the National Institute for Clinical Excellence (2002). This approach has been specifically adapted to address the needs of psychotic patients who have a history of violence (Haddock *et al.*, 2004). A typical CBT intervention would be based on an individualized and shared cognitive formulation of the patient's difficulties, negotiated after the patient has been invited to generate his own problem list (Morrison *et al.*, 2003). The intention is that this formulation is therapeutic in its own right, allowing the patient to see how his fears and difficulties have arisen as a consequence of his life experiences. For example, Zeppi would be helped to see how his assumption that other people want to harm him has arisen as a consequence of genuine experiences of victimization. The interventions that follow would be driven by the formulation, but might involve Zeppi keeping thought diaries to identify triggers for paranoid thinking, and possible alternative interpretations of paranoia-provoking events and conducting behavioural experiments, for example testing out predictions about threats from other people. It is important that, throughout this process, the therapist avoids the temptation to tell the patient that his beliefs are irrational. The therapist approaches the patient's statements as puzzling, even bizarre, but 'just possibly true', thereby engaging him or her in a joint project to test their veracity. Of course, in Zeppi's case, it would help enormously if the therapist had some understanding of his cultural background.

Single case studies of CBT for psychotic symptoms began to appear in the 1990s, but the first randomized controlled trials (RCTs) of this approach only appeared at the beginning of this decade. Given the novelty of the approach, continuing innovation is required but the existing outcome data is promising. At the time of writing, about 30 RCTs of CBT for psychosis have been published, varying from open trials with a few tens of patients, to large, rigorously blinded studies with a few hundred. A recent meta-analysis comparing medication alone with CBT plus medication reported a modest effect size of about 0.4 in the treatment of positive symptoms (Wykes *et al.*, 2008).

CONCLUSIONS

Formulations of patients' difficulties should be grounded, not only in detailed analyses of their behaviour and histories, but also in the findings from psychiatric research. When the research literature and the information we have about a patient are concordant, we can have a high degree of confidence in the validity of the formulation; of course, this confidence will be increased if a resulting intervention is effective. The story of Zeppi is striking in the extent to which it is consistent with recent research on the development of psychosis in general and paranoid delusions in particular.

REFERENCES

Agid, O., Shapira, B., Zislin, J. *et al.* (1999) Environment and vulnerability to major psychiatric illness: a case control study of early parental loss in major depression, bipolar disorder and schizophrenia. *Molecular Psychiatry*, **4**, 163–72.

Alleman, A. and Laroi, F. (2008) *Hallucinations: The Science of Idiosyncratic Perceptions*, American Psychological Association, Washington, DC.

American Psychiatric Association (1980) *Diagnostic and Statistical Manual of Mental Disorders*, 3rd edn, American Psychiatric Association, Washington, DC.

American Psychiatric Association (2000) *Diagnostic and Statistical Manual for Mental Disorders*, 4th edn – Text revision, American Psychiatric Association, Washington, DC.

Andreasen, N.C., Roy, M.-A. and Flaum, M. (1995) Positive and negative symptoms, in *Schizophrenia* (eds S.R. Hirsch and D.R. Weinberger), Blackwell, Oxford, pp. 28–45.

Anthony, W. (1993) Recovery from mental illness: the guiding vision of the mental health service system in the 1990s. *Psychosocial Rehabilitation Journal*, **16**, 11–23.

Ayllon, T. and Michael, J. (1959) The psychiatric nurse as a behavioral engineer. *Journal of the Experimental Analysis of Behavior*, **2**, 323–34.

Beauchamp, T.L. and Childress, J.F. (2001) *Principles of Biomedical Ethics*, 5th edn, Oxford University Press, Oxford.

Bentall, R.P. (2003) *Madness Explained: Psychosis and Human Nature*, Penguin, London.

Bentall, R.P., Corcoran, R., Howard, R. *et al.* (2001) Persecutory delusions: a review and theoretical integration. *Clinical Psychology Review*, **21**, 1143–92.

Bentall, R.P. and Fernyhough, C. (2008) Social predictors of psychotic experiences: specificity and psychological mechanisms. *Schizophrenia Bulletin*, **34**, 1009–11

Bentall, R.P., Kinderman, P., Howard, R. *et al.* (2008) Paranoid delusions in schizophrenia and depression: the transdiagnostic role of expectations of negative events and negative self-esteem. *Journal of Nervous and Mental Disease*, **196**, 375–83.

Bentall, R.P., Kinderman, P. and Moutoussis, M. (2008) The role of self-esteem in paranoid delusions: the psychology, neurophysiology, and development of persecutory beliefs, in *Persecutory Delusions: Assessment, Theory and Treatment* (eds D. Freeman, R.P. Bentall and P. Garety), Oxford University Press, Oxford, pp. 145–75.

Berry, K., Wearden, A., Barrowclough, C. and Liversidge, T. (2006) Attachment styles, interpersonal relationships and psychotic phenomena in a non-clinical student sample. *Personality and Individual Differences*, **41**, 707–18.

Bleuler, E. (1911/1950) *Dementia Praecox or the Group of Schizophrenias* (E. Zinkin, Trans.), International Universities Press, New York.

Bonta, J., Law, M. and Hanson, K. (1998) The prediction of criminal and violent recidivism among mentally disordered offenders. *Psychological Bulletin*, **123**, 123–42.

Boydell, J., van Os, J., McKenzie, J. *et al.* (2001) Incidence of schizophrenia in ethnic minorities in London: ecological study into interactions with environment. *British Medical Journal*, **323**, 1–4.

Bresnehan, M., Begg, M., Brown, A.S. *et al.* (2007) Race and risk of schizophrenia in a US birth cohort: another example of health disparity? *International Journal of Epidemiology*, **36**, 751–8.

Brockington, I. (1992) Schizophrenia: yesterday's concept. *European Psychiatry*, **7**, 203–7.

Brune, M. (2005) 'Theory of mind' in schizophrenia: a review of the literature. *Schizophrenia Bulletin*, **31**, 21–42.

Bucci, S., Startup, M., Wynn, P. *et al.* (2008) Referential delusions of communication and interpretations of gestures. *Psychiatry Research*, **158**, 27–34.

Cantor-Graae, E., Pedersen, C.B., McNeil, T.F. and Mortensen, P.B. (2003) Migration as a risk factor for schizophrenia: a Danish population-based cohort study. *British Journal of Psychiatry*, **182**, 117–22.

Chadwick, P., Trower, P., Juusti-Butler, T.-M. and Maguire, N. (2005) Phenomenological evidence for two types of paranoia. *Psychopathology*, **38**, 327–33.

Cooper, M.L., Shaver, P.R. and Collins, N.L. (1998) Attachment style, emotion regulation, and adjustment in adolescence. *Journal of Personality and Social Psychology*, **74**, 1380–97.

Corcoran, R., Mercer, G. and Frith, C.D. (1995) Schizophrenia, symptomatology and social inference: investigating 'theory of mind' in people with schizophrenia. *Schizophrenia Research*, **17**, 5–13.

Corcoran, R., Rowse, G., Moore, R. *et al.* (2008) A transdiagnostic investigation of theory of mind and jumping to conclusions in paranoia: a comparison of schizophrenia and depression with and without delusions. *Psychological Medicine*, **38**, 1577–83.

Dozier, M., Stovall, K.C. and Albus, K. (1999) Attachment and psychopathology in adulthood, in *Handbook of Attachment* (eds J. Cassidy and P. Shaver), Guilford Press, New York, pp. 497–519.

Fearon, P., Kirkbride, J.B., Morgan, C. *et al.* (2006) Incidence of schizophrenia and other psychoses in ethnic minority groups: results from the MRC Aesop Study. *Psychological Medicine*, **36**, 1541–50.

Freeman, D., Bentall, R.P. and Garety, P. (eds) (2008) *Persecutory Delusions: Assessment, Theory and Treatment*, Oxford University Press, Oxford.

Freeman, D., Garety, P.A. and Kuipers, E. (2001) Persecutory delusions: developing the understanding of belief maintenance and emotional distress. *Psychological Medicine*, **31**, 1293–306.

Freeman, D., Garety, P.A., Kuipers, E. *et al.* (2002) A cognitive model of persecutory delusions. *British Journal of Clinical Psychology*, **41**, 331–47.

Garety, P.A., Hemsley, D.R. and Wessely, S. (1991) Reasoning in deluded schizophrenic and paranoid patients. *Journal of Nervous and Mental Disease*, **179**, 194–201.

Haddock, G., Lowens, I., Brosnan, N. *et al.* (2004) Cognitive-behaviour therapy for inpatients with psychosis and anger problems within a low secure environment. *Behavioural and Cognitive Psychotherapy*, **32**, 77–98.

Harrison, G., Owens, D., Holton, A. *et al.* (1988) A prospective study of severe mental disorder in Afro-Caribbean patients. *Psychological Medicine*, **18**, 643–57.

Hodgins, S., Hiscoke, U.L. and Freese, R. (2003) The antecedents of aggressive behavior among men with schizophrenia: a prospective investigation of patients in community treatment. *Behavioral Science and the Law*, **21**, 523–46.

Hodgins, S., Mednick, S., Brennan, P.A. *et al.* (1996) Mental disorders and crime: evidence from a Danish birth cohort. *Archives of General Psychiatry*, **53**, 489–96.

Janssen, I., Hanssen, M., Bak, M. *et al.* (2003) Discrimination and delusional ideation. *British Journal of Psychiatry*, **182**, 71–6.

Johnstone, E.C., Crow, T.J., Frith, C.D. and Owens, D.G.C. (1988) The Northwick Park 'functional' psychosis study: diagnosis and treatment response. *Lancet*, **ii**, 119–25.

Kendell, R.E. (1975) *The Role of Diagnosis in Psychiatry*, Blackwell, Oxford.

Kirk, S.A. and Kutchins, H. (1992) *The Selling of DSM: The Rhetoric of Science in Psychiatry*, Aldine de Gruyter, Hawthorne, NY.

Kraepelin, E. (1899/1990) *Psychiatry: A Textbook for Students and Physicians. Volume 1: General Psychiatry*, Watson Publishing International, Canton, MA.

Liddle, P.F. (1987) The symptoms of chronic schizophrenia: a re-examination of the positive-negative dichotomy. *British Journal of Psychiatry*, **151**, 145–51.

Link, B.G. and Stueve, A. (1994) Psychotic symptoms and the violent/illegal behaviour of mental patients compared to community controls, in *Violence and Mental Disorder: Developments in Risk Assessment* (eds J. Monahan and H.J. Steadman), Chicago University Press, Chicago, pp. 137–60.

Link, B.G., Stueve, A. and Phelan, J. (1998) Psychotic symptoms and violent behaviours: probing the components of 'threat/control-override' symptoms. *Social Psychiatry and Psychiatric Epidemiology*, **22**, S55–60.

MacBeth, A., Schwannauer, M. and Gumley, A. (2008) The association between attachment style, social mentalities, and paranoid ideation: an analogue study. *Psychology and Psychotherapy: Theory, Practice, Research*, **81**, 79–83.

McGorry, P.D., Mihalopoulos, C., Henry, L. *et al.* (1995) Spurious precision: procedural validity of diagnostic assessment in psychotic disorders. *American Journal of Psychiatry*, **152**, 220–3.

McKenna, P.J. and Oh, T. (2008) *Schizophrenic Speech: Making Sense of Bathroots and Ponds That Fall in Doorways*, Cambridge University Press, Cambridge.

Meins, E., Jones, S.R., Fernyhough, C. *et al.* (2008) Attachment dimensions and schizotypy in a non-clinical sample. *Personality and Individual Differences*, **44**, 1000–11.

Mickelson, K.D., Kessler, R.C. and Shaver, P.R. (1997) Adult attachment in a nationally representative sample. *Journal of Personality and Social Psychology*, **73**, 1092–106.

Mirowsky, J. and Ross, C.E. (1983) Paranoia and the structure of powerlessness. *American Sociological Review*, **48**, 228–39.

Morgan, C., Kirkbride, J., Leff, J. *et al.* (2007) Parental separation, loss and psychosis in different ethnic groups: a case-control study. *Psychological Medicine*, **37**, 495–503.

Morrison, A.P., Renton, J., Dunn, H. *et al.* (2003) *Cognitive Therapy for Psychosis: A Formulation-Based Approach*. Brunner-Routledge, Hove.

Moutoussis, M., Williams, J., Dayan, P. and Bentall, R.P. (2007) Persecutory delusions and the conditioned avoidance paradigm: towards an integration of the psychology and biology of paranoia. *Cognitive Neuropsychiatry*, **12**, 495–510.

Myhrman, A., Rantakallio, P., Isohanni, M. and Jones, P. (1996) Unwantedness of pregnancy and schizophrenia in the child. *British Journal of Psychiatry*, **169**, 637–40.

National Institute for Clinical Excellence (2002) *Schizophrenia: Core Interventions in the Treatment and Management of Schizophrenia in Primary and Secondary Care*, National Institute for Clinical Excellence, London.

O'Kane, A. and Bentall, R.P. (2000) Psychosis and offending, in *Behaviour, Crime and Legal Processes: A Guide for Forensic Practitioners* (eds J. McGuire, T. Mason and A. O'Kane), John Wiley & Sons, Ltd, London, pp. 161–76.

Parnas, J., Teasdale, T.W. and Schulsinger, H. (1985) Institutional rearing and diagnostic outcome in children of schizophrenic mothers. A prospective high-risk study. *Archives of General Psychiatry*, **42**, 762–9.

Pickering, L., Simpson, J. and Bentall, R.P. (2008) Insecure attachment predicts proneness to paranoia but not hallucinations. *Personality and Individual Differences*, **44**, 1212–24.

Priebe, S. and McCabe, R. (2006) The therapeutic relationship in psychiatric settings. *Acta Psychiatrica Scandinavica*, **119** (Suppl. 429), 66–72.

Selten, J.-P. and Cantor-Graae, E. (2005) Social defeat: risk factor for psychosis? *British Journal of Psychiatry*, **187**, 101–2.

Selten, J.-P., Veen, N., Feller, W. *et al.* (2001) Incidence of psychotic disorders in immigrant groups to The Netherlands. *British Journal of Psychiatry*, **178**, 367–72.

Shaw, J., Hunt, I.M., Flynn, S. *et al.* (2006) Rates of mental disorder in people convicted of homicide: national clinical survey. *British Journal of Psychiatry*, **188**, 143–7.

Skinner, B.F. (1945) The operational analysis of psychological terms. *Psychological Review*, **52**, 270–7.

Skinner, B.F. (1957) *Verbal Behavior*, Copely Publishing, Acton, MA.

Smith, G.N.J.B., Murray, R.M., Flynn, S. *et al.* (2006) The incidence of schizophrenia in European immigrants to Canada. *Schizophrenia Research*, **87**, 205–11.

Spitzer, R.L. and Fliess, J.L. (1974) A reanalysis of the reliability of psychiatric diagnosis. *British Journal of Psychiatry*, **123**, 341–7.

Stompe, T., Friedman, A., Ortwein, G. *et al.* (1999) Comparisons of delusions among schizophrenics in Austria and Pakistan. *Psychopathology*, **32**, 225–34.

Tamminga, C.A. and Davis, J.M. (2007) The neuropharmacology of psychosis. *Schizophrenia Bulletin*, **33**, 937–46.

Thewissen, V., Bentall, R.P., Lecomte, T. *et al.* (2008) Fluctuations in self-esteem and paranoia in the context of everyday life. *Journal of Abnormal Psychology*, **117**, 143–53.

Thewissen, V., Myin-Germeys, I., Bentall, R.P. *et al.* (2007) Instability in self-esteem and paranoia in a general population sample. *Social Psychiatry and Psychiatric Epidemiology*, **42**, 1–5.

van Os, J., Gilvarry, C., Bale, R. *et al.* (1999) A comparison of the utility of dimensional and categorical representations of psychosis. *Psychological Medicine*, **29**, 595–606.

Veling, W., Selten, J.P., Susser, E. *et al.* (2007) Discrimination and the incidence of psychotic disorders among ethnic minorities in the Netherlands. *International Journal of Epidemiology*, **36**, 761–8.

Veling, W., Susser, E., van Os, J. *et al.* (2008) Ethnic density of neighborhoods and incidence of psychotic disorders among immigrants. *American Journal of Psychiatry*, **165**, 66–73.

Whittington, R. and Wykes, T. (1994) An observational study of associations between nurse behaviour and violence in psychiatric hospitals. *Journal of Psychiatric and Mental Health Nursing*, **1**, 85–92.

Whittington, R. and Wykes, T. (1996) Aversive stimulation by staff and violence by psychiatric inpatients. *British Journal of Clinical Psychology*, **35**, 11–20.

Wilder, D.A., Masuda, A., O'Connor, C. and Baham, M. (2001) Brief functional analysis and treatment of bizarre vocalizations in an adult with schizophrenia. *Journal of Applied Behavior Analysis*, **34**, 65–8.

World Health Organization (1992) *ICD-10: International Statistical Classification of Diseases and Related Health Problems*, 10th revision edn, World Health Organization, Geneva.

Wykes, T., Steel, C., Everitt, B.S. and Tarrier, N. (2008) Cognitive behavior therapy for schizophrenia: effect sizes, clinical models, and methodological rigor. *Schizophrenia Bulletin*, **34**, 523–7.

Zolkowska, K., Cantor, G.E. and McNeil, T.F. (2001) Increased rates of psychosis amongst immigrants to Sweden: is migration a risk factor for psychosis? *Psychological Medicine*, **31**, 669–78.

PART IV

Eating Disorders

10

A Case of Eating Disorder: Antoinette Hilbert-Smith

JONATHON T. NEWTON

PRESENTING COMPLAINT

The client, Antoinette Hilbert-Smith, attended the outpatient clinic with her mother, Maria Hilbert-Smith. Antoinette had been referred by a general physician for extreme weight loss over a 2-year period. The referral letter from the physician, which was dated 2 weeks previously, stated her weight as 91 lbs and asked for an opinion regarding the patient's possible eating disorder. The physician had run tests to rule out inflammatory bowel disease, tuberculosis, human immunodeficiency virus, and endocrinological disorders (hypopituritism, diabetes and Addison's disease). All test results were negative. At presentation, Antoinette offered a greeting but said very little throughout the assessment unless directly questioned. Her mother stated that Antoinette has anorexia, eats 'hardly anything' and exercises 'all the time'.

CLIENT DEMOGRAPHIC DATA

Antoinette was aged 17 years and 7 months at first appointment and her weight measured in the clinic was 87 lbs (39.5 kg). Her height, also measured in the clinic was 66 inches (1.68 m). Her body mass index at assessment was 14.

Information on the family background was obtained from the mother Maria Hilbert-Smith. Antoinette's parents were Maria Hilbert (mother, aged 48) and David Smith (father, aged 54). Both are alive, have no history of diagnosed

Clinical Case Formulation: Varieties of Approaches.   Edited by Peter Sturmey.
© 2009 John Wiley & Sons, Ltd.

psychiatric illness, and no remarkable medical history in either parent. Her parents divorced when Antoinette was 14. Both children of the marriage lived with their mother. The arrangement was that both children were to spend a weekend with their father once a month. This was often cancelled, either because David was away on business, or either child did not wish to go. Antoinette has not been to stay with her father for over a year. Her stated reasons for this were that she has a strong dislike of her father's new wife and that they 'force' her to eat 'disgusting food'.

Maria Hilbert-Smith was a member of the corps de ballet for a national ballet company in her 20s. She left the ballet shortly after marrying David Smith, in order to 'support his career'. She is tall, slim and well groomed. She said that appearance is important for her, 'as it is for any woman'. Following her divorce from David, Antoinette retained possession of the family home together with an annual maintenance stipend on the grounds that she had sacrificed her career to maintain the family home. Both children were to receive financial support from their father whilst they remain in full-time education. Maria has been seeing a man called Jeremy for about a year. He used to stay over occasionally but this has declined recently because Antoinette does not like him, and he made some 'unhelpful' comments about her weight. It emerged that he insisted that Maria take Antoinette to the doctor.

David Smith is a successful corporate lawyer who has always worked long hours, and attends a great number of social events with his firm. He is of average height and overweight. He has struggled with his weight. He has a healthy appetite and finds it difficult to lose weight given his sedentary work and the large number of work-related social events he attends. He remarried when Antoinette was 15 and has a 2-year-old daughter with his second wife. His second wife, Catherine Smith, is a junior lawyer who works part-time. The couple employ a full-time nanny to care for their daughter.

Antoinette's siblings include her older brother, Giles. He is currently at Cambridge University studying classics, intends to study law and follow in his father's footsteps into corporate law. He also has political ambitions. Giles has a very active social life at Cambridge and consequently his visits to the family home have been relatively infrequent. Giles also had a girlfriend and finds the time to visit her family quite often. Giles has seen more of his father than Antoinette. They have attended sports events sponsored by David Smith's firm, and occasionally met in London for a meal with his father and stepmother. Maria Hilbert-Smith stated that, 'She doesn't mind that at all.' In a rare interruption, Antoinette stated that Giles 'doesn't care about the family at all and has broken Mummy's heart'. Maria replied, 'He does care Darling, he does. And he loves you.'

Antoinette's paternal grandparents are both alive. They live a long way away, a journey of about 5 h by car. Antoinette sees them at Christmas when they usually plan a visit to see the children. The last time they saw Antoinette was 6 months ago and they were shocked at her weight. They have been telephoning Maria once a week to ask after Antoinette's health. Maria felt that she should 'try to be positive for them' and so has not told them the full extent of Antoinette's weight loss. She has not told them about the appointment today.

Maria's mother died when Maria was 15. She was very close to her mother and was very upset. She was living away at ballet school at the time and never saw her mother after she died. Both the school and Maria's father felt it would be best for Maria if she did not attend the funeral. Maria says that she felt she 'never got the chance to say goodbye'. She became tearful as she told this story. Antoinette betrayed no emotion and made no attempt to comfort her mother at this point. Maria's father was described as 'cold and aloof'. He remarried when Maria was 30, at the time she was married to David. Maria's father now has two children who are teenagers. Maria sees her father, his wife and children once a year when she makes a special visit to him on the anniversary of her mother's death. He rarely sees his grandchildren and does not know that Antoinette is ill.

CLIENT DEMEANOUR AND PERSONAL APPEARANCE

Antoinette wore multiple layers of thick clothing, most of which was either grey or black in colour. It was reasonably warm in the clinic but she declined to remove her coat. She stated that she is constantly cold. She wore gloves. She was asked to remove her gloves at one point and there was no sign of callouses or bite marks on the fingers or back of either hand. She had long hair which reached to about midway down her back. She sat very upright in her chair with her hands in her lap and looked at her hands for most of the time, including when answering questions. She wore no make-up. Her face for much of the time was screened by her hair. Her legs fidgeted continuously. Her cheekbones were prominent.

Antoinette spoke in a very low voice which was often difficult to hear, especially since she spoke down into her hands. She responded to direct questions but gave the impression of being guarded in her answers. She betrayed little emotion. Any feelings of sadness or anger are usually related to her perceptions of the treatment of other people, for example when discussing her brother Giles.

When asked about her family, Antoinette said that she was closest to her mother, and discussed how badly her mother has been treated by other members of the family, most notably her ex-husband and her son, Giles.

Antoinette stated that her father shows no interest in her, and is too busy at work to care about his family, and that he is now only interested in his new wife and daughter. She says that her little sister is very sweet.

Antoinette stated that she has never had a boyfriend, though she was once asked out by a boy from school but she turned him down and he never asked again. She says that she has never thought about her long-term future, but cannot see herself ever having a family of her own. She says that she would find it hard to trust somebody.

CLIENT CURRENT LIFESTYLE

Maria described her daughter's lifestyle as 'entirely regimented'. On weekdays, her routine is to wake at 6.00 a.m. and run for 30 min. She takes a bottle of water with her when she runs. She takes the same route everyday, which takes her through a local park. Maria expressed concern that in the winter months, it is very dark and she worries about her daughter's safety. However, she has not been able to persuade Antoinette to run at a different time or take a different route. She has considered buying a treadmill so that Antoinette can run at home. Antoinette has agreed that this would be a good idea and they have looked at several machines together.

After running, Antoinette does stretching exercises for a further half an hour in her bedroom. This involves using light weights. She then showers and dresses, which takes about 1 h. Antoinette has her own bathroom in the house. At about 8 o'clock, Antoinette eats her breakfast which consists of a 200 ml carton of orange juice, one small portion of breakfast cereal and skimmed milk. It takes approximately 40 min for her to prepare and eat this meal. At 8.40 a.m. during school term, Antoinette is taken to school by her mum. Antoinette has a packed lunch at school, which she prepares for herself each evening. It consists of one apple, one banana, two low-calorie crisp breads (no spread) and a portion of cottage cheese. School lunchtime is from 12.30 p.m. to 2 p.m.

Antoinette has been studying mainly arts-based subjects at school – English literature, German, History and French. Her last report from the school expressed concern that Antoinette was socially withdrawn and did not appear to be mixing with her old friends. Antoinette said that her friends are 'immature' and 'jealous' that she is doing so well. She said that most of the people that used to be her friends are simply interested in boys and dating and neglected their schoolwork. She expressed no interest in meeting young men. The teachers at the school also commented that Antoinette was doing extremely well in her studies and confidently predicted that she will get excellent grades. She has applied to study at a very prestigious university, but has deliberately chosen not to apply to Cambridge where her brother is studying.

School finishes at 3.30 p.m. Maria picks Antoinette up from school and takes her home. Antoinette then studies for an hour. On Tuesday and Thursday evenings at 5.00 p.m., Antoinette attends an aerobics class for an hour. On other weekday evenings, Antoinette stays at home and does her own version of the aerobics class in her bedroom.

Antoinette prepares her own evening meal at 6.30 p.m. each evening. The meal is essentially the same each evening but the protein source is varied on a predictable basis. The core elements are a large salad comprising lettuce, cucumber, tomato, celery, red pepper (no dressing), two crisp breads (no spread) and one from the following: cottage cheese, smoked salmon, thinly sliced ham, thinly sliced chicken or tuna in brine. Following this, Antoinette has a portion of fruit for her dessert.

Antoinette weighs all the portions for this meal. She prepares her packed lunch for the next day at the same time. She refuses to allow her mother or any other member of the family to be present in the kitchen while she is preparing the meal. Once her food is prepared, she calls her mother, who sits with her whilst Antoinette eats. They talk during the meal but discussion of what Antoinette is eating is not allowed. Maria says that if she tries to comment, Antoinette becomes very upset and refuses to eat. Preparation of the meal and eating it takes one and a half hour.

Antoinette stated that her daily calorie intake is 750 kcal. She drinks 2 l of water and has a total of five portions of fruit and vegetables every day. She describes her diet as 'very healthy'.

After her evening meal, Antoinette goes to her room to study. For 1 h each evening, she plays her cello. She is an accomplished cello player.

During weekends, Antoinette keeps her mealtimes and exercise routines the same. She attends cello lessons on Saturday morning, and in the afternoon, she studies. On Saturday evenings, she allows herself to watch TV or DVDs. Her favourite television programme is 'Friends', and she is also fond of 'The O.C.' and 'Lost'. She has a large collection of DVDs and watches them in her room. On Sundays, Antoinette spends her time studying or reading novels, though recently she has found that she is having difficulty concentrating when reading, she finds her mind wandering to thoughts of food and how much she has eaten. Antoinette said that she feels that if she just sits and reads, the calories will start to lay down fat under her skin. When she feels like this, she goes to her room to do some more exercise until she feels that she has used up the excess calories.

Antoinette's lifestyle shows very little variation from week to week, though Maria reported that it has probably become even more regimented in the last few months. If anything happened that interferes with this pattern, for example school holidays, family events and Christmas, Maria reported that Antoinette becomes very agitated and typically eats even less. When asked about this, Antoinette stated that she becomes overcome with panic if anything happens to change her routine, even if she is 5 min late for one meal. She finds the predictability of the routine comforting. She would also panic if she did not have her scales to weigh her food and had to guess how many calories are in a meal. As a result of this, the family members have started to restrict their lifestyles to fit around this routine. They no longer accept social invitations, do not invite family or friends to stay and have not been on a summer holiday since it would involve being away from the family home. Maria was concerned that if they did not stick to the routine, Antoinette would not eat anything at all.

Family members avoid discussing food and weight with Antoinette. There is a tacit agreement that no one should talk to Antoinette about these matters and that any discussion would only make matters worse. Maria reported that when she had made the appointments with the physician and the outpatient clinic, there had been a terrible scene when she told Antoinette. When questioned further, it emerged that Maria had told Antoinette about the appointments when they were sitting eating their dinner one evening; Antoinette had refused to eat anything further, had thrown all her food in the bin, screamed and shouted for half an hour and was inconsolable. She and her mother had argued for hours, and eventually Antoinette had agreed to go to the appointments only when her mother agreed that she would not allow the doctors to put her in hospital or make her put weight on. She had gone to bed that night without eating. It had been extremely distressing for Maria.

CLIENT HISTORY

Antoinette was born at full term and weighed 8 lbs 2 oz at birth. Maria found breastfeeding difficult and Antoinette was bottle-fed from 2 weeks of age. Weaning was uneventful. She was a fussy eater during her first 2 years, but maintained her weight and height at or around the fiftieth percentile on standard pediatric charts.

Antoinette started school at age 4 years and had enjoyed school until recently. She has always been in the top 5% of her year in all subjects. She used to have many friends, again until recently when she appears to have lost contact with them. Occasionally, one of her friends will call at the house but Antoinette usually asks her mother to tell the friend that she is out.

Maria would have liked Antoinette to take up ballet, but despite being a capable dancer in her local classes, her parents were advised that Antoinette was unlikely ever to have the right physical shape for a ballet dancer. Antoinette's ballet teacher was quoted as saying that Antoinette 'is going to be short and muscular like her father, rather than tall and elegant like her mother'. Antoinette has had no major childhood illnesses. All immunizations were up to date. Antoinette has had one operation when she had her ears surgically corrected under general anaesthetic. She had prominent protruding ears, and her parents paid for these to be corrected. Antoinette had the operation at age 11 during her summer holidays; she spent a week in hospital and then a week on holiday with her parents recovering. Three years previously, Antoinette started orthodontic treatment to straighten her teeth. She wore fixed braces which made eating difficult at first. At the time, she lost some weight. The treatment was completed after 18 months.

Antoinette listed her favoured activities as exercise, studying and playing the cello. She is interested in health and reads articles on health and fitness on the Internet. She would like to develop an 'artistic' hobby such as photography. She likes romantic comedies, particularly anything with Audrey Hepburn – her all-time favourite film is *Breakfast at Tiffany's*. She reported that she loves to spend time with her mother.

When asked about her dislikes, Antoinette listed the following foods: chocolate, cake, fatty foods such as chips and greasy food, puddings generally, hard cheeses. When asked for more general dislikes, Antoinette said that she does not like going out to noisy clubs or parties, getting drunk, or smoking. She reported that she hates girls that gossip and judge you by how you look and where you shop. Antoinette complained that she feels bloated and uncomfortable after eating bread or potatoes. Her mother is concerned that Antoinette may have a wheat allergy or be gluten intolerant.

Psychometric assessment

Antoinette was asked to complete the Eating Disorders Inventory (EDI) scale. Her scores are as follows:

EDI – dieting	21 (High)
EDI – bulimia	3 (Low)
EDI – body dissatisfaction	11 (High)
EDI – ineffectiveness	10 (High)
EDI – perfectionism	12 (High)
EDI – interpersonal distrust	16 (High)
EDI – interoceptive awareness	12 (High)
EDI – total score	12 (High)

Overall, this pattern of results indicates anorexia nervosa marked by extreme dieting and control of food intake in the absence of purging and vomiting behaviour. The key diagnostic features of anorexia nervosa are suggested by dieting and abnormal attitudes to food and weight. The score for the bulimia subscale is within the range for non-eating disordered adult women. In addition, key cognitive features of anorexia nervosa are also present such as perfectionism, interpersonal distrust, a sense of ineffectiveness and poor interoceptive awareness.

Antoinette reported that she never binges and has never self-induced vomiting, though she does report that she feels nauseous if she eats anything fatty or greasy. She does not use laxatives or any other form of purging.

CLIENT GOALS

Antoinette reported that she feels that her weight is probably at the right level now. She considers herself to be fit and healthy. She did not want to lose any more weight. She reported that she might consider gaining weight to 'make Mummy happy', but she could not consider going back to her weight of 118 lbs (53.5 kg) because she thought that she looked 'gross' at that weight. She reported that she wants to eat healthily by reducing the amount of fat in her diet, particularly saturated fats, and by eating good foods containing fibre, vitamins and minerals.

Antoinette's personal goals were to achieve the highest possible grades in her examinations and to secure a place at an excellent college. She reported that she would like to be a university teacher.

Maria reported that she would like her daughter to return to 'normal'. When asked for more detail she said that she would like Antoinette to gain weight. She said that Antoinette has always been 'slight, like me'. She also wanted Antoinette to be happier and to 'stop going around looking so sad all day'. She reported that she would like her daughter to 'do all the normal things girls do', such as going shopping with her friends, going out with boys and having fun. Maria was less concerned about Antoinette's academic goals, stating that she can always catch up with that later.

ADDITIONAL INFORMATION

A report from Antoinette's School was requested. They described Antoinette as academically gifted. She has always been in the upper fifth percentile of her school since the age of 11 and was expected to perform very well in her examinations. Her homework was exemplary and beautifully presented. She was polite and obedient. There had been some discussion of her being made Class President, but since her illness, the teachers felt that this would be an unnecessary additional burden. The staff were concerned that Antoinette was becoming increasingly socially isolated. She did not appear to interact with other members of her class and did not have a confidant among the staff. She was excessively active during the school physical education sessions, and there had been some talk among the staff of prohibiting Antoinette from these lessons. During school breaks, Antoinette spent long periods walking around the school grounds wrapped in warm clothing. The school believe that Antoinette was suffering from anorexia nervosa, having had some experience with a student who had this disorder 5 years previously. In that case, the young woman left the school before completing her studies and was hospitalized for inpatient treatment. They subsequently lost touch with the family.

Mr David Smith was asked to attend a session to discuss his elder daughter's condition. He was unable to attend but agreed to speak on the phone for half an hour. He expressed grave concerns about his daughter's condition. He said that Antoinette had stopped coming to see him since his remarriage and at the time he thought it was because his ex-wife was reluctant to let Antoinette see him, stating that, 'Maria was afraid; Toni might like being with me and Catherine more than her.' As a result, he had not realized as early as he should have that Antoinette was ill. He would like to 'get it sorted' and expressed his love for his daughter. He expressed the opinion that the problem was caused by his ex-wife's desire to have a daughter in her own image, and that in contrast, Antoinette was quite like him – 'more academic than artistic'. He stated that he would do whatever was in his power to help, even if this meant attending treatment with his daughter. When asked whether he felt there was anything that made his daughter's condition better or worse, he said that he could not think of anything.

AN EVENT

At the first session following assessment one week later, Antoinette's mother, who attended with Antoinette, announced that she now realizes that she was 'anorexic' during her adolescence and gave a history of her eating and exercising behaviour whilst at ballet school. She said that this was unresolved and that she wished to enter therapy to address it. She believed that the lack of resolution of this issue interfered with her ability to form relationships in her adult life and was directly relevant to her divorce from Antoinette's father. She has read books and Internet sources about eating disorders. She wished to enter therapy to address this issue and asked if she could be taken on as a client.

At this appointment, Antoinette's weight was 86 lbs (39.0 kg). She complained of an Achilles' tendon injury. She has been asked not to attend the aerobics classes anymore since the woman who ran the class was concerned about Antoinette's weight.

11

A Formulation of the Case of Antoinette: A Multiperspective Approach

PRIYANTHY WEERASEKERA

THEORETICAL EXPLANATION AND RATIONALE

A formulation is a tentative explanation or hypothesis as to why an individual presents with a particular condition at this point in time (Weerasekera, 1993). Formulations supplement the diagnostic classification system, as this diagnostic system does not infer pathogenesis or predict the course of disorder. A formulation should be testable, predict prognosis and suggest treatment. Treatment should be comprehensive, integrative and evidence based. As treatment progresses and new information is obtained, the formulation should be re-examined, re-evaluated and perhaps revised. The formulation is therefore fluid and always changing as response to treatment is observed.

The Multiperspective Model presented in this case considers a variety of orientations (Weerasekera, 1996). It is similar to the 'biopsychosocial' model, in that it considers the relevant biological, psychological and social variables important in understanding a particular case. It differs in that it examines the patient's presentation from several theoretical frameworks, and integrates this into one unifying formulation. The formulation is organized to provide a hypothesis of the important predisposing, precipitating, perpetuating and protective factors relevant to the case. Under the multiperspective umbrella, the model examines individual and systemic perspectives. Individual variables include biological, behavioural, cognitive and psychodynamic perspectives.

Clinical Case Formulation: Varieties of Approaches.   Edited by Peter Sturmey.
© 2009 John Wiley & Sons, Ltd.

Systemic perspectives include couple, family, occupational/school and the social perspective. It is not essential that all perspectives be considered, but rather the relevant ones are selected and integrated. This approach to formulation also pays attention to the patient's coping-response style, and more importantly, this model includes treatment.

The rationale for this approach to formulation is that with any given condition or disorder, biological, psychological and social factors all play a role in the development, maintenance and outcome of the disorder. Therefore, it is difficult to see how one theoretical approach can capture all aspects of a case. If a formulation is an explanation or hypothesis as to why an individual presents with a particular condition at a particular time, then it is important that multiple variables are addressed in the explanation.

RELEVANT AND IRRELEVANT VARIABLES

The variables chosen for inclusion were those that related to the predisposing, precipitating, perpetuating and protective factors, and the coping-response style since this framework is used in multiperspective case formulation (Weerasekera, 1996). The four Ps have been used to evaluate biological, psychological and social factors in the commonly used 'biopsychosocial' grid. The predisposing factors are those that make an individual vulnerable to a particular condition. These factors increase the probability of a specific condition occurring if the specific factors prevail. Precipitating factors have a temporal relationship with the onset of the disturbance. A precipitant occurs just prior to the onset of the disorder. A perpetuating factor maintains the condition. They are chronic in nature and contribute to the longevity of the condition. Protective factors buffer the course of the disorder. Therefore, these factors when integrated provide the 'story' or formulation as to why this individual is presenting with this condition at this particular time. It identifies both biological and psychological risk factors, with similar variables that explain onset, and maintenance of the condition. The attention given to protective factors also pays attention to prognosis. The coping-response style identifies individual variables that help tailor treatment to each client. This approach then integrates the important variables in a developmental narrative so that all factors can be attended to in treatment. Antoinette's mother, Maria, reported having a cold father. Maria also reported not being able to attend her mother's funeral. It is possible that this background led Maria to have difficulties around issues of illness and death, and with expressing emotions, but this is speculative. Further information would be required regarding Maria's history before one can confidently make these statements. For this reason this information was not included in the formulation.

ROLE OF RESEARCH AN CLINICAL EXPERIENCE

A formulation should be guided by both research and clinical experience. Research tells us what has been empirically investigated and what is the most plausible hypothesis or explanation of the patient's current difficulties. Research, however, deals with efficacy studies, and the results of these controlled trials are not always generalizable to the real world. Clinical experience is obtained from the real world, but is subject to bias due to individual experience. Research helps us understand the predisposing, precipitating, perpetuating and protective factors. Prospective research particularly informs us about variables that may be important in the development of a condition. Both biological variables and psychological variables can be studied. Genetic studies, biological markers and other studies that look for biological antecedents or correlates of a disorder help us understand how biological vulnerabilities contribute to a disorder. In the case of anorexia, there is evidence to show that the condition runs in families (Polivy and Herman, 2005; Spelt and Meyer, 1995). Whether this is a result of modelling or a biological vulnerability, or both, is unclear. In this particular case, there is a family history of anorexia providing some positive support for a biological vulnerability towards the disorder.

Psychological factors have also been studied in anorexia, either as antecedents to the disorder or as maintaining factors. These include sociocultural, familial and a variety of individual variables (Polivy and Herman, 2002). The relentless pursuit of thinness in certain societies has been identified as a causal factor in leading some cultures to have a higher prevalence of eating disorders than others. Although this has been a popular theory of causality, it is hard to consider it as a powerful predictor given the low incidence of the disorder. Therefore, other factors are likely important for one individual to internalize these values and not another.

Perhaps the most controversial risk factor identified in the onset and maintenance of an eating disorder is family dysfunction. Clients with eating disorders have been identified as having families that are enmeshed, hostile, intrusive and unable to meet the emotional needs of the client. These patterns have been identified through case reports and poorly controlled studies, making them difficult to interpret. Recent studies do identify insecure attachment patterns in these families, but this is now considered to be a consequence rather than a cause of the disorder. Specific maternal behaviours, however, have been found to be important in the development and course of the disorder. Mothers of clients who suffer from eating disorders have been found to spend more time attending to their daughter's weight, making remarks connecting attractiveness to thinness and being critical of their daughter's appearance (Hill and Franklin, 1998). In addition, these mothers have been found to be unhappy with overall family functioning and show evidence of eating disordered symptoms themselves. It has been found that specific maternal comments made regarding appearance and weight carry more significance than modelling of eating behaviour in the development and maintenance of specific eating behaviours, even at the elementary school level (Ogden and Steward, 2000). Therefore, maternal comments are important in the development and maintenance of the disorder, and family dysfunction is common, whether this precedes or is a consequence of the illness is controversial.

In this particular case, there is evidence that maternal comments regarding weight, shape and attractiveness have predated the onset of the illness as this occurred when Antoinette was very young, and did not have active symptoms of an eating disorder. It is also apparent that a close, enmeshed relationship currently exists between mother and daughter, and a dysfunctional one with her father. Her brother has also disconnected himself from the family. Whether these patterns predated or are a consequence of the illness is less clear.

Individual risk factors have also been studied although the evidence here is mixed. Certain personality features such as the need to have control over oneself or one's body, and poor identity formation have been implicated as precursors to the development of eating disorders, as programmes aimed at improving self-esteem have been found to improve weight gain (Fairburn, Shafran and Cooper, 1999). Therefore, it has been hypothesized that it is the presence of body dissatisfaction and identity disturbances as well as the need to regain control that makes one vulnerable to the development of an eating disorder. It is apparent that these factors are evident in this case.

Research also indicates that the obsessional preoccupation with eating and weight is similar to the thought patterns of clients with obsessive–compulsive disorder (OCD). Although many anorexic clients find these thoughts comforting, and over half see them as ego-syntonic indicating the divergence from true OCD (Sunday, Halmi and Einhorn, 1995). Perfectionism has also been found to be associated with clients with anorexia even after weight is restored, leading researchers to consider this characteristic as a precursor to the development of the illness (Hewitt, Flett and Ediger, 1995; Forbush, Heatherton and Keel, 2007). Antoinette certainly demonstrates ritualistic eating behaviours, an obsessional preoccupation with weight, a rigid lifestyle and evidence of perfectionism.

From a clinical standpoint, Antoinette presents with the common features of a case of Anorexia Nervosa. She is preoccupied with the need to be thin, and with the typical family issues that centre on separation and individuation. She appears to have an enmeshed relationship with her mother, and is physically cut off from father. She has unrelenting standards, and is driven to attain the 'perfect' physique of a ballerina, similar to her mother. There is evidence that she is distant from her emotional experiences and this was also modelled in the family. Therefore, her clinical presentation and family dynamics are consistent with clients diagnosed with this condition.

THE FORMULATION

In formulating this case, it is important to consider the significant biological and psychological factors leading Antoinette to present with Anorexia Nervosa, obsessive–compulsive personality disorder (OCPD) and a parent–child problem. From a biological perspective, she is vulnerable to anorexia given that her mother has suffered from this condition. In addition, her father struggles with weight issues indicating further biological vulnerabilities towards weight instability.

Given this biological vulnerability, certain psychological factors also predispose her towards Anorexia Nervosa, OCPD and parent–child problems. The client's early developmental years indicate a mother who wished her daughter to follow in her footsteps: to be thin and to be a ballerina. Antoinette, however, was unable to pursue her mother's dream, for she was seen as having a muscular physique rather than the thin, tall, elegant body type needed to be a ballerina. It is possible that the rejection of her body type set the stage for her obsessional preoccupations with thinness, perfectionism, ritualistic eating and exercising. If she could be thin, she would be like mother, and obtain her approval. Being rejected as a ballerina may have contributed to her feeling unattractive, unlovable and unworthy, leading to chronic low self-esteem. Others are likely experienced as only loving her for her external features, for what she looks like, rather than for who she really is. This would contribute to poor identity formation as personal characteristics are ignored. It would also make it difficult for her to have intimate relationships. Not having experienced anyone as being truly interested in her, she would be distrustful of anyone who showed interest, as this may not have happened to a significant degree given the emphasis on physical appearance.

Family factors that likely contributed to her conditions include parental separation in the context of her mother also suffering from an eating disorder, and loss of acceptance and support from father who may not have emphasized her having to be thin. Her father and brother leaving shattered her family as she knew it, leading her to feel even more helpless about her ability to control the world around her. Her ritualistic eating behaviour and struggle to be perfect may be seen as her attempt to exert some control over a life which is perceived as unpredictable and chaotic. Significant attachment figures have been lost and potential new ones have arrived, and she has had no say in any of this. This revolving door at home will contribute to insecure attachment patterns in later life, and difficulties with relationships. There is evidence that she already avoids close relationships with both males and females.

Socially she did have positive relationships until recently. This suggests that she did trust at one point and was able to access social relationships for leisure and support. It will be important to re-establish this in the future. However, her social interaction patterns changed after her recent losses in her life, and the onset of her illness.

From an occupational and school perspective she has always done well, always maintained high standards and an excellent performance record. This is important in that it contributes to positive self-esteem and has likely protected her from becoming severely depressed. However, her unrelenting standards in this area makes her vulnerable to depression should she not perform perfectly in all subjects in the future.

Given this developmental course and underlying biological vulnerability, the recent occurrence of her father's remarriage, having to accept his new wife and especially their 2-year-old daughter, as well as her mother's new boyfriend and her brother leaving, may have all precipitated the disorder. These events likely created significant feelings of anxiety regarding loss of all her significant attachment figures, feelings of loss of control and low self-worth.

Once precipitated, the disorder was likely maintained by reinforcement, given the attention she must have received from mother for being slim, and avoidance of visiting father and his new family, which was likely too painful for her. Having to see her father with a new woman and particularly a new daughter may have heightened her feelings of rejection and loss of control over her life. Her anorexia was also reinforced by her mother cancelling social engagements, lessening contact with her own boyfriend and generally attending more to her. Antoinette's rigid study habits were also reinforced by excellent grades and positive comments from teachers. This would further increase time and energy put into studying. It is also possible that once anorexia was established it was maintained by certain hormonal factors that have been implicated in sustaining reduced intake. Additionally, once anorexia has been established, the ingestion of food has been associated with multiple gastric symptoms, such as bloating and general gastric distress that would further decrease the intake of food.

On a positive note Antoinette possesses a number of protective factors that could buffer the course of the illness, thereby predicting a good prognosis. First, she is an intelligent young girl and intelligence has been shown to be a protective factor in many conditions. How intelligence exerts its effect is less clear, but has been speculated to produce resilience in the midst of adversity. Her focus on her schoolwork, her need to perform well and her wish to get into a prestigious university indicate that she has academic and occupational goals for the future. Whether or not she adheres to a treatment plan focused on weight gain is another question. Other protective factors include the absence of certain negative prognostic signs that have been found to be associated with a poorer outcome. There is no evidence of vomiting, bulimia or purging. There were no premorbid developmental or clinical abnormalities in childhood. The illness is of shorter rather than longer duration. She is nutritionally stable. She is not clinically depressed or suicidal. In addition, although the parents are separated, both parents are willing to be involved in treatment. Antoinette herself is also willing to be involved in treatment although her motivations are somewhat unclear as she states she is doing it for her mother.

Negative prognostic signs include the presence of OCPD and perfectionism. Her lack of insight and avoidant behaviours related to social connections may also be seen as a negative prognostic sign, as this does not give her the opportunity to connect with peers and receive social support as well as opportunities to receive feedback regarding what is considered normal eating behaviours and weight. Also her goals for therapy do not include change in weight or eating habits as she states she is happy with the way she is, but is pursuing this for her mother, a poor motivation for treatment.

Her coping-response style indicates that she is someone who utilizes a variety of defences to deal with her difficulties. Feelings of loss, sadness and anxiety over the inability to control her world are displaced onto activities she can control such as eating, exercising and weight control. She is also a doer, in that she involves herself in activities to deal with her problems. The exercise, engagement in activities and inordinate amount of time given to food preparation indicate that she has a behavioural coping-response style. There is no evidence that she discusses any of her true feelings with anyone – either with her parents, brother or friends. Her most important coping style involves the occupational school system in that her self-esteem needs are mostly met here. She has channelled her difficulties into her schoolwork; this can be seen as displacement and an occupational school coping-response style. Therefore, many coping styles are utilized. She does not access anyone as a confidant, does not discuss her feelings or thoughts, and although her restriction of food and excessive exercise could be seen as a biological coping-response style, they are more behavioural in that they are activity oriented. This coping-response style should help determine where treatment should begin. At this point we would consider treatment, for according to this model it is part of the formulation. However, given the format of this chapter, it is discussed below.

HISTORY

The history contains all the significant information necessary for constructing a formulation. It provides the identifying data, the chief complaint, the history of the presenting complaint, any past psychiatric problems, medical problems, family psychiatric history, the past personal history and the mental status. The above information is key in that it provides the essential information necessary to form a clinical diagnosis. In this approach, it is the diagnosis and the individual's history that is formulated. The information in the history helps us discuss the relevant predisposing, precipitating, perpetuating and protective factors. It also informs us about the individual's coping strategies.

CURRENT FACTORS

The current factors help us understand the precipitating, perpetuating and protective factors that contribute to the formulation. The current factors in this case include parental separation, father's remarriage and the arrival of his new daughter, mother's new boyfriend and his decreased presence once the eating disorder began, loss of brother as a result of his departure to university and increased attention delivered by mother to Antoinette regarding weight, eating and lack of social behaviours. All these current factors have been woven into the formulation as illustrated above.

TREATMENT PLAN

In considering treatment, the first issue is that of safety. She is not suicidal, and she is nutritionally stable. Therefore, treatment can begin as an outpatient. Given the lack of strong evidence for the use of medication in the treatment of anorexia, and the likelihood that she would initially refuse, there does not appear to be a strong indication for this at this time (Attia and Schroeder, 2005). Therefore, treatment to consider initially is a behavioural one that takes advantage of her activity-oriented coping style. This will help with the development of a positive therapeutic alliance. Treatment should be individually focused in the beginning with a clear decision being made by both parties as to the goal of treatment being a minimum weight gain, the beginning of menses and improvement in quality of life. Once an alliance is developed a discussion can ensue regarding the addition of group treatment to supplement the individual treatment. This will also encourage socialization, identity formation and separation–individuation. Cognitive therapy to challenge her distortions regarding body image and unrelenting standards will also help once an alliance is established (Fairburn, 2005). There is positive evidence for individual plus group treatment for eating disorders. Evidence also exists for including parents in the feeding process at home so that power struggles are prevented and parents become part of the behavioural refeeding programme (Lock and Le Grange, 2005). It may be important not to include family in formal family therapy until eating behaviours are established. Family involvement to discuss the issues at home will be important, but the timing of this will be up to the therapist and client to decide. A strong alliance will be needed prior to dealing with these issues. Antoinette may also need time to deal with her own issues before dealing with the family. Eventually, however, family sessions to discuss affective issues around the parental separation and father's reconstituted family may be needed if Antoinette is to work through her feelings of rejection, sadness and loss. This is speculative but testable in a family meeting. To not attend to family variables may be counter-therapeutic, for returning her to this environment with individual treatment alone may predict relapse once she has returned. Once weight gain is stabilized, Antoinette should be encouraged to participate in extracurricular activities at school. Participation in sports, music and the arts with other students will facilitate the development of friendships and romantic relationships. Medications may be integrated once weight gain has been established; specifically a selective serotonin reuptake inhibitor (SSRI), given that there is some evidence that this may help maintain weight gain after weight is restored (Attia and Schroeder, 2005).

After initial treatment, ongoing integrated treatment will be required. This will involve the following:

(a) Cognitive-behavioural and psychodynamic therapy or cognitive-analytic therapy to deal with eating behaviour, since the formulation indicates that Antoinette has a distorted body image, unrelenting standards, identity and separation–individuation issues and family of origin issues (Dare *et al.*, 2001).

(b) Experiential techniques to facilitate the expression of affect, specifically anxiety over the loss of control of all the changing events in her life as indicated in the formulation. Expression of these feelings would hopefully diminish the need to self-starve to regain control.

(c) Family therapy on an infrequent basis initially to ensure feeding patterns are maintained (Lock and Le Grange, 2005), and later to deal with family issues as indicated in the formulation (reinforcement of 'thinness', enmeshment with mother and being estranged from father).
(d) Medications to maintain weight gain (Fairburn, 2005) as she may have a biological vulnerability to anorexia.
(e) Ongoing participation in social activities at school and booster sessions with an eating disorder group should also be encouraged, given the importance of social factors in helping her with identity and separation–individuation issues, as well as reinforcing a proper body image.

This integrated approach will help deal with the multiple variables important in the development and maintenance of these disorders, and it will help in preventing relapse. Integration can proceed sequentially and later simultaneously, as each component is dealt with, and over time. Simultaneous integration of therapies can be seen as additive and synergistic in enhancing outcome.

THE EVENT

The event is the mother's disclosure of her own past personal history, her own struggle with anorexia and her wish to pursue therapy with her daughter's therapist. This provides support for Antoinette having a biological and psychological (modelling) predisposition towards anorexia. It also indicates that mother has a need to maintain a close, enmeshed relationship with her daughter as she is requesting to see the same therapist, rather than seeking her own. This offers some support to the hypotheses that there are separation–individuation issues, as it appears difficult for Antoinette to have her own, independent treatment. It likely strengthens the treatment plan that promotes individual treatment first for Antoinette *before* any family involvement is prescribed. It is probably best that mother pursue her own independent therapist.

OTHER ISSUES

Other information to be gathered includes her early relationships with her mother and father, any separation issues, particularly in the early school years, any history of abuse or other traumas and any difficulties with expressing sadness and anger. Information regarding these issues should be obtained either as part of the assessment or later as treatment begins, as she may become more comfortable to provide more valid and sensitive information once an alliance is established.

SUMMARY

Antoinette presents with a 2-year history of anorexia, OCPD, perfectionism, social isolation and family problems. The history suggests a biological predisposition towards anorexia. Additionally, eating behaviours, values regarding thinness and perfectionism were likely modelled and reinforced. The family struggles indicate insecure attachments with parents, and loss of a significant attachment figure prior to the onset of the illness. Father's absence and the new daughter is likely perceived as further rejection, which reinforces her low self-esteem, and negative view of herself. These factors, coupled with the arrival of mother's new boyfriend, and loss of brother, likely led to feelings of loneliness and unimportance, which were not expressed. Difficulties with identity issues, separation and individuation no doubt followed. As the world around her changes and significant attachment figures are lost, she finds the one thing she can control: her weight and eating. Attachment figures are seen as unreliable and distrustful which leads to social isolation, solitary activities and preoccupation with weight. At least these things can be controlled. Her eating behaviours and rigid lifestyle keep her emotions at bay, and attachment figures close and interested (mother and father), as attention is now diverted to her.

REFERENCES

Attia, E. and Schroeder, L. (2005) Pharmacologic treatment of Anorexia Nervosa: where do we go from here? *International Journal of Eating Disorders*, **37**, S60–3.

Dare, C., Eisler, I., Russell, G. *et al.* (2001) Psychological therapies for adults with anorexia nervosa: randomized controlled trial of outpatient treatments. *British Journal of Psychiatry*, **178**, 216–21.

Fairburn, C.G. (2005) Evidence-based treatment of Anorexia Nervosa. *International Journal of Eating Disorders*, **37**, S26–30.

Fairburn, C.G., Shafran, R. and Cooper, Z. (1999) Invited essay: a cognitive behavioural therapy of anorexia nervosa. *Behaviour, Research and Therapy*, **37**, 1–13.

Forbush, K., Heatherton, T.G. and Keel, P.K. (2007) Relationships between perfectionism and specific disordered eating behaviours. *International Journal of Eating Disorders*, **40**, 37–41.

Hewitt, P.L., Flett, G.L. and Ediger, E. (1995) Perfectionism traits and perfectionistic self-presentation in eating disorder attitudes, characteristics, and symptoms. *International Journal of Eating Disorders*, **18**, 317–26.

Hill, A.J. and Franklin, J.A. (1998) Mothers, daughters and dieting: investigating the transmission of weight control. *British Journal of Clinical Psychology*, **37**, 3–13.

Lock, J. and Le Grange, D. (2005) Family-based treatment of eating disorders. *International Journal of Eating Disorders*, **37**, S64–7.

Ogden, J. and Steward, J. (2000) The role of the mother-daughter relationship in explaining weight concern. *International Journal of Eating Disorders*, **28**, 78–83.

Polivy, J. and Herman, C.P. (2002) Causes of eating disorders. *Annual Review Psychology*, **53**, 187–213.

Polivy, J. and Herman, C.P. (2005) Mental health and eating behaviours: a bi-directional relation. *Canadian Journal of Public Health*, **96** (Suppl. 3), S43–53, S49–53.

Spelt, J. and Meyer, J.M. (1995) Genetics and eating disorders, in *Behavior Genetic Approaches in Behavioral Medicine* (eds J.R. Turner, L.R. Cardon and J.K. Hewitt), Plenum, New York, pp. 167–85.

Sunday, S.R., Halmi, K.A. and Einhorn, A. (1995) The Yale-Brown-Cornell eating disorder scale: a new scale to assess eating disorder symptomatology. *International Journal of Eating Disorders*, **18**, 237–45.

Weerasekera, P. (1993) Formulation: a multiperspective model. *Canadian Journal of Psychiatry*, **38**, 351–8.

Weerasekera, P. (1996) *Multiperspective Case Formulation: A Step Towards Treatment Integration*, Kreiger Publishing, Malabar, FL.

12

The Functional Analysis and Functional Analytic Clinical Case Formulation: A Case of Anorexia Nervosa

RAIMO LAPPALAINEN, TERO TIMONEN, AND STEPHEN N. HAYNES

THEORETICAL ORIENTATION AND RATIONALE

The functional analysis is a case formulation model based on learning theory, evidence-based assessment and treatment, basic research on psychopathology and applied and experimental behaviour analysis (Haynes and O'Brien, 1990, 2000; Haynes and Williams, 2003; Virus-Ortega and Haynes, 2005; see also http://www2.hawaii.edu/~sneil/ba/ for PowerPoint slides and functional analytic clinical case model (FACCM) case presentations). The functional analysis is illustrated with a FACCM, a vector diagram that presents behaviour problems and goals, functional relations among behaviour problems, the relative importance of behaviour problems, the strength and form of causal and non-causal relations for behaviour problems and the modifiability of causal variables.

The functional analysis and FACCM are most useful in three contexts: (1) with complex clinical cases, especially with clients with multiple problem areas and multiple, interacting causal variables; (2) with cases in which standardized treatment is failing; and (3) in treatment team settings in which treatment goals for a client are discussed. This chapter discusses the functional

Clinical Case Formulation: Varieties of Approaches. Edited by Peter Sturmey.
© 2009 John Wiley & Sons, Ltd.

analysis with a particularly challenging set of problems, Anorexia Nervosa (Fairburn, Cooper and Shafran, 2003).

The functional analysis can be used together with the American Psychiatric Association's (APA, 2000) *Diagnostic and Statistical Manual (Fourth Edition) Text Revision* (DSM-IV-TR) and the related *Structured Clinical Interview for DSM-IV Axis I and Axis II Disorders* interviews (First *et al.*, 1997a,b). The main difference between these approaches is that the functional analysis looks beyond the diagnoses and description of behaviour problems and uses mainly functional information in order to make a client's problems and other behaviour problems understandable. The main goal of the functional analysis is to *explain* behaviour problems and suggest the best treatment focus.

Although diagnosis can be useful in case formulation, there are several limitations when using diagnoses in clinical practice from the functional or behavioural point of view (see review of the role of diagnosis in behavioural assessment in Nelson-Gray and Paulson, 2004). A diagnosis is often needed when transferring information between professionals within the health care system. However, a diagnosis is often insufficient for understanding and effectively treating the disorder. The descriptions of a disorder, such as Anorexia Nervosa, included in a diagnosis are too non-specific and give little information on specific behaviours of a particular client. Of particular importance for a functional analysis, a diagnosis provides no information about how these behaviours vary across situations and contexts, what maintains the behaviour problems and how different psychological problems may interact with each other.

Diagnosis-based explanations for behaviour disorders are often circular. For example, an observation that a client eats very small amounts of food can be one indication that the client is anorexic. The term 'anorexic' is then used to *explain* why the client eats small amounts of food. This kind of reasoning may give clinicians a false belief that they understand a behaviour problem even though variables having a causal relationship with anorexic behavioural patterns are not identified (Lappalainen and Tuomisto, 2005). This may lead to treatment that is not optimally effective.

The main limitation of diagnosis-based case formulations is that they are *descriptive* rather than *explanatory*. Effective therapies must address the causes of behaviour problems and many studies have demonstrated that causes can differ across clients with the same behaviour problem. The aim of the functional analysis is to first specify a client's behaviour problems and treatment goals and then to identify variables that affect him or her in order to explain the behaviour problems by identifying variables that account for variance in the behaviour problems across time, settings and contexts.

The validity of the functional analysis depends on the validity of the assessment data upon which it is based. Data should be acquired through multiple methods and multiple sources using validated interviews, analogue and naturalistic observations, questionnaires and self- and ambulatory monitoring (Haynes and O'Brien, 2000). Ultimately, the validity of the functional analysis is evaluated via the effects of the treatment based on it. If the treatment is effective in modifying causal variables identified in the functional analysis and expected changes in the behaviour problems do not occur, some elements of the functional analysis are invalid and require modification. Important causal variables may have been missed, there may be moderator variables operating that were not identified, or the importance of, or relations among, behaviour problems, or the strength of relations may have been misestimated.

As illustrated by the case presented in this chapter, clinicians often fail to acquire valid data on important variables, from multiple sources, and using multiple methods. Without valid data on functional relations, case formulations and treatment decisions are often strongly based on the clinician's biases and assumptions or follow standard practice. When we are missing valid assessment information, which is often the case in clinical practice, we must rely more on hypothetical causal relationships based on available information, research knowledge and practical experience.

In the context of insufficient data, functional hypotheses can be tested during treatment. From this perspective, the missing data may not be so serious a problem, but can still increase the chance of misdirected treatment in early sessions. It is important to monitor the effects of the treatment and frequently evaluate and refine the pretreatment functional analysis.

Even in cases where there is insufficient validated data, the functional analysis can still provide a valuable tool to test hypotheses about variables and the relationships between variables. Practically, the functional analysis and FACCM can be considered to be a tentative process model – a model based on available clinical evidence and the results from nomothetic research, where hypotheses lead to further testing and refinement during additional assessment and during treatment. Research by Greg Mumma illustrates the process of validating cognitive behavioural case formulations using multivariate time-series regression designs (Mumma, 2004; Mumma and Smith, 2001).

Relevant and irrelevant variables

The FACCM is a vector-graphic visual model of a functional analysis. It uses a variety of symbols to make the functional analyses clinically useful. The different symbols and their meaning are described in Figure 12.1. Briefly, the rectangle indicates a behaviour problem; a circle indicates a causal

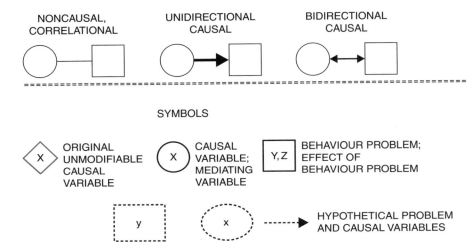

IMPORTANCE/MODIFIABILITY OF VARIABLES
(using width of variable boundary and coefficients)

| X1 .2 | LOW IMPORTANCE /MODIFIABILITY | | X1 .8 | HIGH IMPORTANCE /MODIFIABILITY |

TYPE AND DIRECTION OF RELATIONSHIP BETWEEN VARIABLES

NONCAUSAL, CORRELATIONAL   UNIDIRECTIONAL CAUSAL   BIDIRECTIONAL CAUSAL

SYMBOLS

ORIGINAL UNMODIFIABLE CAUSAL VARIABLE   CAUSAL VARIABLE; MEDIATING VARIABLE   Y, Z BEHAVIOUR PROBLEM; EFFECT OF BEHAVIOUR PROBLEM

y   x   HYPOTHETICAL PROBLEM AND CAUSAL VARIABLES

Figure 12.1   The basic symbols used in the FACCM.

variable (an antecedent variable, a consequence or a moderator variable) and a diamond indicates a historical causal variable that cannot be modified. These symbols illustrate a client's problem areas as well as contextual and situational variables, moderator variables and contingencies. The functional relations between the variables are arrows and lines that indicate the strength, direction and form of functional relation.

The overall goal of the functional analysis and the FACCM is to estimate the relative *magnitude of effect* of each causal variable. This can often be done through visual inspection, but estimates of the magnitude of effect can be calculated by assigning values to the variables and functional relations in the FACCM. Clinical judgements from the FACCM can be more precise by adding judgements of the importance of a problem by using a 0–10 scale where 0 = not difficult at all and 10 = very difficult. The modifiability of causal variables can be illustrated on 0–1.0 scale where 0 = not modifiable – 0.8 = very modifiable. The strength of the connection between variables can be estimated by using a 0–1.0 scale where 0 = no relation and 0.8 = strong relation. These estimates can be made observable in the model also by using different line thicknesses. These values are illustrated in Figure 12.2.

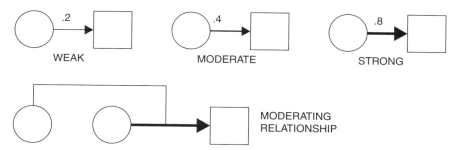

Figure 12.2 The basic illustration of strength estimation and relationships between variables.

As we discussed earlier, and as will be evident in the case formulation to be presented, clinicians often have insufficient information to identify behaviour problems or causal variables or to estimate the strength of the functional relations. In cases where there is insufficient information, dashed lines indicate hypothesized variables and functional relations, reflecting the situation in which variables and relations among variables are still unclear and the assessor needs to collect more data.

In some cases, the validity of the FACCM model can be improved by showing it to the client. The FACCM helps the clinician describe to the client how she/he has understood the client's situation, and illustrates to the client the possible causal relationships. This discussion serves several purposes. It prepares and motivates the client for the treatment. It illustrates for the client the importance of treatment evaluation and planning, and encourages the client to make changes and to test hypotheses illustrated in the FACCM. FACCMs are also useful when shown to hospital staff, teachers and other mental health professionals to get feedback, explain treatment options and motivate the professionals to provide evidence-based treatment. The model is also very useful in supervision. The supervisor can very quickly get a general picture of the client's situation and of the hypothesis made by the therapist.

There are several other characteristics of a functional analysis approach to case formulation.

1. Causal variables can differ across different *dimensions of a behaviour* problem. For example, the causes for the original onset of a client's eating disorder can differ from the causes for its maintenance over time.
2. Although a functional analysis stresses the importance of immediate antecedent conditions, contexts and consequences, *social systems and*

distal variables can serve important causal functions. For example, in the case formulation that follows, life stressors and social support for the client's mother may affect her behaviour towards the daughter, thereby affecting the daughter's eating-related thoughts and behaviour.

3. Case formulations can be presented at different *levels of specificity*. Higher order, less-specific formulations can be more useful in making initial treatment decisions. More specific, lower level, formulations can be more useful once a treatment focus has been determined. The FACCMs for the current case illustrate a more specific case formulation for cognitive/emotional variables, which followed a less-specific case formulation that included many types of causal variables and treatment targets.

4. A functional analysis is *flexible, conditional and dynamic*. Causes for a behaviour problem can vary across settings, contexts and time. For example, the variables affecting a client's eating behaviour may be different now than in the past and may be different as a function of the social context in which eating occurs. Also, the functional analysis can change as additional data are acquired during assessment and treatment.

5. *Moderator variables*, variables that affect the strength of relations between two other variables, are often important elements in a functional analysis. This will be illustrated in the case of the woman with anorexic behaviours discussed later in this chapter.

ROLE OF RESEARCH AND CLINICAL EXPERIENCE

As indicated above, the FACCM is meant to help clinical decision-making in cases involving multiple clinical problems. One of the most difficult set of behaviour problems to assess and treat is Anorexia Nervosa. Thus, the functional analysis and FACCM are designed to draw attention to the most important aspects of the case.

The functional analysis is an idiographic approach, focusing on variables and functional relations for a specific client. However, the assessment and case formulation are also guided by nomothetically based research. Therefore, it is important to be knowledgeable of the research relevant to clinical case prior to conducting a functional analysis.

There is an enormous amount of research on Anorexia Nervosa (Fairburn, Cooper and Shafran, 2003). We focus here on several findings from learning paradigms that are especially relevant to the case of Anorexia Nervosa under consideration. Excessive attention to and overevaluation of eating, shape and weight and their control are common. Persons with anorexic behaviour patterns typically restrict their food intake in a rigid and extreme way.

An anorexic client may also have bulimia-type behaviours. He or she may vomit, misuse laxatives or diuretics and overexercise. The anorexic client may also exhibit various forms of body checking and avoidance behaviours, and be preoccupied with thoughts about eating, shape and weight. In a subgroup of clients, binge eating is also present.

Fairburn, Cooper and Shafran (2003) and Garner (1997) argued that the starvation syndrome is a maintaining factor for Anorexia Nervosa. This includes social withdrawal from external influences that might diminish overevaluation of eating, shape and weight, and their control. Other maintaining factors could be perfectionism, low self-esteem and interpersonal difficulties (Fairburn, Cooper and Shafran, 2003), all of which may be relevant to the current case.

Lappalainen and Tuomisto (2005) argued that several processes should be taken into account when analyzing the anorexic behaviour. For example, because the anorexic client eats a very limited variety of foods and has often decreased the number of eating occasions, an extinction process of conditioned anticipatory responses associated with food intake may have occurred. As a result, an extinction of the process preparing the anorexic client for food ingestion may influence meal initiation. That is, the anorexic client may not report feelings of hunger or desire to eat when seeing food.

Furthermore, humans easily associate upper gastrointestinal discomfort (nausea) with food items that have been consumed prior to the symptoms. In anorexic clients, the aversive gastrointestinal symptoms may originate from the state of energy depletion or poor health status of the body. The appearance of aversive gastrointestinal symptoms could negatively shift the hedonic value of the food. Thus, the anorexic client may feel ill as a direct result of energy restriction or may feel discomfort, such as feeling cold, after eating. Gastrointestinal discomfort could be associated with the food eaten, as well as with verbal descriptions of food or body. For example, word 'fat' could be associated with negative symptoms.

One possible reason why an anorexic client prefers some foods to others may be that non-preferred foods have previously been consumed only rarely. The anorexic client may alter food intake by limiting the variety of food items. It has been shown that sensory-specific satiety is an important determinant of human food intake, and the variety of foods is an important factor in determining the amount of food eaten (Rolls, 1994). Therefore, increasing the number of food items that a client eats may lead to increased intake of energy (Rolls, 1985).

Some anorexic clients may drink large amounts of liquids either between meals, at the beginning of a meal or during the meal, which should be one focus of assessment and treatment. The amount of water drunk during a meal affects self-reported feelings of hunger and satiety during a meal (Lappalainen *et al.*, 1993). Thus, this suggests that feelings of hunger and satiety can be altered during a meal by altering the amount of liquid intake.

Studies of concurrent schedules in humans show that the response rates and allocation of time are sensitive to different response-reinforcer contingency relationships. The rate of a given response alternative varies reciprocally with the reinforcement rate obtained for responding to a second alternative (Lappalainen and Sjödén, 1992). In normal weight participants, when work requirements for the food were increased under deprivation conditions, participants decreased their responding to food and increased responding to an alternative reinforcer (Lappalainen and Epstein, 1990). In other words, alternative reinforcers can compete with the reinforcing value of food. Thus, for the anorexic clients alternative reinforcers, such as physical activity, may compete with the reinforcing value of food, when more effort is required for eating. Eating may be more difficult because of the aversive consequences of eating and rituals associated with food preparation. The anorexic client decreases eating and allocates more time for physical or other activities. Epling and Pierce (1992) have suggested that food deprivation increases the reinforcement effectiveness of physical activity, and spontaneous or forced activity decreases the reinforcement effectiveness of food. They have also pointed out that these two relationships partially explain the high rates of physical activity in some persons with anorexia.

The point is that changing alternative reinforcers might change the reinforcing value of food. That is, the targets for treatment might not be limited to anorexic eating behaviour itself, but might also include behaviours that are functionally related to eating via the complex schedules. In clinical practice we can, for example, observe that for some clients food is too reinforcing. The client can be occupied with eating and food even when she is consuming very little energy. Increasing the value of alternative reinforcers might change the situation. Limiting physical activity or increasing alternative activities, increasing alternative verbal behaviours and thoughts, and doing little with eating might be the solution. The anorexic client may have limited her activities, resulting in a value increase of food and eating. For example, planning pleasant activities using weekly plans, participating in social activities, doing studies, going to movies or seeing sports could decrease the value of food and eating. Thus, an increase in concurrent activities may affect eating. Accordingly, it has been suggested that the analysis of Anorexia Nervosa should be concentrated on the reduced food intake and enhanced physical activity (Berg and Södersten, 1996). A separate FACCM can be used to illustrate interactions between food intake and physical activity.

THE FORMULATION

The assessment data upon which this case formulation has been constructed comes from Kings' College, London. The data represent typical practice in clinical assessment, in which most of the data are derived from interviews with the client. There are two problems with this strategy for illustrating a functional analytic approach to case formulation. First, and a problem that is true to some degree in all clinical assessments, we cannot be sure of the validity of the data. Many studies have documented problems with self-report data, which are associated with biased reporting, memory lapses and selective attention, suggesting a cautious approach to inferences based solely on self-report. As assessment progresses, we often acquire new information from the client, we acquire data on the same variables from different sources, clients change their reports and some data that we acquire conflict with earlier data. Second, and more importantly, the types of data that are necessary for a functional analysis are missing in this case description. Based on initial information and best practice recommendations in behavioural assessment (Haynes and O'Brien, 2000; Hersen, 2006), a clinical assessment for this client would include the following:

1. Analogue observation of the client interacting with her mother on several topics using, for example, video tapings including topics such as the client's and mother's eating patterns.
2. Observation of the client and her mother eating together to gather more data on how mother–daughter interaction may maintain the eating disorder.
3. Analogue observation and description of the client's eating patterns, when she is eating with the therapist, to gather more data on emotional reactions and thoughts before, during and after eating, for example of anxiety associated with food intake, and verbal rules associated with eating.
4. Questionnaire measures and additional interviews focused on the client's depression, social anxiety and avoidance, life stressors, obsessive and controlling behaviours and family functioning to obtain more data on other behaviour problems and causal variables.
5. Medical evaluations of multiple physiological effects of low caloric intake to obtain data on physiological effects of her restricted caloric intake and evaluate medical complications that might require immediate attention.
6. Self-monitoring of caloric intake, food items consumed and not consumed, family and social interactions using up-to-date methods of palm-top computer monitoring to obtain data on these potential causal factors and to use as treatment outcome.

Although functional analyses are always tentative and dynamic best guesses, they are usually grounded in valid assessment data. The absence of validated data on important variables and relations in this case renders our functional analysis of this client speculative to an unusual degree. Consequently, the functional analysis should be viewed as an example of how a case formulation is constructed, rather than as a case formulation for this particular client.

We present the case formulation at three levels of specificity. First, we indicate from the basic description global or higher level, less-specific behaviour problems, causal variables and the functional relations between variables. The goal of this first level is to assist the clinician in making decisions about initial treatment foci. Then, two more specific levels of functional analyses expand on a subset of causal variables and relations contained in the first as well give hypotheses for main treatment targets.

The functional analysis has several steps, all of which have the same ultimate goal – to guide initial treatment decisions by allowing the clinician to estimate the relative magnitude of effect of focusing treatment on any of the multiple causal variables involved with her case:

1. It begins with the identification of her behaviour problems and assets. We are particularly attentive to the possibility of multiple behaviour problems because they can have important causal relations with one another. For example, consider the bidirectional causal relations often found between a client's marital distress and depression. Behaviour problems can be excesses or deficits.

2. We then estimate the relative importance of each behaviour problem. In this case, as indicated by some physical symptoms she is experiencing, weight loss is the most important of several identified problems.

3. We look for consequences of the behaviour problems. For example, organ damage or physiological dysfunction for severe and long-term calorie restriction.

4. We next estimate the functional relations among behaviour problems. For example, what are the functional relations between caloric intake and depression, substance use and social isolation?

5. We then identify causal variables associated with each behaviour problem.

6. We then estimate the form and the strength of relationships between the causal variables and the behaviour problem – how powerful are these variables in affecting the behaviour problem? Are the relations unidirectional, bidirectional or correlational?

7. We then estimate chains of causal variables – causal relations and sequences among causal variables that may affect the behaviour problem.
8. We estimate the role of moderator variables – for example, variables that affect the impact of family distress on her eating behaviour.

A list of behaviour problems might include: insufficient caloric intake; slow eating patterns; eating in restricted environments; excessive attention to caloric intake; excessive time spent in food preparation; misperception of eating behaviours; excessive exercise; physical symptoms, such as feeling cold; avoidance of social interaction, especially during and about eating; excessive clothing; dysfunctional thoughts about eating, body and calories; social anxiety and social skills deficits; restricted emotional expression; hyper-reactivity to changes in environment or routine; sadness and anger about her brother; family conflicts and concerns (father, father's wife, brother, mother's partner); and inflexibility in lifestyle. We can note in this list how some of the behaviour problems can also function as causal variables for other behaviour problems.

We also take note of her assets. She has yet to develop severe bulimic behaviours such as purging, laxative use; she does not intend to loose additional weight; she has artistic interests and goals; she performs well academically and has goals for college; and she enjoys reading, movies and TV, and time with her mother.

HISTORY AND CURRENT FACTORS

Historical causal factors could include early experiences with fussy eating or dieting, previous life stressors, such as family conflict and parental divorce; her mother's past history with dieting; and early parent–child interactions around eating. No history of overeating and weight concerns was identified in the case description.

Figures 12.3–12.5 present the visual case formulation models of the A's possible situation. We will use three levels of analyses when describing the case. First, the global level case formulation describes the case on a more general level. It gives a general picture of all relevant variables and their relationships. Second, the treatment focus case formulation describes which causal variables could be the first targets for the treatment. Last, the specific-level case formulation makes a specific analysis of the variables that are the first focus for the treatment.

The Figure 12.3 represents the global or higher level, less-specific case formulation and is based on the most likely variables and functional relations

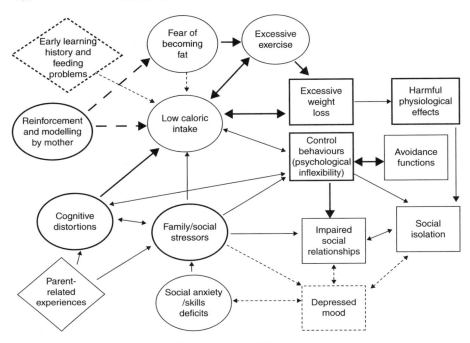

Figure 12.3   Global level case formulation of A's situation.

provided in the case material. It includes also some more tenuous variables, informed by past research, to render the clinical picture understandable. Figure 12.3 illustrates how the FACCM model could be used to create hypotheses for the treatment. It points out possible key interactions to be analyzed and treated more closely. Figure 12.4 is more speculative about a subset of variables from Figure 12.3. The hypotheses can be verified, or not, with more assessment data and as her treatment progresses. The focus in Figure 12.5, presenting the specific-level case formulation, is on the possible cognitive distortions and their relationships to her controlling behaviours as well as relevant familial and contextual situations. Because of insufficient data, we have excluded the more exact calculation using coefficients of modifiability, importance and strength of relations from the models and rely on visual presentation.

Table 12.1 lists some areas where additional assessment data would help clarify and validate our functional analysis. For example, it may turn out that some of these variables have only minor effects although, based on the initial data provided, there are indications that they may be important in the clinical case formulation. We have also noted some other possible causal and moderating variables that may turn out to be important as the data collection continues.

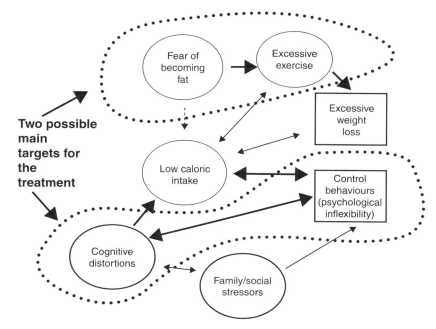

Figure 12.4 Treatment focus case formulation for main treatment targets.

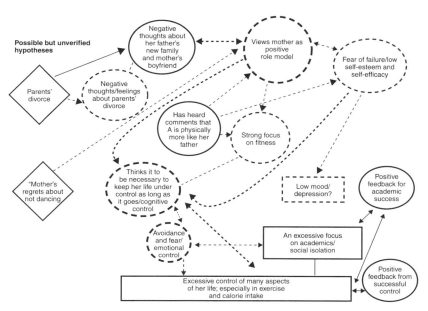

Figure 12.5 Specific-level case formulation that focuses on cognitive distortions and controlling behaviours.

Table 12.1   Additional assessment data that would be useful in testing and developing a FACCM for this case.

Behaviour problems, consequences and assets

1. Harmful physiological effects of chronic caloric restriction

Acrocyanosis, increased cold sensitivity, lower leukocyte counts and lower eosinophils, metabolic abnormalities, electrolyte disturbances, ventricular arrhythmias or major organ damage is possible. A thorough medical evaluation may provide data on these effects. Eating may produce immediate negative effects such as feeling cold, pain or other negative experiences. Additional assessment via an interview or/and by analogue observation involving eating together with the client might be helpful

2. Cognitive distortions

Body image distortion and dislike, distrust of others, lack of insight into own behaviour and its causes, denial of behaviour and health risks, ideas that 'thin is good and rewarded', and expectancies of rejection if not thin. Several questionnaires may provide data on these variables. Also, interviewing the client while she is looking at herself in a mirror will produce more data on her body image

3. Family/social stressors

Research supports significant covariance between life stressors and most causal variables in the FACCM (e.g. obsessive, depressive, distortion, eating, exercise behaviours, some stressors may include within-family conflicts). Data from life-stress questionnaires and daily monitoring of life stressors, mood and thoughts, may provide data on these hypotheses

4. Mother's reinforcement and modelling

Mother's modelling behaviour (e.g. for eating, body image, perfectionism, and controlling behaviours), comments regarding weight, eating patterns, body size, attention to food and eating. Analogue observation of mother–daughter interactions, and semi-structured interviews may provide data on this hypothesis

5. Controlling behaviours

Control associated with eating, weight, physical exercise and social relations may be one of the key issues for maintenance of the problem. This hypothesis is supported both from clinical assessment data and from evidence-based literature

Control often serves avoidance functions? What are the functions?

Controlling eating and excessive physical activity may co-vary (concurrent schedules). Semi-structured interviews may provide data on this hypothesis, as well as behavioural tests (i.e. interrupted time-series interventions) in which the client changes either her physical activity or controlling eating

More data on her checking behaviour would also help clarify aspects of the functional analysis (checking her body from mirrors or windows is needed, as well as if she is totally avoiding mirrors)

6. Social anxiety/skills deficits

Fear of rejection and negative evaluation; poorly developed positive social skills

---

Table 12.1 (*Continued*)

Analogue observation of social interactions, self-monitoring and social anxiety and avoidance questionnaires may help investigate these hypotheses

Hypotheses (not clearly verified), and missing data

Mother may reinforce excessive physical activity (has considered buying a treadmill). Is mother reinforcing other behaviours?

Low self-confidence and self-image. What are her thoughts and feelings about herself? How are they related to eating and other problems?

Problems with learned hunger feelings? Does she report feelings of hunger or desire to eat when seeing food (an extinction process of conditioned anticipatory responses associated with food intake may have occurred)? If this is the case, how relevant is this for the treatment?

Is the client limiting the variety of food items during a meal? Thus, is she affecting the satiety mechanisms with the poor variety?

Is the client misinterpreting bodily sensations (e.g. emotional changes) as feeling overweight? Can this be tested during the session by producing emotional changes?

TREATMENT PLAN

The global functional analysis in Figure 12.3 points out several treatment foci and guidelines for treatment. From this approach to case formulation, treatments are selected that promise to have the maximum magnitude of effect – a function of the relative importance of the behaviour problems, the relative modifiability of causal variables, the relative strength of causal relations and the number of causal paths. The fact that there are several alternatives for treatment is usually an advantage, since there might be practical difficulties arranging or managing treatments or the client may prefer certain alternatives. These issues can be discussed with the client before the treatment is started.

Inspection of Figure 12.3 suggests that treatment foci with the highest expected magnitude of effect would be the modification of cognitive distortions, low calorie intake, control behaviours, such as psychological flexibility, and family or social stressors. Based on the assessment data and additional hypothesized variables and causal relations, these causal variables or behaviour problems lead to several other problems, such as harmful physiological effects, social isolation, impaired social relationships and depressed mood. The magnitude of treatment effects from modifying a causal variable such as 'cognitive distortions' is increased because many problems and effects would be affected.

Further, the functional analysis suggests that the client's low calorie intake, which produces weight loss, is affected by her cognitive distortions, control behaviours and family or social stressors. There is a bidirectional relationship between cognitive distortion and control behaviour as well as between cognitive distortion and family and social stressors, indicating that cognitive distortions could be an initial focus for the treatment, because it has a relatively high estimated magnitude of effect. These possible key targets for treatment are illustrated in the Figure 12.4.

The alternative way to select initial treatment foci is to focus on the variables in the upper part of Figure 12.3 – fear of becoming fat, excessive exercise and low calorie intake. This part of the functional analysis suggests that dealing with the fear of becoming fat may help reduce excessive exercise and low calorie intake. Since low calorie intake and excessive exercise are related, both of these behaviours might change when affecting the other. Taken together, this hypothetical functional analysis suggests that good candidates for the targets for the treatment are cognitive distortions and fear of becoming fat. Figure 12.4 illustrates how the model could be used to focus the treatment on those causal relationships that are expected to have the greatest magnitude of effect.

Figure 12.5 illustrates a more specific FACCM on cognitive distortions. This analysis suggests that behaviours related to cognitive and emotional control would be the main targets for further analysis and treatment. This is in accordance with Fairburn *et al.*'s data that suggest that control seems to be one of the key mechanisms affecting eating disorders. In terms of the functional analysis, we can change cognitive and emotional control associated with eating by changing also other controlling behaviours. This means that, in clinical practice, we may have several different behaviours other than eating that can be the target for the treatment. For example, breaking the rules associated with daily activities at home or at school could be the target for the treatment before dealing with eating. Since this functional analysis suggests that when the client breaks rules she will experience strong emotional reactions, it is possible that compliance for the treatment procedures is better when the client learns to deal with her emotional reactions successfully. Acceptance of aversive emotional reactions when making behaviour changes and increasing psychological flexibility seem to be the key issues for treatment.

THE EVENT

There seems to be no specific event or information in the event that could lead us to change the FACCMs proposed in this text. However, as we have pointed out, such information can be found if we could check directly some hypotheses and test our ideas during an early phase of the treatment process.

It could be possible to test directly the formulation made during the assessment period or early during therapy. Basically, in case formulation and especially in the FACCM, the goal is to collect, summarize and compare existing individual data continuously against case-related situational and historical knowledge as well as research-based evidence. One of the advantages of a behavioural analytic case formulation is that it summarizes the collected information and data in a concrete way. The case formulation makes hypotheses of possible interactions and helps clinicians to pay attention to these interactions also during the session. For example, the therapist could take up the issues of fear of becoming fat (see Figure 12.4) as well as fear of failure and problems of self-esteem (see Figure 12.5). It could be expected that these discussions lead to unpleasant emotional reactions. The therapist could then just carefully pay attention to what happens. The therapist could wait and see if the client is willing to discuss the topics or is she showing some kind of avoidance behaviours or controlling behaviours. Alternatively, the therapists could first (before this discussion is taking place) teach the client to describe her thoughts and emotional reaction using different exercises. For example, there are several exercises in acceptance and commitment therapy (ACT), which would be used such as the observer exercise in which the client is noticing her thoughts and feelings without controlling them. After training of these skills the therapist could take up the issues leading to emotional reactions, and ask the client to use the learned skills and to describe what happens when the therapist is asking these questions. Thus, this kind of behavioural test during the sessions may give rise to an opportunity to confirm or reformulate the case formulation made earlier.

Sometimes new interesting theoretical considerations can lead us to look at things from a different viewpoint even if it would not change the basic FACCM in the case it is carefully constructed. One of these possible theories is acceptance and commitment therapy. ACT is based on the same functional analytic model as the FACCM model. Thus, ACT is easily combined with the analysis model used in this chapter. Experiential exercises challenging and affecting control using ACT offer many productive alternatives for treatment (Hayes and Strosahl, 2004). Working with psychological flexibility, cognitive and emotional control may require more specific analysis of thoughts and emotional reactions related to activities which the client is controlling. Sources of psychological flexibility could be analyzed using the following questions (see Hayes *et al.*, 2004).

What private events (thoughts, feelings, memories and sensations) is the client unwilling to have? Is the client overly attached to beliefs, expectations

Table 12.2   Some limitations to the current case formulation.

- We do not know how or to what degree the mother may be affecting her behaviour, how the eating may co-vary with depressed states, what her social anxieties/skills are, the physiological variables that are important and so on
- The assessment does not conform to recommendations by APA for assessment of anorexia. At the minimum, we would need self-monitoring and ecological momentary assessment strategies (Engel *et al.*, 2005)
- Data on some, possibly relevant, variables that may affect the case formulation may be obtained from the following assessments:
  - Self-report measures of mood/depression – BDI, PANAS (positive and negative affect scale)
  - Family relationship scales (Ronen, 2003)
  - Stressful life events scales, social anxiety/fear of negative evaluation
  - Eating and weight pattern questionnaires – for example, questionnaire of eating and weight patterns (QEWP), three-factor eating questionnaire (TFEQ-18), Dutch eating behaviour questionnaire (DEBQ)
  - Body image evaluation, contour drawing rating scale (Thompson and Gray, 1995)
  - Psychological acceptance and avoidance measurements, acceptance and action questionnaire (AAQ; Hayes and Strosahl, 2004)
  - Analogue observation, mother–daughter interaction (Heyman and Slep, 2004)
  - Time-line follow-back interview (to identify changes and events across time)
  - Biological assessments

and right–wrong, good–bad evaluations? What are they? How are they related to other problem behaviours?

1. Does the client seem preoccupied with the past or future or engage in lifeless storytelling?
2. Is client's identity defined in simplistic, judgemental terms, by problematic content or a particular life story?
3. Does the client see a discrepancy between current behaviours and her values?
4. Can the client change course when her actions are not working?

OTHER ISSUES

We discussed earlier the difficulties in making a valid case formulation on the basis of second-hand information and limited data. However, this situation is common in many clinical settings – clinicians must rely on many different types of data and often they are of the kind that may not be specific enough for valid clinical judgements. In the best case, clinicians collect the type of data necessary for their approach to case formulation. Table 12.2 summarizes the limitations for this case formulation.

SUMMARY

The functional analysis is an approach to clinical case formulation that emphasizes the identification of important and modifiable causal variables. The FACCM is a method to visually summarize the functional analysis and is especially useful in complex cases. The FACCM illustrates how different variables are connected to each other with the emphasis on the functional relations among causal and moderating variables and an individual's behaviour problems. The functional analysis is flexible in that it considers many types of variables including cognitive, behavioural, environmental and physiological variables. The main aim of this chapter has been to give an example how FACCM behavioural analytic case formulation model could be applied in the treatment of eating disorders. We have illustrated how the FACCM could be used to reorganize the available data, and how it then could be used to give ideas for treatment planning. We have used a stepwise three-level analyses model. This model includes global level, treatment focus and specific-level case formulations.

Even though the FACCM, as well as other clinical case formulation models, is based on constructing hypotheses from the actual case situation, it strives for verifiability of the existing assumptions. This leads to process-based orientation to clinical cases and the formulation remains flexible and tentative until the relevant data have been gathered or the treatment is in process, showing the effects of affecting the variables hypothesized in the functional analysis. During the process of case formulation, it is important to continuously check the assumed connections between variables. Eating disorders, and especially Anorexia Nervosa, are clinical problem areas that are complex ones with multiple associated behaviour problems and multiple causal variables. Thus Anorexia Nervosa is well suited to the FACCM model. However, here again the emphasis must be on verifiability of the assumed hypotheses. In the related case description we can see lots of concrete data but also many vague points. We would like to collect additional data in order to possibly identify more relevant connections, for example between the influence of familial conflict and interactions to A's mood and how this in turn effects her behaviour. Further, A's emotional and physiological reactions and thoughts during and before meals might be crucial for the treatment. It may be that some of the assumptions must be abandoned, but certainly there will be many things that help to find new ideas for a suitable treatment package.

A functional analysis model offers many benefits in comparison to traditional diagnostic models. It is more specific and it helps to explain the complex interaction between causal variables as well as between different behavioural problems. Presenting the case formulation model to the client during different phases of the treatment, and taking into account her views connects the client into the assessment process and treatment planning would be helpful. This may facilitate motivation to change old habits and increase motivation to tolerate aversive emotional reactions connected to those changes. For example, the FACCM may give reasons for the client to do difficult homework tasks. It is also important to notice that the FACCM model makes it easier to connect the basic research findings, and theoretical considerations into the clinical practice.

Knowledge of basic mechanisms associated with eating or other disorders could be more effectively used when applying the FACCM model. The visual summary of the case could be based both on available assessment data and on the theoretical knowledge of the disorder. One more benefit in the functional analysis model is that it is contextual. Thus, it takes into account interaction between different contexts, behaviours and causal variables. For example, for an anorexic client emotional reactions associated with eating may be dependent on several factors that also may interact with each other, such as the number of people present during eating or physiological states of the body prior eating.

Especially in complex cases, such as Anorexia Nervosa, understanding complex interactions might be crucial for successful treatment. The FACCM offers a practical tool for doing a complex contextual analysis. Furthermore, for the beginning therapists the model gives an important advantage. It gives more time for the novice therapist to decide treatment goals and what methods could be used in the treatment. As many psychology students in the training have mentioned, '[I]t is good to know that you do not need to know at once what should be done.' It must be remembered that the functional analysis model is, at least partly, a hypothetical model. Thus, it describes hypotheses on the basis of available data. Since in clinical practice the data are often limited or missing, hypothesis made during the assessment process may be too limited or even wrong. The model made at the beginning of the treatment may be misleading. For that reason, it is important to evaluate and to follow that the treatment has those effects as expected.

We expect that in the future the relational frame theory and the new wave cognitive behavioural therapies will affect all case formulation models (Hayes and Strosahl, 2004). For example, we may have new alternatives as to how to describe complex psychological problems such as inappropriate evaluation of body size or rigidly following one's own rules. Accordingly, new treatment alternatives will emerge based on specific individual behavioural analysis.

REFERENCES

American Psychiatric Association (2000) *Diagnostic and Statistical Manual of Mental Disorders. DSM-IV-TR*, 4th edn, text revision, APA, Washington, DC.

Berg, C. and Södersten, P. (1996) Anorexia nervosa, self-starvation and the reward of stress. *Nature Medicine*, **2**, 21–2.

Engel, S.G., Wonderlich, S.A., Crosby, R.D. *et al.* (2005) A study of patients with anorexia nervosa using ecologic momentary assessment. *International Journal of Eating Disorders*, **38**, 335–9.

Epling, W.F. and Pierce, W.D. (1992) *Solving the Anorexia Puzzle: A Scientific Approach*, Hogrefe & Huber, Toronto.

Fairburn, C.G., Cooper, Z. and Shafran, R. (2003) Cognitive behaviour therapy for eating disorders: a "transdiagnostic" theory and treatment. *Behaviour, Research and Therapy*, **41**, 509–28.

First, M.B., Spitzer, R.L., Gibbon, M. and Williams, J.B.W. (1997a) *Structured Clinical Interview for DSM-IV Axis I Disorders (SCID-I). Clinician Version, User's Guide*, American Psychiatric Publishing, Arlington, VA.

First, M.B., Spitzer, R.L., Gibbon, M. and Williams, J.B.W. (1997b) *Structured Clinical Interview for DSM-IV Axis II Personality Disorders (SCID-II), User's Guide*, American Psychiatric Publishing, Arlington, VA.

Garner, D.M. (1997) Psychoeducational principles in treatment, in *Handbook of Treatment for Eating Disorders* (eds D.M. Garner and P.E. Garfinkel), Guilford Press, New York.

Haynes, S.H. and O'Brien, W.H. (1990) Functional analysis in behavior therapy. *Clinical Psychology Review*, **10**, 649–68.

Haynes, S.H. and O'Brien, W.H. (2000) *Principles and Practice of Behavioral Assessment*, Kluwer, New York.

Haynes, S.N. and Williams, A.W. (2003) Clinical case formulation and the design of treatment programs: matching treatment mechanisms and causal relations for behavior problems in a functional analysis. *European Journal of Psychological Assessment*, **19**, 164–74.

Hayes, C.S. and Strosahl, K.D. (eds) (2004) *A Practical Guide to Acceptance and Commitment Therapy*, Springer, New York.

Hayes, C.S., Strosahl, K.D., Luoma, J. *et al.* (2004) ACT case formulation, in *A Practical Guide to Acceptance and Commitment Therapy* (eds C.S. Hayes and K.D. Strosahl), Springer, New York, pp. 59–73.

Hersen, M. (ed.) (2006) *Clinician's Handbook of Child Behavioral Assessment*, Elsevier/Academic Press, Amsterdam.

Heyman, R.E. and Slep, A.M.S. (2004) Analogue behavioral observation, in *Comprehensive Handbook of Psychological Assessment: Vol. 3. Behavioral Assessment* (M. Hersen (ed.), E.M. Heiby and S.N. Haynes (vol. eds)), John Wiley & Sons, Ltd, New York, pp. 162–80.

Lappalainen, R. and Epstein, L.H. (1990) A behavioral economics analysis of food choice in humans. *Appetite*, **14**, 81–93.

Lappalainen, R. and Sjödén, P.-O. (1992) A functional analysis of food habits. *Scandinavian Journal of Nutrition*, **36**, 125–33.

Lappalainen, R. and Tuomisto, T. (2005) Functional behavior analysis of anorexia nervosa: applications to clinical practice. *The Behavior Analyst Today*, **6**, 166–77.

Lappalainen, R., Mennen, L., van Weert, L. and Mykkänen, H. (1993) Drinking water with a meal: a simple method of coping with feelings of hunger, satiety and desire to eat. *European Journal of Clinical Nutrition*, **47**, 815–9.

Mumma, G.H. (2004) Validation of idiosyncratic cognitive schema in cognitive case formulations: an intra-individual idiographic approach. *Psychological Assessment*, **16**, 211–30.

Mumma, G.H. and Smith, J.L. (2001) Cognitive-behavioral interpersonal scenarios: interformulator reliability and convergent validity. *Journal of Psychopathology and Behavioral Assessment*, **23**, 203–21.

Nelson-Gray, R.O. and Paulson, J.F. (2004) Behavioral assessment and the DSM system, in *Comprehensive Handbook of Psychological Assessment: Behavioral Assessment*, vol. **3** (M. Hersen (Series ed.), S.N. Haynes and E.H. Heiby (vol. eds)), John Wiley & Sons, Inc., New York, pp. 470–89.

Rolls, B.J. (1985) Experimental analysis of the effects of variety in a meal on human feeding. *American Journal of Clinical Nutrition*, **42**, 932–9.

Rolls, E.T. (1994) Neural processing related to feeding in primates, in *Appetite: Neural and Behavioural Bases* (eds C.R. Legg and D. Booth), Oxford University Press, Oxford.

Ronen, T. (2003) *Cognitive-Constructivist Psychotherapy with Children and Adolescents*, Kluwer Academic/Plenum Publishers, New York.

Thompson, M.A. and Gray, J.J. (1995) Development and validation of a new body-image assessment scale. *Journal of Personality Assessment*, **64**, 258–69.

Virus-Ortega, J. and Haynes, S.N. (2005) Functional analysis in behavior therapy: behavioral foundations and clinical application. *International Journal of Clinical and Health Psychology*, **5**, 567–87.

13

Commentary on Formulations of Eating Disorders

MYRA COOPER

Our current knowledge of how best to treat patients who present with eating disorders, especially Anorexia Nervosa (AN) is limited, not least because we lack an agreed and effective framework within which to understand the complexities of the disorder. Two ways to conceptualize Antoinette's problems were presented here, outlined respectively by Weerasekera as a multiperspective approach (MPA), and by Lappalainen and colleagues as a functional analytic clinical case model (FACCM). Both offered a framework within which to understand and treat Antoinette's eating problems.

The task of commentator is not to determine which formulation represents the truth, as Burroughs (1981) noted in *Cities of the Red Night*, 'nothing is true', but to compare and contrast, and reach at a preliminary conclusion. I have elected to do this along a number of dimensions, highlighting in particular those that are likely to be clinically relevant.

On first reading, I was struck by the apparent similarity between the two formulations. Clinically, both appeared to focus on similar content including eating behaviour, cognitions and family/systemic factors. Both used similar or overlapping terms, for example cognitive distortions (Lappalainen *et al.*) and distorted body image (Weerasekera). Both appeared relatively complex in that they contained multiple layers, levels or factors many of which were interrelated. Both were keen to indicate a clear preference for an individual or idiographic approach to the patient, and noted that formulation and subsequent treatment should be tailored to the individual patient's unique circumstances. After outlining the case formulation, both recommended the use of cognitive treatment strategies, together with additional techniques, and

Clinical Case Formulation: Varieties of Approaches. Edited by Peter Sturmey.
© 2009 John Wiley & Sons, Ltd.

both emphasized the value of choosing models and strategies based on empirical evidence. Some of the similarities and differences I noticed are discussed below, followed by a brief summary, in which I suggest that contrary to my first impression, the apparent similarities may mask significant differences in orientation. These differences are likely to be linked to different value systems. Thus, it is important for clinicians to be aware of their value systems in their professional practice. These differences between the formulations are also associated with rather different approaches to treatment, including at least two areas of current debate. The similarities will be discussed first.

SIMILARITIES BETWEEN THE TWO FORMULATIONS

Idiographic versus manualized treatment

Idiographic or individualized treatment was emphasized in both case formulations. This has been contrasted unfavourably with manual-based treatment by some researchers interested in eating disorders. Manual-based treatments have a number of advantages in the treatment of eating disorders, and do not necessarily mean that treatment is not individualized, or that a formulation cannot capture the idiosyncratic features of a specific case (Wilson, 1996). However, while we have some good evidence-based manualized treatments for Bulimia Nervosa (BN) (Schmidt and Treasure, 1993), this is not the case for AN. The clinician is often obliged to work at Level 5 in Wilson's (1997) stepped care model, using an 'empirical hypothesis testing approach'. This involves using a set of complex skills to treat a problem where there is no empirically supported treatment. Moreover, even in BN, there is some evidence that individualized approaches, including the development of an individualized formulation, may be more beneficial, than adherence to a standardized protocol (Ghaderi, 2006).

Research

Both formulations made use of evidence from outside the psychotherapy, clinical psychology and the psychiatric field. The FACCM case formulation, for example drew on basic research on food and eating, while the MPA formulation referred to the stress and coping literature. A number of the theoretical constructs and principles referred to, as well as some of the links believed to exist between them, have at least some empirical support. This is particularly true for the cognitive and behavioural constructs and ideas identified, but it also applies to some of those from the psychodynamic and systemic fields which are emphasized in the MPA formulation.

Research on case formulation

In contrast to evidence for the theoretical constructs and ideas, there is little evidence, not only here, but in general, that either case formulation is reliable, clinically valid or related to outcome. The field is a long way from achieving many of the goals that a research programme into clinical case formulation might set out to achieve. See for example, Bieling and Kuyken (2003). This includes establishing 'bottom-up' evidence, or reliability of formulation between individual therapists, demonstration of a relationship between key theoretical constructs and the presenting problems, improved treatment and treatment outcome as well as usefulness.

Cognitive approaches

Treatment guidelines for eating disorders often recommend the use of cognitive behaviour therapy (CBT) (American Psychiatric Association, 2006; National Institute for Clinical Excellence, 2004). However, it is easy to forget that the evidence for a good outcome with CBT is confined to BN (Agras *et al.*, 2000). Moreover, even with the best CBT treatment, many patients still have an eating disorder at the end of treatment, and the longer term outcome remains relatively poor (Cooper, 2005). Perhaps not surprisingly, and particularly given its lack of proven efficacy in relation to AN, the MPP case formulation recommended a cognitive behavioural approach as one of only several possible approaches, while the FACCM formulation preferred a primarily behavioural approach, with work on cognitive distortions embedded and justified within a learning theory framework.

Neurobiological factors

Both formulations included some reference to biological factors, but neither formulation integrated neurobiological findings in any detail. While no specific drug is indicated for AN, the disorder has features, such as anxiety and mood disturbance, that may usefully respond to pharmacological intervention under some circumstances. Both serotonin and dopamine systems have been implicated in eating disorders and drugs targeting these systems continue to be widely employed in practice. Some understanding of how their use might be integrated or explained in relation to psychological aspects would be helpful for the clinician. Research on basic eating and feeding, touched on in the FACCM formulation might be relevant in adding to our understanding of such links.

Sociocultural issues

One significant factor that was not given much attention was cultural issues, both in terms of ethnicity and social class. This is perhaps surprising given the demographic distribution of eating disorders. In the MPA formulation, it was noted that such factors do not in themselves explain the development or persistence of an eating disorder. Nevertheless, many examples of values and attitudes that might be socioculturally based were mentioned in the case formulation, and relatively little attention was paid to their role and significance. A third factor that received little attention is lifespan issues, as outlined for example by Erikson (1950). Both Antoinette and her parents face issues common to others of a similar age and life stage and some discussion of their significance might add to our understanding as well as suggest potential avenues for intervention.

Therapeutic relationship

Both formulations noted the importance of the therapeutic relationship in understanding and working with Antoinette, but both saw this as a means to an end, rather than a vehicle for change in itself. While learning theory has traditionally given less emphasis to the therapeutic relationship, dynamic formulations specifically include it as a key source of information. It is thus perhaps surprising that it did not receive more attention in the FACCM approach. Its relative neglect might be an important omission in both understanding and treatment, particularly in the light of the observation that the therapeutic relationship is often fraught with difficulties in those with AN (Geller, Williams and Srikameswaran, 2001).

DIFFERENCES BETWEEN THE FORMULATIONS

The similarities in the two formulations are balanced by a number of differences, including in presentation and level of detail, but also in values and orientation. These are considered below.

Representation of the formulation

The relationships between symptoms in the FACCM formulation were represented mathematically in a vector diagram with arrows and lines indicating the strength, direction and form of the relationships between problems and their causes. Visual representation is often very useful for the client as well as for the therapist, and while no equivalent diagram was provided for the MPA formulation it would be relatively easy to represent the relationships it hypothesizes schematically and visually. However, the FACCM diagram has the advantage that weights can be allocated to indicate the strength and likely modifiability of any links, although the information to do this was not provided here. This identifies the goals that are likely to be easier to achieve. Thus, it provided a ready focus for initial intervention. However, the representation might be considered unduly complex and unwieldy for use in everyday clinical practice, although it may provide a useful basis for the development of theory and research. The reliability and validity of any relative weights was also unclear.

Detail and specificity

The level of detail in the functional analytic case formulation (FACCF) approach is striking. Problems were analyzed into smaller parts, as illustrated by the discussion of how dysfunctional eating patterns might be maintained. See also Lappalainen and Tuomisto (2005). This identified very specific targets for intervention, for example breaking the rules associated with daily activities in order to learn strategies for dealing with strong emotional reactions.

The MPA approach, in contrast, suggested certain approaches or techniques rather than specific targets. For example, it suggests use of a behavioural re-feeding programme, but did not identify the components that this might involve. Such programmes are, of course, widely used, thus those wishing to proceed will find relevant examples in many clinical settings. One of the more sensitive applications of such a programme is outlined by Duker and Slade (2002).

Scientist–practitioner model

The emphasis on research suggests that both would endorse the 'scientist–practitioner' model, the idea proposed more than 50 years ago by the Boulder conference (Raimy, 1950) that clinicians should be trained as both scientists and practitioners. Both apply scientist–practitioner principles to the process of developing and testing out the formulation. However, while in the MPA case formulation this was stated as a general principle, in the FACCM model it constituted an iterative and recursive process that formed an integral part of the assessment and formulation process. This was demonstrated, for example in how self-monitoring a range of different behaviours, thoughts and feelings before, during and after eating might yield data that can then be used to alter the focus of the intervention.

Assessment

The FACCM formulation placed great emphasis on assessment, particularly using multi-modal strategies and the use of data to refine and develop the formulation. A range of very detailed methods of acquiring this data were suggested. It also emphasized the importance of checking the formulation against the data. The scientific method was thus an inherent part of the process of constructing the formulation. This contrasts with the MPA formulation where the scientific method was used primarily to choose the relevant constructs and links to be included in the final formulation.

Integration and eclecticism versus theoretical purism

Unlike the FACCF formulation, the multi-systemic formulation drew on several theories including cognitive, systemic, psychodynamic and learning theories. For example, the importance of an 'enmeshed, hostile, intrusive' family environment was noted, which may be associated with negative comments about a daughter's weight and appearance, and which may then 'teach' specific eating disorder behaviours. In contrast, the FACCM took learning theory as its main framework, and transformed Antoinette's symptoms into a series of learned behaviours. In this way, family and parent-related factors were expressed in specific patterns of reinforcement and modelling. This gave a continuity in the causal chain that is absent in MPA, where the story moves between concepts taken from different theories. While the FACCM formulation has the advantage of requiring proficiency in only one theory and language, in practice many clinicians appear to find a single theoretical framework too constraining, including in eating disorders, where most employ an integrative approach (von Ransen and Robinson, 2006). As with cognitive approaches, which the FACCM formulation subsumes within broadly defined learning theory, this approach also has limited empirical support, including as an effective treatment.

Historical roots

The MPA formulation was organized within a traditional psychiatric framework that involves predisposing, precipitating, perpetuating and protective factors (Gelder, Harrison and Cowen, 2006). As such it formulates the diagnosis of AN together with making and formulating a further diagnosis of obsessive–compulsive personality disorder. In contrast, the FACCM approach explicitly eschewed diagnosis and focused on the specific behaviour problems that Antoinette was described as having when assessed. The FACCM specifically noted that the use of diagnosis is often uninformative when making practical decisions about treatment, while the MPA case formulation, in contrast, works closely with diagnosis, including both Axis 1 and 2 disorders (APA, 1994).

The two formulations are associated with not only theoretical divisions but also, in broad terms, with discipline boundaries, notably the medical versus the non-medical. Clinicians often, perhaps understandably, prefer to practise what they were trained in, and this is also true in the eating disorder field (von Ransen and Robinson, 2006). Thus those trained in a medical, diagnostic and psychiatric tradition might identify more readily with, and possibly also prefer to work with, the MPA case formulation, while those with a non-medical background might identify with and prefer the FACCM focus on specific behaviours.

Philosophical stance

There is a philosophical divide between the two approaches. The MPA case formulation made both a structural and functional analysis of Antoinette's problem. It identified causes such as 'poor identity formation' and 'perfectionism' and the presence of an obsessive–compulsive personality disorder. These suggested structures or entities that exist beyond what can be observed. At the same time, however, the function of what can be seen was also noted, for example that some of Antoinette's symptoms are reinforced by her parents' behaviour. The MPA formulation thus reflected both structural and functional approaches to psychopathology, perhaps inevitably, given that it draws on most of the main theories that have been used to understand eating disorders in recent years, and which themselves have different philosophical roots. The FACCM, as its name implies, was functional in orientation, and made little use of abstract structures to explain Antoinette's symptoms. It focused primarily on more observable behaviour, including the antecedents, consequences and moderators of the symptoms reported, and how each affects the other.

TREATMENT

Of particular interest is exactly what one does having formulated the problems. While there was considerable overlap in the specific methods recommended, there was also significant divergence. Two areas of current debate will be considered.

Sequencing of interventions

A particular concern in treating those with eating disorders, especially those with AN, is what should form the initial focus of treatment. The MPA formulation proposed initial focus on weight gain, beginning of menses and improvement in quality of life. The FACCM suggested focusing on cognitive distortions and fear of becoming fat/excessive exercise. While these may not necessarily be mutually exclusive, in that weight gain might be achieved by focus on cognitive distortions, the MPA formulation suggested that a behavioural re-feeding programme should precede any cognitive intervention. Many clinicians will be familiar with this dilemma in planning treatment for those with eating disorders. A common belief in approaching AN is that psychological treatment cannot be useful until a minimum weight gain has been achieved. While not explicitly ruling this out, the MPA formulation and proposed treatment plan were consistent with this view. In contrast, the FACCM might be viewed as more compatible with the view that psychological treatment should commence early on, and that weight gain is unlikely without it.

Cognitive treatment – new developments

The interventions suggested by the FACCM approach were, in general, rather more cognitive, for example aimed at acceptance of emotional reactions and increasing psychological flexibility. They also reflected recent developments in cognitive therapy that incorporate experiential strategies, as, for example in acceptance and commitment therapy (Hayes and Strohsal, 2005), and developments in AN that seek to decrease rigidity in thinking, as for example in cognitive remediation therapy (Davies and Tchanturia, 2005), or indeed those suggested for altering the patient's relationship to her thoughts using detached mindfulness, as described for BN (Cooper, Todd and Wells, 2008). In contrast, the MPA approach suggested a more traditional, tried and tested CBT and for which, in BN, if not AN, and as noted above, there is some empirical evidence of efficacy.

CONCLUSIONS

Formulations can be evaluated on a number of dimensions, the most crucial being whether or not they result in a successful outcome for the patient. As suggested above, the role of commentator is not to judge which formulation is best. The field is a long way from being able to answer the question of what is best by most, if not all, criteria that might be considered relevant. In practice, given our lack of certainty in relation to AN, and eating disorders more generally, it is likely that the important message is that it is vital to remain open-minded when formulating cases like those described here. Both formulations outlined here will thus be useful heuristics for clinicians, both for those who are less experienced and knowledgeable about eating disorders, but also for those seeking to work with very complex cases using some of the more innovative techniques that are currently being developed for this group. Such guidance is currently lacking in the literature.

REFERENCES

Agras, W.S., Walsh, T., Fairburn, C.G. *et al.* (2000) A multicentre comparison of cognitive behavioural therapy and interpersonal psychotherapy for bulimia nervosa. *Archives of General Psychiatry*, **57**, 459–66.

American Psychiatric Association (1994) *Diagnostic and Statistical Manual of Mental Disorders*, 4th edn revised, American Psychiatric Association, Washington, DC.

American Psychiatric Association (2006) *Practice Guidelines for the Treatment of Patients with Eating Disorders*, 3rd edn, American Psychiatric Association, Washington, DC.

Bieling, P.J. and Kuyken, W. (2003) Is cognitive case formulation science or science fiction? *Clinical Psychology: Science and Practice*, **10**, 52–69.

Burroughs, W.S. (1981) *Cities of the Red Night*, Henry Holt, New York.

Cooper, M.J. (2005) Cognitive theory in anorexia nervosa and bulimia nervosa: progress, development and future directions. *Clinical Psychology Review*, **25**, 511–31.

Cooper, M.J., Todd, G. and Wells, A. (2008) *Cognitive Therapy for Bulimia Nervosa*, Taylor & Francis, London.

Davies, H. and Tchanturia, K. (2005) Cognitive remediation therapy as an intervention for acute Anorexia Nervosa: a case report. *European Review of Eating Disorders*, **13**, 311–6.

Duker, M. and Slade, R. (2002) *Anorexia Nervosa and Bulimia: How to Help*, Open University Press, Milton Keynes.

Erikson, E. (1950) *Childhood and Society*, Norton, New York.

Gelder, M., Harrison, P. and Cowen, P. (2006) *Shorter Oxford Textbook of Psychiatry*, 5th edn, Oxford University Press, Oxford.

Geller, J., Williams, K.D. and Srikameswaran, S. (2001) Clinician stance in the treatment of chronic eating disorders. *European Eating Disorders Review*, **9**, 365–73.

Ghaderi, A. (2006) Does individualisation matter? A randomised trial of standardised (focused) versus individualised (broad) cognitive behaviour therapy for bulimia nervosa. *Behaviour, Research and Therapy*, **44**, 273–88.

Hayes, S.C. and Strohsal, K.D. (2005) *A Practical Guide to Acceptance and Commitment Therapy*, Springer, New York.

Lappalainen, R. and Tuomisto, M.T. (2005) Functional analysis of anorexia nervosa: applications to clinical practice. *The Behaviour Analyst Today*, **6**, 166–77.

National Institute for Clinical Excellence (2004) *Core Interventions in the Treatment and Management of Anorexia Nervosa, Bulimia Nervosa and Related Eating Disorders*, National Institute for Clinical Excellence, London.

Raimy, V. (1950) *Training in Clinical Psychology* (by the staff of the conference on graduate education in clinical psychology, Boulder, Colorado, August 1949), Prentice Hall, New York.

Schmidt, U. and Treasure, J. (1993) *Getting Better Bit(e) by Bit(e)*, Psychology Press, Hove, East Sussex.

von Ransen, K.M. and Robinson, K.E. (2006) Who is providing what type of psychotherapy to eating disorder clients? A survey. *International Journal of Eating Disorders*, **39**, 27–34.

Wilson, G.T. (1996) Manual-based treatments: the clinical application of research findings. *Behaviour, Research and Therapy*, **34**, 295–314.

Wilson, G.T. (1997) Treatment manuals in clinical practice. *Behaviour, Research and Therapy*, **35**, 205–10.

PART V

Older Adults

14

A Case of Problematic Behaviour in an Older Adult

HELEN DEVRIES

PRESENTING COMPLAINT

Mrs Lewis was referred for evaluation by the manager of her seniors-only apartment complex. The reason for the referral was the manager's frustration with the condition of Mrs Lewis's apartment. The manager indicated that Mrs Lewis collected 'junk' and refused to get rid of any of the stuff that was cluttering her apartment. The apartment complex consisted of government-subsidized housing for low-income seniors and was subject to periodic inspections by the staff of the government agency. The apartment manager was anticipating an inspection in the next few months and was upset with Mrs Lewis for letting her apartment become so cluttered. All attempts by the apartment manager to encourage or help Mrs Lewis clear out the clutter had been resisted. As a last resort, the apartment manager referred her to a neighbourhood community older adult centre that, in addition to case management and educational/social services, provides psychological services. The apartment manager asked that Mrs Lewis be evaluated to determine if her cognitive functioning had deteriorated so much that she was no longer able to maintain her apartment or live independently. If the evaluation indicates that Mrs Lewis's cognitive functioning is within normal range, the manager will request assistance to motivate Mrs Lewis to clean out her apartment.

Clinical Case Formulation: Varieties of Approaches. Edited by Peter Sturmey.
© 2009 John Wiley & Sons, Ltd.

CLIENT DEMOGRAPHIC DATA

Mrs Lewis was a 76-year-old Caucasian female. She was divorced and had two surviving daughters who lived several hours away. Her only son had died approximately 20 years ago in an automobile accident. Mrs Lewis had a high school education and had worked in retail sales for many years. She had an income of less than $20,000 per year and relied on subsidized housing to enable her to live independently. She owned a car and was able to drive locally during daylight. She currently volunteered in many activities, including childcare at her church and sales at a local resale shop run by her church to raise funds for the community centre. Her health was good, although she did report some problems with joint pain.

CLIENT DEMEANOUR AND PERSONAL APPEARANCE

Mrs Lewis appeared clean and neatly dressed, although her clothing looked worn and outdated. She wore no make-up and her hair was clean but not particularly well styled. She spoke in a very soft voice, kept her eyes down, only briefly made eye contact and conveyed an almost child-like demeanour. Her diminutive stature and deferential self-presentation combined to convey an impression of timidity and meekness. She had adequate social skills, was appropriate in her speech and affect, and gave no evidence of delusions or hallucinations. She seemed eager to please, was cooperative about answering questions, but tended to be tangential and indirect in her responses to direct questions.

CLIENT CURRENT LIFESTYLE

Mrs Lewis lived alone in a one-bedroom apartment in a complex consisting of all government-subsidized units for low-income older adults. The complex housed over 350 seniors. She volunteered at her church by providing childcare during church functions and activities. She also volunteered at a resale shop run by the church to benefit the community centre. She participated in several of the activities offered through the older adult programme at the neighbourhood community centre, including their monthly 'lunch and learn' series, an exercise class and a healthy behaviours class.

Despite her involvement in multiple activities, she had no close friends. Mrs Lewis never invited anyone to her apartment for a social visit and did not seem to have any social interaction with neighbours in her building, except through her participation in planned activities at the senior centre. When she attended activities at the community centre, staff members had observed that she tended to assume the role of 'helper,' by offering to set up or clean up or by serving others. She tended to remain on the fringes of social interactions with other seniors, preferring to serve as a kind of junior staff person rather than as a guest or a participant. She was pleasant, courteous and cooperative, but she rarely joined in conversations with the other seniors who participated in the programmes. Rather, she kept getting up from the table to bring more food or drink to the others at the table, cleared away plates or cups, cleaned up any spills and generally sought to take care of everyone. This behaviour prevented her from engaging in conversation with others. When she was at the table, she tended to be very quiet and only spoke when someone addressed her directly.

The apartment manager reported that Mrs Lewis had never developed any close relationships with other residents during her years of living in the complex. She seemed to have little interaction with neighbours in the building other than polite interchanges at the mailboxes or in the halls. She had never had any negative or hostile interactions with neighbours, but neither had she developed any friendships or informal relationships with them, despite having lived in the complex for over 10 years. Over the years, she had always been quiet and non-intrusive, seeming to prefer to keep to herself. Other than her volunteer activities, she spent her time quite alone, according to the apartment manager.

At her church, Mrs Lewis kept very busy and attended many functions, but often worked behind the scenes in the kitchen or nursery, and did not join in the actual activities as a participant. Despite her frequent attendance at church functions, she had no informal social relationships with any of the church members outside the planned activities or the helper role. She attended a weekly Bible study, but seemed to be a passive listener who did not enter into the discussions. She indicated that she preferred to be in the role of volunteer or helper and that she was uncomfortable initiating informal conversations or relationships with peers. She found it less stressful and more comfortable if she carried out a defined task that gave her a function and reason for being there. This lack of informal social relationships with peers seemed consistent across many settings. She seemed to prefer staying in the background rather than joining in as an active participant. She did not appear to have a negative impact on others. Rather, she seemed almost invisible to others.

Mrs Lewis had very little contact with her two adult daughters who both lived several hours away. She described her daughters as very busy and indicated that she did not want to bother them with her concerns. One of the daughters called her once every week or two to check on Mrs Lewis, but rarely visited. The other daughter's husband had significant health problems, and this daughter rarely called or visited her mother. Mrs Lewis had no contact with her former husband, and neither did her daughters.

CLIENT HISTORY

Following the referral for evaluation, Mrs Lewis was contacted and agreed to come to the senior centre for an initial intake and screening. She drove herself to the centre for the intake evaluation, was on time, and found the office with no difficulty. During the intake assessment, the psychologist completed a clinical interview to gather developmental and psychosocial history. In addition, Mrs Lewis was given the *Mini Mental State Examination*, Trails A & B, and the *Geriatric Depression Scale*. Scores on these screening measures were within normal limits. Mrs Lewis was oriented, had good attention/concentration and evidenced no language or memory difficulties. She clearly understood the reason for the referral, acknowledged that the accumulation of clutter in her apartment was an ongoing problem and understood that she was in danger of being evicted if the situation did not improve. Mrs Lewis reported the following developmental history in a matter-of-fact tone with little to no affect being expressed.

Mrs Lewis's mother died during an influenza outbreak when Mrs Lewis was 6 years old. Her 3-year-old brother also died during the epidemic. Her father remarried within a year, and his new wife had two young daughters from a previous marriage who came with her into the new household. Eventually, Mrs Lewis's father and his new wife had a child of their own. Mrs Lewis reported that she was excited about the new baby and wanted to help take care of her. Despite her efforts to be helpful and cause no trouble, the family situation was not harmonious. At the age of 8, she was sent to live with her grandmother. Mrs Lewis reported feeling very close to her grandmother and said that she liked living with her. This arrangement continued for several years, but things changed when Mrs Lewis was about 11, when her grandmother became ill and died rather suddenly.

After her grandmother's death, Mrs Lewis was sent, as a 'special student', to live at a local orphanage that was run by her uncle. While there, she was assigned several 'jobs' to help pay for her room and board, including helping with the laundry and meal preparation. She lived there until finishing high school, at which time she was on her own. She had almost no contact with her father during those years, except for brief visits at holidays. When asked why her father did not maintain better contact with her, she replied that she was a difficult child and that her father had his hands full caring for the new family. When asked what she meant by being 'difficult', Mrs Lewis indicated that she liked to go off on her own without telling anyone where she was and that this caused her caregivers to become upset. She never disappeared for long – a few hours at most – but they always seemed angry with her when she returned and would take away privileges as punishment. She also said that she would sometimes say rude things or ask too many questions. She noted that she had learned to be more kind and polite as she got older so as not to upset people.

After completing high school and leaving the institution where she had been living, Mrs Lewis found lodging in a boarding house for women. She said that she liked school and had done well, but there was no support for her to go on for further education or special job training. She got a job in a factory where she met her future husband. They eventually married and, after their daughter was born, moved to their own home in a suburban area. She described those years as happy for her and her family. She loved being a mother and enjoyed raising her three children. She stated that she considered her husband to be a good provider. She described her marriage as a partnership, with her husband providing security and financial stability and with her providing the child and home care. When her children were in junior high school, she began to work part-time in retail clothing sales. When she was in her early 50s, her son was killed in an auto accident. A year or two later, her husband told her that he wanted a divorce. He told Mrs Lewis that he had been having an affair with another woman for many years and wanted a divorce so that he could marry this woman. The divorce was devastating for her. She was taken completely by surprise and noted how foolish she felt for not being aware of his plans to leave the marriage. The divorce also imposed significant financial constraints. She could not afford to keep the house and it had to be sold. Mrs Lewis also had to sell or give away much of her furniture and household goods when she moved into a small apartment. Both daughters had moved out of state by then, so she had to handle most of this alone since she did not want to bother them with her problems. She reported that all of this happened very rapidly and abruptly with little time for her to adjust to the new situation or make alternate living arrangements.

The financial constraints imposed by the divorce required that Mrs Lewis find full time work. She eventually found a job with K-Mart, which she held for many years until the store closed and she lost her job. By then she was in her mid-60s and was unable to find a new job. The loss of income forced her to find a more affordable apartment and, at that time, she moved into her current apartment in a government-subsidized complex for low-income seniors. This apartment was quite tiny, and once again required her to get rid of some of her household belongings before moving in.

She reported that she finds it difficult to keep the apartment organized since it is so tiny and has so little storage space. In addition, she stated that her busy schedule of volunteering makes it difficult to find time to sort through things to clear out the clutter. She spends little time in the apartment during the day and keeps busy volunteering at church and the resale shop. Mrs Lewis acknowledged that things had gotten quite cluttered and out of control and that she found it impossible to make decisions about what to keep and what to throw away. When asked how she had managed in the past, she said that over the past 10 years, her daughters had visited periodically to help her sort through things. These visits tended to involve little socialization since the majority of their time together was spent clearing away much of the clutter that had accumulated since their last visit. Mrs Lewis indicated that she found the process upsetting since her daughters were in a rush to get rid of things and she worried that they may have inadvertently discarded something of value. In response to their mother's concerns and agitation when they tried to help clear away the accumulated clutter, the daughters decided to rent a storage unit where they could put her belongings. Mrs Lewis appeared to have accepted this solution, although she was not totally confident that all of her stuff made it to the storage unit and worried that the daughters were still throwing away many of her things. Over the years, the daughters have filled two storage units. The current build-up of the clutter in her apartment that prompted the referral by the apartment manager had happened because her daughters were too busy with their own life situations to make their usual visits to remove the accumulated clutter and take it to the storage unit.

CLIENT GOALS

After the intake assessment and psychosocial history were completed, an appointment was set to visit Mrs Lewis in her apartment. The purpose of the home visit was to assess the status of the apartment and to help Mrs Lewis consider options regarding how to deal with the situation.

The home visit revealed that the situation was even worse than had been anticipated. There were no uncluttered surfaces in the entire apartment. No furniture was visible since it was all buried under piles of papers, clothes, books and other objects. The psychologist could not tell what kind of furniture was in the apartment since all the furniture was covered with piles of stuff. There was a narrow path from the front door to the patio slider doors with just enough room between the waist high piles to squeeze through. At the patio door, there was one recliner chair that was available for sitting with no other seats visible under the stuff that was piled everywhere. The open counter looking into the kitchen was piled high and the view into the kitchen revealed that the counter tops and stove were also piled high with junk mail, old newspapers, magazines and books. The bedroom was inaccessible and seemed equally buried under piles of clutter. The implication was that Mrs Lewis never slept in her bed since it, too, was presumably covered with piles of paper, books and clothes. To conduct the assessment, the psychologist had to sit on the floor next to the one available chair by the patio door where Mrs Lewis sat. There were absolutely no other places to sit or walk.

When asked about how things had gotten to this point and how she might want to proceed given the threat of eviction if she did not clear the clutter, Mrs Lewis became agitated. She acknowledged that the clutter was a problem, but indicated that she did not want to be rushed in sorting through things because she might throw away something of value. On further questioning regarding where much of the stuff had come from, Mrs Lewis stated that she did not like it when the resale shop where she volunteered discarded donations and so would often take things home until she could find someone who might need them. She felt that she needed to sort through the discarded books or clothes so that she could decide who to donate them to. In particular, she felt strongly that the children's programme at her church should take the books or she should give the clothes to a needy family. Once these items got into her apartment, however, she did not give them away. In addition, there were piles of junk mail dating back months. When asked if perhaps she could start by throwing away some of these piles of mail, she became quite distressed, stating that she could not be rushed through the sorting process. Mrs Lewis indicated that she wanted to bring order to her apartment and that she was hoping that her daughters would soon be able to come and help her with this as they had done in the past.

After completing the home visit, the psychologist asked Mrs Lewis if she might want help with the cleaning up task since she was at risk for eviction if she did not make some improvements in the apartment immediately. She said that would be okay. The goal was to establish a behavioural change plan with targeted goals and rewards to encourage and maintain her efforts at cleaning out the clutter. The plan called for an initial approach of setting time limits to work on the sorting and throwing away of the 'junk' mail that was piled in the kitchen. Mrs Lewis agreed that she could spend half an hour every morning sorting through the old mail. As a reward for spending half an hour per day on this plan, she would treat herself at the end of the week to a latte and muffin from the Starbucks in the neighbourhood, a rare treat for her.

After several attempts to implement this plan, it became clear that Mrs Lewis was not responding well and the clutter was continuing to accumulate. She eliminated only a very few pieces of the junk mail and worked so slowly that it became clear that half an hour a day would not be enough time to make any difference. She felt she had to go through every piece, no matter how long it had been there, to be sure she did not miss a coupon or an important message. In the meantime, new junk mail was arriving and piling up at a faster rate than she was eliminating the old. An emergency call to the daughters resulted in one of them coming and spending several days hauling away most of the stuff to the storage unit. It was not a pleasant visit, and Mrs Lewis reported feeling embarrassed and ashamed that she could not do better at managing to keep things neat.

AN EVENT

Following her daughter's visit, the psychologist met with Mrs Lewis to review the situation and check in to see how she was feeling. Mrs Lewis indicated that she was worried that her daughter had not taken everything to the storage unit but, instead, had thrown much of it into dumpsters. She indicated that she was worried that important papers were mixed in with the junk and that she would lose these important papers or objects. When the psychologist asked whether she had ever lost important things in the past, Mrs Lewis began to talk about some of the major losses in her life, especially the death of her mother and grandmother, the death of her son and her divorce. For the first time, she evidenced emotion and began to cry. She apologized for being emotional and seemed embarrassed to be crying. She stated that she should act like an adult and not be such a baby. She did not like to have people feel sorry for her or to think she was only thinking about herself. When asked why she felt this way, she said that people were supposed to focus on helping others and not be selfish or demanding of attention. The psychologist asked if she would like to meet to talk more about her concerns and worries. Mrs Lewis agreed that she would like to do that.

15

A Cognitive Analytic Formulation

MARK DUNN

THEORETICAL ORIENTATION AND RATIONALE

The cognitive analytic therapy (CAT) model was originated and developed by Dr Anthony Ryle, Consultant Psychotherapist at St Thomas's Hospital, London, UK and Emeritus Fellow at Kings College Medical School, London (Ryle and Kerr, 2002). He originally trained as a medical doctor as well as in both cognitive and analytic models of psychotherapeutic intervention. He worked as an NHS General Practitioner and then in the Student Medical Centre at Sussex University. His interest lay in integrating different models of therapy and in finding a common language for the practice of psychotherapy. Over time he researched and wrote papers on the integration of cognitive theory, personal construct psychology, British object relations school of psychodynamic theory and the dialogical theories of Russian psychologists Vygotsky and Bahktin. Ryle employed primarily the language of cognitive psychology; analytic theory and concepts are restated in that language. Ryle integrated theories through restatement; practices are integrated pragmatically both generally and specifically depending on the case. This has resulted in the integrative model of theory and practice known as CAT. CAT continues to be open to further integration and development as Ryle and others work to build more bridges to different models as psychotherapy research in general moves forward.

CAT operates from the belief that human relations and individual consciousness are dialogic. In the Cartesian assumptions of cognitive psychology,

Clinical Case Formulation: Varieties of Approaches. Edited by Peter Sturmey.
© 2009 John Wiley & Sons, Ltd.

the centre of experience and action is in the head of the individual. In a dialogical view, the self and the processes of consciousness came into being and operate at the interface between self and others and higher order others such as 'culture'. The self-to-self relation is an internalized form of the ongoing dialogue between self, other and higher order forms of the other. The relational nature of dialogue and dialogic positions is seen as more important than the locus of consciousness. From 'I think therefore I am' to 'we communicate therefore we are.'

From birth and before, babies are treated as having minds and they are communicated with on that basis. Babies are born into relationship, into relational communication, into a dialogue of complex signalling both verbal and non-verbal that is cultural and language based. The brain has evolved to produce the mind. The mind is what the brain does, but it does it in dialogue with other minds. If we would have been raised by wolves we would have the mind, language and culture of wolves. As modern cognitive research shows, the mind is made up of complex, combinatorial, computational routines or structures (Pinker, 1998). We develop these innate structures in dialogue with other human minds and thereby acquire a repertoire of thoughts, feelings and actions in relation to situations and other people. These are backed up by the complex subroutines of cognitions, emotions, reflexes, perception and processing preferences, memories and so on that inform and shape how we think, feel and act. CAT describes these as *procedures*, like steps in a recipe. Procedures are considered to be either adaptive and in tune with the situation and relationship or maladaptive and out of tune with them and in need of adaptive adjustment or tuning. Procedures that are adaptive in childhood may cease to be so in the new situations and relationship we meet in adult life.

The concept of the 'self' in CAT is also dialogic. The representation of the self to the self by others in dialogue results in the acquisition of a 'self' concept, the coming into being of a self-conscious 'I' – 'Oh! They're talking to me; they're talking about me.' Language allows a relationship between the 'I' and the 'me'; it allows self-reflection to become possible and for the self to dialogue with the self. As this skill develops, the mind is able to have intrapersonal relations with the self and inter-personal relations with others. We become able to take up positions in relation to others and we experience people taking up positions towards us; we can influence and be influenced by others. We can also take up positions towards ourselves and try to influence ourselves in various ways (for better and for worse). CAT calls these positionings *roles* or *voices* and proposes that we acquire a repertoire of role positionings as we are growing up. The extent and flexibility of our repertoire has a direct impact on the extent and flexibility of our functioning in the world. The role positionings are the place from which we experience and voice our thoughts, feelings and behaviours; shifting roles shifts these correlates. A role combines both the relational position and the correlates. This is an important concept particularly when things go wrong or are not working well for a person or a relationship. Therapy depends on the clear description and understanding of the role positions or voices and the procedures (thoughts, feelings and behaviours) that they produce.

CAT and case formulation

Case formulation in CAT is seen as a dialogic and collaborative process between patient and therapist seeking out and describing accurately the procedures and role positions that the patient gets into, that do not work, and have brought about the need to seek help. When these descriptions are agreed, then patient and therapist negotiate about what can or should be made the focus of change. From this a plan can be made and goals set for the therapy.

Relevant and irrelevant variables

In CAT nothing would be excluded in consideration of a case formulation. The mind–body system of the individual is understood as being in relation to many other systems including other peoples' mind–body systems, group and social systems and geographical and physical systems. CAT includes the remembered mind systems of others not present, that is others who are dead, lost or otherwise absent. These may also include spiritual and transpersonal belief systems as well as phantasmagorical and delusional systems about minds generally.

Traditionally, CAT pays most attention to the patient's roles and procedures in terms of his or her beliefs, thoughts, feelings and actions. Recently increasing attention is being paid to information from the body. CAT allows information from other involved people with the patient's permission. That said, the main focus of a case formulation is formed by the conclusions the patient has drawn from his or her life, in particular his or her early life experience, his or her conclusions from history. Then, together, patient and therapist look at what role positions the patient takes up and what procedures are enacted in relation to his or her present life situation. During sessions with the patient the therapist pays careful attention to the interactions between patient, therapist and other involved persons as a main source of direct information about roles and procedures.

CAT pays less attention to the search for psychoanalytic information. CAT sorts and sifts historical psychoanalytic information for what is seen to be germane to the patient's problem. It does not ignore what seem to be meaningful communications from the patient, of which the patient is not aware. Nor does CAT ignore the implications of certain kinds of interactions and responses that appear to be defending against important or painful realizations in the patient. Such information is noted and discussed, but is not seen as paramount or the key to transformation. Self-sabotage is seen as a typical procedure to be described and understood. The patient who responds with 'yes, but. . .' is not resisting, but may be not yet aware of what he or she is afraid of, or, for example not yet aware of a core negative belief preventing motivation or investment. Analytic situational descriptors such as 'oedipal triangle' are avoided and restated as role positionings.

CAT avoids reaching too swiftly for behavioural solutions or a premature solution focus. People are understood to be relational, so for any treatment to be effective it must be in the context of a therapeutic relationship with the therapist. This takes time to develop as the patient has to experience the therapist refraining from enacting harmful or painful roles and procedures in relation to the patient, that is not stumbling into blindly re-enacting the patient's early history with him or her or painfully imposing anodyne or demanding procedures on him or her ('Don't worry, be happy,' 'Pull yourself together. . .' and so on).

ROLE OF RESEARCH AND CLINICAL EXPERIENCE

Research into CAT has been patchy. There have been some studies of CAT in the United Kingdom and elsewhere with specific patient groups which have shown CAT to be positively effective (Brockman *et al.*, 1987; Dunn *et al.*, 1997; Fosbury *et al.*, 1997; Pollock, 2001; Treasure *et al.*, 1995).

CAT was developed in the UK National Health Service for the NHS. In the NHS, resources for psychotherapy treatment are rare and limited. In the equation of time and money, CAT was developed to provide a time-limited amount of structured input to the maximum number of patients per pound, so most get 16 sessions plus follow-up. Research into CAT is mostly on this 16-session model. However, with the success of General Practitioner counselling, many cases sent to specialist psychotherapy treatment in the NHS have diagnoses of personality disorder, most commonly borderline and narcissistic personality disorders. Much of the research into CAT involves multiple and single case studies and is of the treatment of personality disorders which tend to be given a longer input of 24 sessions and extended follow-up (Ryle and Marlowe, 1995; Pollock, 1996; Golynkina and Ryle, 1999; Sheard *et al.*, 2000).

The uptake of CAT in the NHS by psychologists, therapists, psychiatrists and social workers has been strong. Repeated practice by full-time staff in CAT-style case formulation has been shown to develop a breadth of clinical experience and intuition that serves patients well. To a certain extent, CAT sees people as somewhat homogeneous as a result of living in a homogeneous culture. Common patterns of roles and procedures occur again and again in clinical practice. CAT uses this fact to cut short the formulation process through questionnaires, such as the *Psychotherapy File*, which lists commonly recurring patterns and roles. CAT takes the approach of off-the-peg tailoring and then shortens or lengthens the sleeves of the formulation rather than the bespoke-tailored formulations of longer and more intensive therapies.

THE FORMULATION

The practice of CAT is to take ample time to develop the formulation. The basis of the treatment is the collaboration of the patient and the therapist on constructing the story of the patient's history, problems and underlying patterns of roles and procedures. The teaming up allows the patient to have ownership of the formulation, particularly where services have given the patient diagnostic labels rather than real help. This ownership creates motivation towards change. The formulation is jointly constructed in dialogue and the process is given at least the first four sessions of the therapy contract.

Information is gathered from a variety of sources: self-report, diary keeping, questionnaires of different sorts, autobiographies and dreams. The therapist synthesizes all of this information and provides a written account of it with her conclusions as to what it all means. This is called a *Reformulation* because it restates whatever formulation the patient has brought to therapy. The therapist may also provide a *Sequential Diagrammatic Reformulation* (SDR) in which the roles and procedures are described in a flow chart or map form showing more clearly how one role leads procedurally to another. The SDR is developed over the first four or so sessions of the therapy. The therapist creates diagrams of the procedures and roles under discussion in the sessions on paper or on a white board. The client is encouraged to join in the process so that the SDR is jointly created. The diagram is road tested between sessions and edited until an agreed accurate diagram is reached. It should describe the client's main roles and procedures and as the therapy progresses exits that are found to work are added. The contribution of the client is vital in giving them ownership of the diagram. The diagram works in the same way as a road or city map in that it helps with orientation and direction finding and helps us to stay out of dangerous and difficult areas that we might otherwise wander into. The aim is that the client should become his or her own map reader rather than simply stopping to ask the therapist for directions when he or she gets lost.

Considering the present case: of Mrs Lewis, the reformulation might be something as follows:

Dear Mrs Lewis,

You have come to therapy seeking help with a problem where you live. You have been collecting all kinds of things and filling up your living space so that your building supervisor is concerned for the health and safety of you and others. Apart from this, you do not see yourself as having any real problems. However, when you speak about your life story and the losses you have suffered you become upset and agree that it would be good to talk more about your life.

When you were a child those closest to you and with whom you were most emotionally involved sadly died: your mother, brother and grandmother. Your father also distanced himself from you. When he remarried, your new stepmother and her daughters did not want to become close to you or let you get involved with the new baby and you were sent away to your grandmother. When she died you were sent to your Uncle's orphanage where you had to work to stay there. This sounds in some ways like the fairy tale of Cinderella. However, you did go to the ball and married your Prince and raised two children. But that too ended in tragedy and loss. Your son was killed in a car crash and your husband betrayed you and left you for another woman. Through all of these tragic events you have always tried to do your best, to be a useful contributor to your community and to responsibly work and look after yourself. In retirement, you have continued to persevere and be useful, keeping busy in the charity shop and looking after other elderly people. However, this has led to a problem; you have started to hang on to all kinds of things because they might be valuable and you feel you cannot risk throwing away things that might be just what someone needs. How has this come about?

My sense is that the experience of these losses in your early childhood was so painful to you that you decided, perhaps without knowing it, to keep your distance from others. This was reinforced by your stepfamily who pushed you out. I imagine it was hard for you to feel like you had any right to belong in any family or any right to have your needs for nurture, protection and support met. It seems that you worked out a strategy to stay attached to others by being useful and helpful without the pain and danger of being emotionally truly involved with them. You had a successful marriage, but this was based upon a clear division of tasks – your emotional needs were suppressed. In addition, when you were a child, whenever you asserted your needs, your opinions or your independence, for example going off for a walk on your own, your parents would get upset and punish you. In the end they rejected and abandoned you. They treated you as if you were of no worth at all and could be just thrown away. So you learned it was best not to assert your needs but to try to please them by serving and being useful, to join in and be present, to be submissive and make no demands so as not to be thrown away. Sadly this strategy does not work so well in adult life and did not stop you being thrown away by your husband.

As a result, you are left with the problem of being unable to decide what things are really worth so you hang onto everything. It is as if you hang on to things just in case something may turn out to be the glass slipper that will magically transform your life, and also because it is the way you can stay attached to people and not be thrown away through your useful recycling role. The result, however, is that your building supervisor now wants to throw you out!

As your tears bear witness, the answer to this problem lies in the direction of sharing your painful story with others and in grieving the losses and longings that are woven into the fabric of your life. In this process, hopefully you will come to realize that you have worth and a right to take your place as an equal with others, not just as a servant. This implies that you have a right to reach for emotional relationship through sharing and the mutual meeting of needs. You need to experiment with building trust through sharing while at the same time watching out for and defending yourself against harm. Communicating effectively and sharing feelings with others will enable you to stay on track and to let others help you know what is valuable and what is not; that things may be thrown away but not people.

Can I propose the following list of targets for our work together expressed as 'I' statements?

1. Avoidance of real emotional connections with others:
   'I don't know how to take my rightful place with others and to share with others.'
2. Submissiveness and placation:
   'I don't know how to stand up for myself. It is as if others are always more important than me. I fear displeasing others and being rejected.'
3. Anxious hoarding:
   'I don't know how to correctly value things. I don't trust myself to judge what is worth keeping and what should be thrown out.'

In this client's case, the diagram (see Figure 15.1) centres on the box describing her main role labelled 'Cinderella'. On this role of placation and

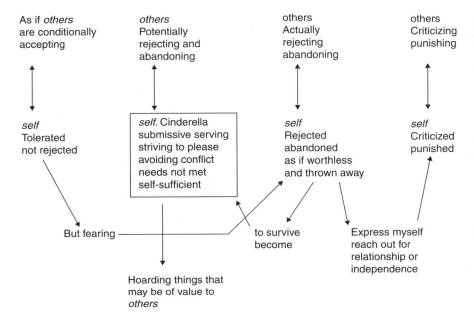

Figure 15.1   Sequential diagrammatic reformulation – SDR for clinical case.

submission depends her 'hoarding' procedure. To the left of the box is described the result of her role in that she is tolerated and not rejected. To the right are described the two outcomes she fears based on her historical experience – rejection and abandonment and criticism and punishment – and shows how these lead back to reinforcing her 'Cinderella' behaviour. Along the top of the diagram are described the ways in which she experienced others and expects them to behave towards her. As therapy progresses, we would expect to add an exit strategy from the lower right corner – express and reach out – whereby with the therapist's support she would find that her feared response of criticism and punishment does not in fact happen.

HISTORY

In CAT formulation the patient's history is of primary importance. What a patient believes and how he or she thinks, feels and behaves is based upon beliefs he or she has learned and thoughts and feelings which have given rise to habitual behaviours in relation to the dialogical processes of socialized learning. The patient's history describes clear patterns of traumatic loss – the death of her mother, younger brother, grandmother and her own son – as well as patterns of abandonment by her father, her stepfamily, her husband and to some extent her daughters and employers. The patient had to adapt to survive this history. Her adaptive behaviours include ways of being with others based on usefulness, submissiveness and making no demands. The adaptations were effective in as much as she had a marriage and children and was able to keep in work. The survival adaptation worked and she survived, but it is hard to conclude that she thrived. On the occasions when she expressed her own nature and personal desires, such as going independently for long walks, she was punished and so adapted further by suppressing her own needs and natural ways of being.

Without an understanding of the history the temptation is to treat the symptoms. It is reported in the case material that a behavioural reward regime designed to encourage throwing things away was not successful. The symptoms in this case prove all too symbolic of the patient's struggle to understand and establish her worth, the worth of things and people around her and the meaning and worth of emotional involvements with others. This struggle can only be understood in the context of her history.

CURRENT FACTORS

The current factors in the patient's story provide a clear picture of the roles and procedures she is caught up in and the ways in which they are ineffective and self-sabotaging. The significant information in this regard would include (a) her personal presentation is clean, neat, submissive, deferential, timid, meek; (b) her responses are tangential, indirect, speaking only when spoken to, passively listening, uncomfortable initiating conversation or relationship, emotionally neutral; and (c) her behaviour is eager to please, cooperative, serving and caretaking, invisible or in the background, present but absent. It is also significant that she is judged to have adequate social skills and is not delusional. She is not in a fantasy world of her own, active in a self-to-self way, or cut-off due to lack of inter-personal skills. Indeed, she would not have been able to hold down the jobs that she did working in retail sales if she were delusional or socially unskilled. She succeeded in retail sales because her adaptive responses fit well in that type of work, serving the needs of both customers and managers. Similarly, one can speculate that her marriage worked for the same reasons. The status quo division of roles allowed her to be an effective wife and mother.

Most significant of the current factors is the presenting problem of hoarding which appears to result from her inability to work out the worth of things. CAT looks for the meaning of behaviour both literal and symbolic. In this case both meanings are important. Hoarding and recycling gives her a valuable role in the community, one in which she can be useful to others. The hoarding is also symbolic of her own personal pain at being so thrown away and abandoned, so it becomes impossible to repeat the painful act and to throw anything away herself. She is ashamed of how untidy her flat is as a result and knows that she has a problem. She says that she should not cry and that adults do not cry. She does not want anyone to feel sorry for her or to think her selfish. All of these observations of her current attitudes give further support to the formulation of self-sufficiency due to loss and abandonment.

TREATMENT PLAN

CAT has been developed to follow a standard treatment plan. This consists of the following five phases. (1) Sessions 1–4: assessment phase: gathering information, establishing relationship. (2) Session 4 or 5: reformulation: sharing and redrafting as necessary the descriptions of roles and procedures causing the problems in written and map forms. (3) Sessions 5–14: recognition and revision: developing awareness of procedures and roles in action in real life and in the treatment room, developing alternative roles and procedures, designing and carrying through experiments with new roles and procedures to create change and produce new information. (4) Sessions 15–16: ending: understanding what has been accomplished and what is still to be achieved, appreciating the ups and downs of the therapeutic relationship, goodbye letters exchanged summarizing the experience. (5) Follow-up 8–12 weeks later: reporting back on progress or relapse, negotiating further therapeutic input.

For this patient, the treatment plan begins with the joint production of and negotiated agreement to the reformulation. The agreed descriptions have clear implications for what might be targeted for change in the remaining therapy sessions. In this case, three are proposed and would have to be agreed between the therapist and client. They are (a) avoidance of emotional connection, (b) submissiveness and placation and (c) anxious hoarding. The patient would be encouraged to recognize the enactment of these with the help of her SDR. Before revision is attempted, recognition must be clear and automatic. In this case, she must be able to clearly recognize when and in what way she acts submissively and then needs to work on reducing the submissive behaviour before being encouraged to act assertively, or she is likely to become frightened and resist. The menu-driven nature of CAT does not mean that other matters arising cannot be looked at; indeed there may be hidden stumbling blocks and sabotage strategies that are revealed and need dealing with. However, focusing on the agreed menu means that real changes have to be attempted rather than just going on adding detail to the overall picture and producing ever greater clarity.

Avoidance of real emotional connections and submissiveness and placation are seen to be common neurotic procedures in CAT. The behaviours that emanate from these strategies can vary in many ways and are the most obvious features of the client's presentation. In this case, the hoarding was the presenting problem and understanding its meaning is key. Hoarding of this kind is not a common presenting problem compared to drug or drink addiction, anxiety and depression and for the treatment to fit the client the hoarding has to be accurately understood for it to become possible to stop doing it. Similarly the general themes of avoidance and placation have to be nailed down to their specific variations in each case for change to be possible. Exactly what is being avoided and when; exactly who is being placated and why.

Regarding her three targets

Avoidance of real emotional connections

The therapeutic relationship is key here. A real connection established between therapist and patient can act as a template for attempting deeper connections with people at her church and social centre. Feeling valued and validated, or understood, by the therapist should enable her to open up to others, to share her feelings and needs and perhaps even a little of her life story with others.

Submissiveness and placation

The aim here would be to plan simple experiments that elicit new information and provide a platform for new interpretation. For example, 'What happens when you are not immediately helpful? Do people reject and abandon you?', 'What small thing can you risk asking someone to do for you?' or 'What happens when you say no to someone?' These are all scary experiments after a lifetime of placatory behaviour, but should be manageable with the therapist's support.

Anxious hoarding

The aim here is not to clear out and throw things away but to find ways of understanding the true value of things. Inside herself she cannot work out a template for judging whether to keep or discard objects so she hangs on to everything. The other solution for her would be to throw away everything. The best strategy might be to suggest that she consult those she can connect to at church or in her social group to develop a sense of consensual value about things, to let others help her work it out. By entering the social group properly she gets the benefit of consensual reality that will in turn allow her to check and limit extreme behaviour. Being valued herself for herself, rather than for her servant role, should contribute to the reorganizing of her value system because her role will have changed. With this the problem behaviour should lessen. A new role, procedure and behaviour have been learned and will in time replace it.

THE EVENT

The meeting with the psychologist is important as it seems to be the first point at which anyone has addressed her history of losses. Simply asking the question whether she had lost important things in the past resulted in an opening up, a connecting and an emotional outpouring. This is the beginning of therapy. By asking the right question, the psychologist demonstrates her trustworthiness and the possibility of real emotional connection and relationship. The patient's responses then include real information about her 'rule book' for relationships which confirm the formulation and the treatment plan.

OTHER ISSUES

There are no other issues.

SUMMARY

This is a 76-year-old divorced woman living in social housing in conflict with her apartment manager for filling her living space completely with junk. She has a long history of traumatic losses from childhood onwards including the death of her mother, brother and grandmother, abandonment by her father and stepfamily, and in adult life, the death of her son and the betrayal and divorce by her husband. She has adapted to these circumstances by becoming self-sufficient and emotionally self-contained, submissive and placatory, perseverant and useful to others, but with an inability to understand the value of objects both human and material, including her own worth, the worth of others and the worth of everyday things. As a result, she holds on to things of marginal value for whatever potential worth they may have. Having been effectively thrown away herself by others in her life she cannot bear to throw anything away. In asking the patient about her and about her losses, she demonstrates an access to feelings and a willingness to engage with others to work towards change.

REFERENCES

Dunn, M., Golynkina, K., Ryle, A. and Watson, J.P. (1997) A repeat audit of the cognitive analytic clinic at Guy's Hospital. *Psychiatric Bulletin*, **21**, 1–4.

Brockman, B., Poynton, A., Ryle, A. and Watson, J.P. (1987) Effectiveness of time-limited therapy carried out by trainees; a comparison of two methods. *British Journal of Psychiatry*, **151**, 602–9.

Fosbury, J.A., Bosley, C.M., Ryle, A. *et al.* (1997) A trial of cognitive analytic therapy in poorly controlled Type 1 patients. *Diabetes Care*, **20**, 959–64.

Golynkina, K. and Ryle, A. (1999) The identification and characteristics of the partially dissociated states of patients with borderline personality disorder. *British Journal of Medical Psychology*, **72**, 429–45.

Pinker, S. (1998) *How the Mind Works*, Allen Lane, The Penguin Press, London.

Pollock, P.H. (1996) Clinical issues in the cognitive analytic therapy of sexually abused women who commit violent offences against their partners. *British Journal of Medical Psychology*, **69**, 117–27.

Pollock, P.H. (2001) Clinical outcomes for adult survivors using CAT, in *Cognitive Analytic Therapy for Adult Survivors of Childhood Abuse* (ed. P.H. Pollock), John Wiley & Sons, Ltd, Chichester, pp. 231–8.

Ryle, A. and Kerr, I.B. (2002) *Introducing Cognitive Analytic Therapy*, John Wiley & Sons, Ltd, Chichester.

Ryle, A. and Marlowe, M.J. (1995) Cognitive analytic therapy of borderline personality disorder: theory and practice and the clinical and research uses of the self states sequential diagram. *International Journal of Short-Term Psychotherapy*, **10**, 21–34.

Sheard, T., Evans, J., Cash, D. *et al.* (2000) A CAT derived one to three session intervention for repeated deliberate self-harm: a description of the model and initial experience of trainee psychiatrists in using it. *British Journal of Medical Psychology*, **73**, 179–96.

Treasure, J., Todd, G., Brolley, M. *et al.* (1995) A pilot study of a randomised trial of cognitive analytic therapy for adult anorexia nervosa. *Behaviour, Research and Therapy*, **33**, 363–7.

16

The Core Conflictual Relationship Theme: A Psychodynamic Formulation of the Case of Mrs Lewis

MARNA S. BARRETT

THEORETICAL ORIENTATION AND RATIONALE

What is the core conflictual relationship theme?

The core conflictual relationship theme (CCRT) provides psychotherapy with a sound measure for study of the central relationship pattern in psychotherapy sessions. The main principle of the CCRT method is that repetition across relationship narratives provides a good assessment of the central relationship pattern. Furthermore, the CCRT reflects an underlying schema of a person's knowledge about how to conduct relationship interactions that is partly conscious and partly unconscious.

From a theoretical perspective, each of the assumptions of the CCRT method is consistent with an object relations perspective on interpersonal and intrapersonal conflicts. In other words, conflicts with others and with self are defined by early patterns of relating. Moreover, the CCRT offers an operational measure of the transference as conceived by Freud (1912/1958).

The CCRT first came about from Luborsky's (Luborsky and Crits-Christoph, 1998) inferences about a central relationship pattern: (1) the relationship pattern of patients focuses on narratives about wishes and responses in relationships with others and self; and (2) the central relationship

Clinical Case Formulation: Varieties of Approaches. Edited by Peter Sturmey.
© 2009 John Wiley & Sons, Ltd.

pattern was best defined by the combination of the most frequent wishes, the responses from others and the responses of the self across relationship episodes. Thus, he viewed the CCRT as a complex interaction of wishes and responses, in combination with the pervasiveness of each of these components. For instance, a patient described an interaction with a co-worker in which the following exchange was reported:

> In fact a girl called me crazy today. And I wanted to cry. I wanted to tell her I think you need to go see a psychiatrist yourself. . . and sometimes people do act crazy. I told her I wasn't ashamed of it.

This relationship episode includes wishes (to be assertive, to retaliate and to be accepted), the response of others (criticize) and the response of the patient (angry, hurt and ashamed). By examining several relationship exchanges between the patient and different people, patterns emerge such that the therapist can recognize the central theme that defines relationship conflicts for the patient.

In using the CCRT method to guide clinical case formulations, four basic assumptions are made. First, the segment of the session to be examined is the narrative about relationship episodes. The narrative includes wishes, the response from other people and/or the response of self. Second, the CCRT can be reliably obtained from the identified relationship episodes. A third assumption is that the CCRT is pervasive; that is, the same wishes, and responses from others and self are repeated in a number of relationship episodes. Finally, the CCRT is a central pattern that is evident across a variety of relationship interactions.

Supportive–expressive psychotherapy (SE) is a form of psychodynamic psychotherapy that focuses on the interpersonal and intrapsychic conflicts representing the CCRT (Luborsky, 1984; Luborsky and Crits-Christoph, 1990, 1998). The CCRT serves as a springboard for the therapist's interventions throughout treatment and is unique to each patient. In this way, the CCRT is utilized to address the patient's idiosyncratic way of relating. In regard to depression, the CCRT is used to address two important dimensions emphasized by psychoanalytic and cognitive theorists (Blatt et al., 1982; Beck, 1983). In anaclitic (Blatt) or sociotropic (Beck) depression, the patient wants to be connected and nurtured but feels abandoned by others and empty. In introjective (Blatt) or autonomous (Beck) depression, the patient wishes to be perfect or flawless, experiences others as punishing, leading to feelings of guilt and self-criticism and a desire to take revenge. Thus, in SE therapy, the therapist addresses the sense of loss, helplessness and inability to live up to the expectations of self or others.

The CCRT is not only applicable to depression but also enables SE therapists to treat patients with a variety of conflicts and disorders. By uncovering the patients' conflictual relationship patterns as manifested in current and past relationships as well as in the therapeutic relationship, the conflicts contributing to distress are brought to light and worked through. Exploring these conflicts helps the patient develop better ways of defending and coping with feelings, expressing one's needs and responding to others. This expressive work is done within a supportive environment where the development and maintenance of a positive therapeutic alliance is considered crucial to treatment effectiveness. The SE model assumes that gains in self-understanding about the CCRT and subsequent change in the CCRT mediate symptom improvement.

RELEVANT AND IRRELEVANT VARIABLES

Narratives about relationship episodes, or interpersonal stories, are routinely told in psychotherapy sessions and remain consistent over the course of treatment and across different relationships (Luborsky and Barrett, 2006). Thus, using these relationship episodes to examine repetitive patterns of interpersonal dynamics, the CCRT can be established. There are eight major categories into which each of the responses of self (RS), responses of others (RO) and wishes (W) have been established. These categories include the following and are the most relevant variables in developing a case conceptualization from the CCRT perspective.

1. *(RS) In relationships, I am* helpful; unreceptive; respected and accepted; oppositional and hurt others; self-controlled and self-confident; helpless; disappointed and depressed; anxious and ashamed.
2. *(RO) In relationships, others respond to me as* strong; controlling; being upset; bad and not trustworthy; rejecting and opposing; helpful; liking me and understanding.
3. *(W) In relationships, I wish* to assert myself and be independent; to oppose, hurt and control others; to be controlled, hurt and not responsible; to be distant and avoid conflicts; to be close and accepting; to be loved and understood; to feel good and comfortable; to achieve and help others.

In regard to the present case, there are several relationships episodes that are highly relevant for determining the CCRT. These episodes include Mrs Lewis's interactions with the apartment manager, members of her church, her daughters, her father and uncle, and her mother and grandmother. Although not central to development of the CCRT, Mrs Lewis's family history is of significance in understanding the possible origins of her repetitive patterns of relating. At age 6 years, she experienced the loss of her mother and younger brother which was closely followed by rejection and punishment from her father and stepmother. She was forced to move in with her grandmother with whom she developed a close relationship. However, at age 11 years her grandmother died, she was again rejected by her father, forced to move in with an uncle, and disregarded.

Mrs Lewis was again traumatized by loss in the death of her son at around age 50 years. Shortly thereafter she was devastated by the dissolution of her marriage (loss and rejection). As a result of the divorce, she faced significant financial losses, was forced to move, and had to relinquish many of her personal possessions. She seemed to recover from these losses only to again experience a loss (unemployment) that resulted in financial hardship, a forced change in living situation and loss of her loved possessions.

From a CCRT perspective, variables of less or no relevance to the case formulation are the factors that are not a part of relationship interactions. For instance, Mrs Lewis's involvement in church activities, the conditions of her living situation or the behavioural change plan are relatively unimportant to the development of the CCRT unless narratives of relationship episodes occurring within these settings were presented. It is the pattern of relating rather than context that holds most importance.

ROLE OF RESEARCH AND CLINICAL EXPERIENCE

Clinical experience informed the development of the CCRT model, but research has sustained it as a way to understand patient problems within the context of interpersonal relationships and as a viable approach to therapy. For instance, SE psychotherapy has demonstrated a positive treatment outcome in general clinical populations (Crits-Christoph and Connolly, 1988) as well as in patients with chronic and non-chronic depression (Luborsky et al., 1996), generalized anxiety disorder (Crits-Christoph et al., 1996) and depression (Crits-Christoph, Mark and Gibbons, 2002).

Whereas reductions in distress or other measures of symptomatic improvement indicate a beneficial outcome in any form of therapy, treatment benefits in SE psychotherapy can also be identified through changes in the CCRT. For example, benefits can be evidenced by (1) changes in the CCRT patterns (Luborsky and Crits-Christoph, 1998), (2) reductions in the pervasiveness of CCRT components (Cierpka et al., 1998), (3) increases in the accuracy of interpretation (Crits-Christoph, Cooper and Luborsky, 1998) and (4) mastery of the central relationship patterns, for example emotional self-control and intellectual self-understanding (Grenyer and Luborsky, 1996). More specifically, CCRT narratives from relationship episodes outside of therapy have shown significant similarity and consistency with CCRT narratives occurring in early psychotherapy sessions (Barber *et al.*, 1995). Additionally, the pervasiveness of CCRT narratives (i.e. frequency across relationship episodes) has demonstrated consistency throughout psychotherapy, with the Wish component most consistent (Luborsky and Crits-Christoph, 1998).

In terms of symptom severity, greater pervasiveness of CCRT components in narratives has been associated with greater psychiatric severity (Cierpka *et al.*, 1998), such that greater distress was associated with fewer positive responses of self (see Luborsky and Crits-Christoph, 1998). In line with a psychodynamic understanding of psychological distress in relationships with others, researchers (De Roten *et al.*, 2004; Luborsky and Crits-Christoph, 1990) have found significant associations between the defences and defensive functioning of individuals and their CCRT.

THE FORMULATION

Core conflictual relationship theme

There are two main phases in developing a CCRT: (1) identify the relationship episodes, and (2) extract the CCRT from the relationship episodes. Although the most usual source of relationship episodes is psychotherapy sessions, they can be inferred from a clinical case presentation. Across narratives, each relationship episode (RE) describes an interaction between the patient and a main other person. It is the therapist's job to determine the main other person and the boundaries of the episode (i.e. where an RE begins and ends). Because the case example of Mrs Lewis does not include verbatim reports of interpersonal exchanges, REs will, by necessity, be inferred. Moreover, although each RE is typically examined independently, development of the CCRT is done with knowledge of the other narratives in the context of the session. Again, these connections will be inferred from the case presented. Having noted each RE, the CCRT components (i.e. wishes (W), response of others (RO) and response of self (RS)) can be identified and a CCRT established.

CASE FORMULATION

The case of Mrs Lewis is quite complicated in that she is likely suffering from a schizoid personality disorder as well as an underlying depression and obsessive–compulsive disorder. From the age of 6 years, Mrs Lewis repeatedly experienced the loss of individuals close to her (mother, grandmother, brother). Although she does not say how she reacted to these losses, it is likely Mrs Lewis felt abandoned and alone. In response, she tried to please and do what was right but was rejected and disregarded (father and uncle). In an effort to explain her father's rejection, Mrs Lewis described times when she would say rude things or wander off without telling anyone where she was going.

On the one hand, such behaviour could be interpreted as evidence of anger and a way of distancing one's self from others to protect against further loss. Her later pattern of focusing solely on helping others without emotional connection would therefore represent an attempt to avoid feelings of guilt and loss. On the other hand, however, Mrs Lewis did not relate any awareness of how distraught a parent might feel in such a situation nor did she offer any explanation except to say that she tried to be kind and polite. Moreover, because of the long-standing nature of this behaviour and its pervasiveness across all social situations (e.g. church, neighbourhood, work and family), it more likely reflects a detached, emotionally withdrawn interpersonal pattern. Indeed, her life has been predominated by emotionally distant relationships. Mrs Lewis was described as being socially active, yet on the fringe of social interactions. She was uncomfortable and rarely participated in conversations, had no close friends, did not engage socially with her neighbours and was seen by others as timid, quiet, eager to please and cooperative. Furthermore, she willingly seemed to accept a physically and emotionally distant relationship with her daughters and reported little socialization when they came to visit. From this perspective, her desire to help others might represent a deflection or projection of her desire not to need help from others, as is evident in her telling the therapist she does not want others to feel sorry for her.

Complicating the picture, Mrs Lewis also seems to be suffering from obsessive–compulsive disorder (OCD) as indicated by her hoarding of papers, items and collectables in response to fears of losing something important. From a psychodynamic perspective, it is likely that her OCD developed after repeated interpersonal interactions in which she experienced a loss (mother, brother, grandmother, marriage), was rejected by others (father, husband) and then forced to give up her material possessions (move with her grandmother and uncle into smaller apartments), which resulted in a loss of stability in her life.

Although Mrs Lewis has functioned quite well with an emotionally distant interpersonal pattern, it belies her underlying fears of abandonment, loss and depression brought on by repeated traumatic loss. In an effort to defend against the anxiety and fear associated with future loss, Mrs Lewis has sought control in the only way she could – through hoarding of her possessions. Only when she is able to explore these interpersonal patterns and develop better ways of coping with her feelings will she form more satisfying relationships and resolve her depressive and compulsive behaviour.

HISTORY

Because of the focus on patterns of relating, history is particularly important in formulating a CCRT conceptualization. Furthermore, research has supported the consistency of CCRTs over the lifespan and across relationships. For example, the CCRT of children has been found to be relatively constant from ages 3–5 years (Luborsky *et al.*, 1995) as well as relatively stable across ages 14–18 years (Waldinger *et al.*, 2002). Consistent with Freud's (1912/1958) observation that the transference template tends to be a general pattern across multiple relationships; fairly similar patterns have been found within narratives across relationships with different people. For instance, in a sample of 35 patients the CCRT for the relationship with the therapist was significantly similar to the CCRT with other people (Fried, Crits-Christoph and Luborsky, 1992).

In regard to Mrs Lewis, one can only infer the possible components of REs with her family since there are no specific interactions presented. Throughout her life, others were consistently rejecting (father, husband), angry (father, stepmother), distant and hurtful (RO). Although she was quite uncertain about their responses, she felt guilty and tried to be helpful (father, uncle and husband; RS). Her efforts were a result of her desire not to be hurt, to be distant from others and to be good (W). These early patterns of relating are evident later in her life in the ways she relates to her daughters, fellow church members, her neighbours and the therapist.

CURRENT FACTORS

In addition to examining relationship patterns in the historical context, current factors are equally important as they provide evidence of the repetitive nature of CCRTs within current REs. For example, in her interactions with the apartment manager, Mrs Lewis was ashamed and embarrassed (RS). The response of the manager was to become frustrated and upset (RO), yet all Mrs Lewis wanted was to be good, helped and respected (W). In her interactions with members of her church she was helpful but unreceptive to their friendship (RS). The church members responded with distance (RO), yet again, all

Mrs Lewis desired was to help others and feel good about herself (W). Similar patterns of relating are evident in her relationships with residents in her apartment complex and members of her community centre.

In contrast to these interpersonal patterns, Mrs Lewis interacted with her daughters in a number of different ways. For example, when she needed to clean out her apartment, Mrs Lewis was anxious, helpless and dependent on her daughters. However, when her daughters were helping her go through her things and throw items away, she responded to their efforts with anger and disappointment (RS). In response to her helplessness and dependency, the daughters seemed to distance themselves and resist her requests for help. However, when they finally did agree to help her clean, they sought to control the situation by deciding what stayed and what was discarded, and, not surprisingly, were seen by Mrs Lewis as unhelpful and not understanding (RO). She wanted her daughters to help her organize things, but also wanted to be respected and not have conflicts (W).

TREATMENT PLAN

Regardless of the diagnosis, SE psychotherapy focuses on developing an understanding of the distressing symptoms in the context of interpersonal and intrapsychic conflicts. In regard to Mrs Lewis's schizoid interpersonal pattern and underlying depression, SE would specifically address issues of helplessness and hopelessness, dealing with loss, anger and poor capacity to recognize her emotional distance. Because the CCRT is a complex formulation, it is unusual for the therapist to present the entire CCRT in one interpretation. Instead, the following guidelines can be useful in deciding how to present the CCRT in small bits so that the patient builds up a concept of the main pattern and attends to the mastery of the problems within it. Facilitating this gradual awareness of the core conflictual pattern gives the therapist considerable flexibility in adapting the treatment plan to the individual patient.

1. *Begin with the aspects of the CCRT that the patient is most readily able to handle.* Typically, patients are better able to handle those aspects of the CCRT that are most familiar or occur most frequently across REs. It is also important to choose interpretations involving the Wish and the Response of Other, as there is more empirical support for the use of these components in interpretations (Crits-Christoph *et al.*, 1998). Therefore, given the frequency and familiarity with which Mrs Lewis presents interpersonal loss, an SE therapist would likely focus on loss

as the first part of the CCRT (a decision confirmed by Mrs Lewis's response to the therapist's query about repeated losses in her life). In particular, the therapist would help Mrs Lewis explore her reactions and feelings to these losses. For instance, she felt devastated, angry and helpless when faced with sudden loss. After allowing Mrs Lewis to fully explore her reactions, the therapist would then help her examine the ways in which others responded to her. For example, in response to her absence, Mrs Lewis was punished by her father and stepmother. Her efforts to repair the relationship and feel loved and cared for were met with anger, rejection and a forced move.

2. *Include the presenting symptoms in some interpretations.* By including some of the patient's symptoms, the person can begin to get an idea about the context in which the symptom appears. In treatment with Mrs Lewis, the therapist could summarize several interactions in the single statement, 'You want to be loved and cared for but feel rejected and so become distant and depressed.' Or, in the case of her hoarding, a therapist might interpret her behaviour in the following way: 'You want to feel loved and in control of your life but are so fearful of losing someone or something that you hang on to material possessions and remain distant from others.'

3. *Significant emotional reactions often accompany negative interpersonal exchanges.* Because attention to negative emotional reactions can advance treatment, it is especially helpful to concentrate interpretations on negative CCRT components. It should be noted, however, that attention to emotionally charged interpersonal episodes risk potential ruptures in the therapeutic alliance that may hinder the progress of treatment.

   In regard to Mrs Lewis's situation, there are two negative interpersonal patterns that involve significant emotional reaction. First, Mrs Lewis has experienced a life predominated by loss and feelings of abandonment. Although she initially sought comfort and support from those individuals that remained, she was often dismissed and rejected leaving her with greater feelings of despair, anxiety and fear. Second, Mrs Lewis responded to the repeated episodes of rejection from others by withdrawing and isolating herself only to perpetually undermine her desire for closeness and love. These exchanges leave her with intense feelings of loss and hurt. Addressing either of these negative interpersonal exchanges within a caring supportive environment can help Mrs Lewis to more fully understand the origins of her relationship patterns and experience the care that she so long has sought but been unable to obtain.

4. *Choose a style of interpretation that strengthens the alliance and does not provoke resistance.* Because of the intense emotional reactions typically associated with CCRTs, developing awareness of CCRT patterns must

be done in a supportive therapeutic environment. For example, Wachtel (1993) has suggested that any tinge of a blaming, confrontational manner in providing interpretations may stimulate resistance. In contrast, presenting interpretations in a way that demonstrates interest, attention and collaboration is likely to enhance the alliance and increase acceptance. One example of this balance between alliance building and resistance can be seen in the interaction between the therapist and Mrs Lewis at her home. In response to the therapist's direct questioning about how things had become so cluttered and what she wanted to do given the threat of eviction, Mrs Lewis becomes quite agitated and insists that she not be rushed into sorting things. Later in the conversation, she again resists the therapist's suggestions to throw away old mail, becomes distressed and states that she does not want to be rushed. In each of these instances the therapist's use of confrontation was met with resistance. However, when the therapist offered to help Mrs Lewis develop a plan for cleaning out the clutter, the effort was met with acceptance.

5. *Where needed, ask the patient to describe more fully some parts of an event or an experience.* Seeking elaboration of interpersonal events from the patient can be helpful to the therapist in formulating a CCRT, thereby helping the patient as well. For example, when Mrs Lewis apologized to the therapist for crying she said that she 'should act like an adult and not be such a baby' and did not like people feeling sorry for her. To better understand Mrs Lewis's response, the therapist might have said, 'Tell me what happened when your mother and grandmother died. Did people tell you how you should act and what you should feel?' 'How did it feel when people felt sorry for you?' From this exchange the therapist can develop a more informed interpretation about Mrs Lewis's experience when faced with loss.

THE EVENT

Consistent with the focus of SE therapy, the event with the therapist can be viewed as yet another example of Mrs Lewis's repetitive pattern of relating. The therapist's efforts to confront Mrs Lewis with the reality of possible eviction are viewed by Mrs Lewis as controlling and unhelpful. She becomes resistant and responds to the therapist with anxiety, worry, guilt and anger. Despite these feelings, Mrs Lewis wants to accept the therapist's help in cleaning her cluttered apartment (e.g. willingness to try the behavioural plan) and to be good. However, she also wants not to be seen as weak and not be hurt (e.g. repeated requests not to rush the process). These relational components are similar to patterns she first established in her relationships with her father, stepmother and uncle. In CCRT terms, the experience of loss and abandonment was met with rejection and disregard that left Mrs Lewis feeling helpless, guilty and alone. Therefore, this event with the therapist only serves to further confirm the struggles Mrs Lewis has in relating to others and does not alter the case formulation or treatment plan.

OTHER ISSUES

One other important issue to consider in examining relational patterns is the therapeutic relationship. By focusing on the core patterns of relationship conflicts, the therapist develops an understanding of the patient's typical ways of relating to others that will almost assuredly be reenacted in the relationship with the therapist. Thus, in response to a developing therapeutic alliance, the therapist can anticipate feelings of helplessness and dependency in Mrs Lewis that will be evident in her attempts to please and be the 'prefect patient'. Similarly, should the therapist challenge Mrs Lewis about her cluttered apartment or her lack of connection with others, it is likely that Mrs Lewis will respond with resistance, withdrawal and quiet anger. An SE therapist would use these exchanges to further highlight the repetitive nature of Mrs Lewis's CCRTs and describe how these ways of interacting block her ability to have her needs met, whether within therapy or in outside relationships.

SUMMARY

Mrs Lewis is likely suffering from a schizoid personality disorder with an underlying depression and OCD. She has experienced repeated and sudden loss of individuals in her life that has resulted in an unstable living situation and, at times, rejection by those that remain. This pattern has resulted in feelings of helplessness, isolation and depression (anaclitic depression). In an effort to manage the anxiety and fear associated with future loss and instability, she has developed an intense need to hold on to material possessions and avoids developing close personal relationships. Even her efforts to gain some sense of control and autonomy have been met with anger and frustration. Once Mrs Lewis is able to recognize and explore these core conflictual patterns, she can then develop better ways of defending and coping with her feelings, more clearly express her needs and respond to others in ways that enhance her feelings of self rather than continuing the cycle of depression and anxiety.

ACKNOWLEDGEMENT

The author wishes to thank Dr David Mark for his insightful comments and input on an earlier version of the paper.

REFERENCES

Barber, J.P., Luborsky, L., Crits-Christoph, P. and Diguer, L. (1995) A comparison of core conflictual relationship themes before psychotherapy and during early sessions. *Journal of Consulting and Clinical Psychology*, **63**, 145–8.

Beck, A.T. (1983) Cognitive therapy of depression: new perspectives, in *Treatment of Depression: Old Controversies and New Approaches* (eds P.J. Clayton and J.E. Barrett), Raven Press, New York, pp. 265–90.

Blatt, S.J., Quinlan, D.M., Chevron, S.M. *et al.* (1982) Dependency and self-criticism: psychological dimensions of depression. *Journal of Consulting and Clinical Psychology*, **150**, 113–24.

Cierpka, M., Strack, M., Benninghoven, D. *et al.* (1998) Stereotypical relationship patterns and psychopathology. *Psychotherapy and Psychosomatics*, **67**, 241–8.

Crits-Christoph, P. and Connolly, M.B. (1988) Empirical basis of supportive-expressive psychodynamic psychotherapy, in *Empirical Studies of the Therapeutic Hour. Empirical Studies of Psychoanalytic Theories*, vol. 8 (eds R.F. Bornstein and J.M. Masling), American Psychological Association, Washington, DC, pp. 109–51.

Crits-Christoph, P., Connolly, M.B., Azarian, K. *et al.* (1996) An open trial of brief supportive-expressive psychotherapy in the treatment of generalized anxiety disorder. *Psychotherapy: Theory, Research, Practice, Training*, **33**, 418–30.

Crits-Christoph, P., Cooper, A. and Luborsky, L. (1998) The measurement of accuracy of interpretations, in *Understanding Transference: The Core Conflictual Relationship Theme Method*, 2nd edn (eds L. Luborsky and P. Crits-Christoph), APA Books, Washington, DC, pp. 197–211.

Crits-Christoph, P., Mark, D. and Gibbons, M.B.C. (2002) Supportive-expressive psychodynamic therapy for depression, in *Comparative Treatments of Depression. Springer Series on Comparative Treatments for Psychological Disorders* (eds M.A. Reinecke and M.R. Davison), Springer, New York, pp. 166–94.

De Roten, Y., Drapeau, M., Stigler, M. and Despland, J. (2004) Yet another look at the CCRT: the relation between Core Conflictual Relationship Themes and defensive functioning. *Psychotherapy Research*, **14**, 252–60.

Freud, S. (1912/1958) The dynamics of the transference, in *The Standard Edition of the Complete Psychological Works of Sigmund Freud*, vol. 12 (ed. and Trans. J. Strachey), Hogarth Press, London, pp. 99–108. (Original work published 1912).

Fried, D., Crits-Christoph, P. and Luborsky, L. (1992) The first empirical demonstration of transference in psychotherapy. *Journal of Nervous and Mental Disease*, **180**, 326–31.

Grenyer, B.F.S. and Luborsky, L. (1996) Dynamic change in psychotherapy: mastery of interpersonal conflict. *Journal of Consulting and Clinical Psychology*, **64**, 411–6.

Luborsky, L. (1984) *Principles of Psychoanalytic Psychotherapy: A Manual for Supportive-Expressive (SE) Treatment*, Basic Books, New York.

Luborsky, L. and Barrett, M.S. (2006) The core conflictual relationship theme (CCRT) – a basic case formulation method, in *Handbook of Psychotherapy Case Formulation*, 2nd edn (ed. T. Elles), Guilford, New York, pp. 105–35.

Luborsky, L. and Crits-Christoph, P. (1990) *Understanding Transference: The Core Conflictual Relationship Theme Method*, Basic Books, New York.

Luborsky, L. and Crits-Christoph, P. (1998) *Understanding Transference: The Core Conflictual Relationship Theme Method*, 2nd edn, APA Books, Washington, DC.

Luborsky, L., Diguer, L., Cacciola, J. *et al.* (1996) Factors in outcomes of short-term dynamic psychotherapy for chronic vs. nonchronic major depression. *Journal of Psychotherapy Practice and Research*, **5**, 152–9.

Luborsky, L., Luborsky, E.B., Diguer, L. *et al.* (1995) Extending the core relationship theme into early childhood, in *Development and Vulnerability in Close Relationships* (eds G. Noam and K. Fisher), Erlbaum, New York, pp. 287–308.

Wachtel, P. (1993) *Therapeutic Communication: Principles and Effective Practice*, The Guilford Press, New York.

Waldinger, R., Diguer, L., Guastella, F. *et al.* (2002) The same old song? – Stability and change in relationship schemas from adolescence to young adulthood. *Journal of Youth and Adolescence*, **31**, 17–29.

17

Commentary on Formulations of a Case of Problematic Behaviour in an Older Adult

KEVIN HOWELLS AND LAWRENCE JONES

Providing a commentary on two formulations of a clinical case by fellow mental health professionals is fraught with danger. The first is that the commentators inevitably bring with them their own, and potentially idiosyncratic, definitions of formulation and their own underlying theoretical and philosophical assumptions about the nature of explanation and causation in psychological science and clinical practice. The original formulators (Dunne and Barrett) may well reject the definitions and assumptions of the commentators. So, it is a good time, therefore, to lay such cards on the table.

The first card to lay down is our own theoretical orientations and conceptions of the clinician's role. We are both clinical psychologists working, broadly speaking, within a scientist–practitioner model of the psychologist's role. The latter typically involves the generation and empirical testing of hypotheses about the causation of clinical problems (Popper, 1963), both nomothetically and idiographically, and using the knowledge generated to plan and evaluate the effectiveness of subsequent treatment interventions. The second card is that we are both broadly cognitive – behavioural in theoretical approach, though one of us (LJ) has an interest in integrative approaches to psychotherapy and has trained in cognitive-analytic therapy (CAT) and the other (KH) has some background in constructivist therapies, such as personal construct therapy. Third, neither of us has any specialist knowledge or clinical experience in relation to hoarding. This would also seem to be the case for

Clinical Case Formulation: Varieties of Approaches. Edited by Peter Sturmey.
© 2009 John Wiley & Sons, Ltd.

Barrett and Dunne, the two formulators. Having no specialist knowledge is a common state of affairs for the generalist clinician and one which necessitates nomothetically oriented information gathering – what do we know from scientific research into hoarding in general – before proceeding to an idiographic analysis, resulting in the clinical formulation. Neither of the formulators appears to have perceived a need to gather such information for the present exercise, though it is possible that they interpreted the requirements of the book as precluding this.

The two formulations reviewed in this chapter are strongly influenced by the psychodynamic tradition and some might argue that applying the kinds of criteria for validity and reliability from a cognitive behaviour therapy (CBT) framework might reflect a fundamental misunderstanding of the kinds of claim to truth being made by assertions in psychodynamic paradigms. There are some who have argued that constructs in psychoanalytic discourse belong more to a hermeneutic paradigm where practitioners are much more interested in meaning than in causal processes. (For a critique see Grünbaum (2004).)

In this chapter it is assumed, however, that there are some criteria that are broadly applicable to all formulations aimed at bringing about significant clinical change – no matter what their theoretical orientation. It is from this perspective that we have endeavoured to enter into a constructive dialogue with the formulations we have been asked to consider. Best practice cognitive behavioural formulation of clinical problems stresses the importance of five principles. First, formulations be evaluated using empirically derived and supported measures that are multi-modal and sensitive to change. Haynes *et al.* (2009) made the important point that '[t]he validity of judgements about behaviour problems and their functional relations depends on the validity of the measures obtained during the clinical assessment – invalid measures are likely to lead to invalid clinical judgements' (pp. 31–2). The second principal is that the clinical problem being addressed is clearly and unambiguously defined. Third, the focus is on determining *causal functional relationships* between the problem and antecedent and consequent events of a social, cognitive, emotional, behavioural, physiological and environmental sort. Fourth, antecedent factors should include both distal historical and proximal current factors. An exclusive emphasis on purely distal historical causal variables is inappropriate, given what is known about the influence of current state and situational factors on normal and abnormal behaviours (Mischel, 2004). It is thus important to specify how proximal variables mediate the impact of distal variables. The final assumption is that problems and their causes are dynamic and change over time (Haynes *et al.*, 2009; Virues-Ortega and Haynes, 2005). (See Chapter 12 by Tero Timonen, Stephen Haynes and Raimo Lappalainen for an example of this approach to case formulation.)

An adequate formulation would specify important functional relationships between the problem and its significant antecedent events and consequences. Not all functional relationships are causal and it might be argued that one of the purposes of a formulation is to specify factors that are genuinely causal as opposed to merely correlational. We suggest that a formulation needs to explicitly address, if only briefly, which of the many variables discussed are causal as opposed to only functionally linked through correlation (Haynes, 1992). This does not occur, explicitly, in the two formulations under consideration.

How adequate are measurements in the two formulations? Do they suggest a need for multiple informants, rather than just self-report, multiple types of measure, such as questionnaires, interviews, case notes, behavioural observation, checklists and multiple settings? Although both formulations make some reference to measures used to collect information relevant to a formulation, the measures and their validity are not comprehensively described, perhaps because of space limitations in a short paper. The information for the core conflictual relationship theme (CCRT) formulation appears to be derived exclusively from 'narratives . . . told in psychotherapy sessions' (Chapter 16, Section 'Relevant and Irrelevant Variables', pp. 215–216). The reliability and validity of this measurement approach or the possible use of other psychometric or behavioural measures are not discussed, with the exception of information about the stability at the nomothetic level of CCRTs over time. In CAT, reference is made to 'self-report, diary keeping, questionnaires of different sorts, autobiographies and dreams' (Chapter 15, Section 'THE FORMULATION'), but these methods are not presented in sufficient detail for their reliability and validity to be known.

The CCRT account is very clear that both historical and proximal relationship factors are the critical causal variables, with other situational and contextual variables having little or no explanatory relevance. Current factors are relevant to examine to the extent that they include possible evidence for the repetitive nature of CCRTs. This relatively narrow conception of relevant causal influences contrasts starkly with the CAT viewpoint that 'nothing would be excluded in consideration of a case formulation' including 'the mind–body system . . . other people's mind–body systems . . . group and social systems . . . spiritual and transpersonal belief systems' (Chapter 15, Section 'Relevant and Irrelevant Variables', pp. 201–202), and so on. In practice, however, the major focus in CAT appears to be on the patient's roles and procedures formed by his or her personal life narratives. Despite the very wide range of causal factors identified in CAT, it is unclear whether and how these would be assessed, apart from the reliance on the patient's self-report narrative and observations of behaviour in the therapeutic session. CAT shares with CCRT an emphasis on the importance of the therapeutic relationship.

The CCRT formulation makes clear reference to structural psychiatric classifications. Mrs Lewis suffers from 'a schizoid personality disorder as well as underlying depression and obsessive compulsive disorder' (Chapter 16, Section 'CASE FORMULATION'), though it is not clear how important these disorders are as explanatory variables. The diagnoses appear to be seen as a consequence of CCRT factors, rather than as a cause of them. There is little reference to psychiatric frameworks in the CAT formulation, apart from the comment that 'services have given the patient diagnostic labels rather than real help' (Chapter 15, Section the Formulation).

The CCRT formulation is shared with the patient, but not in the entirely collaborative way proposed in the CAT formulation paper, where the aim is to facilitate in a careful and planned manner gradual awareness that does not provoke resistance and which is likely to strengthen the therapeutic alliance. This contrasts with the CAT formulation where the formulation is explicitly seen as 'a dialogic and collaborative process' (Chapter 15, Section 'HISTORY').

DO THE FORMULATIONS MEET KUYKEN AND COLLEAGUES' CRITERIA?

Recent work by Kuyken and colleagues (Kuyken, 2006; Bieling and Kuyken, 2003; Kuyken *et al.*, 2005) provides a framework for evaluating the two formulations. These criteria have been applied mainly to CBT formulations, though there is no obvious reason why they should not be applied to formulations from other theoretical perspectives. Indeed, Bieling and Kuyken (2003) cite both the CAT and CCRT literatures, the latter being viewed as a case formulation method that is reliable, valid and related to improved outcomes.

Is the theory on which the formulation is founded evidence based?

Whilst both of the theoretical models have a generic theoretical and evidence base supporting their use, which is discussed briefly by the authors, there is no reference to CAT or CCRT theory or to empirical findings relating to hoarding or its treatment. These observations are unsurprising, given the rarity of the problem and the relatively early stages of theoretical and empirical validation of CAT and CCRT. Given the multiplicity and wide range of possible causal influences in formulating any clinical problem, the clinician needs to gather information from three possible sources: (1) the general nomothetic literature on causes of this *class* of problems, in this case obsessive–compulsive problems; (2) literature relating to the specific problem (hoarding) and (3) idiographic, individual-specific factors revealed by the assessment and analysis of the case at hand. It is possible, of course, that the causal factors revealed by (3) would have no overlap with (1) and (2), though for a longer series of such cases, individual-specific formulations would necessarily reflect what has been found in nomothetic studies. Both present formulations are restricted to information from category (3). There is, however, a reasonably substantial literature on hoarding that could usefully be accommodated in the present formulations (Frost and Hartl, 1996; Grisham *et al.*, 2006; Luchins *et al.*, 1992; Samuels *et al.*, 2007; Seedat and Stein, 2002; Steketee and Frost, 2003; Wu and Watson, 2005). Such papers suggest a need to consider factors such as attentional problems, information-processing deficits, decision-making, beliefs about possessions, distress and avoidance in formulating hoarding. In their review of obsessive–compulsive disorder, Steketee and Frost (2003) did not identify interpersonal issues around loss as an aetiological factor. Whilst grief-like reactions to the loss of possessions are identified, they are not linked with developmental experiences of loss, but are linked with strong emotional attachment to objects, memory-related concerns about losing objects and desire for control and responsibility; there is thus no evidence, as yet, in the literature that this is an important feature, as suggested by the formulations.

Is the formulation reliable?

For this exercise, there is no information available as to the reliability of the formulations, as is often the case in clinical practice, though supervision, including peer supervision, allows an opportunity to expose two clinicians to the same assessment information and to compare the formulations made. The CCRT account does refer to a literature which includes investigation of the reliability of CCRT analyses. Luborsky and Diguer (1998), for example suggest that there is a significant degree of reliability in CCRT formulations. It is possible to compare the two present formulations with each other to assess their reliability.

The CCRT formulation generated the following hypotheses:

H1. *The function of interpersonal emotional distance is to avoid distress associated with loss.*
H2. *Anticipation of future loss of relationship and possessions is associated with anxiety and fear.*
H3. *Anxiety and fear are about loss offset by hoarding possessions.*
H4. *Anxiety and fear about loss offset by avoiding relationships.*

The CAT formulation, on the other hand, hypothesized:

H1. *Distances self from others to avoid emotional impact of losses.*
H2. *Submission and placation associated with avoidance of anxiety about rejection and loss.*
H3. *She has a lack of understanding of the value of objects and people and throwing things away associated with aversive sense that she might be throwing something away that is valuable.*
H4. *She cannot throw things away because she felt thrown away herself.*

Both the formulations arrived at the hypothesis that the function of inter-personal emotional distance, for this individual, is to avoid distress associated with loss. This agreement could be evidence of reliability. Other hypotheses, however, are entertained by only one clinical model, for example the CAT hypothesis that Mrs Lewis cannot throw things away because she felt thrown away herself.

Kuyken (2006) wrote that 'the work on the reliability of case formulations suggests that practitioners should stay closer to the descriptive levels of formulation because the further they move from description to inference the more likely they are to form idiosyncratic understandings' (p. 29). Both of these formulations are heavily reliant on inference, it would be important to establish whether other practitioners within the same theoretical framework would develop similar formulations. Both manualization of the formulation process and use of formal professional guidelines have been recommended as potentially enhancing reliability of formulations (Bieling and Kuyken, 2003). The CCRT therapy is a manualized approach whereas the CAT approach does not appear to have a manual but does have a ready literature to which practitioners can turn. Contemporary practice guidelines are not referred to by either practitioner.

Is the formulation valid?

As suggested above, the validity of a formulation is dependent on the ade-quacy of measurement of variables. Another way of assessing validity is to determine whether the formulation is consistent with the client's experience and perceptions of his or her problem. Both accounts highlight the importance of obtaining the patient's own view of the formulation. The CAT formulation puts greater emphasis on the notion of collaborative working and, as such, may be seen as more likely to consider the patient's own experience in developing the formulation. However, the CCRT account also emphasizes the importance of understanding the patient's perspective when developing a formulation. The suggestion that other therapists' and supervisors' impressions be used to validate the formulation (Bieling and Kuyken, 2003; Kuyken, 2006) is not evidenced in either case, however, both therapies generally place a significant emphasis on supervision and peer review of formulations.

Does the formulation improve the intervention and therapy outcome?

Whilst it is not possible to determine whether the formulations would improve therapy outcome, there are clear links between both formulations and the specification of treatment targets. In addition, there is evidence in the literature that interventions based on high-quality CCRT theme formulations led to better treatment outcomes (Crits-Christoph, Cooper and Luborsky, 1988) with some patient groups.

Is the formulation acceptable and useful?

For CAT the formulation appears to be, in part, an explicit attempt to engage the patient on the patient's own terms, rather than an expert-generated, objective analysis. The CAT reformulation letter is a sophisticated attempt to communicate to the patient the formulation that has been arrived at mutually in the session. In the reformulation letter to Mrs Lewis, there is a careful teasing out of the kinds of issues that Mrs Lewis is willing to address, such as the problems with where she lives, and wanting to talk about her life, from those she is clearly not interested in addressing, such as her hoarding. The acknowledgement of the patient having come into therapy as a consequence of pressure from others, rather than out of a personal sense that her hoarding was a problem is potentially validating for the patient. The CAT emphasis on not taking a 'one up' or 'magistral' stance with the patient contrasts strongly with the CCRT emphasis on using interpretations where the formulation is asserted – the acceptability and utility of these stances is an empirical question and may vary from individual to individual. As suggested above, both papers draw clear treatment targets from the formulation, thus the formulations have shown themselves to be useful.

Science and clinical formulation

If a formulation is a hypothesis, or series of hypotheses about the causes of a problem, then it follows that an adequate formulation should have certain characteristics. By definition, a hypothesis is tentative or provisional (Kuyken, 2006) rather than a definitive statement about causality. Haynes *et al.* (2009)

have described case formulations as inevitably incomplete and imperfect. Reasons for this include the intrinsic error inherent in any measures, whether the latter are formal, such as a psychometric test score, or informal, such as a clinical judgement. In addition, the dynamic and unstable relationship between important functional variables and the limited domain of formulation validity (formulations may vary in different settings) add to the tentative nature of any formulation. Formulations are also difficult to evaluate empirically. Validation typically requires sophisticated methods of single-case analysis. There is little indication that either formulation is written in a tentative or provisional way. There is a sense in which they both have been developed *as the* rather than *a* formulation. This may however be due to a model of change in which presenting the formulation as definite is considered to be necessary in order to challenge effectively. Therapists who do not believe their interpretations wholeheartedly may not be as effective as those who do. Alternatively, this definiteness may be an artefact of how the nature of the exercise has been perceived by the two authors.

Recognition that a formulation is an initial and tentative hypothesis is congruent with accepting that alternative hypotheses are possible and may prove to be more valid (Kuyken, 2006; Haynes *et al.*, 2009). It has been suggested that any formulation should be written in pencil (R. Ledger, 2008, Personal communication, 1 June).

Grünbaum (2004), in his critique of psychoanalytic conceptions of science, argued that '... it is always fallacious to infer a causal linkage between thematically kindred events from their mere thematic kinship. Yet it *may* happen that *additional* information will sustain such a causal inference in certain cases' (p. 158). Thematically kindred events may be causally linked but further work needs to be done in order to test such hypotheses. The procedure of identifying thematically kindred events belongs firmly to the domain described by Popper (1963) as the 'context of discovery' – the stage in scientific enterprise where hypotheses are generated – and not to the 'context of justification' – where hypotheses are tested against logical and empirical criteria. It is a moot point whether, in the application of scientific thinking in the idiographic context, it is possible to apply the same criteria for testing hypotheses as those applied in the broader nomothetic context. The necessity for action in the moment makes it difficult to implement the same kind of rigorous criteria. It is surely important, however, for practitioners to specify some way of at least attempting to test their hypotheses and to indicate the necessity to reformulate, should the hypothesis be refuted.

In the CCRT model, there is a systematic account of the process of identifying themes for Mrs Lewis. Theses are summarized in Table 17.1. This

Table 17.1 A summary of the core conflictual relationship themes for Mrs Lewis and their links.

Loss of cared persons and possessions	Rejection/punishment	Forced to move
Mother and younger brother died	Rejection and punishment from father and stepmother	Forced to move in with grandmother
Grandmother dies	Rejected by father. Uncle disregarded her	Forced to move in with uncle (disregarded)
Loss of son		
Loss due to dissolution of marriage	Rejection due to dissolution of marriage	Forced to move due to financial losses
Loss of possessions due to financial losses		
Loss of employment		Forced change in living situation
Loss of loved possessions		

thematic analysis is then used to develop the CCRT formulation of characteristic ways of relating to others.

Tests of formulations are seen, in both therapies, as the kinds of responses that are obtained to interpretative comments/reflections or reformulations. These are not, however, examined systematically in either account and there does not seem to be an active attempt to seek refutation of core therapist assumptions. CAT would additionally encourage the individual to generate exits from his or her characteristic patterns of relating and the efficacy of these interventions would also be seen as a test of the formulation. Ideally, the two formulations would include explicit predictions which follow from the formulation which are capable of testing and refutation in the clinical setting. As currently stated, the formulations do not suggest what future events or behaviours would prove the formulation wrong and indicate the need to pursue an alternative hypothesis.

There is no reference in the formulations to attempts to avoid bias (Kuyken, 2006). It might be argued that for both interventions the formulation was framed strictly within the interpersonal domain and thereby excluded a whole range of other potential variables. Contemporary approaches to formulation emphasize the need to include multiple domains, including environmental, cognitive, affective, biological and behavioural (Haynes *et al.*, 2009; Morton and Frith, 1995; Morton, 2004). Both of the present formulations highlight environmental (distal developmental experiences) and cognitive/relational factors (subsequent beliefs about self in relation to others) as forming the main causal pathway, without a wider reference.

CONCLUSIONS

For clinicians to offer their clinical reasoning and formulation strategies to public scrutiny is brave indeed – doubly so when there are major and inevitable constraints in the formulation exercise, likely to make even the best of formulations appear inadequate. The formulators in this exercise were limited to the written case description provided, had no opportunity to interact with or observe the patient and were not able to follow the case through time to observe change and variation in the clinical picture. In addition, word limits for the case formulators precluded detailed accounts of the theoretical and empirical background and of assessment methods. Finally, the formulations were subjected to a critique by commentators (LJ and KH) from a different theoretical orientation! It is very likely that many of the critical points we have made above reflect the constraints of any such exercise rather than inherent deficiencies in the formulations reported.

For the commentators, this exercise has been instructive in alerting us to the difficult problem of how we render disparate theoretical perspectives commensurable. It has also raised some perplexing questions. Is it desirable, and possible, for example to translate statements from different theoretical approaches into an integrated framework, within which, for example some agreement could be achieved as to what are verifiable causal influences for the person's problems? (See, for example an attempt to do this by Morton and Frith (1995) and Morton, 2004.) Integration may be desirable in some clinical settings because a shared understanding of the causes of a problem is required, so that diverse staff may work together to bring about change. This is more than an academic issue in that in mental health services it is not uncommon for the patient's problems to be formulated by a series of professionals from a number of theoretical persuasions. How is an integrative formulation to be achieved which will facilitate a collective, coherent and consistent approach to treatment and clinical management?

REFERENCES

Bieling, P.J. and Kuyken, W. (2003) Is cognitive case formulation science or science fiction? *Clinical Psychology: Science and Practice*, **10**, 52–69.

Crits-Christoph, P., Cooper, A. and Luborsky, L. (1988) The accuracy of therapists' interpretations and the outcome of dynamic psychotherapy. *Journal of Consulting and Clinical Psychology*, **56**, 490–5.

Frost, R.O. and Hartl, T.L. (1996) A cognitive behavioural model of compulsive hoarding. *Behaviour, Research and Therapy*, **34**, 341–50.

Grisham, J.R., Frost, R.O., Steketee, G. *et al.* (2006) Age of onset of compulsive hoarding. *Journal of Anxiety Disorders*, **20**, 675–86.

Grünbaum, A. (2004) The Hermeneutic versus the scientific conception of psychoanalysis, in *Psychoanalysis at the Limit: Epistemology, Mind, and the Question of Science* (ed. J. Mills), State University of New York Press, New York, pp. 139–60.

Haynes, S.N. (1992) *Models of Causality in Psychopathology: Toward Dynamic, Synthetic and Nonlinear Models of Behaviour Disorders*, MacMillan, New York.

Haynes, S.N., Yoshioka, D.T., Kloezeman, K. and Bello, I. (2009) Clinical applications of behavioural assessment: identifying and explaining behaviour problems in clinical assessment, in *Oxford Handbook of Clinical Assessment* (ed. J. Butcher), Oxford University Press, New York.

Kuyken, W. (2006) Research and evidence base in case formulation, in *Case Formulation in Cognitive Behaviour Therapy: The Treatment of Challenging and Complex Clinical Cases* (ed. N. Tarrier), Brunner Routledge, London, pp. 12–35.

Kuyken, W., Fothergill, C.D., Musa, M. and Chadwick, P. (2005) The reliability and quality of cognitive case formulation. *Behaviour, Research and Therapy*, **43**, 1187–201.

Luborsky, L. and Diguer, L. (1998) The reliability of the CCRT measure: results from eight samples, in *Understanding Transference: The Core Conflictual Relationship Theme Method*, 2nd edn (eds L. Luborsky and P. Crits-Christoph), Basic Books, New York, pp. 97–108.

Luchins, D., Goldman, M.B., Lieb, M. and Hanrahan, P. (1992) Repetitive behaviors in chronically institutionalized schizophrenic patients. *Schizophrenia Research*, **8**, 119–23.

Mischel, W. (2004) Towards an integrative science of the person. *Annual Review of Psychology*, **55**, 1–22.

Morton, J. (2004) *Understanding Development Disorders. A Causal Modelling Approach*, Blackwell, Oxford.

Morton, J. and Frith, C. (1995) Causal modelling a structural approach to developmental psychopathology, in *Developmental Psychopathology* (eds D. Cicchetti and D.J. Cohen), John Wiley & Sons, Inc., New York, pp. 357–90.

Popper, K. (1963) *Conjectures and Refutations: The Growth of Scientific Knowledge*, Routledge and Kegan Paul, London.

Samuels, J.F., Bienvenu, O.J., Pinto, A. *et al.* (2007) Hoarding in obsessive–compulsive disorder: results from the OCD collaborative genetics study. *Behaviour, Research and Therapy*, **45**, 673–86.

Seedat, S. and Stein, D.J. (2002) Hoarding in obsessive–compulsive disorder and related disorders: a preliminary report of 15 cases. *Psychiatry and Clinical Neurosciences*, **56**, 17–23.

Steketee, G. and Frost, R. (2003) Compulsive hoarding: current status of the research. *Clinical Psychology Review*, **23**, 905–27.

Virues-Ortega, J. and Haynes, S.N. (2005) Functional analysis in behavior therapy: behavioral foundations and clinical application. *International Journal of Clinical and Health Psychology*, **5**, 567–87.

Wu, K.D. and Watson, D. (2005) Hoarding and its relation to obsessive–compulsive disorder. *Behaviour, Research and Therapy*, **43**, 897–921.

PART VI

Intellectual Disabilities

18

A Case of Anger in a Person with Intellectual Disabilities

BETSEY A. BENSON

PRESENTING COMPLAINT

Mr B was referred for treatment by Mrs Smith, a vocational training counsellor at the day habilitation programme for people with intellectual disabilities that Mr B attended. She said that Mr B was learning janitorial skills in this programme, but he had problems interpersonally. He talked back to supervisors, responded poorly to criticism and had poor relationships with other workers. These problems were interfering with Mr B's successful completion of the training programme and job placement. When asked why he came to the initial appointment, Mr B said, 'Mrs Smith said that it will help me get a job. I want a job.'

CLIENT DEMOGRAPHIC DATA

Mr B was 32 years old and single. He was never married and had no children. He lived with his grandmother. Mr B was diagnosed with hemiplegic cerebral palsy which affected the right side of his body. He walked with a slight limp, but had no difficulty in climbing stairs or walking short distances. He had some limitations in the use of his right hand; he could pick up a pencil but he wrote with his left hand. He had some articulation difficulties, although he could be understood. He wore glasses for near-sightedness. His hearing was normal. Mr B took no medications.

Clinical Case Formulation: Varieties of Approaches.   Edited by Peter Sturmey.
© 2009 John Wiley & Sons, Ltd.

A psychological report written when he was a 17-year-old described Mr B as a young man with mild intellectual disabilities and impulse control problems. He obtained a Full Scale IQ score of 65, with a higher Verbal than Performance IQ score. His scores on timed subtests were lower than on untimed tests. His reading skills were reported to be at the 3rd grade level and his math skills were at the 2nd grade level. Adaptive behaviour strengths identified were in the areas of independent functioning and domestic activity. Weaknesses identified included number concepts, socialization and economic activity.

Client demeanour and personal appearance

Mr B was of average height and build. He wore work clothes, was clean-shaven, neat and well groomed. He carried a copy of the daily newspaper folded in his right hand. He smiled a broad smile, made eye contact and extended his left hand when introductions were made. "Call me Mike," he said.

Upon first meeting, he seemed friendly and relaxed. He commented on the bus service and the route he followed from the vocational programme to the office where he arrived on time for the appointment. He openly glanced around the room and took in the surroundings. When asked for routine personal data, he took out his wallet and retrieved a folded piece of paper. It contained his name, birth date, address, phone number, grandmother's name and other information that he said he usually needed when he completed job applications.

CLIENT CURRENT LIFESTYLE

Mr B and his grandmother lived in a two-bedroom apartment. The neighbourhood had experienced an increase in crime in recent years. Mr B received disability checks and his grandmother was supported by an old age pension. Mr B also received a small stipend for participating in the vocational training programme that would end in three months or when he completed the programme.

Mr B reported that he did some cooking and cleaning in his home, mostly, he made microwave meals, but he said that he could make great pancakes. He reported that his grandmother did most of the shopping and paid the bills. He said that it was a good arrangement for both of them; they helped each other.

Mr B went to church with his grandmother weekly. He accompanied her to other community events that she wanted to attend. He had a few acquaintances in his neighbourhood with whom he is friendly, although his interactions with them might simply be to nod and wave to one another when passing on the street. There was a local bar that he frequented from time to time, but he said he did not like some people who spend all their money on drink. He also disapproved of people who gamble or buy lottery tickets in the hope of winning a large amount of money. "It is like throwing your money away," he said. He denied drug use and smoking. When the subject of drugs was brought up, Mike said that he sees a lot of it on the street and tries to avoid those people. He stated, "they are just trouble."

For the last 9 months, he attended the vocational training programme 5 days a week, 6 hours per day. When asked what he learned at the vocational centre, he described various pieces of equipment that he operated to wax and clean floors and rugs, as well as several chemical cleaning agents that he used. Some of his statements sounded like repetitions of instructions he had been given in the training programme, such as 'you don't open up that bottle in the janitor closet, you would pass out.' He proudly stated that he is one of the best workers in the programme to operate the floor polisher. "Some people let it get away from them," he said, "you really have to hold on tight to the handles."

When asked about the other trainees in the programme he said, "Most of them are OK." One of the reasons he liked this programme is because they did not take any 'low functioning people'. 'There were a few young guys in the programme. They think they know it all. I knew more before I started the programme than they will ever know,' Mr B said. 'And there are a couple of women who are friendly enough, but one of them likes to play one guy against another. That's not right. One of the best trainees finished the programme a few weeks ago and left for a job.'

Mr B said that the young guys joked around too much. One day in the break room, one of them knocked over Mr B's drink and did not clean it up. Mr B complained that the guy should have bought him another beverage. In retaliation, he took the worker's lunch and threw it in the trash. Mr B had to replace the lunch after the worker complained to the supervisor. Mr B's beverage was also replaced by the other worker, but by then he said it was 'too little, too late'. Another thing that bothered Mr B was that a worker in the programme liked to make jokes about people's names. He had a nickname for everyone and repeated it whenever he saw the person. Mr B told him to stop because he did not like the name he was called, but the guy kept doing it. Mr B swore at him and threatened to 'take you outside'. Mr B was reprimanded by the vocational training counsellor for threatening and using foul language. "Tell me that was fair," he said.

Probably the most bothersome aspect of the programme for Mr B was that some of the workers had 'silly competitions' to see who could finish a job the fastest. Mr B said that although he was not the fastest worker, he did the best job. "What is the point in hurrying when you'll just have to do it over?" he said. It was during one of the 'silly competitions' that Mr B pushed another worker who was trying to pass him in the hallway. The person fell down and blamed Mr B for some bruises on his elbows and knees. Mr B had to apologize to him in front of the other workers. He did not think that it was his fault because the other worker was trying to go too fast and Mr B said that he barely touched him before he fell down.

Mr B missed the worker who finished the programme and left for a job. They talked during breaks about music and radio shows and found that they liked some of the same things. Mr B thought that the worker got a good job and he hoped that he was doing well. He did not know how to contact him, but he might like to meet him sometime, maybe after he finished the programme and had a job.

He described Mrs Smith, the supervisor who referred him, as a nice lady. He said, "She takes her time with everyone. She knows how to show you what to do. She does not have a chip on her shoulder. She had me show a new guy how to run the floor-polishing machine. He did not catch on right away." He reported that if there was any disagreement between Mr B and his instructor, it was that Mr B thought he was ready to finish the programme and move on while his instructor did not think he was ready yet.

He reported that on Saturday mornings he goes to a school for radio announcing. He said that the tuition for the school was rather expensive, but he thought it was worth the cost because he was learning a lot about radio. The teacher at the school told him that he would not get a position in radio. Mike said that he knew it, but he wanted to continue anyway. He said that he listened to and repeated commercials and other announcements while at the school, liked to talk about his favourite radio stations and favourite shows and described his home audio system in some details.

Mr B also had a membership in a health club where he exercised about three times a week. He said that he liked using different machines that were designed to improve one's strength. 'That's how I stay in shape,' he said.

When asked about his dating history and his relationships with women, Mike said that he did not date much. He reported that when he was younger, he would go out with some of his friends from school to see a movie or go to a party although there was not anyone special. He reported that then, there was a lady at church whom he liked, but he did not know if he should ask her out. Had she said 'No,' he would have been embarrassed and had she said 'Yes' but it did not go well, then he would have to see her at church every week and that would be awkward.

CLIENT HISTORY

Mr B's maternal grandmother was the parental figure in his life. He provided few details about his parents. The psychological report from his school years stated that his father left his mother before he was born and that his mother died when he was young. Mike simply said, "My Gran raised me. That is how it is." He had no siblings. He had some elder cousins who lived in the same city, but he seldom saw them. A few of his cousins have spent time in jail. While he was growing up, Mr B was close to an uncle who would take him to places and lived with them briefly. The uncle died 3 years ago from a heart ailment.

Mr B attended public school special education classes until 18 years of age. He did not enjoy his time at school, especially during the teen years when he said that students teased each other. When asked if he was teased, he said, sometimes, but he did not let it bother him. "People who do that are ignorant," he said. Mr B was disciplined at school for talking back to teachers, throwing things and noncompliance. He was suspended from school on two occasions for fighting in the lunchroom. His happiest times at school were when they went on field trips to visit various museums and other attractions. He also liked career exploration activities in which the students learned about different jobs.

During his 20s, he attended some adult education classes in the evening. He said that he wanted to learn about computers and electronics.

Prior to enrolling in the vocational training programme, Mr B had several short-lived jobs at restaurants and small businesses where he performed janitorial work. He left these positions due to disagreements with supervisors. Sometimes he quit. Other times he was fired for insubordination. There were long periods between jobs when he had no formal employment. Sometimes, he worked at a small neighbourhood store by sweeping and cleaning up at the end of the day for which he was paid a few dollars.

Mr B's most recent employment was discussed in some details. He worked 20 h per week at a fast food restaurant for approximately 3 months. His job was to clean the restaurant lobby, the rest rooms and around the outside of the restaurant. He emptied the trash, mopped the floors, cleaned the tabletops and chairs, and so on. His immediate supervisor was a young woman in her 20s who was recently promoted to shift manager. According to Mr B, she fired him for calling the restaurant too often to ask about his work schedule. Apparently, Mike called each morning and asked if he was on the schedule to work that day. There was a schedule posted in the restaurant, but Mike said that there were several Mike's on the schedule and he was never sure which line on the schedule was for him. He also complained that his supervisor told him to do things differently than the other manager did and, his co-workers did not always do what they were supposed to do. Mike thought that he was sometimes assigned tasks that other workers should be doing. He complained about some of the customers who were sloppy and dropped food on the floor. He was reprimanded for telling a customer to throw his trash away.

When pressed for further details about his relationship with his previous supervisor, Mr B admitted that once he told her that she did not know what she was doing. The incident occurred after she criticized him for the way he had cleaned the restaurant lobby. He raised his voice, threw his mop on the floor and walked to the rear of the restaurant. The restaurant was open for business at the time and there were customers seated in the lobby. He regretted the incident, but did not want to return there to work. He did not understand why the manager would put such an incompetent person in charge. He sounded irritated when he said this.

Prior to working at the fast-food restaurant, Mr B held a part-time janitorial position at a large company. He was a member of a crew of workers with disabilities who cleaned the building in the evening. Mr B held this position for about a year. He said that he liked working there until his supervisor left. He did not get along with the new supervisor and disagreed with the changes that the new person instituted. He was fired after refusing to change the order in which he completed his assignments. He complained about the partner that the new supervisor assigned him to work with and said that the other worker was too slow and was always trying to take a break. "That job didn't pay too well, anyway," he said.

Mr B continued to compare the second supervisor unfavourably to the first. The first week on the job, the second supervisor told the crew to clean the rooms in a different order than before and a week later changed the routine again. The first supervisor would say, 'Hi, how are you doing?' while the second supervisor 'never had a good word for you. He only spoke to you to give you an order or to tell you that you were doing something wrong.' Mr B was given a warning after mumbling under his breath and walking away from the new supervisor while he was giving instructions. The new supervisor also did not care that Mr B liked to do some jobs more than others. 'It didn't matter to him what you liked, he just told you what you had to do.' The second supervisor assigned Mr B to work on a different floor and it took Mr B longer to finish the work in the new location. Mr B complained that the second supervisor favoured some workers over others and let his favourite workers do what they wanted. Mr B asked for a transfer to a different crew, but he was told that there were no openings. He was fired 2 weeks later.

He reluctantly admitted to other difficulties with anger control. He purchased a new stereo system and found that it did not work properly. When he returned it to the store, he said that he had to 'yell a lot' to get his money back. The store manager was called over to settle the dispute. At the local laundermat, he argued with the manager about the machines not working properly and he demanded a refund. Here, too, he succeeded in eventually getting what he wanted, but he did not think he should have to yell to make it happen. "The customer is always right," he said.

When questioned directly about any involvement with law enforcement, Mr B said that the police were indeed called one time when he was having an argument. A neighbour in the apartment building was making too much noise and Mr B told the person to be quiet. Mr B admitted that he threatened to harm the neighbour. They argued in the hallway and another building resident called the police. The police told both of them to calm down and no charges were filed. His grandmother was upset about the incident. She said that he should just leave it alone because there was no point in making trouble.

When asked if he ever has arguments with his grandmother, he said, "Sure, we argue, but it all blows over." When they argued, he left the apartment and walked around the block or went to a nearby park. When he calmed down he went back home and they talked it over. They usually worked it out. Many of their arguments occurred after he lost a job. She told him that he could do better if he would just try to get along with people.

He admitted that he brought his frustrations home with him. If he had a bad day at work, he complained to her about it. Sometimes he was angry and cursed when he talked about his day. She did not like cursing. One time, he was so mad that he threw a vase and broke a window in the apartment. She told him to get out and not to come back until he was able to behave himself. He left for 2 days, walking the streets much of that time. When he came back, he apologised to her and she said he could stay. He promised her that he would not do something like that again and he kept his promise.

At this point, Mr B added that he only used his fists to defend himself. "Nobody gets hurt," he said, "Those fights at school were a long time ago." He stated that he does not do that anymore and walks away instead.

Mr B's medication history includes stimulants during childhood, antipsychotic medications during the teen years, and most recently, a beta blocker. Mr B said he does not want to take pills. He complained of the side effects of medication and stated that medications made him feel 'different'. There have been no psychiatric hospitalizations. He refused previous referrals for individual counselling by saying that he is not crazy. Group therapy had also been offered, but he said that he 'doesn't want to tell his business' to everyone.

CLIENT GOALS

Mr B's stated goal for therapy was to get a job. When it was explained that the therapist would not be assisting with his job search, he replied that he knew it, but his vocational counsellor said that he needed to come to therapy and that it would help him get a job. He stated that he needed a job to buy the things he wanted and to help his grandmother. "She is not getting any younger," he said.

AN EVENT

As Mr B was most interested in improving his job prospects, the initial focus in the assessment phase was on interpersonal skills at work, specifically interactions with supervisors. Various role-playing scenarios were designed and enacted with Mr B taking the part of the worker while the therapist played the supervisor or vice versa. The therapist first described the situation and then would give Mike his assignment. Mike and the therapist enacted the situation and then discussed it. The initial scenes were portrayed in a rather stiff and awkward manner, but after a few attempts, Mike seemed to be able to get caught up in the scene and to shift from acting to the discussion more easily.

In one scenario, the supervisor of a janitorial crew told a worker that he needed to work faster. To provide background information for the situation, the therapist said, 'This supervisor was told that if his crew doesn't finish cleaning all the offices by the end of the shift, he will get in trouble with his boss and might get fired. Now, Mike, you be the supervisor and tell the worker that he needs to work faster.'

Mike stood up to begin role-playing the situation, stopped, and said, 'He's really in a jam, isn't he?' 'Who, Mike?' the therapist replied. 'The supervisor. He's really in a jam if his crew doesn't get the job done. And, if someone in the crew called off work, then he's really got problems,' Mike explained. 'I guess that's right, Mike. What can the supervisor do?' Mike walked over to the therapist, now playing the worker, and said with some urgency, 'Hey, we've got to move fast tonight. Can you speed it up? We've got to finish it all by the end of the shift. Let's get going!' The therapist, pretending to be the worker, replied, 'I'm working as fast as I can.'

During the discussion that followed, the therapist asked Mike, 'What do you think the worker should say or do in that situation?' Mike thought for a moment and said, 'Well, if the supervisor tells him in a nice way to pitch in and do the job, the worker should try to do it as long as the supervisor is not putting on a bad attitude and if he is not just picking on that worker and no one else. If he treats the worker like a person and gives him some respect, then the worker should give it back to him. He's got to make a living, too.'

19

A Psychodynamic Formulation

NIGEL BEAIL AND TOM JACKSON

Whilst there is a relative paucity of literature around psychodynamic inter-ventions for people who have intellectual disabilities, we believe that the perspectives afforded by psychodynamic investigation may be of particular benefit to such individuals, due to the cognitive limitations and barriers to communication implicit in working with this clinical group.

Stiles *et al.*'s (1990) pan-theoretical model of the way people assimilate their problematic experience used the *Assimilation of Problematic Experiences Scale and* found that most people in the general population enter psychotherapy at what they call the 'problem statement' level, at which stage they can articulate what they feel is their problem. Prescriptive therapies tend to work from the basis that clients have this awareness of their problems and are able to make a problem statement in response to questions about their difficulties. In our experience, clients with intellectual disabilities fre-quently present for treatment without such understanding, particularly in the early stages of therapy. Research using Stiles' model found that people with intellectual disabilities typically presented for treatment at the lower levels of assimilation, such as 'warded off', experiencing 'unwanted thoughts', or having some 'vague awareness' of the problem, and that psychodynamic psy-chotherapy enabled them to progress towards and beyond problem statement in a few sessions (Newman and Beail, 2002, 2005; see Figure 19.1).

Mr B presents as a man with good verbal ability and has the adaptive skills to engage in employment. He asserts his goal is to obtain further employment, has some insight into his anger and has rules regarding using his fists. His needs may therefore be most appropriately met by a prescriptive intervention, such as cognitive behavioural therapy, rather than exploratory psychodynamic

Clinical Case Formulation: Varieties of Approaches.   Edited by Peter Sturmey.
© 2009 John Wiley & Sons, Ltd.

Level
0 – Warded off
1 – Unwanted thoughts
2 – Vague awareness
3 – Problem statement/clarification
4 – Understanding/insight
5 – Application/working through
6 – Problem solution
7 – Mastery

Figure 19.1 Levels of assimilation of problematic experience.

psychotherapy. Mr B's presentation does not contraindicate the use of a psychodynamic intervention and, if offered a choice, people with intellectual disabilities like Mr B may choose exploratory psychotherapy rather than a prescriptive treatment. If Mr B chose this approach he would be invited to an outpatient setting for assessment and then, if deemed appropriate, treatment would commence.

Typically psychodynamic therapy with people with intellectual disabilities consists of three stages:

Stage 1. Pre-assessment. This occurs prior to meeting the client. The therapist considers the person's route to therapy, history, reason for referral, consent issues, potential risks and benefits, practicalities of him or her attending an outpatient appointment and the availability of support.

Stage 2. Assessment. At this stage the therapist and client meet at the anticipated time and place of therapy and consider both of their abilities to tolerate and make use of the therapeutic environment, boundaries and relationship. The therapist provides information about the therapy, identifies commitments and responsibilities for effective working and ensures that consent is given for therapy to commence. At this stage, the therapist begins to gauge the client's developmental level and cognitive abilities so that he or she can adapt his or her technique to best meet his or her client's individual needs during the course of the therapy, such as making communication aids available and using appropriate language. Within the pre-assessment and assessment stages, the therapists specifically concern themselves, in a way similar to other models of therapy and as in the case example, with exploring the client's problem, his or her individual circumstances and his or her history. However, in psychodynamic therapy this exploration is an ongoing process which extends throughout the entire course of the therapy.

Stage 3. Treatment. This is the predominant part of therapy, in which the therapist and client meet alone, in a private place, away from the person's home or work environment. They will typically meet weekly at the same place and time, for 50 min each week.

THEORETICAL ORIENTATION AND RATIONALE

Psychodynamic psychotherapy aims to facilitate therapeutic action through the formation and experiencing of a consistent, safe and boundaried relationship between client and therapist. This relationship focuses specifically on the client, and through exploration of whatever happens between client and therapist, attempts to identify the client's own psychological reality. This involves integration of unacceptable aspects of clients and their important relationships, into their understanding of themselves. These unacceptable aspects often reside within clients' unconscious and act to prevent reconciliation with more acceptable perceptions of themselves and their relationships. The boundaries and therapeutic stance adopted in psychodynamic therapy function to contain the client and therapist in a manner whereby previously intolerable psychological states, such as anger, and aspects of the self and relationships, can be safely acknowledged, becoming held within the session, clarified, understood and, where possible, resolved and reintegrated in a tolerable form by the client. Psychodynamic therapists use a number of different sources of information in their attempts to understand clients' presentations. These include third-party information, prior knowledge and experience of the client, prior knowledge and experience of others, including relevant theoretical models, verbal communication, non-verbal communication and behaviour, most notably, they pay particular attention to transference and counter-transference feelings. Sessions begin with the therapist providing the client with space to free associate. This involves inviting the client (either explicitly or implicitly) to say whatever is in his or her mind and whatever comes to mind. The therapist will be interested in anything that the client says or does, including information and behaviour relating to his or her current problem, circumstances, current and past relationships, dreams, fantasies and so on. The therapist is concerned with the patient's mental representation of himself or herself within the world and seeks to identify the origin, meaning and resolution of difficult feelings and inappropriate behaviours. The work entails making links between early life experiences and relationships and identifying how these experiences influence unconscious and conscious expectations of relationships in the present day. The therapist resists giving the client personal information, and instead presents him- or herself as a type of screen onto which the client can project his or her imagined perceptions of the therapist, or intolerable aspects of themselves. The therapist may provide information giving responses about clients' treatment, reason for referral and about matters such as the time left in the session and so on; however, advice and instruction are not usually within the remit of a psychodynamic model. The therapist will attend carefully to his or her client's verbal and non-verbal communications and encourage him or her to tell his or her story, and then formulate interpretations aimed at accessing and making sense of unconscious content.

Making sense of the information

Third-party information

From the information contained within Mr B's referral and assessment report, we are told that he has few friends and acquaintances and has not dated much. He has few family contacts. An uncle with whom he had a good relationship died a few years ago.

History is very relevant to the psychodynamic approach. Mr B's history contains details of aggressive behaviour in school. The severity of this is not reported, but it was such that he was disciplined and also suspended on two occasions. At school, he seemed to prefer non-academic classes and career exploration. He had several short-lived janitorial jobs and long periods of no employment. His work history highlights several difficulties which seem to arise from interpersonal difficulties in his relationships with peers, supervisors and customers. The psychodynamic psychotherapist would ask more questions about childhood, parental relationships, including fantasies and beliefs around these, and his relationship with his grandmother and other key figures.

Third-party information can often be seen as polluting the relationship between the therapist and client in psychodynamic therapy, as it introduces other people's subjective judgements into the therapeutic relationship. However, in the predominance of cases there is an element of third-party information and this is particularly true of people with intellectual disabilities who bring with them a network of carers and a considerable quantity of written information. The impact and influence of this information on the therapeutic process is important to reflect on and be considered by the therapist.

Prior knowledge and experience

Prior knowledge and experience includes knowledge and experience of the client and others with similar presentations. This source of information includes a broad range of psychodynamic and other psychological theories, including models of attachment, developmental theories and theories around trauma, as well as considering different perspectives and understandings of the experiences of people with intellectual disabilities.

We have no prior information about Mr B specifically. However, reports of therapy with people with intellectual disabilities similar to Mr B guide us to consider the role of a person's disabilities in his or her presenting problems, and to attend to the associated issues of dependency, loss, sexuality and ultimately annihilation/believing that it would have been better if he or she had not been born (Sinason, 1992). Reports also describe many adults with intellectual disabilities living within a paradoxical situation of being enmeshed with lots of others, such as carers and other service users, whilst feeling isolated, lonely and separate. This perspective might give some insight into Mr B's experience of the world and his relationships with others.

Verbal communication

The client may talk about a range of things and the therapist does not interrupt. The therapist attends to the factual content of what the person says, the words used and also what is not said. In the session, Mr B talked about the bus route to the session and he talked about his various jobs in some detail; distinguishing himself from 'low-functioning people', and about relationships and difficulties with co-workers and supervisors. He also talked about other non-work activities, such as radio, school and his liking for computers and going to the gym, and that he stays in shape. He disapproves of behaviours such as drinking and gambling. He also cannot tolerate things that do not work, such as the radio and washing machine.

Attending to what Mr B fails to verbalize in sessions identifies that he did not talk about his parents and how he came to be cared for by his grandmother, his disability and the impact of this on his life and any anxieties he may feel about coming to therapy or the issues which might be considered.

Non-verbal communication

In psychodynamic therapy, the therapist observes not only the client's mood, as communicated through what he or she says, but also by the way he or she says it and how he or she behaves. This is difficult to discern through a transcript; however, some information from the transcript is useful in this regard. Mr B arrived in his work clothes and carried a newspaper. This may tell us about his representation of himself and his identifications; that he wants to be seen as a typical worker and someone competent who reads the paper and keeps up. Thus he presents an image of being like everyone else. Is he trying to pass as non-disabled? He also has a physical disability and speech difficulty which are apparent within sessions.

No angry incidents or acts of aggression occurred in the session. Thus, Mr B has some control of his behaviour and is able to communicate through words. However, what he says and accompanying reports show that he cannot control his angry feeling at all times.

Transference and counter-transference feelings

Psychodynamic therapists seek to understand with the client the latent or unconscious meaning of the client's communications. In order to do this, they recontextualize the manifest content of the communications as transference (Smith, 1987). Freud (1912) described transference as occurring when psychological experiences are revived and, instead of being located in the past, are applied to dealings with a person in the present. In psychodynamic psychotherapy the establishment, modalities, interpretation and resolution of the transference are, in fact, what define the cure (Laplanche and Pontalis, 1988). Transference within therapy allows the therapist to identify interpersonal issues and deal with them as empirical data in the here-and-now. This process allows early traumatic experiences and empathic failures on the part of parents and other caregivers to be relived and worked through. Thus, in the session the therapist would not only explore Mr B's account of his anger but also explore those issues that are unsaid in an attempt to develop a fuller history of the role of anger and aggression in his life.

In psychodynamic psychotherapy, the way the patient talks to and interacts with the therapist is seen as an example of how he or she interacts with others. Whilst listening to the client, the therapist monitors his or her own feelings, fantasies and reactions in response to the client's material. These are accepted as meaningful elements in the communications between client and therapist. How the client makes the therapist feel in session may very likely reflect his or her impact on others outside of the session. This is referred to as the counter-transference. There is little information on the therapist's reaction to this client, but there is an indication that perhaps one reaction to this man is that he presents as a little boring, which may give some insight into the fact that he has few friends.

Developing a formulation

In psychodynamic therapy, the therapist relates all that is said and done by the client to its potential meaning with respect to past and present relationships and their psychological underpinnings. They then develop hypotheses based on links within and between the available material. In sessions, the therapist makes exploratory and information-seeking responses which attempt to draw out more information from the client. These are generated from hypotheses about what the client might not be saying in words, but could be hinting at through his or her behaviour or tone of voice. Information-seeking responses aim to aid clarification, and help sort out what is happening by questioning and rephrasing. As evidence-supporting links between the material emerges, hypotheses develop.

The initial referral described that Mr B was having difficulties interpersonally. He was described as 'talking back to supervisors, responding poorly to criticism and having poor relationships with other workers'. It appeared that Mr B had specific difficulties with authority figures, which was supported by later accounts of his school life in which he had been disciplined for talking back to teachers, throwing things and non-compliance. Previous work experiences mirrored this pattern, with Mr B either quitting posts or being fired following insubordination and disagreements with supervisors. Based on knowledge and experience of other people with similar difficulties, we hypothesized that Mr B did not experience a strong paternal influence during his formative years. This influence typically provides children with clear boundaries of appropriate behaviour and models adaptive stress management strategies as well, accustoming children to criticism and authority figures. Within Kleinian theory, these figures, which are often referred to as *objects*, and typically reflect key people from a person's life are internalized by children and become a part of their own psychological make-up. This enables them to tolerate criticism and relate to authority figures more easily in later life, and develop an 'inner parent' which helps to moderate their behaviour. Aspects of the case description point to occasions where Mr B has had to rely on external moderators of his behaviour; such as the occasions where supervisors at work, the police or his grandmother have had to dictate to him how to behave. Paternal influences also provide a sense of security and protection for children and it is possible that Mr B's aggressive behaviour may be a sign of an underlying sense of vulnerability – that the world is a dangerous place.

The hypothesis that Mr B had failed to internalize a consistent paternal object during his childhood and was subsequently struggling to relate to authority appropriately was supported by later revelations contained within his school report that Mr B's father had left his mother before he was born. Mr B's behaviour in sessions also reflected an absence of a paternal figure, descriptions of which were notable by their absence from his accounts. Indeed, he did not mention either of his parents or how he felt about their absence, which may reflect an anxiety about making himself available to consider the feelings associated with this. From a psychodynamic perspective, there is evidence that the absence of his parents in his childhood may be a source of anxiety for Mr B, as he appeared to defend against engaging emotionally with dialogue about his parenting: *'My Gran raised me. That's how it is'*. This is an area that a psychodynamic psychotherapist would seek more information around, by reflecting back, paraphrasing or précising what the client has told him or her or acted out, before exploring the issue further. Other areas of exploration may then arise. For example, what are his fantasies regarding the origin of his disability and are these linked in any way to his absent parents? How did the loss of his parents when he was so young impact on his attachments and emotional development? These are hypotheses that a psychodynamic psychotherapist may silently hold and wish to obtain more information on at a later time.

Psychodynamic psychotherapy seeks to understand unconscious communications through models of the internal world. Most significantly, psychodynamic therapy works on the premise that we all have an ego, which is the location of the anxiety caused by intolerable unconscious material, and which employs a range of defences to ward off anxiety. People with intellectual disabilities generally have poorer ego development and therefore tolerate anxiety less well than non-disabled people. Mr B is known to have significant physical disabilities, sensory impairments and mild intellectual disabilities including a slower processing of information than his peers, however, in the case description he uses a range of defences to distance himself from these difficult aspects of his life, instead presenting an image of himself as a particularly competent and able man with abilities exceeding those of his peers. Attention to these defences lead to a hypothesis that Mr B finds his disabilities so traumatic and intolerable that he defends against integrating them as part of himself; instead preserving a sense of himself as someone whose life is not affected by the limitations and barriers of having multiple disabilities. We would hypothesize that he tries to keep these anxieties at bay by attempting to pass as 'normal'. He presents with a broad smile to indicate that he is perfectly well and not in need of help, but this is in conflict with the opinions of his referrer and supervisor as well as what is communicated by his attendance to therapy. He also engages in activities such as radio announcing, working with computers and seeking particularly masculine employment, which feed his fantasies of being someone who is not disabled. He describes attending a health club where he exercises about three times a week, particularly using machines designed to improve his strength, and despite having hemiplegic cerebral palsy describes himself as being 'in shape'. Notably, he acknowledges people with disabilities, but devalues them by referring to them as 'low functioning' and 'incompetent'. This provides an insight into how Mr B perceives disability and how difficult it would be to tolerate integration of disabled aspects into

his sense of himself. Instead he projects and displaces his anger and deroga-
tion of disability outwards, into others with disabilities and objects that do
not function properly such as the stereo system he returns to the shop, and
washing machines at the laundermat. When he is confronted with aspects of
his disabilities, he makes poor rationalizations for the intolerable elements
he cannot project outwards. He devalues the quick working that he cannot
achieve, *'What's the point of hurrying when you'll just have to do it over'*;
and asserts that regardless of speed, he does the best job. He also negates the
impact of any losses resulting from his disabilities by denigrating that which
was lost: *'That job didn't pay too well anyway'*. Consistently, he counters
any representation of a disabled, needy self with descriptions of himself as
competent and able. This was evident when he showed the therapist the piece
of paper with his name, birth date, address, phone number and grandmother's
name on, which is evidence of disability, and immediately asserted that he
went to lots of job interviews, which assert his ability. In the accounts of his
sessions, Mr B focuses on his adaptive skills and strengths in independent
functioning, employment and domestic activity and prevents interaction between these aspects and the support needs he has. He keeps apart in his mind
things that he sees as good and bad, trying to see himself in his fantasies as
good and others as bad. His psychic defences serve the function of protecting
him from his anxieties which include his fear of rejection as communicated
through his desire to be accepted as normal and his rationalization as to why
not to enter into relationships; because it would be painful to be rejected or for
the relationship to fail. He struggles to acknowledge any negative emotions
or conflicts in relationships, and when confronted with conflict or negative
judgements, he either loses control – becoming angry, or flees – as in the
times when he goes for a walk around the block or quits/storms out of work.
We also see that Mr B finds some pleasure from fantasizing about himself
as non-disabled; enjoying thinking about different careers and even pursuing
training in a field in which he knows he cannot gain employment, such as
radio broadcasting. Mr B minimizes his history of aggressive behaviour and
has little understanding of his interpersonal difficulties in the workplace and
elsewhere, projecting limitations to his work performance into the aptitude of
his supervisors.

The psychodynamic model guides therapists to explore all relationships,
especially those with significant carers. In Mr B's case, his main carer has
been his grandmother, and it is interesting to note the manner in which he
talks about this relationship. He is able to acknowledge some dependency
on his grandmother, but there is a sense from the case description that he
struggles with this and seeks to rid himself of any feelings of being a burden
on her. He parallels his dependency on his grandmother with her dependency

on him, asserting that his staying with her is a good arrangement for both of them and that they help each other. Thus, he is able to protect his perception of himself from the threat of being a disabled dependent, to preserve an image of himself as an able, competent person. In this interaction, he demonstrates two defensive strategies of projection – casting out intolerable aspects of the self into others – and interojection – taking in positive aspects of another person which serve to protect the ego against the anxieties and conflicts of their absence. In this case, Mr B takes in – interojects – aspects of others who are competent carers, to defend against feelings of dependency on his grandmother and anxieties around not being able to care for her as her own support needs increase. He also appears to have interojected a part of the successful worker who was able to graduate from the training course, and identifies himself with this worker rather than his current peers. This seems to link to his feelings of omnipotence and of being ready to graduate the course himself, and of already knowing more than the other workers could ever learn.

Malan's approach to case formulation

There are several ways in which psychodynamic psychotherapists depict their formulation. The formal completeness model is widely used as exemplified by Malan (1979). Thus, we have used this to help illustrate our formulation. Malan (1979) depicts psychotherapy in the form of the two triangles which stand on their apexes (see Figure 19.2). The two triangles describe the process of psychodynamic psychotherapy. The aim of the therapeutic endeavour is to reach beneath the defence and anxiety to the true feeling. At this point, the true feeling can be traced back from the present transference location, the therapy room, to its origin in the past, usually to the relationship with parents or significant carers. For Malan (1979) 'The importance of these two triangles is

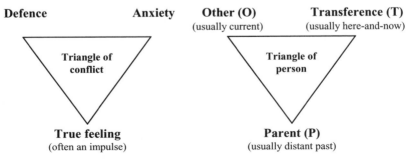

Figure 19.2 Malan's two triangles.

that between them they can be used to represent almost every intervention that a therapist makes; and that much of the therapist's skill consists of knowing which parts of which triangle to include in his interpretation at any given moment' (p. 91). For an illustration of this process with a client who has intellectual disabilities, see also Beail and Newman (2005).

From the case description of Mr B, only tentative beginnings of a formulation can be made as the writers do not have direct transference and countertransference material to work with. The model we have largely drawn on is based on the developmental theories of the Kleinian School of Psychoanalysis (Klein, 1975). We work from the assumption that people with intellectual disabilities develop the same psychic structures as everyone else; but at a slower rate. Thus, their psychic structures can be understood better through theories of early development such as Klein's. Kleinian theory is useful in formulating people who present with difficulties like Mr B, as it provides a framework for understanding anger based on primitive intellectual and emotional development. Central to Kleinian theory is the idea that anxieties arise from the unbearable nature of conflicts in the young child stimulated by recognition that he or she contains both love and hate within himself or herself and that his or her parents and others contain both good and bad within themselves. Klein asserted that these conflicting feelings and anxieties arouse primitive unconscious defences in the form of *projection, introjections, idealization, denial, related identifications, omnipotence* and *splitting*, which serve to protect the child against anxieties. Kleinian theory guides us to look at anger in terms of its utility in defending the client against feelings of dependency, inadequacy, fear of rejection or annihilation and envy. These primitive defences operate by fragmenting and keeping apart those conflicting parts or by denying their existence. The defence of '*splitting*' is considered to be central to this process, and describes the unconscious separating of conflicting aspects of other people and the self (ego), so that they are perceived as either entirely good (loved) or entirely bad (hated). Hence, with Mr B we would hypothesize that his parents and his disability are split off from conscious thought.

'*Projection*' and '*introjection*' are the processes in which the child either casts out into other people (projects) aspects of himself or herself which do not assimilate with his or her existing understanding of himself or herself (Mr B's physical and intellectual disability, the rejected part of him), or takes into himself or herself (introjects) aspects of other people which serve to preserve their existing perception of him or her (a good and competent worker, a radio announcer, a man in good shape, someone who could care for his grandmother). '*Denial*' and '*idealization*' are the defensive processes with which we deny the existence of negative aspects of real objects (the lost and absent parents, the disabled part of himself and the angry part of himself), and which may also result in their idealization (but not so far for Mr B). However, Mr B also used the defence of *omnipotence* to preserve an image of himself as competent and not impaired/disabled; presenting himself as ready to leave his training programme – a view not shared by the programme organizers or supervisors – and as being in '*good shape*'. In the course of time, Kleinian thought has come to view the person as having an internal world that contains a full arena of varied objects (people) in various degrees of synthesis and separateness. Mr B only mentions some people in his internal world, but from other information we are aware of other people. Those he mentions are split into good and bad, and able and disabled. The therapist would need to explore his relationships with those mentioned and also those not mentioned (mother and father). Kleinian theory asserts that it is the experience that we have people (objects) inside ourselves that gives us a sense of existence and identity. The struggle to attain a secure and stable good internal object inside ourselves is seen as the core of a stable personality that can weather emotional disturbance. To achieve this, the self (ego) has to form an integration of the various part objects and of the parts of the self. The basic tenet of our hypothesis is that Mr B has had significant difficulties in this integration. We would want to explore why his parents and his disabilities are out of reach of his conscious communication to help develop our formulation. Thus, from the available information in the case study we have begun to hypothesize the nature of Mr B's anxiety, his fear of rejection and abandonment, and defences, such as splitting, projection, denial, omnipotence, fantasy identifications and the possible hidden issues that lie at the apex of the triangle of conflict (rejection by parents, his disability and possible links between them).

TREATMENT PLAN

In psychodynamic psychotherapy, there is less explicit distinction between the phases of assessment, formulation and treatment, and following formulation of Mr B's presentation, sessions would proceed as already described. Mr B would be invited to continue to free associate and the therapist would continue to listen and observe. At appropriate times, the therapist would reflect back, seek further information and ask exploratory questions. At the same time the therapist will be monitoring his or her feelings that are aroused in them by the client (the counter-transference). The therapist would see the client's behaviour and communication through the concept of transference and consider the material in terms of the client's internal world and the development of that internal world. Following formulation of hypotheses about aspects of the client that are hidden and disowned, the therapist would think carefully how to communicate these to the client. Is the client ready and able to be made aware of unconscious aspects of his or her thinking and life? Exploration of his parental relationships and his disability may result in further resistance, and this would need to be drawn to Mr B's attention by the therapist. This would then be linked to his anxiety and subsequently to the hidden parts of his psyche. In this process, the here-and-now issues of the therapy session are gradually linked to problems in current relationships and those that are the basis of the problems from the past, usually with the parents. The therapist needs to consider whether or not the client could retain the interpretation in full or whether it needs to be delivered in parts. Freudian therapists prefer to wait until the client is in a state of positive transference; however, Klein recommended making interpretations when people are at their maximal level of anxiety. As people who have intellectual disabilities have more difficulties in life with their memory and also are more prone to primitive defences such as splitting, we would argue from a pragmatic point of view that the Kleinian approach is more likely to be effective.

The personality evolves through the internalization and integration of the people who care for us and those we have relationships with over time. Thus, the therapist would be concerned to explore the impact of the lost and absent parents on the development of Mr B's internal world and personality. There are also a range of psychodynamic theories of development, which the therapist may also employ to understand the origins or development of difficulties and conflicts, as well as coping styles. Clarkson (1993) highlights the reparative/developmentally needed relationship and defines this as the internal provision by the therapist of a corrective/reparative or replenishing parental relationship or action where the original parenting was deficient, abusive or overprotective. Such a relationship modality is a further facet of the therapist's intervention and style. Only through exploration with Mr B of the internal representation of his parents and other carers can the therapist help him with any difficulties that may be located in his past but impacting on his behaviour now. Potentially for Mr B, his fear of rejection may stem from his own fantasies about his rejection by his parents, and he may have to face difficult and painful emotions regarding his lost and absent parents, including his feelings of abandonment and rejection. He also has to come to terms with his intellectual and physical disabilities. There may also be fears that his parents rejected him or wished him dead because of his disability, or that they caused his disability through bad sex. These are not fanciful hypotheses but based on the themes that have emerged in therapy and from the clinical experience of the psychotherapists who works with people who have intellectual disabilities.

ROLE OF RESEARCH AND CLINICAL EXPERIENCE

Psychodynamic psychotherapy has a long tradition of theoretical development based on detailed case studies. This tradition is also evident in the literature on psychodynamic psychotherapy with people with intellectual disabilities. The case studies contain narrative accounts of treatment or parts of treatment and rarely refer to outcomes or effectiveness (Beail, 1995). There is also some hostility to evaluating the effectiveness of psychodynamic psychotherapy as practitioners feel that the process of evaluation interferes with the client–therapist relationship. Thus, there is a body of knowledge built on clinical experience and theoretical development (see, for example De Groef and Heinemann, 1999; Sinason, 1992). However, not all have taken this view and a small number of studies have evaluated the effectiveness of this approach with adults who have intellectual disabilities (Beail, 2003; Willner, 2005). Since then Beail *et al.* (2005) have published an open clinical trial and Newman and Beail (2005) have looked how people with intellectual disabilities assimilate their problems during treatment. Whilst research is limited, all studies suggest that people who have intellectual disabilities make positive gains after receiving psychodynamic therapy.

THE EVENT

The role-play described in the case study would not be part of a psychodynamic approach. The psychodynamic psychotherapist works from the position that key interpersonal relationships in the client's current and past are re-enacted in the relationship with them. However, the scenario is helpful in informing us that Mr B can work well with his therapist and can use his imagination to think about others and situations. He also demonstrated his capacity to talk about situations and then to understand that others have internal worlds, emotions and feelings like him. The event shows that he has the capability to moderate his anger by thinking more about the other people involved; seeing things from another person's perspective. Mr B was able to describe and role-play a 'good supervisor' who is reasonable when under pressure, but notably his own behaviour when under pressure is markedly different from this and he tends to become aggressive and demanding.

For the psychodynamic psychotherapist, there are a number of potentially unresolved issues such as these that need to be addressed to enable a deeper understanding of Mr B's anger and aggression in order to facilitate better personal management of these feelings in the future.

OTHER ISSUES

Another relevant issue for Mr B would be the apparent desynchrony between his physical, cognitive and emotional development. This may be a source of anger as he sees other men of his age in employment, whilst he is held back. Mr B's intellectual disability is the main cause of this, a cause he does not acknowledge.

It would also be interesting to consider Mr B's rigid beliefs about how people should behave and which prompt such harsh judgements on others, such as spending money on drink, drug use, disability, other workers and supervisors. Do these reflect harsh value judgements he feels from others, and underlying feelings of injustice and unfairness related to his disabilities? Is a sense that he is and will be judged negatively related to his decision not to attend group therapy or start a relationship? What sense has Mr B made of the losses including his uncle, the good/successful worker and his parents, which have occurred in his life?

The function of anger and aggression as an adaptive strategy would also be useful to explore, as this has been reinforced in situations where aggression has meant that he gets his own way, such as in the stereo shop and laundermat, and goes unpunished, for example by the police or by his grandmother.

SUMMARY

We have constructed a tentative psychodynamic formulation based on the information in the case study. The formulation is a hypothesis that would guide our exploration with Mr B in his therapy sessions. Through exploration we would be able to confirm or refute their relevance.

Using Malan's triangles, we have established that Mr B is using a range of defences, such as splitting, projection, denial and omnipotence. The defences in Kleinian theory are associated with such anxieties as fear of rejection and concerns about dependency. We hypothesized that Mr B has been unable to integrate aspects of his past and himself, notably his disabled self, his lost mother and his absent, abandoning father and any fantasies about relationships between the two such as hatred for the disabled child or bad sex between the parents creating the disability.

Psychodynamic psychotherapy may be an appropriate treatment for people like Mr B whose anger may continue until he develops an integration of those aspects of himself that he finds intolerable.

REFERENCES

Beail, N. (1995) Outcome of psychoanalysis, psychoanalytic and psychodynamic psychotherapy with people with intellectual disabilities. *Changes*, **13**, 186–91.

Beail, N. (2003) What works for people with mental retardation? Critical commentary on cognitive behavioral and psychodynamic psychotherapy. *Mental Retardation*, **41**, 468–72.

Beail, N. and Newman, D. (2005) Psychodynamic counselling and psychotherapy for mood disorders, in *Mood Disorders in People with Mental Retardation* (ed. P. Sturmey), NADD Press, New York, pp. 272–92.

Beail, N., Warden, S., Morsley, K. and Newman, D.W. (2005) Naturalistic evaluation of the effectiveness of psychodynamic psychotherapy with adults with intellectual disabilities. *Journal of Applied Research in Intellectual Disabilities*, **18**, 245–51.

Clarkson, P. (1993) *On Psychotherapy*, Whurr Publishers, London.

De Groef, J. and Heinemann, E. (eds) (1999) *Psychoanalysis and Mental Handicap*, Free Associations Books, London.

Freud, S. (1912) The dynamics of transference, in *The Standard Edition of the Complete Psychological Works of Sigmund Freud*, vol. **12** (ed. J. Stratchey.), Hogarth Press, London, pp. 97–108.

Klein, M. (1975) *The Writings of Melanie Klein*, vol. **3**, Hogarth Press, London.

Laplanche, J. and Pontalis, J.B. (1988) *The Language of Psychoanalysis*, Karnac Books, London.

Malan, D.H. (1979) *Individual Psychotherapy and the Science of Psychodynamics*, Butterworth, London.

Newman, D.W. and Beail, N. (2002) Monitoring change in psychotherapy with people with intellectual disabilities. The application of the Assimilation of Problematic Experiences Scale. *Journal of Applied Research in Intellectual Disabilities*, **15**, 48–60.

Newman, D.W. and Beail, N. (2005) An analysis of assimilation during psychotherapy with people who have mental retardation. *American Journal on Mental Retardation*, **110**, 359–65.

Sinason, V. (1992) *Mental Handicap and the Human Condition: New Approaches from the Tavistock*, Free Association Books, London.

Smith, D. (1987) Formulating and evaluating hypotheses in psychoanalytic psychotherapy. *British Journal of Medical Psychology*, **60**, 313–6.

Stiles, W.B., Elliott, R., Llewelyn, S.P. *et al.* (1990) Assimilation of problematic experiences by clients in psychotherapy. *Psychotherapy*, **27**, 411–20.

Willner, P. (2005) The effectiveness of psychotherapeutic interventions for people with learning disabilities: a critical overview. *Journal of Intellectual Disability Research*, **49**, 75–85.

20

A Cognitive-Behavioural Formulation of Anger in a Man with an Intellectual Disability

PAUL WILLNER

THEORETICAL ORIENTATION AND RATIONALE

Cognitive-behavioural therapies (CBT) represent the dominant modality of psychological treatment in adult mental health services where they have been shown to be effective in a very wide range of psychological disorders, in both group and individual settings (Hawton *et al.*, 1989; Roth and Fonagy, 2005). The basis of a CBT formulation, derived from behaviour therapy, is a functional analysis, which describes the Antecedent stimuli that elicit the behaviour, the Behaviour itself, and the Consequences that reinforce and maintain the behaviour. This ABC model can be expanded to include not only Precipitants (antecedent stimuli) and Perpetuating (maintaining) factors, but also Predisposing factors that make the behaviour more likely to occur, and Protective factors (strengths) that decrease the likelihood of the behaviour occurring, or mitigate adverse consequences. A formulation built along these lines consists of (a) a list of problems, (b) a set of provisional hypotheses concerning predisposing, precipitating, perpetuating and protective factors (the 4Ps) and (c) some further hypotheses concerning potential interventions (Persons, 1989).

The cognitive model of psychopathology (Beck, 1976; Ellis, 1973) is based on the principle that people's emotions and behaviour are influenced by their perceptions and appraisals of events. ('There is nothing either good or bad

Clinical Case Formulation: Varieties of Approaches.   Edited by Peter Sturmey.
© 2009 John Wiley & Sons, Ltd.

but thinking makes it so': Shakespeare, 1602). It is further assumed that psychological disorders are characterized by distorted or dysfunctional thinking. Therefore, mood and behaviour can be improved by working with the patient to modify thinking in the direction of more realistic evaluations of events (Beck, 1976). A cognitive-behavioural formulation seeks to build a mental map that explains the processes by which the identified or hypothesized predisposing and precipitating factors influence the behaviour in question. This is done by identifying the cognitions, and in particular, the cognitive distortions that may mediate these relationships. In a recent extension of this approach, Kinderman has argued that the primary focus should be on the psychological processes that give rise to maladaptive cognitions, rather than their content (Kinderman, 2005; Kinderman and Tai, 2007).

Cognitive-behavioural therapy for anger is based on an approach developed by Novaco and colleagues (Novaco, 1975; Novaco, Ramm and Black, 2000; Taylor and Novaco, 2005) that conceptualizes anger as an emotion with physiological, behavioural and cognitive components, which is triggered by discrete environmental events. This conceptualization gives rise to two related but distinct therapeutic approaches: anger management and anger treatment (Novaco, Ramm and Black, 2000). Anger management is a psychoeducational approach that aims to teach people skills that they can use to cope with provocation. It is based on a psychoeducational-deficit model: people become angry because they lack coping skills. Anger management is usually delivered in a group format. It is guided by CBT principles but typically not by individual analysis and formulation. Anger treatment, by contrast, does require individual analysis and formulation, and is delivered individually. It aims to modify cognitive structures that promote and maintain anger, enhance self-monitoring and develop self-control. It is recommended for clients with deep-rooted anger problems that disrupt their interpersonal functioning and cause psychological and physical distress (Taylor and Novaco, 2005). Both interventions include physiological (relaxation), behavioural and cognitive elements, but whereas the cognitive elements are a relatively minor component of anger management, in anger treatment, they predominate.

RELEVANT AND IRRELEVANT VARIABLES

As the purpose of a formulation is to integrate all of the relevant information (British Psychological Society Division of Clinical Psychology, 2001), none of the information presented in a case description would be assumed automatically to be irrelevant. However, three types of information would be of particular interest which are as follows:

(a) The information that would provide the basis for an initial functional analysis: the triggers that elicit anger episodes, the nature of the challenging behaviour and any factors that might reinforce and maintain it.
(b) Factors that might increase (predisposing) or decrease (protective) the likelihood of anger being expressed inappropriately, including any information about the availability and utilization of coping skills.
(c) Any information, derived primarily from the client's self-report, that would enable inferences to be drawn or hypotheses developed concerning maladaptive or dysfunctional cognitions.

ROLE OF RESEARCH AND CLINICAL EXPERIENCE

There have been many studies demonstrating the effectiveness of cognitively based anger interventions in the general population: Taylor and Novaco (2005) reviewed six published meta-analyses, which found medium to large effect sizes. It is only recently that CBT has been implemented in people with intellectual disabilities (Stenfert Kroese, Dagnan and Loumidis, 1997), and there is a paucity of evidence to demonstrate effectiveness in this population (Willner, 2005). However, anger is the one area where there is a significant research literature, which includes controlled trials. There are six published studies in people with intellectual disabilities comparing group-based anger management with waiting-list controls, all of which demonstrate effectiveness (Taylor and Novaco, 2005; Willner, 2007). Support for the skills-deficit model is provided by evidence that improvements in anger management are related to the extent to which anger-coping skills have been acquired (Willner, 2007). There is also a series of studies, all from the same research group, providing evidence for the effectiveness of individual formulation-based anger treatment in people with intellectual disabilities, again, in comparison to waiting-list controls (Taylor and Novaco, 2005).

While there is evidence that cognitive-behavioural treatments for anger are effective in the general population and in people with intellectual disabilities, there is very little research focusing on processes of change during therapy. None of the studies of anger interventions in people with intellectual disabilities have included any rigorous measures of cognitive change. Neither has there been any research that has attempted to assess directly the significance of the formulation to the outcome of anger interventions. One way to address the significance of an element of a therapeutic intervention is to compare the effects of the intervention with and without that element. For example, there is discussion, albeit inconclusive, of the relative contributions of the physiological, behavioural and cognitive components of anger management (Willner, 2007). In the case of anger treatment, however, the formulation is so integral to the treatment that without the formulation, there could be no intervention. Therefore, the evidence that cognitive-behavioural anger treatment is effective in people with intellectual disabilities could also be interpreted as evidence in support of a cognitive-behavioural approach to the formulation of anger problems in this population.

This said, the formulation developed below, which uses the 4Ps approach (Persons, 1989), is considerably more complex than the type of formulation envisaged by Taylor and Novaco (2005), which is based very largely on an enumeration of the situations that trigger anger, the internal events that these situations evoke and the behaviours that follow, leading to a simple, linear formulation of situation–thoughts–feelings–behavioural reaction–consequences. As the therapy progresses, the therapist introduces and works on the role of thoughts in mediating between events and behaviour, and cognitions such as attention, expectations and attributions. These form part of an implicit formulation that guides the therapist's work with the client, but the published manual does not require a reformulation in which these relationships and processes are made explicit (Taylor and Novaco, 2005). To the extent that the research evidence relates to a much simpler formulation, the complex formulation described below is based on clinical experience, supported by the evidence, in many indications and many populations, that CBT interventions based on formulations of this kind are generally effective (Hawton *et al.*, 1989; Roth and Fonagy, 2005).

FORMULATION

The formulation of Mike's anger problems is summarized in Figure 20.1. It is presented in two parts: an enumeration of the predisposing, precipitating, perpetuating and protective factors that can be identified from the case description (Benson, 2009), followed by a narrative account of Mike's anger that incorporates identified or hypothesized cognitive mediators.

Predisposing factors

The case description outlines or suggests at least six important factors that combine, as described below, to predispose Mike to react in an angry fashion to provocation.

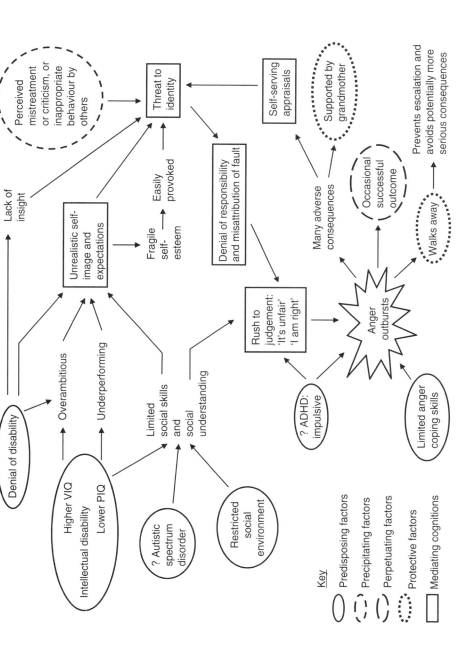

Figure 20.1 A cognitive-behavioural formulation of Mike's anger, based on the 4Ps approach and clinical experience.

First, Mike has an intellectual disability. His full-scale IQ (FSIQ) score of 65 places him towards the top of the 'extremely low' range of abilities required for a diagnosis of intellectual disability (FS IQ < 70). Indeed, his particularly poor performance on timed tests may reflect his mild physical disability (cerebral palsy), so his true FSIQ score may be higher than that reported. It is unclear from the case description whether the poor performance on timed tests is entirely responsible for the discrepancy between Mike's Verbal and Performance IQ scores. For the purposes of this formulation, it will be assumed that Mike has a lower Performance IQ score even after discounting timed tests.

Second, one of the most telling points in the case description is Mike's statement that he likes his vocational programme because it does not cater to 'low-functioning people'. This suggests strongly that Mike does not see himself as a person with a learning disability. Denial of disability is relatively common among people whose abilities are only just within the 'extremely low' range. As described below, this will become one of the most significant features of the formulation.

Third, a number of the facts provided suggest that Mike may be somewhere on the autistic spectrum. He is something of a loner, with few friends, and no close friends and poor relationships with workmates. His interests in electronics, computers, audio systems and radio announcing, which avoids direct social contact, are consistent with an autistic spectrum disorder, as is his choice of working out at the gym, rather than participating with others in sports. The presence of autistic features, if confirmed by further assessment, would go some way to explain Mike's need for routine and intolerance of change, as demonstrated in the failure of his most recent work placement.

Fourth, Mike inhabits a relatively impoverished social environment and his social understanding and social skills are poor. His main social contact throughout life has been his grandmother. He was teased at school, where the thing he enjoyed most was trips out to visit museums. His only male role model seems to have been his uncle, who lived with him briefly. We can only speculate on what Mike might have learned from the uncle about how to deal with provocation, bearing in mind that Mike lives in a high-crime neighbourhood and several other family members have spent time in gaol.

Fifth, Mike was diagnosed as a young man having 'impulse control problems'; the fact that he was prescribed stimulants as a child suggests that he was also diagnosed with attention-deficit hyperactivity disorder (ADHD). His more recent anti-psychotic medication would be consistent with this diagnosis. Judging from the behavioural problems that Mike has experienced over the years, it appears that problems of impulse control have followed him throughout his life: there is no indication that he ever stops to take stock before responding to provocation.

Sixth, Mike seems not to have learned any useful anger-coping skills, other than walking away, which he does only after an outburst, not before.

Precipitating factors

Mike's anger outbursts are preceded by a consistent set of triggers: perceived slights or wrongs; disagreement with others about how things should be done; and an inability to accept criticism. More generally, Mike's outbursts are precipitated by perceived violations of his expectations of how things should be done or how he should be treated.

Perpetuating factors

The case description identifies a single overt factor that sustains Mike's angry behaviour: anger occasionally works in achieving his goals, particularly when displayed towards shopkeepers. While behaviour maintained by partial reinforcement is notoriously difficult to extinguish, it is unlikely that this factor alone is sufficient to explain the persistence of Mike's confrontational behaviour, given the volume of adverse consequences that his behaviour also engenders. We return below to the question of whether Mike's anger might provide him with additional less obvious benefits.

Protective factors

Mike's presentation is very short on protective factors. His one major strength is that he is able to restrain his anger, which, since his schooldays at least, does not progress from verbal aggression and occasional destruction of property to direct physical aggression. He is able to manage this by using his one anger-coping skill – walking away. This strategy protects Mike from the very serious consequences, such as prosecution, that would be likely to follow if his anger were to escalate to the point where he committed physical assaults. Mike's grandmother also protects him from the consequences of his anger by providing emotional support when he gets into trouble, with the exception of the occasion when he broke her vase and window. It is notable that while Mike still brings his frustration home, he has been able to keep his promise to her not to repeat this behaviour. It appears that Mike has some sense of proportionality and within his own frame of reference, is careful not to over-respond.

Narrative formulation including an account of cognitive mediators

Mike is a man with an intellectual disability, with autistic features and possible ADHD. He has grown up in a restricted and dangerous social environment, with no friends and little company other than his grandmother. As a result of his disability, his autistic features and his social environment, he has learned few social skills and he has a poor understanding of social situations.

Mike's verbal ability is relatively high, which allows him to deny his disability. It is important for Mike to see himself, and to be seen by others, as able. He carries a newspaper as a visible badge of his ability. He looks down on drinkers, drug users, gamblers and 'low-functioning people'. He has learned all that the vocational programme has to teach him; he knows more than his teachers or supervisors. He outperforms his fellow workers and knows more than they will ever know. Most tellingly, Mike believes that 'the customer is always right': by this, he means himself, since this belief does not extend to the customers he serves.

Because he sees himself as able, Mike sets himself overambitious goals and has unrealistic expectations of what he should achieve. While he is able to learn practical tasks and takes pride in performing them, his low non-verbal ability, compounded by his physical disability and his poor social skills, puts him frequently into difficulty in work situations because of his inappropriate social behaviour. His self-esteem is fragile as a result of these repeated challenges, and he goes through life on a very short fuse. Mike's grandmother tells him that he 'could do better if he would just try to get along with people', but there is no evidence that she tells him home truths about the changes that would be needed in order to bring this about.

Mike has very fixed ideas of how others should behave, particularly towards him, and he is easily provoked. He has great difficulty in accepting instruction from teachers or supervisors because he believes that he knows better than they how things should be done. He cannot tolerate any challenge to his fragile self-esteem, such as criticism by teachers or supervisors, someone knocking over his drink, or being called by a nickname. He is firmly attached to his routines, perhaps reflective of an autistic spectrum disorder, and cannot tolerate them being changed. Mike is also intolerant of others who fail to meet up to his exacting standards of behaviour: workmates and customers who make a mess, women who 'play off one guy against another', young guys who 'joke around too much' or have 'silly competitions', shopkeepers who overcharge him, neighbours who make too much noise.

Mike is very heavily invested in the belief that his personal rules of behaviour should be respected and he has a low threshold to respond to provocation. Because he denies his intellectual disability, he lacks insight into the extent to which his own behaviour contributes to his repeated failures of so-cial performance. When his rules are violated, he cannot contemplate that he may be wrong because this would threaten the core of his identity as an able person who always knows best. He protects his identity and self-esteem, by denying responsibility and blaming others.

Mike's low Performance IQ implies an impairment of the ability to process non-verbal cues that is essential for a proper reading of social situations. His social understanding is further compromised by his restricted social experi-ence and, possibly, a degree of autism. Mike's dual impairments of social understanding and impulse control ensure that when he misattributes fault to other people he does not stop to question his reasoning, but jumps straight to the conclusion that he is being treated unfairly, and to his salient core belief that he is right and therefore others should agree with him and do things his way. Mike lacks anger-coping skills and knows of no way to express his feelings other than shouting, and his sense of conviction together with his im-pulsivity prevent him from pausing to consider the consequences of behaving in this way.

In recent years, Mike's outbursts have been restricted to verbal aggression and occasional damage to property. He is able to terminate episodes of anger though not to avoid them by walking away. By this means he prevents the episode from escalating to physical assault, and so avoids the potentially more serious consequence of criminal charges.

Although Mike's anger has many adverse consequences, particularly being fired from jobs, his angry behaviour is intermittently reinforced by occasional success in achieving his objectives. However, as noted earlier, it is implausible that this factor alone can account for the persistence of Mike's compulsion to behave in ways that lead to him being harmed. Another less obvious, but probably more important, maintaining factor is that, following an incident, Mike appraises the event in self-serving ways that justify his behaviour ('that supervisor was incompetent'), minimize its impact ('the job didn't pay very well anyway') and suppress any doubts ('too little, too late'). This enables him to feel a sense of pride that he has done the right thing. Whatever the objective outcome, he has defended himself successfully against the threat to his iden-tity, and he emerges from the encounter with his self-esteem bruised but intact.

ROLE OF HISTORY VERSUS CURRENT FACTORS

It is a moot point whether Mike's formulation reflects historical or current factors, as his presentation has been much the same throughout his adult life. However, in two important respects this should be seen as a formulation based on current, rather than historical, events.

First, we are missing some crucial historical information about the development of Mike's problems. Specifically, we do now know how or from whom he learned the two sets of beliefs that lie at the core of the formulation: his perception of himself as an able person without an intellectual disability, and his particular expectations about how others should behave. Presumably Mike's grandmother, his church and perhaps his uncle, have influenced the development of these beliefs, but further assessment would be needed to clarify the nature of these historical influences. Second, because Mike's problems have not changed significantly over the past 15–20 years, all of the information necessary to construct the formulation and design an intervention is available in his current presentation. Indeed, a more detailed assessment confined to, say, the past 6–12 months would lead to exactly the same conclusions.

There is one additional current factor, of crucial importance, that has not yet been considered. This is the question of why Mike has accepted the present referral having declined several previous opportunities. What we know about the circumstances of the referral is that Mike has accepted it because 'his vocational counsellor said that he needs to come to therapy and that will help him get a job'. There is no suggestion that Mike is presenting himself for therapy because he has come to identify himself as a person with anger problems. He appears to have no understanding of how the therapy would help him, what the therapeutic targets would be or that there is any linkage between his behaviour and his job prospects. While Mike certainly wants a job, he displays no motivation to deal with his anger issues.

TREATMENT PLAN

The formulation calls for three distinct interventions: motivational interviewing, anger management and anger treatment. Mike displays no motivation to change, so this must be the first therapeutic target, using motivational interviewing (Miller and Rollnick, 2002) to help him recognize that anger is a problem for him that he would benefit from addressing. Provided he engages with treatment, the next stage should be to teach him some anger-coping skills. He needs first to learn to recognize that he is becoming angry. When he is able to do this, the particular coping skills that would be of benefit to him in provocative situations are: (a) stopping to think before expressing his feelings; (b) assertiveness skills that would enable him to express his anger in a socially acceptable manner; and (c) learning how to use his range of hobbies and interests to distract himself, rather than bringing his frustrations home and ruminating on incidents. The major part of Mike's therapy will involve helping him to restructure his cognitions around his self-concept and his perceptions that the world treats him unfairly. This would involve helping him (d) to gain a more balanced view of his abilities and recognize that others may sometimes know better, so that his identity is not threatened by difference; and (e) to address his self-serving appraisals and misattributions of fault, through learning that responsibility in social situations is shared between the participants and that there may be legitimate reasons why people sometimes behave differently to how he thinks they should.

Mike's case is in fact one fairly typical presentation of individuals with intellectual disabilities referred for individual anger treatment, and most of his needs will be met by a standard individual anger treatment programme. Taylor and Novaco (2005) described an 18-session programme designed to be delivered through twice-weekly 1-h sessions. The intervention begins with a 6-session preparatory phase aimed at developing an understanding of anger and other emotions and establishing motivation to change, followed by a 12-session treatment phase. Treatment is based on stress inoculation, using therapist-guided graded exposure to a hierarchy of individual triggers for anger. The major components of the programme are cognitive restructuring and problem-solving, supported by behavioural-coping skills training. Taylor and Novaco (2005) emphasized that their protocol was intended to guide but not to determine treatment, which should be adapted to meet the needs of the individual client. Mike may need a greater emphasis in the preparatory phase on building motivation to change – the manual devotes only one session to this issue – and the addition of input around assertiveness, which the manual does not address systematically.

While Mike's treatment would largely conform to a published treatment manual, it would include a variety of modifications to compensate for the difficulties that Mike may experience as a consequence of his intellectual disability. It is standard practice, when working with people of limited intellectual ability to use a range of modifications to improve communication. These include: (a) use of simple words and short sentences; (b) repetition, frequent recapitulation and constant checking for understanding; and (c) use of pictures and gesture (Lynch, 2004; Prosser and Bromley, 1998). In addition to the obvious modifications aimed at slowing down and simplifying delivery, there would be other more subtle differences from the therapy that would be offered to a more able person. In particular, Mike may well need the therapist to provide alternative cognitions for him to use as a basis for cognitive restructuring, rather than expecting Mike to do this work himself (Taylor and Novaco, 2005; Willner and Goodey, 2006). Also, there is evidence that anger interventions are more effective if carers attend sessions and support homework completion (Rose *et al.*, 2005; Willner, 2006). In Mike's case, there is little prospect of involving his grandmother, but his vocational counsellor may be willing and able to help.

THE EVENT

Several aspects of the event are unexpected. First, Mike is clearly motivated to work on his anger, provided this is within a vocational context, so the apprehension that he may need motivational work before engaging with therapy is allayed. Second, Mike shows himself readily able to take another's point of view. Perhaps Mike's autistic symptoms do not have an overwhelming impact on his ability to engage in interpersonal problem-solving. Third, Mike appears amenable to changing his position, provided he perceives that the other person has a good attitude and is not picking on him. However, there is no evidence yet that he is able to deal with situations that he perceives as not meeting these criteria. All in all, this further information is encouraging; but the road ahead of Mike and his therapist will be long and hard.

OTHER ISSUES

As discussed earlier, the choice of the complex 4Ps formulation, as outlined in Figure 20.1 and above, rather than a simple linear formulation, was based more on clinical experience than on research evidence. Having used the complex formulation to develop a treatment plan, it is worth comparing it to a linear formulation (Figure 20.2) and asking whether the more complex formulation has any clinical advantage.

It is apparent that there are some important issues that could be overlooked in a treatment plan derived from the simple linear formulation. These include a specification of the common feature of Mike's triggers for anger, violation of his rules of behaviour, and a consideration of why this is such a serious issue for him, leading to one of the most important treatment targets, Mike's denial of his disability and the ensuing tendency to set unrealistic targets that he cannot meet. If this problem is not addressed, then Mike is likely to display intense resistance to challenges to his ideas about his right and others' wrong behaviour. The 4Ps formulation also links Mike's rules of behaviour and his resistance to change to a possible autistic spectrum disorder, which would have implications for the way in which challenges to Mike's thinking are presented and pursued. A third issue suggested by the complex formulation,

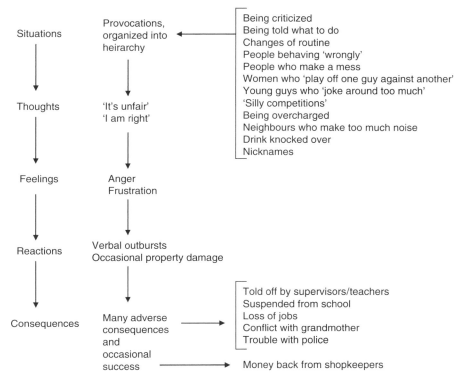

Figure 20.2 A simpler linear cognitive-behavioural formulation of Mike's anger, based on a functional analysis.

but absent from the simple formulation, is the implication that at some stage Mike may need some psychoeducational input around social relationships. Finally, the linear formulation provides no insight into the persistence of a pattern of behaviour that creates many difficulties for Mike and provides few tangible benefits. For several reasons, therefore, the complex formulation is likely to lead to a richer therapeutic intervention – though it is impossible to know how much more effective, if at all, this would be.

It is also pertinent to reflect that Mike's perception of being treated unfairly is one that is in reality accurate for many people with intellectual disabilities in many aspects of their lives. There is nothing unreasonable in Mike's wish to be treated with respect: indeed, the tenacity with which he pursues this aspiration could be seen as a triumph of hope over experience. Mike has encountered real prejudice – at school and almost certainly elsewhere – and he is entitled to feel distressed and frustrated when his efforts to do what is required of him are unappreciated. Mike's anger would be lessened if the people around him were more mindful and considerate of the many difficulties that he encounters in trying to live his life on their terms. Mike is not the only person in this scenario with a problem, but he is the only one whose problem is recognized and referred for treatment.

SUMMARY

Mike is a man with an intellectual disability, with autistic features and possible ADHD. His relatively high verbal ability allows him to deny his disability, but his low non-verbal ability and poor social skills let him down and his self-esteem is fragile as a result. He has little tolerance of change or criticism, and when challenged by events that violate his expectations of how people should behave, he defends these threats to his identity by denying responsibility and misattributing blame to others. His limited social understanding leads him to jump to the conclusion that he is being treated unfairly and the only way he knows to express his feelings is to respond with outbursts of anger. He restrains himself by using his only anger-coping skill, walking away, before he commits a physical assault, so avoiding criminal consequences. His anger is occasionally successful in achieving his objectives. More frequently, the consequences are adverse, but he appraises these episodes in a self-serving manner that confirms him in the belief that he has done the right thing. Mike displays no motivation to change, so this must be the first therapeutic target. Subsequently, he will benefit from interventions to teach him anger-coping skills, particularly stopping to think, distraction and assertiveness, and to restructure his cognitions around his self-concept and his perceptions that the world treats him unfairly.

REFERENCES

Beck, A.T. (1976) *Cognitive Therapy and the Emotional Disorders*, International Universities Press, New York.

Benson, B.A. (2009) A case of anger in a person with intellectual disabilities, in *Clinical Case Formulation: Varieties of Approaches* (ed. P. Sturmey), John Wiley & Sons, Ltd, Chichester, pp. 241–266.

British Psychological Society Division of Clinical Psychology (2001) *The Core Purpose and Philosophy of the Profession*, British Psychological Society, Leicester.

Ellis, A. (1973) *Rational-Emotive Therapy*, Cornell University Press, Itaska.

Hawton, K., Salkovsis, P.M., Kirk, J. and Clark, D.M. (1989) *Cognitive Behaviour Therapy for Psychiatric Problems: A Practical Guide*, Oxford University Press, Oxford.

Kinderman, P. (2005) A psychological model of mental disorder. *Harvard Review of Psychiatry*, **13**, 206–17.

Kinderman, P. and Tai, S. (2007) Clinical implications of a psychological model of mental disorder. *Behavioural and Cognitive Psychotherapy*, **35**, 1–14.

Lynch, C. (2004) Psychotherapy for persons with mental retardation. *Mental Retardation*, **42**, 399–405.

Miller, W.R. and Rollnick, S. (2002) Motivational Interviewing: Preparing People for Change (2nd edition). Guilford Press, New York.

Novaco, R.W. (1975) *Anger Control: The Development and Evaluation of an Experimental Treatment*, D.C. Heath, Lexington, MA.

Novaco, R.W., Ramm, M. and Black, L. (2000) Anger treatment with offenders, in *Handbook of Offender Assessment and Treatment* (ed. C. Hollin), John Wiley & Sons, Ltd, Chichester, pp. 281–96.

Persons, J.B. (1989) *Cognitive Therapy in Practice: A Case Formulation Approach*, Norton, London.

Prosser, H. and Bromley, J. (1998) Interviewing people with learning disabilities, in *Clinical Psychology and People with Learning Disabilities* (eds E. Emerson, C. Hatton, J. Bromley and A. Caine), John Wiley & Sons, Ltd, Chichester, pp. 99–113.

Rose, J., Loftus, M., Flint, B. and Carey, L. (2005) Factors associated with the efficacy of a group intervention for anger in people with intellectual disabilities. *British Journal of Clinical Psychology*, **44**, 305–17.

Roth, A. and Fonagy, P. (2005) *What Works for Whom? A Critical Review of Psychotherapy Research*, 2nd edn, Guilford Press, New York.

Shakespeare, W. (1602) Hamlet, in *Shakespeare, Complete Works*, Oxford University Press, Oxford.

Stenfert Kroese, B., Dagnan, D. and Loumidis, K. (eds) (1997) *Cognitive-Behaviour Therapy for People with Learning Disabilities*, Routledge, London.

Taylor, J.L. and Novaco, R.W. (2005) *Anger Treatment for People with Developmental Disabilities: A Theory, Evidence and Manual-Based Approach*, John Wiley & Sons, Ltd, Chichester.

Willner, P. (2005) The effectiveness of psychotherapeutic interventions for people with learning disabilities: a critical overview. *Journal of Intellectual Disability Research*, **49**, 73–85.

Willner, P. (2006) Readiness for cognitive therapy in people with intellectual disabilities. *Journal of Applied Research in Intellectual Disabilities*, **19**, 5–16.

Willner, P. (2007) Cognitive-behavioural therapy for people with intellectual disabilities: focus on anger. *Advances in Mental Health and Learning Disabilities*, **1**, 14–21.

Willner, P. and Goodey, R. (2006) Interaction of cognitive distortions and cognitive deficits in the formulation and treatment of obsessive–compulsive behaviours in a woman with an intellectual disability. *Journal of Applied Research in Intellectual Disabilities*, **19**, 67–74.

21

Commentary on Formulations of Anger in a Person with Intellectual Disabilities

ROBERT DIDDEN

Case formulations for psychological and behavioural problems have been developed for a wide range of therapeutic approaches, such as cognitive-behavioural and psychodynamic therapies (see Eells, 2007). A case formulation has at least two aims. First, it provides a comprehensive and coherent model or set of hypotheses about the causes and maintaining factors that explain a person's psychological and behavioural problems. These hypotheses should be testable and based on a psychological theory. Second, a case formulation provides directives for designing an intervention that is based on these hypotheses and which is supported by empirical research. A formulation may be considered the bridge between clinical practice and theory and empirical research (Kuyken *et al.*, 2005).

In case formulations, there is a tight linking between assessment and intervention. Individualized case formulation-driven psychotherapy is considered an alternative for manualized treatments and protocols. In manualized treatments and protocols, this linking often is less tight. A formulation approach is usually also more flexible than a manualized approach, but may also be more prone to inferential biases by the therapist who processes complex information (Eells and Lombart, 2003). A therapist's experience and skill is strongly related to the quality of a formulation. Preliminary studies in this area show that agreement between therapists decreases when moving from the descriptive level (e.g. symptom description) to the inferential level (e.g. inferring causal relationships between variables within a comprehensive model)

Clinical Case Formulation: Varieties of Approaches. Edited by Peter Sturmey.
© 2009 John Wiley & Sons, Ltd.

in a formulation (e.g. Mumma and Smith, 2001). There is a debate whether a reliable formulation is necessarily also a qualitatively good formulation as to the comprehensiveness of the structure and usefulness for designing an intervention (see Kuyken *et al.*, 2005). Therapy may be seen as a type of hypothesis testing and a formulation has some validity if outcomes of the intervention are in line with the predictions that follow from the hypotheses. However, studies examining the validity of case formulation or its impact on treatment outcome are scarce (Bieling and Kuyken, 2003). The evidence for the greater effectiveness of case formulations over manualized approaches in the general psychology literature is equivocal (Chadwick, Williams and Mackenzie, 2003).

Cognitive-behavioural and psychodynamic therapies have been reported in the treatment literature of individuals with mild intellectual disabilities (Beail, 2003; Willner, 2005). These therapies differ in the way therapists from each approach consider variables, such as childhood history, target behaviour, causal events and aetiology of current problems, and client's level of control, as important and essential to the understanding and treatment of a person's problems (Eells and Lombart, 2003). These approaches also often differ in the duration of treatment.

In this chapter, the two case formulations of anger in a person with intellectual disabilities from cognitive-behavioural and psychodynamic approaches will be commented upon. Similarities and differences in conceptualization and treatment between these case formulations will be discussed from an applied behavioural analytic account of psychological and behavioural problems. Finally, the evidence base of each treatment implied by the case formulation will be shortly reviewed.

PSYCHODYNAMIC AND COGNITIVE-BEHAVIOURAL CASE FORMULATION

Benson (Chapter 18) describes a man with mild intellectual disabilities who showed verbal aggressive behaviour such as swearing and threatening. Mr B had problems in controlling his anger and had been referred for outpatient therapy. He exhibited verbal aggressive behaviour when he felt that he was not treated appropriately or when he was teased or provoked. He was especially sensitive about other people behaving inappropriately. Because of his outbursts, he had had inter-personal problems keeping jobs and relating to other people, such as his grandmother, teachers or vocational trainers.

Beail and Jackson (Chapter 19) provided a psychodynamic case formulation of Mr B's anger and aggression. The basic assumption was that his aggression was the symptom of an underlying inner conflict that should be identified and disclosed. His inner conflict originated from early, negative life experiences that caused present day functioning. Mr B was not aware or conscious of these conflicts and his current problems with controlling anger and aggression were the result of these unconscious feelings. Through transference and counter-transference, the therapist had to form an understanding of the meaning of Mr B's verbal and non-verbal behaviours in the past and present. The key to understanding the present communications lies in the past. It was hypothesized that Mr B's anger problems and aggression were caused by an underlying sense of vulnerability, insecurity and anxiety which in turn was caused by absence of his parents at a young age. Many of Mr B's behaviours were interpreted as defence mechanisms that served to protect him from his anxieties. Treatment aimed to 'reaching beneath the defence and anxiety to the true feeling' that could be traced back to Mr B's relationships with his parents when he was still a young child. Mr B's treatment consisted of making him aware of these unconscious conflicts and feelings.

Willner (Chapter 20) presented a case formulation of Mr B's anger and aggression from a cognitive-behavioural treatment approach. In this approach, principles of cognitive and behavioural theory are combined to explain and treat emotional and behavioural problems. The basic assumption was that Mr B's behaviour was caused by current environmental events and the way he perceived and appraised these events. In this case formulation, Mr B's aggression was evoked by certain antecedent stimuli, such as being treated in a disrespectful manner, and was maintained by its reinforcing consequences, for example escape from and avoidance of being treated disrespectfully. Furthermore, Mr B lacked appropriate social skills and had a poor understanding of social situations. These variables were causally related to the development of his aggression. His poor social network and features of autism were precipitating factors. Prior to treatment, relationships between these variables were investigated through a functional analysis. Cognitive-behavioural treatment has many behavioural and cognitive elements. It consisted of teaching Mr B appropriate assertive and other adaptive skills, restructuring his distorted cognitions and educating him about social relationships.

SIMILARITIES AND DIFFERENCES IN THE FORMULATIONS

As may be expected, there are many differences between case formulations of psychodynamic and cognitive-behavioural therapies. However, both therapies have also some elements in common. Below, we will discuss the most important similarities and differences in case formulations between these two therapies.

SIMILARITIES

Both therapies are usually implemented in an outpatient setting, although adaptation to inpatient settings is easy. To some degree, self-reports about own feelings and thoughts are considered important in both therapies. In psychodynamic therapy, Mr B's verbal communications are central to the understanding and treatment of his anger problems and aggression. Also, attention is given to non-verbal behaviours as well. For example, both case formulations noted that Mr B behaves like a non-disabled person. He carries a newspaper that he probably is not able to read. Such non-verbal behaviours may give the therapist clues as to how Mr B sees himself and how this relates to the cause of his problems. Mr B does not see himself as a person who has significant disabilities. He finds that he is able and sets high goals for himself.

Both case formulations noted that his understanding of relationships and social situations is poor. He has fixed ideas about how people have to behave. His self-esteem or ego is judged to be fragile and his verbal behaviours were interpreted as possible threats to his identity. Both therapies aimed, albeit through different pathways, at changing his cognitions around his self-concept and denial of his disabilities. Both acknowledged that cognitions and behaviours originate from earlier experiences in interacting with significant others, such as parents or other family members. In both formulations, some thought is given to the development of anger problems.

Differences

There are important differences between the psychodynamic and cognitive-behavioural case formulations to Mr B's anger problems and aggression. A distinct difference lies in defining and selecting the target behaviour. In psychodynamic therapy, Mr B's anger and aggression was viewed as a symptom of an underlying cause based on adverse early life experiences and thus treatment should be directed at this underlying, yet unobservable cause. When explaining his anger and aggression a central role was given to early life experiences. His anger and aggression were conceptualized as defence mechanisms to protect his vulnerable self or ego. For example, walking away from a situation was viewed as a flight. The deeper cause of his anger was some inner conflict of which Mr B was not yet aware of. During therapy, the therapist had to reveal these conflicts and make the client aware of them. In cognitive-behaviour therapy the client has to be aware that anger and aggression itself is the problem and should be changed, while in psychodynamic therapy the client has to become aware that his anger is the symptom of an underlying conflict that has to be faced.

Psychodynamic therapy is implemented individually and often does not make use of manuals or protocols. The therapist refrains as much as possible from giving directives or advice and from judging or evaluating the content of what a client communicates to him. By contrast, anger and aggression are the main focus of cognitive-behaviour therapy. Causal relationships between Mr B's behaviour and current environmental events were identified. Anger and aggression are caused by distorted cognitions and deviant learning processes. For example, walking away from a situation was viewed as a form of self-control or coping skill that prevents Mr B from displaying physical aggression. The therapist evaluated the distorted cognition as something that has to be changed. While it was acknowledged that deviant behaviour patterns may originate from childhood, the client's behaviour was explained by current learning processes. Willner's formulation suggested that distorted cognitions may be strongly related to low IQ, poor learning and possibly autism.

Cognitive-behavioural therapy makes use of manuals and may be implemented both individually and in groups (see Willner, Chapter 20). Its approach is directive and prescriptive. Therapists often use rating scales and methods to collect descriptive data to evaluate progress of treatment. Unlike psychodynamic therapy, an important role is given to carers and significant others. They play an important role in generalization of newly learned client skills, collecting data and providing client information, such as client history. In psychodynamic therapy, others may not be involved in the therapy as this may pose a potential threat to the secure relationship or alliance between client and therapist.

COMMENTS ON THE TWO FORMULATIONS OF ANGER

As stated in the introduction, a case formulation should present an internally coherent and comprehensive account for a person's emotional and behavioural problems. Each formulation provides a more or less coherent account for Mr B's anger problems and aggression. While the model proposed by Willner (Chapter 20) is comprehensive, it contains variables that are not or have not been shown to be causally related to one another. Some explanations are circular. The presence of one variable (e.g. attention deficit hyperactivity disorder (ADHD)) is inferred from another variable (e.g. rush to judgement), however, the presence of ADHD is inferred from the observed behaviour of rushing to judgement. Therefore, this inference of causation is circular. Also, it is still unclear and untested whether non-observable variables, such as threat to identity, act as mediating cognitions and are both sufficient and necessary for the explanation of anger and aggression. Recent studies have shown that, for example aggression and anger are associated with a hostile bias, self-concept or a person's socio-emotional understanding. For example, individuals with aggressive behaviour interpret social events as more hostile than individuals without aggressive behaviours. In the case of Mr B, he might interpret feedback on his work from his vocational supervisor as an effort to humiliate him. Several researchers working in the area of cognitive theory have given such variables the status of causal factors in the explanation of aggression and anger. However, the question of whether they are the cause of the problem, the consequence of the problem or part of the problem itself has yet to be resolved.

The above critical comments hold especially true for researchers and clinicians that have adopted a psychodynamic approach to emotional and behavioural problems. According to Sturmey *et al.* (2007), psychodynamic therapies are a structuralist approach to psychopathology in which verbal behaviour is the result of underlying and unconscious structures. The therapist infers these structures from observation of verbal behaviour.

We believe that Mr B's anger and aggression would best be explained and addressed by a functionalistic approach. Cognitive-behavioural therapies are to a large degree functionalistic, but they also have structuralist elements based on cognitive theory, e.g. inferred cognitive structures such as cognitive schemata (Sturmey, 2006). In an applied behaviour analytic account, its basic assumption is that environmental events are causing the target behaviour (i.e. Mr B's aggression) (Didden, 2007). A change in a person's behaviour would be the result of a change in the person's environment and his adaptive skills. In such an account, distorted cognitions are not considered causal factors but may be conceptualized as covert behaviour. While such cognitions may somehow be related to the target behaviour and its antecedents and consequences (i.e. environmental events), restructuring cognitions alone would be unlikely to produce significant changes in the person's behaviour. Cognitive-behavioural treatment consists of a package of behavioural and cognitive elements. It still has not been shown that the cognitive elements in cognitive-behavioural treatment are effective. Relaxation training alone may be sufficient in decreasing anger and aggression. No component analysis of such treatment packages has been performed with people with intellectual disabilities, although see Jacobson *et al.* (1996) for a component analysis of cognitive-behaviour therapy for depression which found that behavioural rather than cognitive components were effective. Thus, there is some indication that positive treatment outcomes are largely predicted by the behavioural elements of such an approach.

Like cognitive-behavioural therapy, applied behaviour analysis emphasizes current behaviours and events, and a functional analysis precedes treatment (Didden, 2007). The main differences between a cognitively oriented therapist and behaviour therapist are that in the latter case: (a) therapy would also be directed at people in the client's network or environment, (b) restructuring cognitions would not be given a prominent place in functional analysis and treatment, (c) functional analysis and treatment are preferably carried out in the natural settings of the client, (d) applied behaviour analysis uses single subject designs and (e) treatment evaluation is based on observational rather than self-report data on behaviour-environment interactions. In the example of Mr B, aggression has been shaped and maintained by a life-long learning process in which this behaviour came under the control of intermittent negative and positive reinforcement. By exhibiting aggression, Mr B succeeded in avoiding and escaping unwanted situations, such as being teased and provoked. Thus, aggression has a history of negative reinforcement through terminating, albeit temporarily, teasing and bullying. At the same time, this behaviour may have resulted in attention which is a strong reinforcer in the absence of otherwise rewarding relationships. Mr B's cognitions are related to both his emotional and aggressive behaviour and environmental events, but not in a causal way. Changing environmental events and adaptive skill will be sufficient in changing the likelihood of Mr B becoming aggressive and probably will change his cognitions as a side effect.

CONCLUSION

Many people with intellectual disabilities have difficulties in controlling their anger which increases the likelihood of verbal and physical aggressive behaviour. Developing effective treatments for anger and aggression are therefore warranted. Undoubtedly, much progress has been made in this area and the landscape of treatment options has widened. Recently, there has been a debate as to the evidence base, in terms of number and quality of studies, for treatments such as described in the present chapter (Beail, 2003; Sturmey, 2006; Willner, 2005). It is agreed that the evidence base for applied behaviour analysis is strong but that studies for the treatment if individuals with mild intellectual disability living in community settings are still relatively few in number. The evidence base for cognitive-behavioural therapies, such as anger management, is growing and this approach has been shown to be effective in the treatment of anger and aggression, although the number of well-controlled studies is still limited (Lindsay *et al.*, 2004). Finally, though uncontrolled studies have reported positive effects for psychodynamic therapies, the processes by which such effects are established are unclear. Nevertheless, such therapies may have potential value in addressing the needs of people with mild intellectual disabilities.

REFERENCES

Beail, N. (2003) What works for people with mental retardation? A critical commentary on cognitive-behavioural and psychodynamic psychotherapy research. *Mental Retardation*, **41**, 468–72.

Bieling, P. and Kuyken, W. (2003) Is cognitive case formulation science or science fiction? Clinical Psychology. *Science and Practice*, **10**, 52–69.

Chadwick, P., Williams, C. and MacKenzie, J. (2003) Impact of case formulation in cognitive therapy for psychosis. *Behaviour, Research and Therapy*, **41**, 671–80.

Didden, R. (2007) Functional analysis methodology in developmental disabilities, in *Functional Analysis in Clinical Treatment* (ed. P. Sturmey), Academic Press, New York, pp. 65–86.

Eells, T. (ed.) (2007) *Handbook of Psychotherapy Case Formulation*, 2nd ed, Guilford Press, New York.

Eells, T. and Lombart, K. (2003) Case formulation and treatment concepts among novice, experienced, and expert cognitive-behavioral and psychodynamic therapies. *Psychotherapy Research*, **13**, 187–204.

Jacobson, N.S., Dobson, K.S., Truax, P.A. *et al.* (1996) A component analysis of cognitive-behavioral treatment for depression. *Journal of Consulting and Clinical Psychology*, **64**, 295–304.

Kuyken, W., Fothergill, C., Musa, M. and Chadwick, P. (2005) The reliability and quality of cognitive case formulation. *Behaviour, Research and Therapy*, **43**, 1187–201.

Lindsay, W., Allan, R., Parry, C. *et al.* (2004) Anger and aggression in people with intellectual disabilities: treatment and follow-up of consecutive referrals and a waiting list comparison. *Clinical Psychology and Psychotherapy*, **11**, 255–64.

Mumma, G. and Smith, J. (2001) Cognitive-behavioral-interpersonal scenarios: inter-formulator reliability and convergent validity. *Journal of Psychopathology and Behavioral Assessment*, **23**, 203–21.

Sturmey, P. (2006) On some recent claims for the efficacy of cognitive therapy for people with intellectual disabilities. *Journal of Applied Research in Intellectual Disabilities*, **19**, 109–17.

Sturmey, P., Ward-Horner, J., Marroquin, M. and Doran, D. (2007) Structural and functional approaches to psychopathology and case formulations, in *Functional Analysis in Clinical Treatment* (ed. P. Sturmey), Academic Press, New York, pp. 1–21.

Willner, P. (2005) The effectiveness of psychotherapeutic interventions for people with learning disabilities: a critical overview. *Journal of Intellectual Disability Research*, **49**, 75–85.

PART VII

Emerging Issues

22

Contemporary Themes in Case Formulation

TRACY D. EELLS

It is a privilege to comment on the preceding chapters and to offer some observations. I congratulate Peter Sturmey on carrying forward the idea of this book and making it a reality. I also congratulate the case formulators who shared their clinical insights and expertise, the commentators who carefully analyzed the formulations and the case presenters who provided rich and clinically realistic material for everyone to work with. The book will serve as an outstanding resource for those interested in learning multiple models of case formulation and seeing these models applied to concrete cases.

After reading and considering the wealth of information and insights offered in the preceding chapters, I have identified five themes about case formulation. They relate to (1) case formulation research, (2) what is formulated, (3) evidence versus theory in formulation, (4) the organization of information in formulation and (5) the nature of explanatory mechanisms. In this chapter, I will discuss these themes as they are reflected in the preceding chapters as well as in the broader context of the current state of case formulation practice and research. I will conclude with some suggestions for future case formulation work.

FORMULATION AS A CORE THERAPY CONCEPT IS DISPROPORTIONATE TO AVAILABLE RESEARCH

As Sturmey points out in his introduction, case formulation is widely recognized as a core competency by multiple professional organizations or task

Clinical Case Formulation: Varieties of Approaches. Edited by Peter Sturmey.
© 2009 John Wiley & Sons, Ltd.

forces of these organizations (American Psychiatric Association (APA), 2004; APA Presidential Task Force on Evidence-Based Practice, 2006; British Psychological Society Division of Clinical Psychology, 2000, 2001). Multiple authors describe formulation as the 'first principle' underlying therapy (Beck, 1995), a 'linchpin concept' (Bergner, 1998), the 'heart of evidence-based practice' (Bieling and Kuyken, 2003) and 'central to the process of undertaking CBT' (Dudley and Kuyken, 2006). The centrality of case formulation extends to manual-driven therapies, which not only contain implicit case formulations (Persons, 1991, 2008) but are often delivered in a more individualized and flexible way than may generally be assumed (Schulte *et al.*, 1992; Wilson, 1997). As exemplified in several chapters, formulation is acknowledged as crucial in treating those with co-morbid psychiatric conditions, those with problems for which there is no manual and others with novel or treatment-resistant conditions (Wilson, 1997).[1]

In light of the central role attributed to case formulation it is puzzling that research in the area has not been more extensive. Few authors of the case formulation chapters in the present volume cite research measuring the reliability or validity of their method. It appears that developers of case formulation models tend not to view them as psychometric instruments subject to the same statistical criteria that other psychometric tools are held to. Would it not be important to know the extent to which clinicians trained in a case formulation method and using the same clinical material agree on the formulations they independently develop? Without this information, how are we to know whether the formulation is arbitrary or generic and to what extent it fits the specific person in question?[2] Would it not also be important to have some assurance that the method measures what it is intended to measure?

---

[1] The current status of case formulation is a relatively new phenomenon. The behavioural and humanistic traditions have historically not considered formulation to be a core concept in therapy (Eells, 2007). Forty years ago Goldfried and Pomeranz (1968) noted the absence of relevant assessment procedures in behaviour therapy and proposed a solution. The solution was to define relevant targets for change and suitable interventions for achieving change. These points resonate in the FACCM model described by Lappalainen, Timonen and Haynes (Chapter 12). Within the humanistic tradition, Rogers (1951) cautioned that 'psychological diagnosis' is not necessary and may harm the psychotherapeutic process by positioning the therapist in a 'one up' relationship to the client. In contrast, many methods described in this book emphasize establishing a collaborative therapist–client relationship. The intellectual heirs of Rogers have now promulgated innovative methods of case formulation (Goldman and Greenberg, 1997, 2007).

[2] On the other hand, reliability should not be achieved at the expense of producing generic 'one size fits all' formulations that might satisfy us psychometrically but not fit the person well, what Meehl (1956) termed the 'Barnum effect'. The right balance should be struck between constructing an idiographic formulation tailored to a specific individual and capitalizing on the available nomothetic research and theories of psychopathology. Overgeneralizing can

The most prominent exception to the absence of reliability estimates is Luborsky's core conflictual relationship theme (CCRT) method, as presented by Barrett (Chapter 16), and for which several reliability studies have been conducted (Barber and Crits-Christoph, 1993; Luborsky and Diguer, 1998). In general, these studies find fair to good agreement based on a weighted kappa of the three main CCRT components: wish of self, response of other and response of self. Other exceptions are the formulation model for cognitive analytic therapy (Bennett and Parry, 2004a) and cognitive-behavioural (CB) methods of case formulation (Kuyken *et al.*, 2005; Mumma and Smith, 2001; Persons and Bertagnolli, 1999; Persons, Mooney and Padesky, 1995). In general, studies of CB-based formulation have found good agreement in identifying a problem list and less agreement regarding underlying cognitive mechanisms.

Not surprisingly, across formulation methods, agreement rises when therapists' formulations are compared with what is considered an ideal or consensually constructed formulation rather than other independently constructed formulations (Horowitz and Eells, 1993; Kuyken *et al.*, 2005), and decreases when agreement is based on judgments of individual judges rather than a panel of judges (Horowitz and Rosenberg, 1994; Horowitz *et al.*, 1989; Rosenberg *et al.*, 1994). In addition, reliability tends to increase when formulations are structured and when the inferential leaps from factual information provided by the person are relatively short (Eells, 2007). In sum, reliability is a well-established psychometric concept used to evaluate instruments designed to measure psychological phenomena, which include case formulation. To date, relatively little work has been done in this area (Garb, 1998). More research on the reliability of psychotherapy case formulation models would benefit the field.[3]

---

also result from stereotyping individuals on the basis of ethnicity, age, gender, appearance, socioeconomic background or education (Eells, 2007).

[3] Some assert that treatment utility (Hayes, Nelson and Jarrett, 1987) of a case formulation is more crucial to assess than the model's reliability (Persons and Tompkins, 2007). The reasoning is that if formulation-guided treatment produces better outcomes than treatment not guided by formulation, then the formulation model has value aside from its reliability. It is further asserted that it may not be critical to achieve an initially reliable formulation since a key feature of formulation is that it is adaptable as new information emerges and as hypotheses are tested. While treatment utility is important in formulation, it is a separate concept than reliability as well as some forms of validity. Collins and Messer (1991) showed that two research groups can independently produce highly reliable case formulations that are based on the same method but differ in content. In a follow-up study, Tishby and Messer (1995) found that sets of equally reliable case formulations constructed according to different theories of therapy predicted patient progress differently. Although not a study of treatment utility, the studies highlight differences between measures of case formulation reliability and validity. Recall also that reliability places a ceiling on validity (Ozer, 2001). Reliability may be considered a necessary but not sufficient measure of a case formulation method.

Similar to reliability, few of the chapter authors discuss evidence of the validity of their case formulation method. Validity in this context refers to the extent to which the formulation measures what it is supposed to measure. Depending on the method, what is measured may be a core conflict or interpersonal dilemma; a functional sequence of events; or a cycle of situation, emotion, thought and behaviour, or other predictions based on other sources of evidence. Case formulation validity could also focus on separate components of a formulation model, for example the three primary component of a CCRT. Again, a primary exception to the general lack of evidence of validity is the CCRT. As Barrett (Chapter 16) summarizes, the CCRT correlates in multiple ways with treatment benefits in supportive-expressive therapy (Section 'Role of Research and Clinical Experience', pp. 216–217). Crits-Christoph, Cooper and Luborsky (1988) found a correlation of 0.44 between the accuracy of CCRT-based interventions and outcome, as measured by residual gain scores. Convergent validity of the CAT formulation model, discussed by Dunn (Chapter 15), has been assessed by comparing a CAT formulation with both a CCRT formulation and one based on a modification of Benjamin's structure analysis of social behaviour (Benjamin, 1974; Schacht and Henry, 1994), although just one person was studied (Bennett and Parry, 1998). Applying an intervention model to resolve maladaptive interpersonal behaviour pattern re-enactments, as identified with a CAT formulation, Bennett and Parry (2004b) also show that good outcome in treating those with borderline personality disorder correlates with identifying these patterns and following the model, whereas the opposite is the case for those with poor outcomes.

The incremental validity (Garb, 1998; Sechrest, 1963) of behavioural and CB case formulation approaches has also been explored to some degree. Some use the term 'treatment utility' (Hayes, Nelson and Jarrett, 1987), defined as the degree to which an assessment method contributes to treatment outcome. With one exception, the few randomized controlled studies that have been conducted comparing standard and individualized treatment show equivalence or give a slight edge to individualized treatment (Jacobson *et al.*, 1989; Schneider and Byrne, 1987). A recent study of CB treatment for Bulimia Nervosa found preliminary support for the superiority of individualized as opposed to manualized treatment for some outcome measures (Ghaderi, 2006). A study by Schulte *et al.* (1992) has been cited as evidence for the superiority of standardized treatment to formulation-guided therapy.[4]

---

[4] One argument for expecting superior outcome in the aggregate by standard application of the manual is that the probabilistic model on which these treatments are based assumes that they will prove effective by addressing the relevant maintaining variables in a majority of cases. The exercise of clinical judgement in developing a case formulation, it is asserted, is likely to introduce error and thus decrease overall effectiveness (Wilson, 1996).

These researchers randomly assigned individuals with phobias to standard exposure therapy, individualized treatment based on functional analysis and a yoked control treatment. At termination, an omnibus test showed significant differences in favour of the standard treatment for three of nine outcome measures. However, further scrutiny of the results suggest more equivocal findings and may even be interpreted as indicating equivalence between the individualized and manualized conditions rather than superiority of the latter. For example, pair-wise comparisons by Kuyken, Padesky and Dudley (2008) suggested that the manualized condition was superior to the individualized condition at termination on two rather than three of the nine outcome measures, with equivalence on the remaining seven. At 6-months post-termination, an omnibus test conducted by Schulte *et al.* (1992) showed differences on two of nine outcome measures, and no differences were found at 2 years post-termination. Thus, taken as a whole these results can be interpreted as consistent with other studies showing no difference between standard and individualized therapy. Other studies have found no difference in outcome (Chadwick, Williams and Mackenzie, 2003; Emmelkamp, Bouman and Blaauw, 1994), although process variables may be affected. Chadwick, Williams and Mackenzie (2003) found that case formulation-guided therapy did not affect delusional and self-evaluative beliefs differently than standard CBT, but did find that therapists using formulation-guided therapy rated the alliance as stronger. This finding was not observed for the alliance as rated by the patient. It is noteworthy that no studies have found case formulation guided treatment to harm patients.

Randomized controlled trials to assess treatment utility are problematic to conduct since, as noted earlier, therapists who ostensibly deliver standard manualized treatment inevitably individualize it (Kuyken, Padesky and Dudley, 2009; Schulte *et al.*, 1992; Wilson, 1996), thus reducing between group heterogeneity. In light of the magnitude of differences shown in a number of studies, Tarrier and Calam (2002) estimated that the difference in effect sizes between the two conditions is likely to be small and that sample sizes would need to be greatly increased to demonstrate superiority of the tailor-made therapies.

For the above reasons, other methodologies have been used to assess the treatment utility of case formulation. Persons and colleagues (Persons, Bostrom and Bertagnolli, 1999; Persons *et al.*, 2006) found that case formulation-driven CB therapy for depression or for a combination of depression and anxiety, delivered in a private practice clinic setting, produced outcomes similar to those achieved with manual-based therapy in randomized controlled trials. Using time-series analysis, Mumma and Mooney (2007) found evidence for the treatment utility of the cognitive formulation in a single case.

Investigations of reliability and validity are just two areas where research in case formulation has been insufficient. Relatively little research has been done on issues such as training in case formulation (Caspar, Berger and Hautle, 2004; Kendjelic and Eells, 2007), the role of case formulation-based interventions in the psychotherapy process (Silberschatz and Curtis, 1993; Silberschatz, Fretter and Curtis, 1986) and the cognitive processes involved in constructing formulations (Caspar, 1997; Eells *et al.*, 2005), among other questions. The methodologies described above and the questions examined could be applied to the case formulation methods described in this text to better understand their contribution to therapy, especially to outcome.

A WIDE VARIETY OF PROBLEMS CAN BE FORMULATED TO INCREASE UNDERSTANDING AND GUIDE TREATMENT

The case formulation methods described in this text are flexible and applicable to a wide range of problems. The chief problem addressed in the case studies ranges from those that are most frequently encountered such as depression, to less frequent problems such as hoarding. Also included as primary problem areas are eating disorders, psychosis and impulsive anger. These are presented in individuals of both genders who range widely in age and socio-economic background. Other problems represented in the cases include possible substance abuse, personality disorder, possible cognitive disorder, family dysfunction, marital conflict, loneliness, social isolation, insomnia and obsessive–compulsive symptoms, among others. Taken together, these problems represent a reasonable gamut of issues that clinicians encounter in practice.

In view of this heterogeneity, it is remarkable that each of the case formulators was able to use their model to shed light on these conditions, sometimes in surprising and surprisingly complementary ways. The formulations of Zeppi by Casey (Chapter 7) and Wilder (Chapter 8) and the commentary by Bentall (Chapter 9) are a case in point. All agreed that Zeppi suffered from paranoid delusions. Casey's primarily biomedical formulation reflects the dominant view that schizophrenia, while its cause is currently unknown, is likely biological in origin, although its course is influenced by psychological and social factors (Patel, Pinals and Breier, 2003). Wilder showed how a functional analysis that tests specific hypotheses about environmental factors could provide insights into Zeppi's complaints about magnet waves burning his body. He proposed specific tests to determine whether these complaints are attention seeking, an attempt to escape demanding tasks or serve as self-stimulating activity. The answer would yield different treatment plans. Bentall's formulation of the delusions from a CB perspective focus was drawn from a research base and addresses whether the delusions reflect a 'bad me' or 'poor me' self-concept. These conceptualizations, though quite different, are mutually compatible in that they operate within different contexts. One addresses biological factors, another addresses a specific pattern of problematic behaviour and the third refers to the self-concept. All could be valid inferences. Further, each contributes to a comprehensive treatment plan for Zeppi. Together, the formulations provide a comprehensive, evidence-based view of Zeppi's delusions. Individually, they each omit aspects of Zeppi that would likely contribute significantly to understanding him and providing optimal treatment.

It is about the evidence although theory is a guide

Ideally, a case formulation strikes the right balance between theory and evidence. Each of the case formulation methods described in this book is rooted in psychological and psychotherapy theories. The methods are theory laden, which is to say that the formulations based on them and the observations supporting them are significantly influenced by the guiding theory. Terminology such as 'underlying beliefs' (Newman, Chapter 3), 'cognitive structures' (Willner, Chapter 20), 'roles' and 'procedures' (Dunn, Chapter 15), 'wishes of the self' (Barrett, Chapter 16) and 'ego' or 'mental models of the self' (Beail and Jackson, Chapter 19) are all linked to specific theories of individual psychological functioning; however, the theory dependence of the models varies. The CB, behavioural, psychodynamic and psychoanalytic models appear more strongly rooted in and guided by theory than the more integrative and eclectic models, such as that of Weerasekera (Chapter 11) or the biopsychosocial paradigm discussed by Casey (Chapter 7), each of which opportunistically capitalize on various theories that are relevant to the case and problem at hand. The theories also differ in the amount and type of evidence that has accrued to support them.

Notwithstanding the theory-laden quality of the formulation methods, the role given to the evidence base supporting the formulations was given equal or greater importance by many authors. A remarkable range of evidentiary sources is suggested including symptom measures; behavioural tests; findings from the nomothetic research literature, including neurobiological research, that are applied to the case; results of randomized clinical trials; therapy session narratives; patient diaries, autobiographies and dreams; epidemiological data; analogue observations; daily activity charting; client self-disclosure through interview; third-party information; observations of non-verbal behaviour; transference and counter-transference feelings; and the therapist's prior knowledge and experience of others.

Apart from this general emphasis on the need for evidence, the chapter authors would probably not agree either on what specific types of evidence are best suited to support a formulation or on the evidentiary value of different types. Thus, the question arises as to what constitutes adequate evidence for a case formulation. I will discuss the question of quality of evidence in the context of evidence-based practice.

The 2005 APA Presidential Task Force on Evidence-Based Practice (2006) defined the term as 'the integration of the best available research with clinical expertise in the context of patient characteristics, culture, and preferences' (p. 273). The purpose of evidence-based practice is 'to promote effective psychological practice and enhance public health by applying empirically supported principles of psychological assessment, case formulation, therapeutic relationship, and intervention' (p. 273). In addition, consistent with the goals of case formulation, the task force stated that empirically based practice in psychology 'starts with the patient and asks what research evidence . . . will assist the psychologist in achieving the best outcome' (p. 273). Thus, with regard to our present focus on case formulation, the task force recommends a patient-focused integration of research and clinical expertise and the application of empirically supported principles of case formulation.

The definition of evidence-based practice provides a context for evaluating the information sources for case formulation suggested by the chapter authors. These sources can be placed on a continuum ranging from nomothetic research sources at one end to idiographic sources at the other. On the research end would lay sources such as nomothetic psychopathology research results, epidemiological information and the results of randomized clinical trials. On the idiographic end would be patient's self-disclosure, it may be through initial interviews, observations of non-verbal behaviour, therapy narratives, diaries, dream reports and so on. Also at the idiographic end would lie derivatives of therapist clinical expertise, which may include prior knowledge and experience with others, and transference and counter-transference feelings. In the middle of the continuum might appear forms of self-disclosure framed in nomothetic contexts, such as psychological testing results and symptom measure results. Empirical analogue observations and daily activity charting might also be placed in the middle of the continuum.

Placed in order as suggested above, how many of these information sources satisfy the definition and intent of the APA task force? It seems indisputable that all sources from the centre of the continuum towards the research end are consistent with the definition. However, these sources ultimately must be translated to an idiographic form, presumably on the basis of clinical judgement, since formulation is always patient specific. This translation from the nomothetic context to the idiographic context has risks since psychology laws are predominantly probabilistic. Problems may also arise with information sources at the idiographic end of the continuum. If we consider private data like therapist counter-transference feelings as evidence-based, for example, what source of evidence would not satisfy the definition?

The resolution of this issue may lie in a component of the APA task force's definition of evidence-based practice, which is the concept of clinical expertise. One element of clinical expertise, or at minimum clinical competence, is the exercise of sound judgement, including knowledge of the constraints on judgement. If sound judgement can be applied to all case formulation information sources, the information is more likely to meet the APA's definition of evidence-based practice. How does one exercise sound judgement?

It has been well documented that human judgement, including that of clinicians, is subject to systematic error (Garb, 1998; Kuyken, 2006; Meehl, 1973; Ruscio, 2007; Turk and Salovey, 1988; Tversky and Kahneman, 1973). These errors include failing to take into account base rates, erroneously inferring causality in similarity-based arguments, overestimating the relative significance of different pieces of information; overestimating the significance of information on the basis of the sequence in which one learns it; miscalculating one's ability to anticipate events (Fischhoff, 1975), exhibiting a confirmation bias, peremptorily and prematurely reaching conclusions on too little information, and making judgements based on the ease with which instances of a phenomenon come to mind.

To illustrate the latter idea, imagine working in a college counselling centre where you occasionally encounter distressed women who report childhood sexual abuse. Since it is commonly believed that childhood sexual abuse causes intense harm later in life (Rind, Tromovitch and Bauserman, 1998), you might overestimate the role of abuse in producing presenting complaints since it is a readily available explanation. Knowledge of meta-analytic research (Rind, Tromovitch and Bauserman, 1998), relevant prevalence data (LeBlanc, Brabant and Forsyth, 1996) and relevant base rates in specific populations, can lead to better judgements and better formulations.

Minimizing the risk of error in clinical judgement can help move the sources of case formulation information at the idiographic end of the information continuum into the class of evidence-based information. It can also aid in converting nomothetic information into the idiographic context that case formulation requires. In light of these tendencies to err in judgement, Ruscio (2007) offers several suggestions including scrutinizing similarity-based arguments, conceptualizing problems in multiple ways, formulating and testing multiple working hypotheses, recognizing that personal experience is anecdotal evidence, learning and applying basic principles of probability, identifying exceptions to statistical trends with caution and playing devil's advocate to one's own judgements.

I would add two other suggestions in response to the question of what constitutes adequate evidence in a case formulation. The first is to look for convergence among information sources. Through a cognitive-bootstrapping process, sources of evidence that by themselves may be weak are strengthened by combination with other sources. Consider, for example a therapist who walks into a session with an angry patient feeling well but the therapist walks out feeling helpless, hopeless and inadequate. Suppose the therapist, in an attempt to understand the patient, first rules out counter-transference, then explains his or her feeling as evidence of projective identification (Ogden, 1979), a defensive mechanism characterized by distorting mental representations of self and others (APA, 1994). This is to say that the therapist infers that the patient is projecting his or her own helplessness and inadequacy onto the therapist, that in effect, the therapist is experiencing the patient's feelings. Is the therapist's experience and interpretation evidence based? Likely not in itself; however, if the patient tells narratives in therapy that lead to a CAT formulation or a psychodynamic formulation that suggests a concept of self as helpless and powerless in relationship with others viewed as powerful, then the case for projective identification might be bolstered. Further, if the therapist was aware of recent research on defensive mechanisms (Cramer, 2000), he or she might stand on even firmer footing in considering the experience of anger as evidence of projective identification.

The second suggestion is to develop and constantly practise clinical expertise, as defined by Chi (2006a). She views expertise as 'the manifestation of skills and understanding resulting from the accumulation of a large body of knowledge' (p. 167). Acquiring an accessible, deep and expansive knowledge of one's field, as well as knowing how and being willing to seek information one does not have, will help the clinician demonstrate sound judgement. We will return to the topic of expertise in the penultimate section of this chapter.

To sum up, both theory and evidence supported the formulations in the chapters, with evidence playing an equal or stronger role in many. Multiple sources of information are offered to use in constructing a case formulation, raising the question of what constitutes adequate evidence for case formulation. Nomothetic sources appear to meet the APA's definition for evidence-based practice, although they still must be converted to idiographic forms. More idiographic types of information require additional support and scrutiny, which can come from bootstrapping other information, from being aware of and correcting for risk of judgement error, and from developing and practising clinical expertise.

Elements organizing a case formulation vary across methods

Considerable information is generated in the course of psychotherapy. The information is of many types, comes from multiple sources, and is sometimes ambiguous and contradictory. The psychotherapist is always working with incomplete information under conditions of uncertainty. For these reasons, eliciting, selecting, prioritizing and organizing information in meaningful, useful, efficient and parsimonious ways is a non-trivial matter and is a critical task in the case formulation process. Sturmey (Chapter 1) writes that a shared feature among case formulation models is that they 'abstract out key features of the case' (p. 8). What is abstracted is the topic of this section. One limiting feature makes the abstraction process more workable: as Bieling and Kuyken (2003) point out, 'formulation is emphatically an account of the person's presenting problems, not of the whole person' (p. 53).

The authors were clear in articulating what is formulated in their method. Each included categories of information that their method requires in order to understand the person's presenting problems. In the case of CB formulation, Newman (Chapter 3) listed a person's automatic thoughts, underlying beliefs, compensatory strategies and diagnostic data. The essential categories of information to generate a functional analysis were the immediate antecedents of problematic behaviour, the behaviour itself, and its consequences. The FACCM method described by Lappalainen, Timonen and Haynes (Chapter 12) is one of the more sophisticated versions of functional analysis in that it included functional relations among behaviour problems, an assessment of the relative importance of these problems, the strength and form of causal and non-causal relationships, estimates of the modifiability of causal variables, moderator variables, consideration of both proximate and distal variables and a recommended visual format for displaying these relationships. Weerasekera's (Chapter 11) multi-perspective model as well as Willner's CB model, required an identification of protective, precipitating, perpetuating and protective factors. As Dunn explained (Chapter 15), the CAT reformulation process involves identifying patterns of roles and procedures (i.e. beliefs, thoughts, feelings and actions) in the context of a dialogic view of human relations and individual consciousness, organizing it into a sequential diagrammatic reformulation (SDR), which is a kind of flow chart showing how one role leads into another. The CCRT method, as described by Barrett (Chapter 16) included three elements that were organized transactionally, as previously described.

These case formulation elements vary in their scope and focus. As Howells and Jones (Chapter 17) pointed out, the CAT and CCRT formulations of Mrs Lewis' hoarding 'are framed strictly within the interpersonal domain that thereby excluded a whole range of other potential variables' (p. 235). These other variables included environmental, cognitive, affective, biological and behavioural factors. As Howells and Jones further pointed out, research on hoarding (Steketee and Frost, 2003) suggests many non-interpersonal factors that may influence hoarding. The same might be said of other methods. For example, those based on functional analysis appear not to recognize the role that defence mechanisms, compensatory strategies or relationship procedures may play in influencing problems. In contrast to the functional analytic methods, those based on psychoanalytic theories tend to downplay situational influences. These concepts are simply not within the theoretical scope of these methods and thus not recognized as categories of information on which to collect information.

The number and choice of organizational categories for a formulation method are related to a series of tensions involved in the case formulation process, one of which is comprehensiveness versus immediacy (Eells, 2007). Since case formulation is foremost a practical task and parsimony is an important goal (Sturmey, Chapter 1), the therapist must formulate quickly and efficiently to develop an idea of the patient's problems. This goal suggests that no more than the minimally necessary organizational elements should be used. However, the therapist also needs a sufficient breadth of categories to organize the information required to understand the person adequately.

Eells and Lombart (2003) distinguish three foci for formulation: The case at a prototypical level such as for a specific diagnosis or a common problem, the case level for a specific person and formulation of a situation or episode that arises in or out of therapy, such as the event described for Sally, Zeppi, Antoinette, Mrs Lewis and Mr B. From this framework, the case formulation elements needed for models presented in the book focus primarily on the individual case level. For example, compensatory strategies, core beliefs, relationship dilemmas and protective factors are global attributes of an individual. One exception may be the functional analytic approaches, particularly the FACCM method described by Lappalainen, Timonen and Haynes (Chapter 12), which focus more on specific behaviour in specific situations. This is illustrated by the comment from Lappalainen, Timonen and Haynes that the case description did not provide them with the information they needed to formulate the case. They needed more concrete, situation-specific, behavioural information, rather than the case-level information that was primarily provided. Ideally, these different formulation foci, and the supporting formulation elements, are interrelated and mutually inform each other, as the authors' analyses of the events described for each case demonstrated. In each case, the authors concluded that the formulation was supported by the event and that the event can be understood better in light of the formulation.

Case formulation explanatory mechanisms vary

The hypothesized explanatory mechanism is the 'heart' (Persons and Tompkins, 2007) or 'linchpin' (Bergner, 1998) of the formulation. It ties the inferred elements together into a succinct account of the person's problems. Ideally, it is a testable statement (Fridhandler, Eells and Horowitz, 1999).

A multitude of explanatory mechanisms are offered in the five cases. Many follow broad, theoretical orientations such as the behavioural, cognitive, psychodynamic, psychiatric and eclectic, as reviewed by Sturmey (Table 1.1, pp. 9–12). The behaviourally oriented authors, including Lejuez, Brown, and Hopko (Chapter 4), Wilder (Chapter 8), Lappalainen, Timonen and Haynes (Chapter 12) and Howells and Jones (Chapter 17), use functional analysis to explain the cases. As explained earlier, the basic explanation from this standpoint is that problematic behaviour is a function of its antecedents and consequences. Other models explain presenting problems in terms of maladaptive interpersonal behaviour patterns (Barrett, Chapter 16; Dunn, Chapter 15); maladaptive beliefs, thoughts and compensatory coping strategies (Newman, Chapter 3; Lappalainen, Timonen and Haynes, Chapter 12); the biomedical paradigm in which problems are viewed as disease-like entities (Casey, Chapter 7; Barrett, Chapter 16); and anxiety-reducing but symptom-producing influences of warded-off thoughts and feelings (Beail and Jackson, Chapter 19).

There are many variations within each broad category, including those that are disorder specific. Lejuez, Brown and Hopko (Chapter 4), in their formulation of Sally, use an operant model based on Skinner (1953) and developed further by others (Coyne, 1976; Ferster, 1973; Lewinsohn, 1974) which conceptualizes depression as the extinction of established sequences of healthy behaviour that previously had been positively reinforced. Depressed affect and behaviour are maintained through both positive reinforcement (e.g. increased attention) and negative reinforcement (e.g. elimination of responsibilities such as household duties when one is depressed); however, as aversive consequences (e.g. social isolation, dysphoric affect) replace positive consequences the individual seeks to regain lost reinforcement through increasing depressive behaviour. Similarly, Lappalainen, Timonen and Haynes (Chapter 12) draw from an evidence-based transdiagnostic theory of maintaining factors in eating disorders (Fairburn, Cooper and Shafran, 2003) to develop their formulation of Antoinette.

Some authors offered partial explanations of the cases in terms of attachment theory (Bentall, Chapter 9; Weerasekera, Chapter 11), modelling (Weerasekera, Chapter 11) and Erikson's (1963) psychosocial theory of lifespan development (Cooper, Chapter 13). Bentall suggested that Zeppi developed an insecure attachment style, which is reflected in his inability to trust others and flows from the absence of a 'secure base' in early life (Bowlby, 1988). Weerasekera (Chapter 11) used attachment theory to understand possible dysfunction in Antoinette's family, but noted research suggesting that insecure attachment style is a consequence rather than a cause of family dysfunction. Cooper (Chapter 13) partially explained Antoinette's eating behaviour in terms of both her and her parents' psychosocial life stages.

Some authors offered explanations based on research findings. Bentall (Chapter 9) cited research on cognitive deficits related to interpreting social cues as a partial explanation of Zeppi's problems. Lappalainen, Timonen and Haynes (Chapter 12) cited basic research in eating behaviour to help conceptualize Antoinette. As mentioned earlier, Howells and Jones (Chapter 17) cited research associating hoarding behaviour with attentional problems, information-processing deficits, decision-making, beliefs about possessions and distress and avoidance in hoarding, rather than with maladaptive interpersonal behaviour patterns, as the case formulators of Mrs Lewis suggested.

Some of these explanations are specific and procedural; others are more general. Examples of the former are functional analysis, the CAT formulation and the CCRT. Each lays out a sequence or chain of events, offering opportunities for therapeutic intervention. For example, in functional analysis, one can change the environment and thus the antecedent conditions or the consequences of behaviour. With the transactional sequences embodied in a CCRT, a therapist can address any of its specific elements, such as the expected response from others to a wish of the self, or how that response is then appraised by the self. The more general explanations are not 'unpacked' in the way that the former are. They include the explanations in terms of cognitive deficits, insecure attachment style and idiosyncratic information-processing styles in those who hoard. The links to treatment are less clear in these explanations. Therefore, they would benefit from further articulation of exactly how these factors express themselves in the lives of those who seek therapy.

Case formulation explanatory mechanisms vary in their complexity (Eells *et al.*, 2005), although those in the present volume all appear relatively complex. In using the term 'complex', I am referring to the extent to which the therapist integrates several facets of the person's problems into a meaningful presentation. Simplicity and complexity may be seen as inherent tensions in the case formulation process (Eells, 2007). A formulation should be complex enough to explain the problems, but no more complex than necessary. If an overly simple formulation is offered, important aspects of a person's problems are not captured in the formulation, which may undermine the therapy. If the formulation is too complex, its reliability and validity is likely to suffer, and the clinician's time is not used efficiently. Research suggests that the formulations of CB and psychodynamic experts tend to be more comprehensive, complex, elaborated and systematically constructed than those of novices and experienced clinicians (Eells *et al.*, 2005).

The heterogeneity of explanatory mechanisms offered for the cases raises two questions. First, how does the therapist generate ideas? And second, how should the therapist choose among the ideas that are generated? The literature on expertise and expert performance can help answer these questions. It demonstrates consistent differences between experts and novices in specific domains of knowledge and skill. In contrast to novices, experts have mastered a massive knowledge base in their field, have cognitive search strategies that are more efficient than those of novices, comprehend problems better, are better at detecting when crucial information is missing and do all of this more quickly (Chi, 2006b; Feltovich, Prietula and Ericsson, 2006; Glaser and Chi, 1988). We have evidence in the area of case formulation that experts generate more and better ideas about a case than novices and experienced therapists (Eells *et al.*, 2005). We also have preliminary evidence that experts tend to reason in ways that closely interweaves data and inference so that they do not stray far from data when making conceptualizations (Eells, 2008).

How does one become an expert? Ericsson and colleagues (Ericsson, 2006; Ericsson and Charness, 1994; Ericsson, Krampe and Tesch-Romer, 1993) suggest that rather than reflecting innate abilities, expert performance is an acquired skill. They found that highly structured, effortful, persistent and goal-oriented activity with specific instructions and with immediate and feedback on the accuracy of performance for at least 10 years is characteristic of those who have achieved exceptionally high performance levels in a specific skill or knowledge domain. The answer then to both questions posed earlier may be the same, although with a qualification, as the answer to the old question, 'How do you get to Carnegie Hall?' Answer: 'practice, practice, practice', the qualification being that the practice must be consistent, effortful, systematic and must include feedback. Expert performance in case formulation might be acquired in the same way. Evidence suggests that experience alone is not sufficient.

Although describing specific methods for attaining expertise in case formulation is beyond the scope of this chapter, a framework is provided by Kahneman (2003), who, in his Nobel Prize lecture, reinterpreted his decades of work on intuitive judgement and decision-making. Kahneman posited two modes of cognitive functioning: an intuitive mode that is rapid, relatively effortless, free flowing, emotional and automatic; and a reasoning mode that is slow, serial, deliberate, effortful, rule-governed and controlled. The best decision-makers are able to benefit from the easily accessible and free flow of ideas offered through the intuitive system, and to balance this with a more deliberate, effortful reasoning system. Kuyken (2006) suggested how these systems may operate in case formulation. The cognition of novices might be dominated by the reasoning mode or by unchecked intuition. Expert case formulators on the other hand, might work primarily in the intuitive mode with appropriate checks from the reasoning mode. When difficulty arises, as when the clinician is presented with a complex case, the reasoning system may dominate both novices and experts.

Once the core explanatory mechanism is chosen, it can be tested, as many authors have suggested. If it is substantiated, then the therapist might assume that the formulation is in some sense the 'correct' one; however, it is possible that another formulation might have been tested and it, too, might have gained support. One conceivably could end up with multiple correct yet conflicting formulations. Suppose, for example that Mrs Lewis' therapist, guided by her CCRT formulation, suggests that the roots of her hoarding lie in fear of abandonment. Suppose further that Mrs Lewis accepts this formulation over time, decreases her hoarding, and develops new and satisfying relationships. Although no one would argue that the therapy was unsuccessful, it is plausible that, as Howells and Jones point out, the root of the hoarding was actually an excessive emotional attachment to possessions and distorted and exaggerated fears about consequences of parting with them, and that exposure to de-cluttering – motivated by the CCRT 'insight' about relationships, is what actually led to the successful outcome. In this case, the wrong formulation adventitiously led to a good outcome. It is for these reasons that attending to multiple sources of information, including outcome studies and case studies, as well as all the other sources described earlier, and also conceptualizing patients in multiple ways, may be the best strategy for enhancing our knowledge of the mechanisms that explain patient's problems.

FUTURE CASE FORMULATION WORK

Sturmey's book has provided much opportunity for reflecting on case formulation and its role in psychotherapy. I will close the chapter with six suggestions for the future, as stimulated by my reading of the book. The first of these, as discussed earlier, is the need for more research on case formulation. An initial step in this direction is to establish the extent to which psychometric properties such as reliability and validity that we expect of other measures of individual psychological functioning should also be expected of a case formulation model. Are case formulation methods similar in this respect to psychological tests or are they different enough that the usual psychometric standards should not be expected? If the case can be made that these measures provide useful information, then work on establishing reliability and validity of case formulations methods should be accelerated. Earlier in the paper, I suggested several other areas of case formulation research. Others have done so as well (Bieling and Kuyken, 2003; Tarrier and Calam, 2002).

A second suggestion is to increase the evidentiary standards for the content of a case formulation. This suggestion is consistent with the trend towards evidence-based practice in psychology, as well in medicine (Institute of Medicine, 2001). It is also consistent with an increased focus in health care delivery on quality of care, accountability, patient-centred care and evidence-based decision-making. Towards this end, for example the explanatory mechanism component of case formulations would benefit if it were influenced more by research in the area of psychopathology, epidemiology, neurobiology and learning theory. In addition, evidence-based decision-making, and the regular use of debiasing techniques will improve judgement.

Third, a set of empirically supported principles of case formulation should be developed, as suggested by the APA Task Force on Evidence-Based Practice. These principles could articulate guidelines for case formulation method construction, could articulate evidentiary standards for the content of a case formulation and could address issues related to the process of developing a case formulation so as to minimize the risk of judgement errors. For example, they might recommend that a plausible alternative formulation be routinely generated and that clinicians consider and provide evidence for why one formulation is preferred over another. The principles might also recommend that hypotheses in case formulations be testable. Since case formulation serves as the crucible (Kuyken, Padesky and Dudley, 2008) for applying nomothetic and other psychological data to the individual, and lies between a descriptive diagnosis and treatment, a set of principles suitable for this important role would be a significant advance.

Fourth, more effort should be made in developing quantitative methods that capitalize on skilled clinical observation, and that result in improved clinical judgement and outcomes. Westen and Weinberger (2004) show that clinicians can provide valid and reliability data if we quantify their inferences using psychometric instruments designed for experts. Westen and Muderrisoglu (2003) found that clinicians using a Q-sort technique achieved highly reliable classifications of patients into personality disorder categories, as well both convergent and discriminant validity. The technique involved quantified judgements of clinically relevant personality characteristics that were then statistically aggregated. It could be possible to develop these methods further to go beyond a DSM-IV diagnosis to a case formulation format that includes categories discussed by the chapter authors in this text.

Fifth, in light of the common elements across many of the case formulations presented in this volume, and as the trend towards psychotherapy integration increases (Norcross, Hedges and Prochaska, 2002), consideration should be given to an integrative model of case formulation. As each of the commentary chapters showed, considerable overlap exists among the models presented, while each also has its distinctive characteristics. An integrative model of case formulation might be able to capture these overlapping concepts while also retaining the distinctive features of each approach. One place to start would be to develop a common language for case formulation (Goldfried, 1995).

Sixth, clinicians constructing case formulations should routinely take into consideration the cultural embeddedness of patients. A number of chapter authors commented on the need to consider culture to understand pressures on patients and to demonstrate understanding of the patient. One driver of this multicultural competence suggestion is the increasingly diverse demographics in the United States (APA, 2003; Committee on Institutional and Policy-Level Strategies for Increasing the Diversity of the U.S. Healthcare Workforce, 2004) as well as evidence that failure to account for culture can have deleterious consequences for clients (Ridley and Kelly, 2007).

REFERENCES

American Psychiatric Association (1994) *Diagnostic and Statistical Manual of Mental Disorders*, 4th edn, American Psychiatric Press, Washington, DC.

American Psychiatric Association (2004) *Practice Guidelines for the Treatment of Psychiatric Disorders*, American Psychiatric Publishing, Inc, Washington, DC.

American Psychological Association (2003) Guidelines on multicultural education, training, research, practice, and organizational change for Psychologists. *American Psychologist*, **58**, 377–402.

APA Presidential Task Force on Evidence-Based Practice (2006) Evidence-based practice in psychology. *American Psychologist*, **61**, 271–85.

Barber, J P. and Crits-Christoph, P. (1993) Advances in measures of psychodynamic formulations. *Journal of Consulting and Clinical Psychology*, **61**, 574–85.

Beck, J.S. (1995) *Cognitive Therapy: Basics and Beyond*, Guilford Press, New York.

Benjamin, L.S. (1974) Structural analysis of social behavior. *Psychological Review*, **81**, 392–425.

Bennett, D. and Parry, G. (1998) The accuracy of reformulation in cognitive analytic therapy: a validation study. *Psychotherapy Research*, **8**, 84–103.

Bennett, D. and Parry, G. (2004a) A measure of psychotherapeutic competence derived from cognitive analytic therapy. *Psychotherapy Research*, **14**, 176–92.

Bennett, D. and Parry, G. (2004b) Maintaining the therapeutic alliance: resolving alliance-threatening interactions related to the transference, in *Core Processes in Brief Psychodynamic Psychotherapy: Advancing Effective Practice* (ed. D.P. Charman), Lawrence Erlbaum Associates Publishers, Mahwah, pp. 251–72.

Bergner, R.M. (1998) Characteristics of optimal clinical case formulations: the linchpin concept. *American Journal of Psychotherapy*, **52**, 287–300.

Bieling, P.J. and Kuyken, W. (2003) Is cognitive case formulation science or science fiction? *Clinical Psychology: Science and Practice*, **10**, 52–69.

Bowlby, J. (1988) *A Secure Base*, Routledge, London.

British Psychological Society Division of Clinical Psychology (2000) *Understanding Mental Illness and Psychotic Experiences. A Report by the British Psychological Society Division of Clinical Psychology*, British Psychological Society Division of Clinical Psychology, Leicester.

British Psychological Society Division of Clinical Psychology (2001) *The Core Purpose and Philosophy of the Profession*, British Psychological Society Division of Clinical Psychology, Leicester.

Caspar, F. (1997) What goes on in a psychotherapist's mind? *Psychotherapy Research*, **7**, 105–25.

Caspar, F., Berger, T. and Hautle, I. (2004) The right view of your patient: a computer-assisted, individualized module for psychotherapy training. *Psychotherapy: Theory, Research, Practice, Training*, **41**, 125–35.

Chadwick, P., Williams, C. and Mackenzie, J. (2003) Impact of case formulation in cognitive behaviour therapy for psychosis. *Behaviour, Research and Therapy*, **41**, 671–80.

Chi, M.T.H. (2006a) Laboratory methods for assessing experts' and novices' knowledge, in *The Cambridge Handbook of Expertise and Expert Performance* (eds K.A. Ericsson, N. Charness, P.J. Feltovich and R.R. Hoffman), Cambridge University Press, New York, pp. 167–84.

Chi, M.T.H. (2006b) Two approaches to the study of experts' characteristics, in *The Cambridge Handbook of Expertise and Expert Performance* (eds K.A. Ericsson, N. Charness, P.J. Feltovich and R.R. Hoffman), Cambridge University Press, New York, pp. 21–30.

Collins, W.D. and Messer, S.B. (1991) Extending the plan formulation method to an object relations perspective: reliability, stability, and adaptability. *Psychological Assessment*, **3**, 75–81.

Committee on Institutional and Policy-Level Strategies for Increasing the Diversity of the U.S. Healthcare Workforce (2004) *In the Nation's Compelling Interest: Ensuring Diversity in the Health Case Workforce*, Institute of Medicine, Washington, DC.

Coyne, J.C. (1976) Toward an interactional description of depression. *Psychiatry*, **39**, 28–40.

Cramer, P. (2000) Defense mechanisms in psychology today: further processes for adaptation. *American Psychologist*, **55**, 637–46.

Crits-Christoph, P., Cooper, A. and Luborsky, L. (1988) The accuracy of therapists' interpretations and the outcome of dynamic psychotherapy. *Journal of Consulting and Clinical Psychology*, **56**, 490–5.

Dudley, R. and Kuyken, W. (2006) Formulation in cognitive-behavioural therapy: 'There is nothing either good or bad, but thinking makes it so', in *Formulation in Psychology and Psychotherapy: Making Sense of People's Problems* (eds J. Johnston and R. Dallos), Routledge, New York, pp. 17–46.

Eells, T.D. (2007) Psychotherapy case formulation: history and current status, in *Handbook of Psychotherapy Case Formulation*, 2nd edn (ed. T.D. Eells), Guilford Press, New York, pp. 3–32.

Eells, T.D. (2008) *The Unfolding Case Formulation: Defining Quality in Development of the Core Inference*. Paper presented at the 39th Meeting of the Society for Psychotherapy Research, Barcelona, Spain.

Eells, T.D. and Lombart, K.G. (2003) Case formulation: determining the focus in brief dynamic psychotherapy, in *Core Processes in Brief Psychodynamic Psychotherapy* (ed. D.P. Charman), Lawrence Erlbaum Associates, Mahwah, NJ, pp. 119–44.

Eells, T.D., Lombart, K.G., Kendjelic, E.M. *et al.* (2005) The quality of psychotherapy case formulations: a comparison of expert, experienced, and novice cognitive-behavioral and psychodynamic therapists. *Journal of Consulting and Clinical Psychology*, **73**, 579–89.

Emmelkamp, P.M.G., Bouman, T.K. and Blaauw, E. (1994) Individualized versus standardized therapy: a comparative evaluation with obsessive–compulsive patients. *Clinical Psychology and Psychotherapy*, **1**, 95–100.

Ericsson, K.A. (2006) Protocol analysis and expert thought: concurrent verbalizations of thinking during experts' performance on representative tasks, in *The Cambridge Handbook of Expertise and Expert Performance* (eds K.A. Ericsson, N. Charness, P.J. Feltovich and R.R. Hoffman), Cambridge University Press, New York, pp. 223–41.

Ericsson, K.A. and Charness, N. (1994) Expert performance: its structure and acquisition. *American Psychologist*, **49**, 725–47.

Ericsson, K.A., Krampe, R.T. and Tesch-Romer, C. (1993) The role of deliberate practice in the acquisition of expert performance. *Psychological Review*, **100**, 363–406.

Erikson, E.H. (1963) *Childhood and Society*, 2nd edn, Norton, New York.

Fairburn, C.G., Cooper, Z. and Shafran, R. (2003) Cognitive behaviour therapy for eating disorders: a "transdiagnostic" theory and treatment. *Behaviour, Research and Therapy*, **41**, 509–28.

Feltovich, P.J., Prietula, M.J. and Ericsson, K.A. (2006) Studies of expertise from psychological perspectives, in *The Cambridge Handbook of Expertise and Expert Performance* (eds K.A. Ericsson, N. Charness, P.J. Feltovich and R.R. Hoffman), Cambridge University Press, New York, pp. 41–67.

Ferster, C.B. (1973) A functional analysis of depression. *American Psychologist*, **28**, 857–70.

Fischhoff, B. (1975) Hindsight is not equal to foresight: the effect of outcome knowledge on judgment under uncertainty. *Journal of Experimental Psychology: Human Perception and Performance*, **1**, 288–99.

Fridhandler, B., Eells, T. D. and Horowitz, M. (1999) Psychoanalytic explanation of pathological grief: scientific observation of a single case. *Psychoanalytic Psychology*, **16**, 1–24.

Garb, H.N. (1998) *Studying the Clinician: Judgment Research and Psychological Assessment*, American Psychological Association, Washington, DC.

Ghaderi, A. (2006) Does individualisation matter? A randomised trial of standardised (focused) versus individualized (broad) cognitive behaviour therapy for bulimia nervosa. *Behaviour, Research and Therapy*, **44**, 273–88.

Glaser, R. and Chi, M.T.H. (1988) Overview, in *The Nature of Expertise* (eds M.T.H. Chi, R. Glaser and M.J. Farr), Lawrence Erlbaum Associates, Hillsdale, NJ, pp. XV–XXVIII.

Goldfried, M.R. (1995) Toward a common language for case formulation. *Journal of Psychotherapy Integration*, **5**, 221–44.

Goldfried, M.R. and Pomeranz, D.M. (1968) Role of assessment in behavior modification. *Psychological Reports*, **23**, 75–87.

Goldman, R. and Greenberg, L.S. (1997) Case formulation in process-experiential therapy, in *Handbook of Psychotherapy Case Formulation* (ed. T.D. Eells), Guilford Press, New York, pp. 402–29.

Greenberg, L.S. and Goldman, R. (2007) Case formulation in emotion-focused therapy, in *Handbook of Psychotherapy Case Formulation* Guilford Press, New York, pp. 379–411.

Hayes, S.C., Nelson, R.O. and Jarrett, R.B. (1987) The treatment utility of assessment: a functional approach to evaluating assessment quality. *American Psychologist*, **42**, 963–74.

Horowitz, L.M. and Rosenberg, S.E. (1994) The consensual response psychodynamic formulation: part 1: method and research results. *Psychotherapy Research*, **4**, 222–33.

Horowitz, L.M., Rosenberg, S.E., Ureno, G. *et al.* (1989) Psychodynamic formulation, consensual response method and interpersonal problems. *Journal of Consulting and Clinical Psychology*, **57**, 599–606.

Horowitz, M.J. and Eells, T.D. (1993) Role-relationship model configurations: a method for psychotherapy case formulation. *Psychotherapy Research*, **3**, 57–68.

Institute of Medicine (2001) *Crossing the Quality Chasm: A New Health System for the 21st Century*, National Academies Press, Washington, DC.

Jacobson, N.S., Schmaling, K.B., Holtzworth-Munroe, A. *et al.* (1989) Research-structured vs. clinically flexible versions of social learning-based marital therapy. *Behaviour, Research and Therapy*, **27**, 173–80.

Kahneman, D. (2003) A perspective on judgment and choice: mapping bounded rationality. *American Psychologist*, **58**, 697–720.

Kendjelic, E.M. and Eells, T.D. (2007) Psychotherapy case formulation training improves formulation quality. *Psychotherapy: Theory, Research, Practice, Training*, **44**, 66–77.

Kuyken, W. (2006) Evidence-based case formulation: is the emperor clothed?, in *Case Formulation in Cognitive Behaviour Therapy? The Treatment of Challenging and Complex Cases* (ed. N. Tarrier), Routledge/Taylor & Francis Group, New York, pp. 12–35.

Kuyken, W., Fothergill, C.D., Musa, M. and Chadwick, P. (2005) The reliability and quality of cognitive case formulation. *Behaviour, Research and Therapy*, **43** (9), 1187–201.

Kuyken, W., Padesky, C.A. and Dudley, R. (2008) *Collaborative Case Conceptualization: Working Effectively with Clients in Cognitive-Behavioral Therapy*, Guilford Press, New York.

Kuyken, W., Padesky, C.A. and Dudley, R. (2009) *Collaborative Case Conceptualization*, Guilford Press, New York.

LeBlanc, J.B., Brabant, S. and Forsyth, C.J. (1996) The meaning of college for survivors of sexual abuse: higher education and the older female college student. *American Journal of Orthopsychiatry*, **66**, 468–73.

Lewinsohn, P.M. (1974) A behavioural approach to depression, in *The Psychology of Depression: Contemporary Theory and Research* (eds R.M. Friedman and M.M. Katz), John Wiley & Sons, Inc., New York, pp. 157–78.

Luborsky, L. and Diguer, L. (1998) The reliability of the CCRT measure: results from eight samples, in *Understanding Transference: The Core Conflictual Relationship Theme Method*, 2nd edn (eds L. Luborsky and P. Crits-Christoph), American Psychological Association, Washington, DC, pp. 97–107.

Meehl, P.E. (1956) Wanted – a good cookbook. *American Psychologist*, **11**, 263–72.

Meehl, P.E. (1973) Why I do not attend case conferences, in *Psychodiagnosis: Selected Papers* (ed. P.E. Meehl), Norton, New York, pp. 225–302.

Mumma, G.H. and Mooney, S.R. (2007) Incremental validity of cognitions in a clinical case formulation: an intraindividual test in a case example. *Journal of Psychopathology and Behavioral Assessment*, **29**, 17–28.

Mumma, G.H. and Smith, J.L. (2001) Cognitive–behavioral-interpersonal scenarios: interformulator reliability and convergent validity. *Journal of Psychopathology and Behavioral Assessment*, **23**, 203–21.

Norcross, J.C., Hedges, M. and Prochaska, J.O. (2002) The face of 2010: a Delphi poll on the future of psychotherapy. *Professional Psychology: Research and Practice*, **33**, 316–22.

Ogden, T.H. (1979) On projective identification. *International Journal of Psychoanalysis*, **60**, 357–73.

Ozer, D.J. (2001) Four principles for personality assessment, in *Handbook of Personality*, 2nd edn (eds L.A. Pervin and O.P. John), Guilford Press, New York, pp. 671–88.

Patel, J.K., Pinals, D.A. and Breier, A. (2003) Schizophrenia and other psychoses, in *Psychiatry* (eds A. Tasman, J. Kay and J.A. Lieberman), John Wiley & Sons, Ltd, Chichester, pp. 1131–206.

Persons, J.B. (1991) Psychotherapy outcome studies do not accurately represent current models of psychotherapy: a proposed remedy. *American Psychologist*, **46**, 99–106.

Persons, J.B. (2008) *The Case Formulation Approach to Cognitive-Behavior Therapy*, Guilford Press, New York.

Persons, J.B. and Bertagnolli, A. (1999) Inter-rater reliability of cognitive-behavioral case formulations of depression: a replication. *Cognitive Therapy and Research*, **23**, 271–83.

Persons, J.B., Bostrom, A. and Bertagnolli, A. (1999) Results of randomized controlled trials of cognitive therapy for depression generalize to private practice. *Cognitive Therapy and Research*, **23**, 535–48.

Persons, J.B., Mooney, K.A. and Padesky, C.A. (1995) Interrater reliability of cognitive-behavioral case formulations. *Cognitive Therapy and Research*, **19**, 21–34.

Persons, J.B., Roberts, N.A., Zalecki, C.A. and Brechwald, W.A.G. (2006) Naturalistic outcome of case formulation-driven cognitive-behavior therapy for anxious depressed outpatients. *Behaviour, Research and Therapy*, **44**, 1041–51.

Persons, J.B. and Tompkins, M.A. (2007) Cognitive-behavioral case formulation, in *Handbook of Psychotherapy Case Formulation*, 2nd edn (ed. T.D. Eells), Guilford Press, New York.

Ridley, C. and Kelly, S.M. (2007) Multicultural considerations in case formulation, in *Handbook of Psychotherapy Case Formulation*, 2nd edn (ed. T.D. Eells), Guilford Press, New York.

Rind, B., Tromovitch, P. and Bauserman, R. (1998) A meta-analytic examination of assumed properties of child sexual abuse using college samples. *Psychological Bulletin*, **124**, 22–53.

Rogers, C.R. (1951) *Client-Centered Therapy, its Current Practice, Implications, and Theory*, Houghton Mifflin, Boston, MA.

Rosenberg, S.E., Horowitz, L.M., Hanks, S. *et al.* (1994) *The Consensual Response Psychodynamic Formulation: Part 2. Application to Case of Ms. Smithfield*, vol. **4**, Routledge, pp. 234–38.

Ruscio, J. (2007) The clinician as subject: practitioners are prone to the same judgment errors as everyone else, in *The Great Ideas of Clinical Science: 17 Principles That Every Mental Health Professional Should Understand* (eds S.O. Lilienfeld and W.T. O'Donohue), Routledge/Taylor & Francis Group, New York, pp. 29–47.

Schacht, T.E. and Henry, W.P. (1994) Modeling recurrent patterns of interpersonal relationship with Structural Analysis of Social Behavior: the SASB-CMP. *Psychotherapy Research*, **4**, 208–21.

Schneider, B.H. and Byrne, B.M. (1987) Individualizing social skills training for behavior-disordered children. *Journal of Consulting and Clinical Psychology*, **55**, 444–5.

Schulte, D., Kunzel, R., Pepping, G. and Schulte-Bahrenberg, T. (1992) Tailor-made versus standardized therapy of phobic patients. *Advances in Behaviour, Research and Therapy*, **14**, 67–92.

Sechrest, L. (1963) Incremental validity: a recommendation. *Educational and Psychological Measurement*, **23**, 153–8.

Silberschatz, G. and Curtis, J.T. (1993) Measuring the therapist's impact on the patient's therapeutic progress. *Journal of Consulting and Clinical Psychology*, **61**, 403–11.

Silberschatz, G., Fretter, P.B. and Curtis, J.T. (1986) How do interpretations influence the process of psychotherapy? *Journal of Consulting and Clinical Psychology*, **54**, 646–52.

Skinner, B.F. (1953) *Science and Human Behavior*, The Free Press, New York.

Steketee, G. and Frost, R. (2003) Compulsive hoarding: current status of the research. *Clinical Psychology Review*, **23**, 905–27.

Tarrier, N. and Calam, R. (2002) New developments in cognitive-behavioural case formulation. Epidemiological, systemic and social context: an integrative approach. *Behavioural and Cognitive Psychotherapy*, **30**, 311–28.

Tishby, O. and Messer, S.B. (1995) The relationship between plan compatibility of therapist interventions and patient progress: a comparison of two plan formulations. *Psychotherapy Research*, **5**, 76–88.

Turk, D.C. and Salovey, P. (eds) (1988) *Reasoning, Inference, and Judgment in Clinical Psychology*, The Free Press, New York.

Tversky, A. and Kahneman, D. (1973) *Judgment Under Uncertainty: Heuristics and Biases*, Oregon Research Institute, Oxford.

Westen, D. and Muderrisoglu, S. (2003) Assessing personality disorders using a systematic clinical interview: evaluation of an alternate to structured interviews. *Journal of Personality Disorders*, **17**, 351–69.

Westen, D. and Weinberger, J. (2004) When clinical description becomes statistical prediction. *American Psychologist*, **59**, 595–613.

Wilson, G.T. (1996) Manual-based treatments: the clinical application of research findings. *Behaviour, Research and Therapy*, **34**, 295–314.

Wilson, G.T. (1997) Treatment manuals in clinical practice. *Behaviour, Research and Therapy*, **35**, 205–10.

Index